The Object Primer
Second Edition

The Application Developer's Guide to Object Orientation and the UML

Scott W. Ambler

CAMBRIDGE
UNIVERSITY PRESS

SIGS
BOOKS

PUBLISHED BY THE PRESS SYNDICATE OF THE UNIVERSITY OF CAMBRIDGE
The Pitt Building, Trumpington Street, Cambridge, United Kingdom

CAMBRIDGE UNIVERSITY PRESS
The Edinburgh Building, Cambridge CB2 2RU, UK
40 West 20th Street, New York, NY 10011-4211, USA
10 Stamford Road, Oakleigh, VIC 3166, Australia
Ruiz de Alarcón 13, 28014 Madrid, Spain
Dock House, The Waterfront, Capt Town 8001, South Africa

http://www.cambridge.org

Published in association with SIGS Books

First edition published by SIGS Books and Multimedia in 1995
First edition published by Cambridge University Press in 1998
Reprinted 1998, 1999
Second edition published 2001

Design by Kevin Callahan and Andrea Cammarata
Composition by Andrea Cammarata
Cover design by Jean Cohn and Andrea Cammarata

Printed in the United States of America

A catalog record for this book is available from the British Library.

Library of Congress Cataloging in Publication data available.

ISBN 0 521 78519 7 paperback

To Clark Kent,
who never made any money saving
the world from Solomon Grundy.*

*With a nod to The Crash Test Dummies
for "Superman's Song."

About the Author

scottAmbler is an instance of an **OOConsultant** for **roninInternational** (*www. ronin-intl.com*) based in **denverColorado**. **roninInternational** implements **objectArchitectureConsulting()**, **componentArchitectureConsulting()**, and **softwareProcessConsulting()** operations. Instances of **HumanoidLifeForm** can send email messages to him at:

scott.ambler@ronin-intl.com

scottAmbler is a very versatile object that will polymorphically change type in order to meet the needs of **roninInternational** clients. For example, he often becomes an **OOMentor**, **OOArchitect**, **OODeveloper**, or **SoftwareProcessMentor** object. Scott has been an instance of an **OOConsultant** since 1991. He used to be a **MastersStudent** object, having received an instance of an **InformationScienceDegree** from the **universityOfToronto**. As a **MastersStudent**, scottAmbler did a lot of work in OO CASE and instantiated a **ThesisPaper** object in computer-supported co-operative work (an academic alias used to describe groupware). The only message his instance of **ThesisPaper** responds to is **sitOnShelfAndGatherDust**, which scottAmbler finds disappointing but predictable. **scottAmbler** has worked at a variety of organizations, including instances of **Bank, InsuranceCompany, TelecommunicationsCompany, InternetStartup, ServicesOutsourcer, MilitaryContractor,** and **Product Distributor.**

Objects that have been declared as friends of **scottAmbler** often send him the message **youTakeThisObjectStuffTooFar,** to which he responds with the text string "It's nothing compared to how far I take *Star Trek.*" In his spare time he likes to write, having instantiated several books about object technology. He also writes regular object columns for **softwareDevelopment** (*www. sdmagazine.com*) and **computingCanada** (*www.plesman.com*). **scottAmbler** is an avid watcher of instances of **StarTrek,** and intends to one day do his **doctorateDegree** at **starFleetAcademy.** His personal web site is *http://www. ambysoft.com,* where he has posted a collection of **WhitePaper** objects and other software development resources.

Contents

Foreword

I was recently surfing the web, and I ran into some very interesting figures. According to the analysts, on the order of 30%-40% of software projects are cancelled. The average software project costs more than double original cost estimates, and a mere 15-20% of all software projects are completed on-time and on-budget. On top of this, there's opportunity cost, which measures the lost business opportunity that could have been seized upon if the project was done correctly from the onset. This opportunity cost is the real problem, and can grow to staggering proportions.

I was befuddled when confronted with this data. Is this really the state of our profession? Apparently so—the numbers do not lie. So what could be the cause of these catastrophic failures?

One obvious answer is lack of sufficient developer resources on projects. We are living in an era where the developer reigns king, and is a highly prized possession, scarce to be found. The result of this is an outstanding supply/demand imbalance in IT.

However, this is only the tip of the iceberg. There are a host of other factors that contribute to failure as well. Examples are poor software developing processes, not engaging users during the development process, and improper use of object-oriented analysis and design.

The good news is that we can change these factors through education. By properly learning correct software development best practices, you can avoid the stumbling blocks that have plagued the rest of the industry. Sidestepping those landmines is critical, especially when time-to-market is measured in the order of weeks, not months or years.

This book is the best starting point for learning object-oriented best practices. When you read this book, Scott Ambler will explain a wide array concepts and paradigms to you which you can apply immediately in your software development. The concepts are conveyed in an easy-to-understand, jovial manner, so that any developer, regardless of background, can harness these concepts.

I firmly believe that reading this book will increase your chances of project success. It will also force you to raise the bar for what you deem acceptable when performing software development, which increases your marketability as an individual developer.

I wish you the best of luck in your projects. Let's work together to better ourselves.

Ed Roman
CEO, The Middleware Company
edro@middleware-company.com

Preface

*T*HE OBJECT PRIMER is a straightforward, easy-to-understand introduction to object-oriented concepts, requirements, analysis, and design methods applying the techniques of the Unified Modeling Language (UML). Object orientation (OO) is the most important change to system development since the advent of structured methods; during the 1990s, it superceded the structured paradigm as the primary approach for software development. While OO is often used to develop complex systems, learning how to work with object-oriented techniques does not need to be complicated. This book differs from many other introductory books about OO—it is written from the point of view of a real-world developer, somebody who has lived through the difficulty of learning this exciting software paradigm.

Who Should Read *The Object Primer?*

If you are a mainframe COBOL or PL/1 programmer who is working on his or her first OO project, *The Object Primer* is for you. If you are a business analyst or user representative involved in the documentation of requirements for an OO application, *The Object Primer* is for you. If you're a project manager who needs to get up to speed on OO, *The Object Primer* is for you. If you are a sys-

xix

tems designer whose organization is migrating to object technology, *The Object Primer* is for you. If you are a student taking your first course in Java or C++, *The Object Primer* is for you. If you're a researcher or an academic interested in arcane software engineering theory, sorry, I can't please everybody.

Throughout this book, I use the term "developer" very broadly: a developer is anyone involved in the development of a software application. This includes programmers, analysts, designers, user representatives, database administrators, support engineers, and so on. While many people would not include user representatives in this list, my experience is that active user involvement is often the key determinant to the success of a software project. Users can actively participate in requirements engineering, analysis, and sometimes design—it is clear to me that users should be considered developers. Call me a radical.

Why Read *The Object Primer?*

By reading *The Object Primer* you will gain a solid understanding of object-oriented concepts and basic objected-oriented modeling techniques. These are the fundamental skills needed to develop object-oriented applications, particularly C++ and Java-based software. Furthermore, these skills are put into the context of a running example—you see how these skills can be applied in the real world.

Why Read This Book Series?

The Object Primer is the first in a five-volume series describing OO development techniques and the OO software process. These books are as follows:

The Object Primer	Introduction to OO concepts and techniques
Building Object Applications That Work	Intermediate OO modeling, programming, testing, patterns, metrics, user interface design, and persistence
The Elements of Java Style	Tips and techniques for writing high-quality Java source code
Process Patterns	Initiate and construct large-scale, mission-critical software using object technology
More Process Patterns	Deliver, maintain, and support large-scale, mission-critical software using object technology

Why a Second Edition?

When I originally wrote the first edition of *The Object Primer*, in the autumn of 1994, the object industry was in relative chaos. The notation wars were raging, and although there were seven or eight well-known modeling notations and more than thirty less-popular ones, there wasn't a clear winner yet. Now when I rewrite this book, in the winter of 1999/2000, the Unified Modeling Language is the industry standard. In 1994, user-centered design was a niche concept in the software development environment at best; now usage-centered design techniques such as essential use case modeling are becoming industry norms. In 1994, organizations were not sure whether object technology was something they should adopt, in 2000 object and component technologies are the standards for new development in most organizations. In 1994 Smalltalk, Eiffel, and C++ were vying for language supremacy and in 2000 Java is the clear market winner with a strong following using C++ for performance-critical applications. Times have changed.

What's New in the Second Edition?

The second edition builds on the strengths of the first, and it is simple and easy to understand. However, it goes beyond the first edition by including usage-centered design techniques such as essential use case modeling and essential user interface modeling. It still includes class-responsibility collaborator (CRC) modeling, a key technique of Extreme Programming (XP). Analysis and design modeling has been expanded to include the primary UML techniques as well as persistence (data) modeling. Chapters showing how to move from design to programming and

---

ADVANTAGES OF THIS BOOK SERIES

- It is short, straightforward, and to the point—it is not wasting your time.
- It presents a full development lifecycle—there is more to OO than just programming!
- It takes complicated concepts and makes them simple—it will shorten your learning curve.
- It is written in the language of developers, not academics—you can understand it.
- It uses real-world examples and case studies—it describes realistic applications.
- It relates new techniques to your current practices—you can see where OO fits in.
- It provides a smooth transition to object technology—your first project can succeed.

then into testing have been added to round out the book. Finally, leading-edge development techniques and processes, including patterns and the Unified Process, are included to provide you with a true introduction to the state of the art. Most important, the second edition reflects my additional experiences over the past five years helping individuals learn how to apply object technology effectively across a variety of problem domains.

Acknowledgments

Special thanks to the people who provided insightful comments that led to significant improvements in this book: John Nalbone, Chris Roffler, Mark Peterson, Susan Ambler, Mike Stefano, Joel Rosi-Schwartz, Dr. Barbara Rosi-Schwartz, and the staff at SIGS Books and Cambridge University Press.

Developers are good at building systems right.

What we're not good at is building the right system.

Chapter 1

Introduction

What You Will Learn in This Chapter

What is object orientation?
The difficulties encountered with traditional development methods
How this book is organized
How to read this book

Why You Need to Read This Chapter

To understand why you should consider embracing object-oriented techniques, you need to understand the challenges of the structured paradigm and how the object paradigm addresses them.

1

This book describes the object-oriented (OO) paradigm, a development strategy based on the concept that systems should be built from a collection of reusable components called *objects*. Instead of separating data and functionality, as is done in the structured paradigm, objects encompass both. While the object-oriented paradigm sounds similar to the structured paradigm, as you will see in this book, it is actually quite different. A common mistake that many experienced developers make is to assume they have been "doing objects" all along, just because they have been applying similar software-engineering principles. The reality is you must recognize that objects are different so you can start your learning experience successfully.

1.1 The Structured Paradigm versus the Object-Oriented Paradigm

The *structured paradigm* is a development strategy based on the concept that a system should be separated into two parts: data (modeled using a data/persistence model) and functionality (modeled using a process model). In short, using the structured approach, you develop applications in which data is separate from behavior in both the design model and in the system implementation (that is, the program).

On the other hand, as you see in Figure 1-1, the main concept behind the object-oriented paradigm is that instead of defining systems as two separate parts (data and functionality), you now define systems as a collection of interacting objects. Objects do things (that is, they have functionality) and they know things (they have data). While this sounds similar to the structured paradigm, it really isn't.

Consider the design of an information system for a university. Taking the structured approach, you would define the layout of a database and the design of a program to access that data. In the database would be information about students, professors, rooms, and courses. The program would enable users to enroll students in courses, assign professors to teach courses, schedule courses in certain rooms, and so on. The program would access and update the database, in effect supporting the daily business of the school.

Now consider the university information system from an object-oriented perspective. In the real world, there are students, professors, rooms, and courses. All of these things would be considered objects. In

---

DEFINITION

Paradigm. (pronounced *para-dime*) An overall strategy or viewpoint for doing things. A paradigm is a specific mindset.

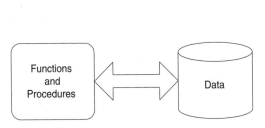

A Structured Application

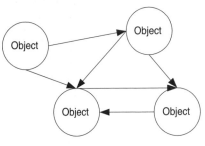

An Object Application

the real world, students know things (they have names, addresses, birth dates, telephone numbers, and so on) and they do things (enroll in courses, drop courses, and pay tuition). Professors also know things (the courses they teach and their names) and they do things (input marks and make schedule requests). From a systems perspective, rooms know things (the building they're in and their room number) and should be able to do things, too (such as tell you when they are available and enable you to reserve them for a certain period of time). Courses also know things (their title, description, and who is taking the course) and should be able to do things (such as letting students enroll in them or drop them).

To implement this system, we would define a collection of classes (a *class* is a generic representation of similar objects) that interact with each other. For example, we would have "Course," "Student," "Professor," and "Room" classes. The collection of these classes would make up our application, which would include both the functionality (the program) and the data.

As you can see, the OO approach results in a completely different view of what an application is all about. Rather than having a program that accesses a database, we have an application that exists in what is called an object space. The *object space* is where both the program and the data for the application reside. I discuss this concept in further detail in Chapter 5 but, for now, think of the object space as virtual memory.

Figure 1-1.
Comparing the structured and object-oriented paradigms

For individuals, OO is a whole new way to think. For organizations, OO requires a complete change in its system development culture.

1.2 How Is This Book Organized?

The Object Primer covers leading-edge OO techniques and concepts that have been proven in the development of real-world applications. It covers in detail why you should learn this new approach called *object orientation*, requirements techniques, such as use cases and CRC modeling, OO

DEFINITIONS
Class. A template from which objects are created (instantiated). Although in the real world Doug, Wayne, and Bill are all "student objects," we would model the class "Student" instead.
Object space. The memory space, including all accessible permanent storage, in which objects exist and interact with one another.
Object. A person, place, thing, concept, event, screen, or report. Objects both know things (that is, they have data) and they do things (that is, they have functionality).
Object-oriented paradigm. A development strategy based on the concept of building systems from reusable components called objects.
OO. An acronym used interchangeably for two terms: Object-oriented and object orientation. For example, when we say OO programming, we really mean object-oriented programming. When we say this is a book that describes OO, we really mean this it is a book that describes object orientation.

The Object Primer *covers everything you need to know to get you started in OO development.*

concepts, OO analysis and design using the UML modeling techniques, OO programming, OO testing, and the OO software process. The book ends with a discussion of how to continue your learning process, including descriptions of common object-oriented technologies and techniques you might want to consider applying on software projects.

Figure 1-2 depicts the organization of *The Object Primer*, showing the individual chapters and the relationships between them. Table 1-1 summarizes the contents of each chapter. On the left side of the diagram are the chapters that describe the fundamental activities of the software process, such as gathering requirements, object-oriented analysis, and object-oriented programming. The arrows between the boxes represent the general relationships between the chapters: you see the chapters describing gathering requirements, validating requirements, and object-oriented analysis are closely related to one another. Chapter 9 covers object-oriented testing and describes testing techniques that should be used to validate your analysis, design, and programming efforts. Along the right-hand side of Figure 1-2 are listed several "supporting" chapters, chapters that present material that is critical to your understanding of the object-oriented paradigm.

DEFINITION
Unified Modeling Language (UML). The definition of a standard modeling language for object-oriented software, including the definition of a modeling notation and the semantics for applying it as defined by the Object Management Group (OMG).

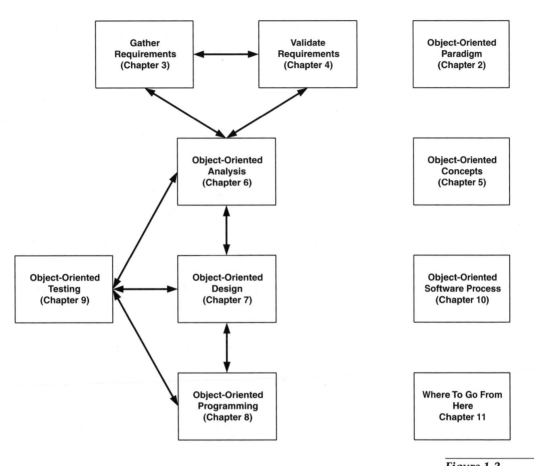

Figure 1-2.
The organization of
this book

1.3 How to Read This Book

Programmers, Designers, and Project Managers

Read the entire book, cover to cover. It's tempting to skip to Chapter 5, which overviews object-oriented concepts, and start reading from there, but that would be a major mistake. Chapter 5 builds on many of the ideas presented in the first four chapters; therefore, reading ahead is not to your advantage.

Business Analysts and User Representatives

Chapters 3 and 4 are written specifically for you, describing in detail the techniques for gathering and validating the user requirements for an OO application. Business analysts should also read Chapter 5, which

Table 1-1. The material contained in each chapter

Chapter	Description
2: A New Software Paradigm	Discussion of the advantages and disadvantages of object orientation, why objects are here to stay, and an overview of the software process.
3: Gathering Requirements	Description of requirements gathering techniques, including use cases, change cases, CRC modeling, interviewing, and user interface prototyping. A discussion of how the techniques work together is included.
4: Validating Requirements	Description of requirements validation techniques such as use case scenario testing and requirements walkthroughs.
5: Object-Oriented Concepts	Description of the fundamental concepts of object orientation, including inheritance, polymorphism, aggregation, and encapsulation.
6: Object-Oriented Analysis	Description of common object-oriented analysis techniques such as sequence diagrams and class diagrams. A description of how to make the transition from requirements to analysis is presented, as well as how all the techniques fit together.
7: Object-Oriented Design	Description of common object-oriented design techniques such as class diagrams, state chart diagrams, collaboration diagrams, and persistence models. A description of how to make the transition from analysis to design is presented, as well as how the techniques fit together.
8: Object-Oriented Programming	Overview of common object-oriented programming tips and techniques. A discussion of how to make the transition from design to coding is presented.
9: Object-Oriented Testing	Overview of the Full Lifecycle Object-Oriented Testing (FLOOT) methodology and techniques.
10: Object-Oriented Software Process	Overview of the Object-Oriented Software Process (OOSP) and the enhanced lifecycle of the Unified Process.
11: Where to Go From Here	Discussion of what you need to do to continue your OO learning process, including a description of leading object technologies and techniques such as Java, Enterprise Java-Beans (EJB), C++, and component-based development.

> **DEFINITION**
>
> *Full lifecycle object-oriented testing (FLOOT).* A testing methodology for object-oriented development that comprises testing techniques that, taken together, provide methods to verify that your application works correctly at each stage of development.

describes the fundamental concepts of object orientation, and Chapter 6, which describes OO analysis techniques. Both groups should also read Chapter 10, which describes the overall software process for object-oriented software—this will help put the overall effort into context for you and give you a greater appreciation of how software is developed, maintained, and supported.

Students

Like the first group of people, you should also read this book from cover to cover. Furthermore, you should read this book two or three weeks before your midterm test on object orientation, and not the night before the exam. This stuff takes a while to sink in (actually it takes much longer than a few weeks, but there's only so much time in a school term).

1.4 What You Have Learned

The object-oriented paradigm is a software development strategy based on the idea of building systems from reusable components called objects. As you saw in Figure 1-1, the primary concept behind the object-oriented paradigm is, instead of defining systems as two separate parts (data and functionality), you now define systems as a collection of interacting objects. Objects do things (that is, they have functionality) and they know things (that is, they have data).

Object orientation is the norm, not the exception.

Objects are here to stay.

Chapter 2

Object Orientation: A New Software Paradigm

What You Will Learn in This Chapter

The potential advantages of object orientation
The potential disadvantages of object orientation
Why objects are here to stay
What object standards exist
The object-oriented software process

Why You Need to Read This Chapter

To understand the object paradigm, you need to understand what its strengths and weaknesses are, and what object standards and software processes exist that are applicable to object-oriented development.

Although object orientation (OO) was first introduced in the late 1960s, for the most part it stayed in the labs until the mid-to-late 1980s when the corporate and system engineering worlds took notice of languages such as Smalltalk and C++. Since then there have been many spectacular successes applying object technologies and techniques as well as several spectacular failures. To be successful applying the OO techniques described in this book you need to understand the potential benefits and drawbacks of OO as well as the basics of the OO software process.

2.1 The Potential Benefits of Object Orientation

OO offers the potential to solve (or at least lessen) many of the problems currently faced by the IT industry. OO was popularized in the corporate world in the late 1980s, it became the de facto development standard in the mid-1990s, and has been growing in use ever since. OO offers many potential benefits:

- Increased reusability
- Increased extensibility
- Improved quality
- Financial benefits
- Increased chance of project success
- Reduced maintenance burden
- Reduced application backlog
- Managed complexity

2.1.1 Increased Reusability

Object orientation offers more opportunities for increased reusability.

The OO paradigm provides opportunities for reuse through the concepts of inheritance, polymorphism, encapsulation, modularity, coupling, and cohesion. While I won't discuss them here, you will see in Chapter 5 that these are all straightforward concepts that lead to better design. Although the use of OO does not guarantee you will develop reusable software or that you will, in turn, reuse software yourself, it does offer significantly more opportunities for reuse than the structured paradigm.

2.1.2 Increased Extensibility

Because classes have both data and functionality when you add new features to the system, you only need to make changes in one place: the applicable class. This is different than in the structured world where a change in a single business rule could affect many programs. For example, say you have four structured programs that access the student data table in a university database. Consequently, you add the attribute "Guardian name" to the table. To support this change, all four structured programs need to be modified to work with the new data. Now say you've developed exactly the same systems using object technology. Instead of coding four different applications to work with the student data, you instead code one single class called "Student," which works with this data that encapsulates (contains) both the functionality and the data appropriate to students. To add "Guardian name" you merely have to modify the definition and source code of the class "Student" in one place, not in four. Clearly, this is easier.

Objects encapsulate both functionality and data, making it easier to maintain your software.

As a second example, you may need to modify your existing system to keep track of university administrators. A university administrator is just like a professor, except that in addition to teaching courses, he or she also schedules them. In a structured application, you would potentially need to add a new data table for administrators and a new program module to handle administrative functions. That is a lot of work. In an OO system, you would define the class "Administrator," which would inherit from "Professor." Granted, you would still need to write code to schedule courses; however, you would not have to worry about all the data and functionality already defined for professors.

Inheritance enables you to reuse existing behaviors, making it easier to enhance your software.

The preceding examples illustrate how easy it is to extend existing OO applications. First, existing classes are easily changed because both the functionality and data reside in one place. Second, through the use of inheritance, new classes are created that take advantage of the behavior implemented by existing classes. No more reinventing the wheel.

Object orientation offers more opportunities for increased extensibility.

2.1.3 Improved Quality

Quality systems are on time, on budget, and meet or exceed the expectations of their users. Improved quality comes from increased participation of users in systems development. As you will see in this book, OO systems development techniques provide greater opportunity for users to participate in the development process (for example, Chapter 3 presents CRC modeling and use case modeling, techniques where users perform the bulk of requirements definition).

Object orientation offers more opportunities for greater software quality.

DEFINITION

Inheritance The representation of an *is a*, *is like*, or *is kind of* relationship between two classes. Inheritance promotes reuse by enabling a subclass to benefit automatically from all the behavior it inherits from its superclass(es).

2.1.4 Financial Benefits

Object orientation enables you to build systems better, faster, and cheaper (BFC).

Reusability, extensibility, and improved quality are all technical benefits. While they all sound like good things (and they are), the reason they are important is because they lead to the business benefits of OO. From the point of view of our users (remember them, they are the people who pay the bills), the real benefits are we can build systems better, faster, and cheaper (BFC).

While most OO books like to concentrate on the technical benefits, the only ones that count are the business benefits, such as BFC. Not only are the BFC benefits applicable to project development, they also apply to production. Systems with high rates of reusability have less code to maintain than systems with low rates of reusability (that's because instead of reusing common code, the same code appears over and over again). The more code, the more effort it takes to maintain it. Furthermore, by definition, a system that is easily extensible is easy to maintain. Finally, a system that meets the needs of its users will receive fewer change requests and fewer support calls than a system that doesn't meet their needs.

The benefits of OO are realized throughout the entire development lifecycle, not just during programming.

It's important to note that the benefits of object orientation are achieved throughout the entire lifecycle. We use inheritance throughout analysis, design, and programming. This means we can reuse our analysis and design efforts, as well as our code. To add new features or to modify existing features in a system, we must first update our analysis and design models, and then modify our code. Therefore, both our models and our code must be extensible (and they are). An indispensable way to improve the quality of systems effectively is to increase the involvement of users throughout the entire development process. That is exactly what OO does. Therefore, because the technical benefits are realized throughout the entire development lifecycle, the BFC ones are also realized (remember, the BFC benefits are the direct result of the technical benefits).

2.1.5 Increased Chance of Project Success

Traditionally, developers have not done a good job at delivering affordable systems in a timely manner that meets the needs of their users. As software professionals, we need to find a way to develop high-quality systems quickly and inexpensively: object orientation is one potential solution. I consider a project successful if it is on time, on budget, and meets the needs of its users. Unfortunately, by this definition, almost every single systems development project has failed. Although, at first glance, my definition may appear harsh, it is actually quite fair. To convince yourself of this, consider the following scenario:

Scenario You and your spouse have decided to take the plunge and have a house custom-built for your family. You go to a house developer, describe your needs and your budget, and tell him to draw up a plan. At your next meeting, the developer shows you something he calls a prototype, which is a scale model of your house that is made out of cardboard. Because it is not what you want, you tell him about a few changes that need to be made. After a few meetings where you evaluate the prototype and suggest changes, you finally have a house design you like. The developer has architectural plans drawn up and, at the next meeting, gets you to sign off on them. You are not an architect, so you really don't understand the drawings. They seem complicated, though, so you think they must be right. You and the developer finally settle on a price of $200,000 and a moving date of June 14th (it's now March 2).

Time goes by, and every second week you receive a progress report from the developer. Although he keeps telling you everything is going well, you begin to suspect something is wrong. Then, during the last week of May, your worst fears are confirmed—you get a call from the developer: "Gee, it seems we're a little behind schedule. Because of unforeseen complications, we've had to tear down and rebuild a few sections of the house, so it won't be ready until July 30th." You stand there in disbelief—your house is going to be seven weeks late, a time slippage of 50 percent! Where are you going to live? To make things worse, the developer tells you "Oh, by the way, we're also a little over budget. Now that we've actually started building the house, we have a better idea of what it will really cost: $400,000." As you try not to faint, you realize that $400,000 is double the original estimate. You are not happy about the situation, but you have already invested a lot of money, so you tell the developer to continue.

August 14th rolls around and you are finally able to move into your house (the schedule slipped an additional two weeks). You don't mind as much, because the final bill came in at only $385,000. You walk through the front door, and as you try to turn on the lights, you realize there's no light switch. You turn to the developer and ask him how to turn on the lights. "You wanted lights in your house? You never told me that!" he exclaims. Angrily, you reply "Of course I wanted lights! Hey, where are the wall plugs? Isn't there any electricity in this house?"

"There wasn't any electrical wiring in the architectural plans or in the prototype, didn't you notice?" says the developer. "You signed off on them. This is the house you've paid for, so you better get used to it."

> Unbelievably, you shout, "This isn't right! You're incompetent! You'll never work in this town again! Get out of my house!" The developer exits quickly, and begins walking to his truck, saying under his breath "That's the problem with people, they don't know what they want. And then when I can't read their minds, they blame me. Boy are people ever stupid."

Users are expert at business and they're the only ones who can tell you what they need.

Sound familiar? How happy would you be if this really had happened to you? How do you think your users feel when the systems you develop are late, over budget, and/or don't meet their needs? In our scenario, the house developer did not get the right specifications from his clients. While prototyping was an effective technique for understanding the basic needs of his clients, it didn't provide him with the full details he needed to produce a complete design for the house. Sure, forgetting to put electricity in a house seems like a fairly obvious problem. However, systems developers often miss features that seem basic and obvious to our users. The reasons developers miss "obvious" features is not that we are incompetent, it's because *we don't know the business well enough to ask the right questions.*

You need models that communicate the required information and that users understand.

The house developer showed his clients drawings (models) that they didn't really understand, but still had to accept anyway. The fundamental problem is the developer didn't have a medium he could use to communicate the design effectively to his clients. What he needed was a model that was simple to understand, but still showed the details necessary to make an educated decision about the design of the house. His prototype was simple, yet lacked the required details, while his architectural plans were too complicated. Just like the house developer, as a system developer, you must have a way to communicate your design to your users in a way they can understand.

You need to work closely with your users.

The developer then went away and built a house that did not meet the needs of its eventual owners. Had the buyer been more involved with the development of the house, he might have realized the house needed to be wired for electricity. This is a fundamental flaw in the way systems are currently developed using structured techniques. Although we know the chance of project success increases as users become more involved in development, users are typically only involved during analysis and user acceptance testing, but not during design and development. You need to find a way to increase the involvement of your users in the development process (in Chapters 3 and 4, you learn techniques to do just that).

DEFINITION

Project success. A project is considered a success when it is on time, on budget, and meets the needs of its users.

Furthermore, the developer delivered the house late and over budget. The main cause for this was he didn't have an understanding of how much it would really cost and how long it would take before he started building. Had he drawn up better design plans, he would not have wasted as much time and materials when he had to rebuild sections of the house. Moreover, had he made use of reusable components (prebuilt walls, kitchens, bathrooms, and so forth), he could have reduced both the time and cost in building the house.

System developers face the same sort of issues. When we don't spend adequate time designing an application, we end up scrapping and rewriting large sections of code. Even when we do spend enough time designing the system, we produce a large amount of documentation that the user doesn't understand, and probably does not have time to read. We could just as well write our design in Latin, for all the good it will do our users. Instead of producing incomprehensible documents, we should find ways to inexpensively communicate our design before we begin construction. Wouldn't it have been nice to find out the light switches were missing before the house was finished?

Time invested in defining requirements and modeling pays off in the long run.

Besides, we are constantly reinventing the wheel by programming the same things repeatedly (how many times have you programmed the logic to go to the next/previous screen?) By using reusable code (and even reusable designs), we can dramatically reduce the time and cost of systems development.

You can reuse a wide variety of artifacts, including code, models, and components.

All software projects can be successful. As a developer, you must use techniques that enable you to work with your users to a greater extent and to communicate your designs to them in a way they understand. You must also invest in reusable components to a greater extent to reduce development time and cost. As you will see, object orientation enables you to do all of these things, and more.

Meanwhile, Back in Reality

Do not get me wrong here, I am not saying this is entirely our fault. It is really difficult to convince users they need to invest the time it takes to get proper user requirements. It also doesn't help that users are constantly changing their minds about what they want (often their needs have changed, but that's another story). Not to mention that users want systems yesterday, often pushing for unreasonable deadlines.

2.1.6 Reduced Maintenance Burden

Software organizations currently spend significant resources maintaining and operating software, and because of the long waiting list of work to be done, it takes significant time to get new projects started. These two problems are respectively called "The Maintenance Burden" and "The Application Backlog." These are problems that object orientation can help you overcome.

DEFINITIONS
Application backlog. The average amount of time it takes for the systems department to start the development of a system as measured from the time that the idea for the project is first conceived.
Maintenance burden. The fundamental need to require software organizations to invest money in the support, operation, and enhancement of existing hardware.
Year 2000 (Y2K) crisis. The need for organizations in the late 1990s to update and/or replace software that was written to store the year as two digits instead of four.

Figure 2-1 depicts one of the most pressing problems facing information system (IS) departments today—most of the department's budget is spent on supporting and maintaining existing "legacy" systems. In fact, some organizations spend upward of 95 percent of their IS budgets on maintenance and support-related activities, although 80 percent is typically the norm. However your IS budget is proportioned, little of it is spent developing new systems, a phenomena called the "maintenance burden." In fact, in the late 1990s, many organizations virtually stopped new development altogether because of the Y2K crisis, an unfortunate example of

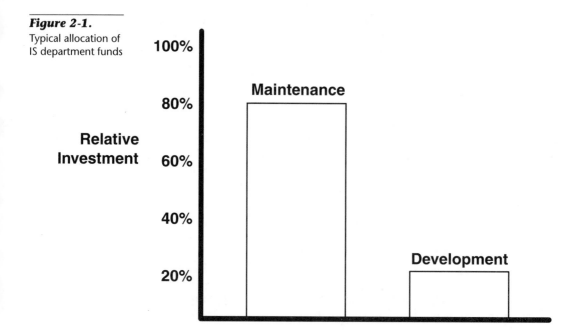

Figure 2-1.
Typical allocation of IS department funds

how dire the maintenance burden can become. The maintenance burden exists for several reasons:

1. **Many systems were developed in the past that are still in use.** Some organizations have been developing systems for more than 30 years, and the maintenance effort has thereby grown over time. Just as you need to spend money occasionally on maintaining your car to keep it going, you need to spend money to keep a computer system going. This is the most common excuse given by developers and, for the most part, it is true, although it does not fully explain why we spend so much on maintenance. The next two reasons do explain.

2. **System documentation is poor, if it exists at all.** Many developers neither like to document their work nor update the documentation, if it does exist. As a result, system documentation is almost always out of date and, in fact, it is common to encounter systems that are completely undocumented. The lack of documentation dramatically increases the cost of maintenance—instead of being able to look at the documentation and determine what is wrong, maintenance programmers need to spend days, and sometimes even weeks or months, looking at the code. That's slow and expensive.

3. **Compared to the standards of today, legacy systems are poorly built.** In the past, developers didn't realize that many of the techniques they were using would lead to systems that are difficult to maintain. They didn't realize the importance of simple strategies such as internal documentation, use of whitespace, intelligent variable naming, loose coupling, and high cohesion. Many of the concepts and techniques of OO specifically address the need to build systems that are easy to maintain.

Meanwhile, Back in Reality
Criticizing is much easier than doing. I'm guilty of all these problems, as you probably are. We can point fingers all we want, but that won't help the situation. The best attitude to take, I believe, is to recognize these problems exist and that we need to deal with them.

2.1.7 Reduced Application Backlog

In many organizations, a two-to-five year "application backlog" currently exists. This is the average amount of time it takes for the systems department to start on the development of a system as measured from the time the idea for the project was first conceived. Figure 2-2 shows that the

---

DEFINITIONS

Cohesion. The degree of relatedness of an encapsulated unit (such as a component or a class); that is, in general, it is better to have high cohesion.

Coupling. The degree of dependence between two items; in general, it is better to reduce coupling wherever possible.

Whitespace. Blanks, such as blank lines or spaces.

---

total implementation time for a system is made up of two parts: the time it takes to get started on the project (the application backlog) and the time it takes to build it. If we can reduce the application backlog, we can get systems out the door faster.

During the recession of the early 1990s, many organizations put off development projects in an effort to reduce short-term expenses, and then, in the late 1990s, their focus on surviving the Y2K crisis motivated them to forgo new projects even further. By putting more projects in the queue, the application backlog naturally increased. While the recession and Y2K don't fully explain the entire application backlog, they did help to increase it.

Fortunately, the application backlog might not be as bad as we think, because if a project has been waiting for five years to get started, chances are it never will. Most organizations take on new projects in priority order, shoving lower-priority projects to the back of the line. Therefore, projects that have been waiting a long time might never actually happen. Projects such as this should be removed from the queue and no longer counted as part of the application backlog. While this will definitely help to reduce the backlog, a serious wait still exists for many projects to get started in most organizations.

Figure 2-2.
How the application backlog affects the total implementation time of a system.

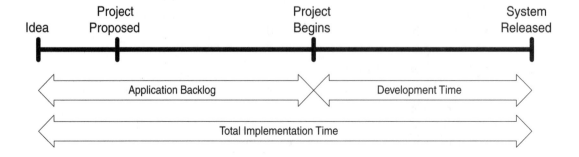

More important, OO can help to reduce the application backlog. The main reason an application backlog exists is that organizations simply cannot get around to working on every new project. Because OO techniques are more productive than structured techniques (developers can create applications faster and spend less effort maintaining them), organizations are able to free up resources sooner to tackle new projects. In the long run, object orientation can help to reduce the application backlog.

Projects that have been waiting for several years most likely will never make it to the top of your organization's priority list.

Meanwhile, Back in Reality

The application backlog is never going to go away. Every time you deliver a new application feature, chances are your users are going to ask for two more. While this can be frustrating, it's human nature. I like to look at it like this: I would rather have my users asking me to continue working on a project than to have them let me go because there's not any more work for me to do.

2.1.8 Managed Complexity

The applications we are being asked to develop are becoming more and more complex. When the structured paradigm was introduced in the 1960s and 1970s, we were developing large, batch, mainframe-based transaction processing systems. While these systems were often huge, they were fairly straightforward—you get the data, you crunch the data, and then you output the data. Systems of today are more complex. Applications are now online and real-time, developed for client/server, peer-to-peer, and Internet-based architectures. They use a wide range of user interfaces, including both graphical and browser-based, and support a complex and swiftly changing business environment. In short, today's development needs are several orders of magnitude more complex than what structured approaches were designed to handle.

On that account, how does object orientation help to manage software complexity? First, consider the way computer hardware is built—you take a collection of industry standard chips, plug them into a motherboard, and put it in a plastic case. The advantage of this approach is the chip designers dealt with the complexity of whatever the chip does. The people who use the chip in their computers don't need to worry about the details of the chip, they only need to know how to use it properly. Think of it like this: It is much easier to build a computer using chips than it is using transistors. So wouldn't it be nice to be able to build computer software like this, too? This is one of the main benefits of object orientation: You can create applications from reusable components called objects. Somebody deals with the complexity of part of the application by creating an object that deals with it. Then other developers use the object as part of their application. This enables you to create complex systems out of a few simple parts (objects).

You can build complex software from well-designed, reusable objects.

Expect the software you build today will need to be changed tomorrow.

Second, you have to design your software with the expectation that it will need to be modified. When you recognize that your systems will need to change over time, sometimes on very short notice, you can take that into account when you initially design them. In this book, you will see that when object-oriented concepts are applied correctly, they lead to systems that are easy to modify and maintain. I also share with you some of my development philosophies, such as the following: You always need to port your software (even "simple" tasks such as operating system upgrades and database upgrades count as ports); also a sign of successful software is when your users conceive new requirements for it, so you must always expect to have to extend your software.

Well-designed, object-oriented software enables you to react quickly to changes in your environment.

Third, part of managing complexity is being able to respond quickly when your environment changes. Business needs change and you need to be able to react quickly to those changes. This means you need to be able to develop new systems quickly and to modify existing ones even more quickly. Gone are the days of two-year, three-year, or even five-year projects. You need to be able to build systems in months, and sometimes even in weeks. By implementing complicated concepts and business rules in objects, you can build complex systems much more quickly.

2.2 The Potential Drawbacks of OO

Nothing is perfect, including object orientation. While many exciting benefits exist to OO, they come at a price:

1. **OO requires a greater concentration on requirements, analysis, and design.** Actually, so did structured techniques, but this reality was often ignored to the detriment of many software projects. You can't build a system that meets the needs of your users if your don't know what those needs are (you need to do requirements). You can't start building a system unless you know how it all fits together (you need to do analysis and design). Both your users and your organization's senior management often underestimate or don't realize the importance of requirements, analysis, and design; consequently, you must be prepared to deal with this issue.

2. **Developers must work closely with users.** Many (but, luckily, not all) developers must completely change their view of the

---

DEFINITION

Software port. The migration of software from one platform to another. You often need to port software to other operating systems, other database systems, and even other hardware platforms.

user community. Users are the experts. Users are your clients. Including these people in the development of a system makes sense. At the same time, both users and senior management must understand this and support the idea that you need to increase user involvement in systems development. This is easier said than done, and it will take months or even years.

"User" is a four-letter word, but that isn't such a bad thing.

3. **OO requires a complete change in mindset on the part of individuals.** Systems are now made up of a bunch of interacting objects that have both functionality and data. This is completely different than the structured approach, which separates functionality and data. Do not underestimate the huge difference between these two approaches.

4. **OO requires the development culture of your IS department to change.** The change in the mindset of individual developers actually reflects an overall change in your development culture. Individual developers will be using a new paradigm, do more analysis and design (and, hence, significantly less programming), and work with their users to a greater extent. If these changes aren't already happening in your organization, then you need to undergo a significant culture change when you introduce OO techniques into your IS department.

5. **OO is more than just programming.** Part of the process of changing your development culture is the realization that there's more to system development than just programming. Don't forget that you achieve the benefits of OO throughout the entire system development lifecycle. This means you can't just go out and download a Java development environment and get the benefits of OO. You actually have to learn how to do OO correctly. This is not easy and it is not quick.

6. **Many OO benefits are long term.** While increased reusability and extensibility help to reduce development time and cost, OO truly pays off when you need to extend and enhance your software. This means you may have to wait several years before you begin to benefit significantly from OO.

7. **OO demands up-front investments in training, education, and tools.** Organizations must train and educate their development staff. They need to buy OO development tools, books, and magazines. These steps require up-front investment. The short-term need for investment, coupled with the long-term payback, may mean senior management will think twice about OO.

8. **OO techniques do not guarantee you will build the right system**. While OO offers the potential for increasing the probability of project success, it still depends on the ability of the people involved. Everyone—developers, users, and managers—must be committed to working together to create an atmosphere in which the OO paradigm can flourish.

9. **OO necessitates increased testing**. To be fair, the real issue is, because object development is typically iterative in nature and because you probably are developing complex software using objects, the end result is you need to spend more time testing. Iterative development requires greater emphasis on regression testing, the validation that existing software still works after changes have been made. The more complex your software, the more effort is required to validate it.

10. **OO is only part of the solution**. Object orientation is not a silver bullet. You still need to use computer-aided system engineering (CASE) tools to help you to model. You still need to perform quality assurance (QA) activities to ensure a system meets the needs of its users. You still need to produce usable interfaces so your users can work with systems effectively. OO is not a panacea; however, it is part of the solution.

2.3 Objects Are Here to Stay

Object languages, such as Java and C++, are the norm for new software development.

My belief is that object orientation is here to stay. In the early 1990s, you could safely claim that objects were merely a fad, but today they are a significant part of the software technology landscape. Object-oriented languages, such as C++ and Java, as well as object-based languages, such as Microsoft's Visual Basic, have long eclipsed traditional structured languages, such as C, COBOL, and PL/1. In fact, C++ is the object-oriented version of C and Object-COBOL is the OO version of COBOL may one

---

DEFINITIONS

Iterative development. A nonserial approach to development where you are likely to do some requirements definition, some modeling, some programming, or some testing on any given day.

Quality assurance. The validation that something was built the right way.

Regression testing. The validation that existing software still works after changes have been made.

Testing. The validation that the right thing was built.

day replace COBOL in many organizations. Whenever I browse through the software section in the magazine rack at my local bookstore, I am inundated by magazines for object languages such as Java and C++, but I would be hard pressed to find any about COBOL programming.

The component paradigm is arguably the logical extension of the object paradigm. With the emergence of component-based software development, you see object-based technologies dominating this market. Yes, developing components using COBOL is possible, but it is much easier to do it in object languages, which is exactly what the majority of component builders are doing.

Objects are the primary enabling technology for components.

2.4 Object Standards

Another reason I believe objects are here to stay is because of the strong standards on which object technology is based. The Object Management Group (OMG) is an industry-recognized standards body, which is responsible for standards such as UML and CORBA that, respectively, are the definition of a standard modeling language for object-oriented software and a standard architecture for supporting distributed objects. The American National Standards Institute (ANSI), *http://www.ansi.org*, has defined a standard for the C++ language, called ANSI C++. Sun Microsystems, *http://www.sun.com*, actively maintains, enhances, and supports a de facto–standard definition for Java and for related standards such as Enterprise JavaBeans (EJB). The Object Database Management Group (ODMG), *http://www.odmg.org*, actively maintains, enhances, and supports a standard definition for object-oriented databases and the Object Query Language (OQL).

2.5 The Object-Oriented Software Process

An increased focus has occurred lately on improving the software process within most organizations. In part, this is because of the Y2K debacle, because of the 80—90 percent failure of large-scale software projects (Jones, 1996), and because of a growing realization that following a mature software process is a key determinant to the success of a software project. A software process is a set of project phases, stages, methods, techniques, and practices that people employ to develop and maintain software, and its associated artifacts (plans, documents, models, code, test cases, manuals, and so forth). Not only do you need a software process, you also need one that is proven to work in practice, a software process tailored to meet your exact needs.

An effective software process enables your organization to increase its productivity when developing software. First, by understanding the fun-

DEFINITIONS

Common Object Request Broker Architecture (CORBA). A standard architecture for supporting distributed objects defined by the Object Management Group (OMG).

Enterprise JavaBeans (EJB). EJB is a component architecture, defined by Sun Microsystems, for the development and deployment of component-based distributed business applications.

Object Database Management Group (ODMG). A standards body responsible for the standard definition for object-oriented databases and the Object Query Language (OQL).

Object Management Group (OMG). An industry-recognized standards body responsible for standards such as the Unified Modeling Language (UML) and the Common Object Request Broker Architecture (CORBA).

The Unified Modeling Language (UML). The definition of a standard modeling language for object-oriented software, including the definition of a modeling notation and the semantics for applying it as defined by the Object Management Group (OMG).

An effective software process dramatically increases your productivity and chances of success.

damentals of how software is developed, you can make intelligent decisions, such as knowing to stay away from wonder tools that claim to automate fundamental portions of the software process. Second, it enables you to standardize your efforts, promoting reuse and consistency between project teams. Third, it provides an opportunity for you to introduce the best industry practices, such as code inspections, configuration management, change control, and architectural modeling to your software organization. Fourth, it enables you to improve your organization's maintenance and support efforts, also referred to as production efforts, in several ways: by defining how to manage change and appropriately allocate maintenance changes to future releases of your software, by defining how to transition software smoothly into operations and support, and by defining how the operations and support efforts are actually performed (without effective operations and support processes, your software will quickly become shelfware).

Although you can choose from many software processes and software methodologies, the two I focus on in this book are the Object-Oriented Software Process (Ambler, 1998b; Ambler, 1999) and the Unified Process (Kruchten, 1999; Jacobson, Booch, and Rumbaugh, 1999). Although Chapter 10 discusses both of these processes in detail, I briefly describe them here to help put the rest of the book into context.

Figure 2-3 depicts the lifecycle of the Object-Oriented Software Process (OOSP), comprised of a collection of process patterns. Similar to the Unified

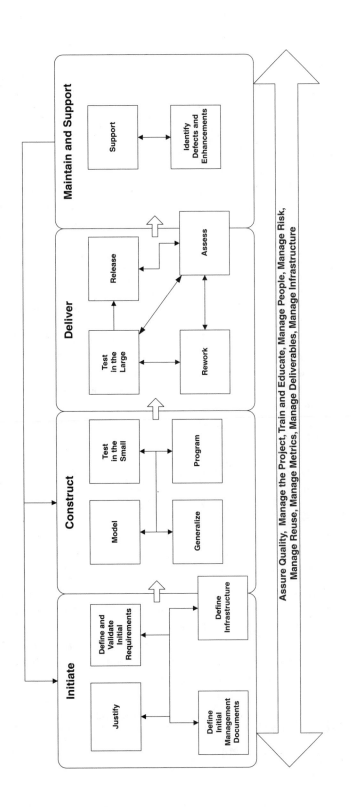

Figure 2-3.
The Object-Oriented Software Process (OOSP) lifecycle

Process patterns are reusable building blocks from which you can tailor a software process to meet your organization's unique needs.

Process, OOSP is based on the concept that large-scale, mission-critical software development is fundamentally serial in the large, iterative in the small, delivering incremental releases in Internet time. A process pattern is a collection of general techniques, actions, and/or tasks (activities) that solve a specific software process problem taking the relevant forces/factors into account. Just as design patterns describe proven solutions to common software design problems, process patterns present proven solutions to common software process patterns.

The Unified Process is likely to become the industry standard for object-oriented software development.

The Unified Process is the latest endeavor of Rational Corporation, the same people who introduced what has become the industry-standard modeling notation, the Unified Modeling Language (UML). Figure 2-4 presents the enhanced lifecycle[1] of the Unified Process (Ambler and Constantine 2000a–c), made up of five serial phases and eleven core workflows. Along the bottom of the diagram you see that any given development cycle through the Unified Process should be organized into iterations. The basic concept is that your team works through appropriate workflows in an iterative manner so at the end of each iteration you produce an internal executable that can be worked with by your user community. This reduces the risk of your project by improving communication between you and your customers. Another risk reduction technique built into the Unified Process is the concept that you should make a go/no-go decision at the end of each phase—if a project is going to fail then you want to stop it as early as possible in its lifecycle.

You need at least a basic understanding of the software process to be a successful developer.

You definitely don't need to be an expert in all aspects of the software process. Few people actually are. But you do need to have at least a broad understanding of how software is developed, maintained, and supported to be effective at your choice of specialties. Few developers even have a basic understanding of the software process, and the vast majority of software projects fail. Perhaps a correlation exists between these two facts? Perhaps so.

2.6 What You Have Learned

You have learned that object orientation offers the potential to solve many of the problems facing the systems industry today, although, as you see in Table 2-1, it also has its drawbacks. You also saw that the object paradigm requires a new approach to software development. OO requires you to work with your users more, as indicated in Table 2-2, and for you to put a greater emphasis on requirements, analysis, and design. The benefits of

---

[1] In mid-1999 I spent significant effort analyzing the Unified Process, comparing and contrasting it with my own work in process patterns and with other leading software processes. The result of my efforts was the enhanced lifecycle, enhanced for the most part by the process patterns of the OOSP, presented in this book and in my Unified Process book series published by R&D Books.

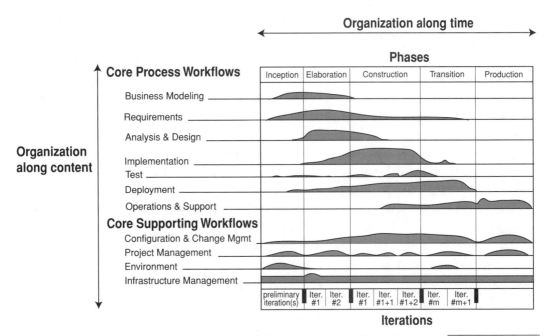

Figure 2-4.
The enhanced lifecycle for the Unified Process

OO are achieved throughout the entire development lifecycle, and OO requires a new mindset on the part of everyone: developers, users, and senior management alike. Furthermore, object orientation's iterative nature requires a culture change within IS departments, including a greater emphasis on testing and quality-assurance activities.

You also learned that object orientation is here to stay, in part, because it is supported by well-defined and accepted industry standards. Finally, you were presented with an overview of two of the leading object-oriented software processes: the Unified Process and the process patterns of the Object-Oriented Software Process (OOSP).

DEFINITIONS

Object-Oriented Software Process (OOSP). A collection of process patterns that, brought together, describes a complete process for developing, maintaining, and supporting software. OOSP is based on the concept that large-scale, mission-critical, software development is serial in the large, and iterative in the small, delivering incremental releases of software in Internet time.

Process pattern. A collection of general techniques, actions, and/or tasks (activities) that address specific software process problems.

Unified Process. A development process for object-oriented and component-based software.

Table 2-1. The potential benefits and drawbacks of object orientation

Potential benefits of OO	Potential drawbacks of OO
• Increased reusability	• Requires a greater concentration on requirements, analysis, and design
• Increased extensibility	
• Improved quality	• Requires developers to work closely with their users
• Financial (bottom-line) benefits enable us to build systems better, faster, and cheaper (BFC)	• Requires a complete change in mindset
	• Requires the development culture of your IS department change
• Increased chance of project success	• Is more than just programming
	• Produces long-term benefits
• Reduced maintenance burden	• Demands up-front investments in training, education, and tools
• Reduced application backlog	
• Managed complexity	• Techniques don't guarantee you'll build the right system
	• Requires more testing
	• Is only part of the solution to our problems

Table 2-2. How to deal with the demands of your users

Our users	So you should
Want less money spent on maintenance	Use OO techniques to reduce the maintenance burden
Don't want to wait for applications	Use OO techniques to reduce the application backlog
Want systems that meet their needs	Make sure you understand what your users want
Want systems on time and on budget	Spend more time in design and get it right before construction
Are the experts, not you	Involve your users in systems development
Pay the bills	Realize your users can get rid of (outsource) you

2.7 Review Questions

1. Which programming language exhibited the first aspects of the object-oriented paradigm?

2. In addition to the Unified Process and the Object-Oriented Software Process described in this chapter, what other software processes are applicable to object-oriented development? Compare and contrast them.

3. Why is extensibility an important feature for software? What must you trade off to achieve extensible software? When do these tradeoff(s) make sense? When don't they make sense?

4. Why should you work closely with your users? What are the trade-offs involved?

5. Why is it important to take maintenance, support, and operations issues into account when you are developing software? What potential trade-offs are involved?

6. What contributions to the object technology field were made by Grady Booch, Peter Coad, Martin Fowler, Erich Gamma, James Gosling, Brian Henderson-Sellers, Ivar Jacobson, Bertrand Meyer, and James Rumbaugh? Why are these contributions important?

Work with your users, not against them.

Chapter 3

Gathering Requirements: From Essential Use Cases to Change Cases

What You Will Learn in This Chapter

How to gather user requirements effectively
How to put together a requirements modeling team
How to interview
How to brainstorm
How to identify essential use cases for your system
How to define an essential prototype for your system
How to domain model using CRC cards
How to develop the supplementary specifications for your system
How to organize a modeling room

Why You Need to Read This Chapter

The more you work together with your users, the greater the chance of project success. CRC modeling, essential use case modeling, and essential user interface prototyping are effective ways to work together with your users to gather requirements.

The first step of software development is to gather user requirements. You cannot successfully build a system if you don't know what it should do. The greatest risk during this stage is that many people don't want to invest the time to elicit requirements; instead, they want to jump right into programming. Your subject-matter experts (SMEs) have their usual jobs to do and don't have the time to invest. Moreover, your developers want to get into the "real work" of coding, and senior management wants to see some progress on the project, which usually means they want to see some code written. You need to communicate with everyone involved that this work is critical to the success of the project and their efforts will pay off in the long run.

Use case modeling, domain modeling, and user interface prototyping are simple, yet effective, techniques for working with SMEs to determine the requirements for your system. A use case model is used to document the behavioral requirements and the functional tasks your system must support. Domain models represent the important business-domain concepts and their interrelationships. A user interface prototype models the user interface for your system, showing the screens/pages, reports, and other aspects of your user interface including their interrelationships.

In Chapter 6, you learn how to evolve your requirements models into analysis models.

In this chapter, I describe how to develop the "requirements versions" of use case models, domain models, and user interface prototypes, whereas in Chapter 6, I show you how to evolve them into their "analysis versions." As a result, I show you how to develop an essential use case model (Constantine and Lockwood, 1999), which is a generalized/high-level use case model for your system, a Class Responsibility Collaborator (CRC) model (Beck and Cunningham, 1989; Ambler, 1998a) for your domain model, and an essential user interface prototype (Constantine and Lockwood, 1999). In Chapter 6, you see how to evolve these models into a system use case model, an analysis-level class model, and a user interface prototype, respectively.

Figure 3-1 depicts the relationships between the artifacts you potentially develop as part of your requirements gathering efforts. The boxes represent the artifacts and the arrows represents "drives" relationships.

TIP *Your models evolve over time*	An important lesson to be learned from this book is object-oriented models evolve throughout development. Your domain model begins as a CRC model, and then evolves into an analysis class model, and then into a design class model and, eventually, into source code. Your user interface model begins life as an essential user interface prototype that evolves into a traditional user interface prototype, and then, eventually, into your user interface design. You get the point. In Chapters 6, 7, and 8, you learn how to evolve the models that you start as part of your requirements efforts.

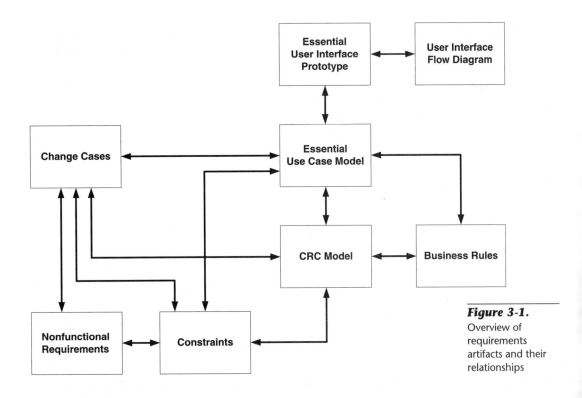

Figure 3-1.
Overview of requirements artifacts and their relationships

For example, you see that information contained in your CRC model drives/ affects information in your essential use case model and vice versa. In addition to the artifacts already described, during requirements gathering you will also potentially identify constraints, business rules, nonfunctional requirements, and change cases. A constraint is a restriction on the degree of freedom you have in providing a solution; a business rule is an operating principle or policy of your organization; a nonfunctional requirement focuses on issues such as standards, integration, and performance; and a change case describes a potential requirement your system may need to support in the future. Constraints, business rules, and nonfunctional requirements compose the supplementary specification (Kruchten, 1999) for your system and all the artifacts depicted in Figure 3-1 compose the requirements model for your system.

Your requirements artifacts are interrelated and drive the development of one another.

What makes a good requirement? Karl Wiegers (1999) believes good requirements are complete, correct, feasible, necessary, prioritized, unambiguous, and verifiable. In other words, they accurately describe what you have been asked to build, they are realistic, they solve one or more needs within your organization, and they can be demonstrably validated.

<table>
<tr>
<td>

TIP

Start at Your Enterprise Requirements Model

</td>
<td>

Some organizations have what is called an enterprise requirements model (Ambler and Constantine, 2000b) that reflects their high-level business requirements. If an up-to-date enterprise requirements model exists within your organization, then it's a perfect starting place to understand both your organization and how your system fits into the overall picture. You should be able to identify which high-level requirements your system will (partially) fulfill; otherwise, it is a clear sign that either the model is out of date or your system is not needed within your organization.

</td>
</tr>
</table>

3.1 Putting Together a Requirements Modeling Team

Requirments teams typically include a wide variety of roles.

Gradually, your requirements team will be composed of SMEs, who will provide you with detailed information regarding the requirements, and one or more requirements analysts. These people are responsible for requirements gathering, documenting, and validation. A formal requirements team often includes a facilitator (someone responsible for managing modeling sessions) and one or more scribes (people responsible for recording information as it is identified).

The first step to putting together a requirements team is to identify your project stakeholders. A *project stakeholder* is anyone who could be materially affected by the implementation of a new system or application (Leffingwell and Widrig, 2000). Your project stakeholders are the pool from which you can identify the SMEs and are often able to provide other sources of requirements, such as documentation regarding existing systems or pertinent regulatory information. They are also the people who help to validate your requirements (requirements validation is the topic of Chapter 4) and the people who "sign off" on the requirements if needed. Project stakeholders include

- The direct users of a system

- The customer/payer of the system

- Anyone who will be affected by the outputs the system produces

- Anyone who will evaluate and bless the system when it is delivered and deployed

- Any internal or external users of the system whose needs must be addressed

- Anyone who will operate or support the system once it is in production.

DEFINITIONS

Actor. A person, organization, or external system.

Behavioral requirement. The functional tasks your system must support.

Business rule. An operating principle or policy of your organization.

Change case. Describes a potential requirement your system may need to support in the future.

Change-case model. The collection of change cases applicable to your system.

Class diagram. Shows the classes of a system and the associations between them.

Class model. A class diagram and its associated documentation.

Class Responsibility Collaborator (CRC) card. A standard index card that has been divided into three sections: one indicating the name of the class the card represents, one listing the responsibilities of the class, and the third listing the names of the other classes with which this one collaborates to fulfill its responsibilities.

Class Responsibility Collaborator (CRC) model. A collection of CRC cards that model all or part of a system.

Constraint. A restriction on the degree of freedom you have in providing a solution.

Domain model. A representation of the business/domain concepts, and their interrelationships, applicable to your system. A domain model helps to establish the vocabulary for your project.

Essential use case. A simplified, abstract, generalized use case that captures the intentions of a user in a technology- and implementation-independent manner.

Essential use case model. A use case model comprised of essential use cases.

Essential user interface prototype. A low-fidelity prototype of a system's user interface that models the fundamental, abstract characteristics of a user interface.

Nonfunctional requirement. The standards, regulations, and contracts to which your system must conform; descriptions of interfaces to external systems that your system must interact with; performance requirements; design and implementation constraints; and the quality characteristics to which your system must conform.

Prototype. A simulation of an item, such as a user interface or a system architecture, the purpose of which is to communicate your approach to others before significant resources are invested in the approach.

Requirements model. The collection of artifacts, including your use case model, user interface model, domain model, change-case model, and supplementary specification that describes the requirements for your system.

Subject-matter expert (SME). A person who is responsible for providing pertinent information about the problem and/or technical domain either from personal knowledge or from research. *continued on page 36*

DEFINITIONS

Supplementary specification. The definition of the business rules, constraints, and nonfunctional requirements applicable to a system.

System use case. A detailed use case that describes how your system will fulfill the requirements of a corresponding essential use case, often referring to implementation-specific features, such as aspects of your user interface design.

System use case model. A use case model comprised of system use cases.

Use case. A sequence of actions that provide a measurable value to an actor.

Use case diagram. A UML diagram that shows use cases, actors, and their interrelationships.

Use case model. A model comprised of a use case diagram, use case definitions, and actor definitions. Use case models are used to document the behavioral requirements of a system.

User interface (UI). The portion of software with which the user directly interacts, including the screens, reports, documentation, and software support (via telephone, electronic mail, and so on).

User interface-flow diagram. A diagram that models the interface objects of your system and the relationships between them; also known as an interface-flow diagram, a windows navigation diagram, or an interface navigation diagram.

User interface model. A model comprising your user interface prototype, user interface flow diagram, and any corresponding documentation regarding your user interface.

Your requirements team may include both active and supporting members.

The next step is to identify the people who will be on your requirements modeling team. You may want to distinguish between active members of your team, such as the full-time requirement(s) analysts and key SMEs, and supporting members, such as SMEs with a focused expertise who are available to your team on an as-needed basis, and actual users who you can talk to and observe. Large organizations may have people who are professional facilitators and scribes, people who act as supporting members for one or more projects running in parallel; smaller organizations designate their requirements analysts to fulfill these roles. Fulfilling several roles on a project is often referred to as "wearing several hats."

Ideally, you want to have, at most, four or five active members on a requirements modeling team. Most software projects face one of two problems when defining a requirements modeling team: either they have too many people who want to be on the team or they have too few. In large organizations, it is common to find that every internal group

Karl Wiegers, in *Software Requirements* (1999), believes users have both rights and responsibilities with respect to software development. These rights and responsibilities effectively define a contract between a development team and its users, a contract that must be honored for the team to be successful.

TIP

Users Have Rights and Responsibilities

Users' rights:

- To expect analysts to speak their language
- To have analysts learn about their business and objectives
- To expect analysts to create a requirements model
- To receive explanations of requirements artifacts
- To expect developers to treat them with respect
- To hear ideas and alternatives for requirements and their implementation
- To describe characteristics that make the product easy to use
- To be presented with opportunities to adjust requirements to permit reuse
- To be given good-faith estimates of the costs of changes
- To receive a system that meets their functional and quality needs

Users' responsibilities:

- To educate analysts about their business
- To spend the time to provide and clarify requirements
- To be specific and precise about requirements
- To make timely decisions
- To respect a developer's assessment of cost and feasibility
- To set requirement priorities
- To review requirements models and prototypes
- To promptly communicate changes to the requirements
- To follow the organization's requirements change process
- To respect the requirements engineering processes that developers use

believes it needs to be involved in a software project, particularly high-profile ones, and insists it must have one or more representatives on the team. This results in "teams" of 10, 20, and sometimes even more people, and such teams have little hope of success because of the management burden of organizing this many people. If this is your situation, you must actively pare down your team to people with the ability to represent several groups. The second problem is the exact opposite of the first: you cannot get enough people on your team. This is often the result of your potential SMEs either being too busy to participate, the problem of a lack of management support for your project, or a lack of understanding of

> ### DEFINITIONS
>
> *Facilitator.* Someone responsible for planning, running, and managing modeling sessions.
>
> *Project stakeholder.* Anyone who could be materially affected by the implementation of a new system or application.
>
> *Requirements analyst.* A person responsible for the gathering/elicitation, documentation, and validation of requirements.
>
> *Scribe.* A person responsible for recording information as it is identified.

how important requirements gathering is. Your recourse here is either to motivate people to get involved with and support your project or to cancel or postpone it. If you cannot identify good requirements for your project, there is little chance of succeeding; therefore, you should stop your project right away, so you don't waste resources on a futile effort.

3.1.1 Choosing Good Subject-Matter Experts

Good SMEs have the following qualities:

1. **They know the business.** This is the definition of SMEs. They understand one or more aspects of the problem domain.

2. **They think logically.** Not only do SMEs need to understand the business, they must also be able to think logically. They should be able to describe what they do systematically in a logical manner. As a general rule of thumb, although this is not always true, someone who finds computers easy to learn and use is most able to think logically.

3. **They can communicate well.** SMEs will be working as a team to develop the requirements model. This means they must have good people and communication skills.

4. **They are willing to invest the time in software development.** SMEs have better things to do than work on a software project. The job of the project manager is to convince the SMEs it is worth their while to invest their time providing expertise to your team. It is important to understand that SMEs who have had bad experiences in the past with broken promises from the systems department may be unwilling to take the time out of their busy schedules.

5. **Most, but not all, of the SMEs come from the user community.** When choosing SMEs, it is important that one or two of them come from outside the user community. While you must have

---

DEFINITION

Joint application development (JAD). A structured, facilitated meeting in which modeling is performed by a group of people. JADs are often held for gathering user requirements or for developing system designs.

---

real users of the system who know the business, it is also a good idea to have relative "outsiders" who have a vision of the future for your application. These people could be developers, system architects, or simply users from a different part of the company.

6. **Good SMEs are not too narrowly focused.** People who believe it is all about them or their respective part of your organization, who only understand how it is done today, who are unwilling or unable to consider new approaches, or who are unable to prioritize their needs seldom makes a good SME.

3.1.2 Choosing Good Facilitators

Good facilitators have the following qualities:

1. **They have good meeting skills.** A formal requirements modeling session is a special type of meeting. Therefore, because facilitators run the session, they need to have top-notch meeting skills.

2. **They understand the requirements modeling process.** Facilitators should ideally understand the entire software process, principally the portion of the process (in this case, requirements gathering) on which the meeting they are facilitating focuses. The software process is the topic of Chapter 10.

3. **They ask valid, intelligent questions.** One important function of facilitators is to help the SMEs explore the various aspects of the system being analyzed. Therefore, facilitators must be able to ask pertinent questions to follow cause-and-effect issues.

TIP

Good Facilitators Are Made, Not Born

Well, perhaps good facilitators are born, I'm not completely sure. My experience is, if you want to become a facilitator, you need to get some training first. If possible, attend another requirements modeling session as an observer, or, if your organization is not currently doing any modeling, consider bringing in a consultant who has experience as a facilitator to run your first modeling session so you can learn from him or her. Second, try to take a course in meeting facilitation. Meeting facilitation courses are reasonably common, as are joint application development (JAD) facilitation courses. Third, try it. Remember, the best teacher is experience.

3.1.3 Choosing Good Scribes

Good scribes have the following qualities:

1. **They listen well.** Scribes are there to listen and record business logic and rules. Therefore, they need good listening skills.

2. **They have good written communication skills.** Scribes are there to write down the business logic.

3. **They have good oral communication skills.** Scribes often need to ask questions to determine exactly what the SMEs mean. This implies that they need good oral communication skills.

4. **They have an ear for business logic.** Scribes must be able to recognize business logic when they hear it if they are going to be able to write it down.

Now that you have seen how to put together a requirements modeling team, you are ready to learn about the fundamental requirements gathering techniques.

3.2 Fundamental Requirements Gathering Techniques

All developers should be adept at two fundamental requirements gathering techniques: interviewing and brainstorming.

3.2.1 Interviewing

Interviewing is an essential part of defining initial requirements.

You usually start defining requirements by interviewing experts, either potential users of the application or people with expertise in either the problem domain or the technical domain. When interviewing these experts, you have several potential goals to accomplish: you might want to broaden your understanding of the application, you might want to determine whom to invite to requirements modeling sessions, or you might want to identify new or existing requirements directly for your

---

TIP

Observe Your Users

I make it a habit to spend a day or two with my users simply to sit and observe what they do. One of the problems with interviewing people is they leave out important details, details that you may not know to ask about because they know their jobs so well. Another advantage of observing your users is you see the tools they use to do their jobs. Perhaps they use a key reference manual or use a notepad to write reminder notes for themselves and/or their coworkers. Taking the time to observe your users doing their work can give you insight into the requirements for the application you are building.

application. The point is you need to sit down and talk with other people about your application.

Interviewing is a skill that takes years to master, one that cannot possibly be taught in a few paragraphs. Here however, are a few helpful pointers to help you to improve your interviewing skills:

1. Send ahead an agenda to set expectations and enable your interviewee to prepare for the interview.

2. Verify a few hours ahead of time that the interview is still on because people's schedules can change.

3. When you first meet the person, thank her for taking time out of her busy day.

4. Tell the interviewee what the project is about and how he fits into the overall process. This lets him know his input is important.

5. Summarize the issues you want to discuss and verify how long the interview will take. This helps to set her expectations and she can help you manage the time taken during the interview.

6. Ask the critical questions as soon as possible. This way, if the interview is cut short, you have the important information.

7. Ask him if you have missed anything or if he wants to add something. This gives him a chance to voice his concerns and often opens new avenues of questioning.

8. Don't assume you know everything, especially if you think you have already heard it before. Your users rarely have a consistent view of the world and part of the requirements definition process is to understand where everyone is coming from. If everyone has the same view on everything, that is great, but it is incredibly rare. Don't shut down your users with a comment like "I have already heard this before…."

9. End the interview by summarizing the main points. This gives you a chance to review your notes and ensure you understood everything.

10. Thank the person again at the end of the interview.

11. Inform the interviewee when you will summarize the interview notes (immediately after the interview when it is still fresh in your mind is best) and tell her you will send her a copy for her review. This helps to put her at ease because she know her input will not

be taken out of context. It also helps to improve the quality of your notes because she will review them and give you feedback.

12. Remember, there is more to interviewing people than just talking; you also need to listen.

13. Identify "needs" versus "wants." It is natural for SMEs to "want" the system to do wondrous and spectacular things. However, it is critical for SMEs to identify the minimum the system "needs" can do to be successful. "Needs" must be satisfied for the application to be a success; "wants" need not be.

3.2.2 Brainstorming

To get people, perhaps your SMEs, thinking on the same wavelength, a good requirements analyst or facilitator can lead a group through a brainstorming session to identify potential requirements for your system. With respect to a requirements model, the main goal is to explore the business objectives for the system you are developing. Brainstorming is a technique where groups of people discuss a topic, and say anything that comes into their minds about it. The rules are simple:

- All ideas are good; ideas are not judged by the group

- All ideas are owned by the group, not the individual

- All ideas immediately become public property, anybody is allowed to expand upon them

TIP *Take the Time to Understand the Long-Term Business Goals*	Over the years, I have noticed the best requirements modelers are those who understand the business where it is today, as well as where it is going. In the mid-1990s, I worked at an American telecommunications (telecom) firm during a time when the regulations were changing. Instead of specializing in one portion of the telecom market, firms would be allowed to compete in the entire spectrum, including long-distance phone, local phone, cable television, cellular phone, and digital phone communications. Knowing this, my team was able to expand our scope to include all aspects of the coming market, enabling us to be ready (and we were) when we were allowed to compete within the entire telecom market. A few years later, I worked at an insurance company that was undergoing a similar change in its business environment but, instead of deciding to become a full-services financial organization, it chose to expand globally to become a leading international insurer. Understanding this business direction, our team was able to focus on requirements pertinent to that vision. The best sources of long-term vision are senior executives within your organization.

The basic idea is a facilitator leads the group through brainstorming. The facilitator starts by explaining the rules of brainstorming and explaining what issues are to be discussed (see the following Section 3.2.2.1). A good idea is to give everyone a copy of the brainstorming rules before a brainstorming session so they are aware of them. When someone suggests an idea, it should be immediately recorded by a scribe onto a publicly visible area, such as flip-chart paper or a whiteboard.

Everyone should be aware of and follow the rules in a brainstorming session.

3.2.2.1 Facilitating a Brainstorming Session

The facilitator is responsible for drawing ideas out of the SMEs and for ensuring that everyone follows the rules. Asking for examples or anecdotes to an idea, asking for the complete opposite of an idea, or asking for details about an idea can draw out clearer or stronger ideas. Because it is easy for the group to go off on tangents following an idea, the facilitator occasionally revisits ideas that have not yet been explored. Brainstorming is an iterative process that does not follow a specific path, so facilitators should be willing to lead the group down multiple avenues of discussion.

To run a brainstorming session effectively, the facilitator should have a good idea what the system and the business needs it is supporting are all about. In other words, the facilitator must prepare before the modeling session. This is often done while the modeling team is being put together. To find good SMEs, you must interview them (either in person or over the phone) and determine what they know about the business. During the interviews, the facilitator picks up valuable knowledge he or she can use during modeling.

3.2.2.2 Potential Issues to Discuss When Modeling Requirements

During the brainstorming session, you want to explore the business objectives for the system. Systems are often developed, or redeveloped, because of changing business needs, so understanding the business process the system will support is critical. In their series of reengineering books (Hammer and Champy, 1993; Champy 1995), Michael Hammer and James Champy discuss several interesting issues that need to be explored during the reengineering process. Table 3-1 lists several of the issues you may want to explore during a requirements brainstorming session.

3.3 Essential Use Case Modeling

An important goal of requirements modeling is to come to an understanding of the business problem that your system is to address to understand its behavioral requirements. With respect to object-oriented development, the fundamental artifact you should develop to model behavioral requirements is a use case model (Jacobson et al. 1992; Schnei-

---

Table 3-1. Potential issues to discuss at a requirements brainstorming session

---

Who is this system for?

What will they do with the system?

Why do we do this?

Why do we do this the way we do?

What business needs does this system support?

What do/will our customers want/demand from us?

How is the business changing?

What is our competition doing? Why? How can we do it better?

Do we even need to do this?

If we were starting from scratch, how would we do this?

Just because we were successful in the past doing this, will we be successful in the future?

Can we combine several jobs ? Do we want to?

How will people's jobs be affected? Are we empowering or disempowering them?

What information will people need to do their jobs?

Is work being performed where it makes the most sense?

Are there any trivial tasks we can automate?

Are people performing only the complex tasks the system cannot handle?

Will the system pay for itself?

Does the system support teamwork or does it hinder it?

Do our users have the skills/education necessary to use this system? What training will they need?

What are our organization's strategic goals and objectives? Does this system support them?

How can we do this faster?

How can we do this cheaper?

How can we do this better?

Two flavors of use case models exist: essential use case models that reflect your behavioral requirements and system use case models that reflect your analysis.

der and Winters, 1998). Use case diagrams are one of the standard Unified Modeling Language artifacts (Rumbaugh, Jacobson, and Booch, 1999). Two basic flavors of use case models exist: essential use case models and system use case models. An essential use case model, often referred to as a *business use case model* or *abstract use case model*, models a technology-independent view of your behavioral requirements. System use case models, also known as *concrete use case models* or *detailed use case models*, model your analysis of your behavioral requirements, describing in detail how users will work with your system, including references to its user interface

	TIP
An important part of the agenda for a brainstorming session is a potential list of issues to consider during the session. Be sure to point out that these issues are merely suggestions and are not meant to be a definitive list.	*Distribute Potential Brainstorming Issues Before Brainstorming Sessions*

aspects. In this chapter, I describe essential use case modeling and, in Chapter 6, I show how to evolve it into a system use case model.

Essential modeling is a fundamental aspect of usage-centered designs, an approach to software development that is detailed in the book *Software for Use* (Constantine and Lockwood, 1999). Essential models are intended to capture the essence of problems through technology-free, idealized, and abstract descriptions. The resulting design models are more flexible, leaving open more options and more readily accommodating changes in technology. Essential models are more robust than concrete representations, simply because they are more likely to remain valid in the face of both changing requirements and changes in the technology of implementation. Essential models of usage highlight purpose, what it is users are trying to accomplish, and why they are doing it. In short, essential models are ideal artifacts to capture the requirements for your system.

When you are doing essential use case modeling, you develop a use case diagram, identify essential use cases, and identify potential actors/ roles that interact with your system. The following describes these tasks in detail.

3.3.1 A Picture Says 1,000 Words: Drawing Use Case Diagrams

The use case diagram in Figure 3-2 provides an example and depicts a collection of use cases, actors, their associations, a system boundary box (optional), and packages (optional). A use case describes a sequence of actions that provide a measurable value to an actor and is drawn as a horizontal ellipse. An actor is a person, organization, or external system

---

DEFINITIONS

Essential model. A model intended to capture the essence of a problem through technology-free, idealized, and abstract descriptions.

Usage-centered design. A modeling methodology that focuses on the work users are trying to accomplish and on what the software needs to supply via the user interface to help users accomplish their goals.

that plays a role in one or more interactions with your system. (Actors are drawn as stick figures.) Relationships between actors and classes are indicated in use case diagrams. A relationship exists whenever an actor is involved with an interaction described by a use case. Relationships can also exist between use cases, although this is typically an issue for system use case models, a topic covered in detail in Chapter 6. Associations are modeled as lines connecting use cases and actors to one another, with an optional arrowhead on one end of the line, indicating the direction of the initial invocation of the relationship. The rectangle around the use cases is called the system boundary box and, as the name suggests, it indicates the scope of your system—the use cases inside the rectangle represent the functionality you intend to implement. Finally, packages are UML constructs that enable you to organize model elements (such as use cases) into groups. Packages are depicted as file folders and can be used on any of the UML diagrams, including both use case diagrams and class diagrams. Figure 3-1 does not include a package because of the narrow scope of the diagram; I use packages only when my diagrams become unwieldy, which generally implies they cannot be printed on a single page, to organize a large diagram into smaller ones. The use of packages is discussed later in Section 3.3.5.

In the example depicted in Figure 3-2, students are enrolling in courses with the potential help of registrars. Professors input the marks students earn on assignments and registrars authorize the distribution of transcripts (report cards) to students. Note how for some use cases there is

Figure 3-2.
A use case diagram
for a simple
university

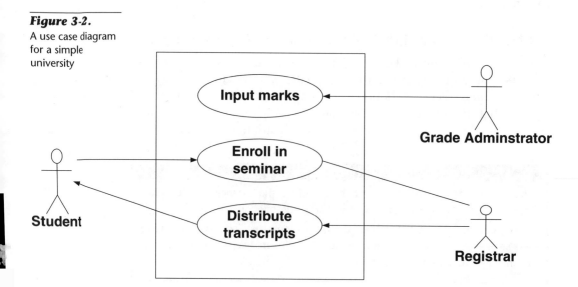

more than one actor involved. Moreover, note how some associations have arrowheads—any given use case association will have zero or one arrowhead. The association between Student and "Enroll in seminar" indicates this use case is initially invoked by a student and not by a registrar (the Registrar actor is also involved with this use case). Understanding that associations don't represent flows of information is important; they merely indicate an actor is somehow involved with a use case. Yes, information is flowing back and forth between the actor and the use case; for example, students would need to indicate which seminars they want to enroll in and the system would need to indicate to the students whether they have been enrolled. However, use case diagrams don't model this sort of information. Information flow can be modeled using UML activity diagrams, covered in Chapter 6. The line between the "Enroll in seminar" use case and the Registrar actor has no arrowhead, indicating it is not clear how the interaction between the system and registrars start. Perhaps a registrar may notice a student needs help and offers assistance, whereas other times, the student may request help from the registrar, important information that would be documented in the description of the use case. Actors are always involved with at least one use case and they are always drawn on the outside edges of a use case diagram.

An important point to be made is, in this chapter, I use a subset of the UML's use case diagram notation for essential use case modeling. The reason for this is straightforward: your goal with essential modeling is to depict the essential aspects of a system and, in the case of essential use case modeling, your goal is to model the essential behavioral requirements for your system. My experience is that although the UML use case diagram notation is robust, not all of it is "essential" for requirements definition. Don't worry. In Chapter 6, I cover the nuances of use case modeling in greater detail but, in this chapter, I focus on the basics.

UML use case diagrams have a robust set of features, not all of which are needed for essential use case modeling.

You will draw a use case diagram while you are identifying use cases, actors, and the associations between them. I like to start by identifying as many actors as possible, the topic of Section 3.3.4. You probably won't identify all the actors right away and all of those you initially identify won't prove to be applicable. Your goal at first is to get a good start. My next step is to ask how the actors interact with my system, enabling me to identify an initial set of use cases. Identifying essential use cases is covered in the following Section 3.3.4. Then, on the diagram, you connect the actors with the use cases with which they are involved. If an actor supplies information, initiates the use case, or receives any information as a result of the use case, then there should be an association between the two. I generally don't include arrowheads on the association lines because my experience is that people confuse them for indications of information flow, not initial invocation.

Drawing use case diagrams is easy. Identifying actors and use cases is the hard part.

DEFINITIONS

Package A UML construct that enables you to organize model elements into groups.

System boundary box A rectangle optionally included on a use case diagram that depicts the scope of your system.

Use case models should reflect the needs of your users, not the desires of developers.

Schneider and Winters (1998) suggest that use case diagrams should be developed from the user's point-of-view, *not* the developer's. Your goal is to model the behavioral requirements for your system, how your users will work with your system to fulfill their needs, not what the developers think they should build.

3.3.2 Identifying Actors

An actor represents anything or anyone that interfaces with your system. This may include people (not just the end user), external systems, and other organizations. Actors are always external to the system being modeled; they are never part of the system. To help find actors in your system, you should ask yourself the following questions (Schneider and Winters, 1998; Leffingwell and Widrig, 2000):

- Who is the main customer of your system?
- Who obtains information from this system?
- Who provides information to the system?
- Who installs the system?
- Who operates the system?
- Who shuts down the system?
- What other systems interact with this system?
- Does anything happen automatically at a preset time?
- Who will supply, use, or remove information from the system?
- Where does the system get information?

When you are doing essential use case modeling, your goal is to use actors to model roles and not the physical, real-world people, organizations, or systems. For example, Figure 3-2 shows that the Student and Registrar actors are involved with the use case "Enroll in seminar." Yes, it is extremely likely that students are people, but consider Registrar. Today, at most modern universities, people are in the role of Registrar. But does it really need to be like this? Consider what registrars do: They mediate the paperwork between a university and a student, they validate the information a student submits, and they provide advice to students regarding which seminars to enroll in. The first two tasks, mediating paperwork and validating information, can obviously be automated. The third task, providing advice to students, could potentially be automated by use of an artificial intelligence (AI) expert system. The point to be made is the Registrar actor could be implemented via either people or systems; it could even be outsourced to another organization specializing in registration activities. If you assume the Registrar actor represents a person, then you have limited your system-design opportunities, going against the grain of essential modeling. Instead, you want to describe the role of what it means to be a Registrar and leave design issues to your design activities. Note, too, that this allows for the possibility that one person could fill multiple roles. For example, if the person employed as the Registrar at a university is also taking courses, he or she may play the roles of both Student and Registrar. This is perfectly valid from a use case point-of-view.

With essential use case modeling actors represent roles. Whether the actor is a person, organization, or system should be left to your analysis and design efforts.

Also important to understand is that actors do not model positions. For example, consider the use case diagram of Figure 3-2. You see those faculty deans, tenured professors, associate professors, and teaching assistants are able both to input marks and adjust marks (perhaps for bell-curving them). Although these people do, in fact, do these things, it is not what you want to depict on your diagram. Instead, you want to ask yourself what role these types of people are playing with respect to the use cases. In this scenario, the users appear to be taking on the role of a Grade Administrator, as you originally saw indicated in Figure 3-2. The advantage of this approach is that it simplifies your diagrams and it doesn't tie you into the current position hierarchy within your organization: next year when the positions of "Tenured Professor" and "Associate Professor" get combined into "Instructor," you won't need to rework all your use case diagrams.

Actors do not model positions.

To describe an actor you want to give it a name that accurately reflects its role within your model. Actor names are usually singular nouns, such as Grade Administrator, Customer, and Payment Processor. You also want to provide a description of the actor (a few sentences will usually do) and, if necessary, provide real-world examples of the actor. Figure 3-4 provides an example of how you might describe the Grade Administrator actor. Notice how the description refers to relevant business rules. Identifying business rules is covered later in Section 3.6.1. Also, notice that examples were not indicated because the descriptions make it clear what a Grade Administrator is.

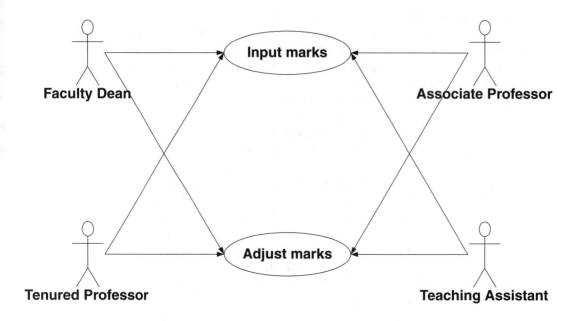

Figure 3-3.
The mistaken
modeling of
positions instead of
actors

3.3.3 Documenting a Use Case

Table 3-2 describes the potential sections you may include when documenting a use case. Although some of the sections are optional, in my opinion, they are still a good idea. When I am documenting essential use cases, I have a tendency to leave out the optional sections and, when I am documenting system use cases, I typically use all sections. Two of the sections, actors and included use cases, can actually be determined by simply looking at your use case diagram. My experience is, however, that it is good to have use cases that can stand on their own—in other words, use cases that contain all the critical information needed to understand them and the context they are in. This enables your SMEs to flesh out use cases individually; perhaps they meet in the mornings to work as a group, and then are assigned use cases to evolve as far as they can on

Figure 3-4.
Description
of the Grade
Administrator actor

Name: Grade Administrator

Description: A Grade Administrator will input, update, and finalize in the system the marks that students receive on assignments, tests, and exams. Deans, professors (tenured and associate), and teaching assistants are all potential grade administrators (see applicable business rules BR123 and BR124).

Examples: –

Table 3-2. The sections of a use case

Section	Purpose
Name	The name of the use case. The name should implicitly express the user's intent or purpose of the use case.
Description	Several sentences summarizing the use case.
Actors [Optional]	The list of actors associated with the use case. Although this information is contained in the use case itself, it helps to increase the understandability of the use case when the diagram is unavailable.
Status [Optional]	An indication of the status of the use case, typically one of: work in progress; ready for review; passed review; or failed review.
Preconditions	A list of the conditions, if any, that must be met before a use case may be invoked.
Postconditions	A list of the conditions, if any, that will be true once the use case finishes successfully.
Extension points [Optional]	Lists of the points in a use case from which other use cases extend. Extensions are covered in Chapter 6.
Included Use Cases [Optional]	A list of the use cases this one includes. Includes are covered in Chapter 6.
Basic Course of Action	The main path of logic an actor follows through a use case. Often referred to as the "happy path" or the "main path" because it describes how the use case works when everything works as it normally should.
Alternate Courses of Action	The infrequently used path(s) of logic in a use case, paths that are the result of an alternate way to work, an exception, or an error condition.
Change History [Optional]	Details when the use case is modified, why, and by whom.

their own in the afternoon, often increasing the productivity of the team. Several examples of use cases that use these sections are depicted in this chapter and in Chapter 6.

As you are modeling, you will often find you are missing information. When this happens, you are left with two options: to stop what you are doing immediately and discover the answer or to make an assumption and move forward. As you would think, it is often more effective to make your best guess now, and then update whatever model you are working on later when you discover the real answer (which is often what you guessed in the first place). Sometimes you never discover the real answer and are forced to accept the potential consequences of your assumption.

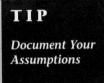

TIP

Document Your Assumptions

DEFINITIONS

Extend association. A generalization relationship where an extending use case continues the behavior of a base use case. The extending use case accomplishes this by inserting additional action sequences into the base use case sequence. This is modeled using a use case association with the <<extend>> stereotype.

Include association. A generalization relationship denoting the inclusion of the behavior described by a use case within another use case. This is modeled using a use case association with the <<include>> stereotype. Also known as a "uses" or a "has-a" relationship.

3.3.4 Use Cases: Essential versus System

Essential use cases capture the intentions of your users in technology independent ways.

A *use case* is a sequence of actions that provide a measurable value to an actor. Another way to look at it is that a use case describes a way in which a real-world actor interacts with the system. An essential use case (Constantine and Lockwood, 1999), sometimes called a business use case, is a simplified, abstract, generalized use case that captures the intentions of a user in a technology and implementation independent manner. An essential use case is a structured narrative, expressed in the language of the application domain and of users, comprising a simplified, generalized, abstract, technology-free and implementation-independent description of one task or interaction. An essential use case is complete, meaningful, and well designed from the point-of-view of users in some role or roles in relation to a system and that embodies the purpose or intentions underlying the interaction.

System use cases often imply decisions about the implementation environment.

Consider the two versions of the use case "Enroll in seminar" presented in Figure 3-5, which presents a simplified system use case (also called a *traditional* or *concrete* use case), and in Figure 3-6, which presents it as an essential use case. The first thing to notice is the "traditional" system use case has many implementation details embedded within it. For example, the concept of *registrar* disappeared and has been replaced with the term *system*, indicating that a decision has been made to automate many of the mundane aspects of enrollment. Don't worry, the concept of a registrar isn't likely to go away completely; in fact, this actor may reappear when the alternate course(s) of action are identified for both versions of the use case (see the following Section 3.3.6). The writer of system use cases is analyzing and describing requirements imposed by the problem, intermingled with implicit decisions about what the user interface is going to be like, whereas the writer of an essential use case is not.

The second thing to notice is the system use case makes references to screens and reports, for example, "UI23 Security Login Screen" and

"UI89 Enrollment Summary Report," and the essential use case does not. Once again this fact reflects implementation details; someone has decided the system will be implemented as screens, as opposed to HTML pages perhaps, and printed reports. However, the essential use case could just as easily have referred to major user interface elements, the essential version of screens and reports, and, truthfully, this is a practice I recommend. I didn't include references to UI elements in Figure 3-6 to provide you with an example where this has not been done. Essential user interface prototyping is described in Section 3.4.

Third, both versions use reference business rule definitions—such as "BR129 Determine Eligibility to Enroll"—because business rules reflect essential characteristics of your domain that your system must implement.

Fourth, the system use case has more steps than the essential use case version. This, in fact, reflects my style of writing use cases: I believe each use case step should reflect one step and one step only. Several advantages exist to this approach: The use case becomes easier to test because each statement is easier to understand and to validate, and alternate courses are easier to write because it is easier to branch from a statement when it does one thing only (which you see in Section 3.3.6).

Fifth, the use case steps are written in the active voice. For example, the statement "The registrar informs the student of the fees" is in active voice whereas "The student is informed of the fees by the registrar" is in passive voice. Writing in the active voice leads to succinct sentences.

Finally, another style issue is that I like to end the basic course of action within a use case with a statement such as "The use case ends" or "The use case ends when…" to indicate that the logic for the course of action has been completely defined.

Essential use cases can be documented as prose or as a structured series of steps.

Traditional/system use cases typically contain too many built-in assumptions, often hidden or implicit, about the underlying technology implementation and the user interface yet to be designed. This is a good feature during your analysis and design efforts, but not so good for your requirements efforts. An essential use case, on the other hand, is based on the purpose or intentions of a user, rather than on the concrete steps or mechanisms by which the purpose or intention might be carried out. Figure 3-7 presents a different approach to documenting an essential use case: instead of writing numbered steps, you simply write prose for the use case. I often take this approach at first to understand what each use case is about, but I believe in tightening up the writing, as you see in Figure 3-6, to ensure that I have truly captured the logic of the use case. Regardless of the style you use, essential use cases are dramatically shorter and simpler than the system use cases for the same interaction. This is because they include only those steps that are essential and of intrinsic interest to the user.

Figure 3-5.

"Enroll in seminar"
as a "traditional"
system use case

Name: Enroll in Seminar

Description: Enroll an existing student in a seminar for which she is eligible.

Preconditions: The Student is registered at the University.

Postconditions: The Student will be enrolled in the course she wants if she is eligible and room is available.

Basic Course of Action:

1. A student wants to enroll in a seminar.

2. The student inputs her name and student number into the system via "UI23 Security Login Screen."

3. The system verifies the student is eligible to enroll in seminars at the university according to business rule "BR129 Determine Eligibility to Enroll."

4. The system displays "UI32 Seminar Selection Screen," which indicates the list of available seminars.

5. The student indicates the seminar in which she wants to enroll.

6. The system validates the student is eligible to enroll in the seminar according to the business rule "BR130 Determine Student Eligibility to Enroll in a Seminar."

7. The system validates the seminar fits into the existing schedule of the student according to the business rule "BR143 Validate Student Seminar Schedule."

8. The system calculates the fees for the seminar based on the fee published in the course catalog, applicable student fees, and applicable taxes. Apply business rules "BR 180 Calculate Student Fees" and "BR45 Calculate Taxes for Seminar."

9. The system displays the fees via "UI33 Display Seminar Fees Screen."

10. The system asks the student if she still wants to enroll in the seminar.

11. The student indicates she wants to enroll in the seminar.

12. The system enrolls the student in the seminar.

13. The system informs the student the enrollment was successful via "UI88 Seminar Enrollment Summary Screen."

14. The system bills the student for the seminar, according to business rule "BR100 Bill Student for Seminar."

15. The system asks the student if she wants a printed statement of the enrollment.

16. The student indicates she wants a printed statement.

17. The system prints the enrollment statement "UI89 Enrollment Summary Report."

18. The use case ends when the student takes the printed statement.

Name: Enroll in Seminar

Description: Enroll an existing student in a seminar for which she is eligible.

Preconditions: The Student is registered at the University.

Postconditions: The Student will be enrolled in the course she wants if she is eligible and room is available.

Basic Course of Action:

1. A student wants to enroll in a seminar.

2. The student submits his name and student number to the registrar.

3. The registrar verifies the student is eligible to enroll in seminars at the university according to business rule "BR129 Determine Eligibility to Enroll."

4. The student indicates, from the list of available seminars, the seminar in which he wants to enroll.

5. The registrar validates the student is eligible to enroll in the seminar according to the business rule "BR130 Determine Student Eligibility to Enroll in a Seminar."

6. The registrar validates the seminar fits into the existing schedule of the student, according to the business rule "BR143 Validate Student Seminar Schedule."

7. The registrar calculates the fees for the seminar, based on the fee published in the course catalog, applicable student fees, and applicable taxes. Apply business rules "BR 180 Calculate Student Fees" and "BR45 Calculate Taxes for Seminar."

8. The registrar informs the student of the fees.

9. The registrar verifies the student still wants to enroll in the seminar.

10. The student indicates he wants to enroll in the seminar.

11. The registrar enrolls the student in the seminar.

12. The registrar adds the appropriate fees to the student's bill according to business rule "BR100 Bill Student for Seminar."

13. The registrar provides the student with a confirmation that he is enrolled.

14. The use case ends.

Figure 3-6.
"Enroll in seminar" as an essential use case

Name: Enroll in Seminar

Description: A student wants to enroll in a seminar so he submits his name and student number to the registrar; therefore, he may be validated to become an eligible student at the university. Once the registrar verifies him, the student indicates the seminar he wants to enroll in from the list of those available. The registrar validates the student is eligible to enroll in the seminar and that the seminar fits into the student's existing schedule. The registrar calculates the fees for the seminar—based on the fee published in the course catalog, applicable student fees, and applicable taxes—and informs the student. The registrar verifies with the student that he still wants to enroll in the seminar, and then enrolls the student in the seminar. The registrar adds the appropriate fees to the student's bill and provides the student with a confirmation that he is enrolled.

Figure 3-7.
"Enroll in seminar" as an essential use case (simple prose).

3.3.5 *Identifying Use Cases*

How do you go about identifying potential use cases? Constantine and Lockwood (1999) suggest that one way to identify essential use cases, or simply to identify use cases, is to identify potential services by asking your SMEs the following questions from the point-of-view of the actors:

- What are users in this role trying to accomplish?

- To fulfill this role, what do users need to be able to do?

- What are the main tasks of users in this role?

- What information do users in this role need to examine, create, or change?

- What do users in this role need to be informed of by the system?

- What do users in this role need to inform the system about?

For example, from the point-of-view of the Student actor, you may discover that students:

- Enroll in, attend, drop, fail, and pass seminars.

- Need a list of available seminars.

- Need to determine basic information about a seminar, such as its description and its prerequisites.

- Need to obtain a copy of their transcript, their course schedules, and the fees due.

- Pay fees, pay late charges, receive reimbursements for dropped and cancelled courses, receive grants, and receive student loans.

- Graduate from school or drop out of it.

- Need to be informed of changes in seminars, including room changes, time changes, and even cancellations.

DEFINITIONS

Cohesion. The degree of relatedness within an encapsulated unit (such as a component or a class).

Hypertext Markup Language (HTML). Industry-standard definition of a platform-independent file format for sharing information. HTML pages are the de facto standard approach for user interfaces on the World Wide Web (WWW).

Similarly, another way to identify use cases is to ask your SMEs to brainstorm the various scenarios, often called use case scenarios (Ambler, 1998a) that your system may or may not support. A use case scenario is a description of a potential business situation that may be faced by the users of a system. For example, the following would be considered use case scenarios for a university information system:

- A student wants to enroll in a seminar, but the registrar informs him that he does not have the prerequisites for it.

- A student wanted to enroll in a seminar that she does have the prerequisites for and seats are still available in the seminar.

- A professor requests a seminar list for every course he teaches.

- A researcher applies for a research grant, but only receives partial funding for her project.

- A professor submits student marks to the system. These marks may be for exams, tests, or assignments.

- A student wants to drop a seminar the day before the drop date.

- A student requests a printed copy of his transcript, so he can include copies of it with his résumé.

You can take either approach, or combine the two, if you like, but the main goal is to end up with a lot of information regarding the behavioral aspects of your system. The next step is to group these aspects, by similarity, into use cases. Remember, a use case provides a service of value to an actor. Furthermore, that service should be cohesive; in other words, it should do one thing that makes sense. For example, you wouldn't want a use case called "Support Students" that does everything a student needs, such as letting them enroll in courses, drop courses, pay fees, and obtain course information. That's simply too much to handle all at once. Instead, you should identify several use cases, one for each service provided by the system. Figure 3-8 presents the start at a use case diagram for a university information system, based on the system aspects listed previously.

A use case provides a service of value to an actor.

Several interesting things are worth noting about the use cases of Figure 3-8:

1. **These are just preliminary use cases.** As you continue to model, you will refactor existing use cases, breaking them apart, combining them, introducing new use cases, and removing ones that don't make sense.

2. **No time ordering is indicated between use cases.** For example, you need to enroll in a seminar before you attend it, and you

Each UML model has its own purpose.

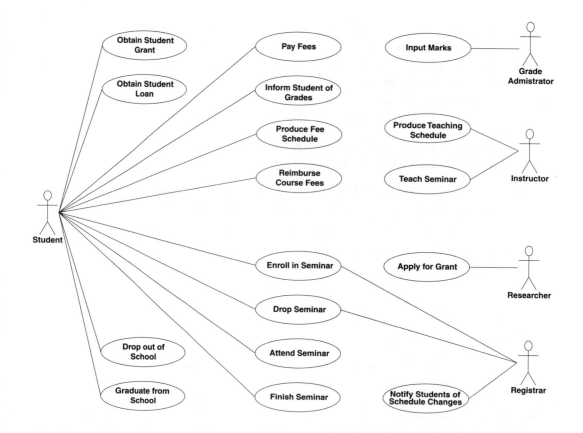

Figure 3-8.
A use case diagram
for a university
information system

need to attend it (I would hope) before you pass it. Although this is important information, it does not belong in a use case diagram. This sort of information, which pertains to the lifecycle of a seminar, is better modeled using a UML state chart diagram (described in detail in Chapter 7). One of the strengths of the UML is it has a wide range of models, each with its own purpose, enabling you to focus on one aspect of your system at a time.

3. **Customer actors are usually involved in many use cases.** The customer of the university, in this case Student, is the center of much of the action in the use case diagram. This is a normal phenomenon—after all, the main goal of most organizations is to provide services to their customers. To be fair, this is also the result of our initial focus on Student.

4. **Use cases are not functions.** I began by listing a series of tasks/functions that the system needed to support, and then used this information to formulate the use case diagram. There is not one-

to-one mapping of functions to use cases, however. For example, the need for an available seminar list is identified as a function, but is modeled simply as a reference in a use case statement (see Figure 3-5, Figure 3-6, and Figure 3-7).

5. **No arrowheads are on the associations.** As I said earlier, showing arrowheads on use case associations can be confusing for people and, frankly, they don't add much value.

6. **The diagram is too big.** A good rule of thumb is a diagram should have 7 +/– 2 bubbles on it. In this case, a bubble would be considered either an actor or a use case. Now, it's time to consider introducing packages, which I have done in Figure 3-9.

7. **Use cases should be functionally cohesive.** A use case should encapsulate one service that provides value to an actor. Accordingly, separate use cases exist for dropping a seminar and enrolling in a seminar. These are two separate services offered to students and, therefore, they should have their own use cases. Looking at Figure 3-8 again, I would expect the use case "Finish Seminar" may be refactored into two separate use cases: one for passing a seminar and one for failing a seminar. When you write the use case for finishing a seminar, if you find the logic for passing a seminar is different than for failing it, then that would be an indication to split the use case in two.

8. **Use cases should be temporally cohesive.** A use case should describe a service whose steps occur during a contiguous period of time. For example, the steps of the use case "Enroll in Seminar" would occur during a short period, likely a few minutes. It wouldn't make sense to have a use case such as "Take a Seminar" that described the enrollment process, attending classes, and passing the seminar. Not only isn't this functionally cohesive, but it isn't cohesive in a time sense either: several steps are taken to enroll, you wait a while, and then you follow several more steps to attend the seminar, and you wait some more time to discover if you passed or failed. The length of time is not the issue; it is the starting, stopping, and starting again that is the problem. If you were to write the logic for the "Attend Seminar" use case, you might find you have temporal cohesion problems.

9. **Every actor is involved with at least one use case, and every use case is involved with at least one actor.** Remember the definition of a use case: it provides a service of value to an actor. If a use case does not provide service to an actor, then why have it? If an actor exists that is not involved in a use case, why model it?

10. I chose not to include a system boundary box. System boundary boxes are optional, so I didn't include it this time to show you it is allowable.

Packages enable you to group similar model elements to simplify complex diagrams.

Figure 3-9 depicts how you would reorganize Figure 3-8 using packages. A UML package is a mechanism for representing a collection of model elements—in this case, the elements of a use case diagram. You can use packages on any type of UML diagram, although their use is most common on use case diagrams, component diagrams, and class diagrams because these diagrams tend to become very large otherwise. By introducing packages, the use case diagram becomes simpler and easier to understand; each package, in turn, would be documented by another use case diagram. For example, Figure 3-10 depicts the resulting use case diagram for the "Manage Seminar Registration" package. Notice how the "Student" and "Registrar" actors both appear on this diagram: They are involved with the use cases that appear on the diagram and, therefore, should also appear on it. In Figure 3-10, I could have included a system boundary box to represent the boundary of the package, although I chose not to because I believe it is superfluous.

Figure 3-9.
Reorganizing the use case diagram with packages

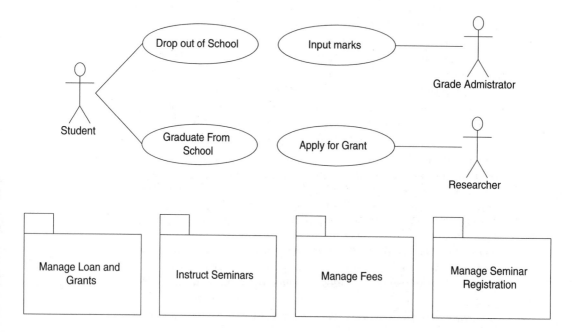

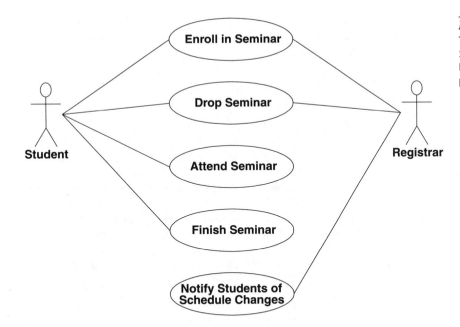

Figure 3-10.
The Manage Seminar Registration package

3.3.6 Modeling Different Logic Flows: Alternate Courses of Action

An alternate course of action is an infrequently used path of logic in a use case. Alternate courses are identified whenever there is an alternate way to work, an exception, or an error condition that must be handled. Figure 3-11 depicts the use case of Figure 3-6 with three alternate courses added to it.

Let's start with style issues. First, an alternate course includes a description of the condition that must be met to invoke the alternate course. Second, notice the identification scheme for each alternate course. The first one is identified as *A,* the second as *B,* and so on. Also, notice the numbering scheme for the steps of the alternate course. Third, each step

Set a standard for numbering alternate courses and stick to it.

DEFINITIONS

Component diagram. A diagram that depicts the software components that compose an application, system, or enterprise The components, their interrelationships, interactions, and their public interfaces are depicted.

Functional cohesion. A measure of how well the behaviors of an item make sense when considered as a whole.

Temporal cohesion. A measure of whether the behaviors of an item occur during the relatively same time period.

Figure 3-11.
The use case of
Figure 3-6 with
some alternate
courses added

Name: Enroll in Seminar

Description: Enroll an existing student in a seminar for which she is eligible.

Preconditions: The Student is registered at the University.

Postconditions: The Student will be enrolled in the course she wants if she is eligible and room is available.

Basic Course of Action:

1. A student wants to enroll in a seminar.

2. The student submits her name and student number to the registrar.

3. The registrar verifies the student is eligible to enroll in seminars at the university according to business rule "BR129 Determine Eligibility to Enroll."

4. The student indicates, from the list of available seminars, the seminar in which she wants to enroll.

5. The registrar validates the student is eligible to enroll in the seminar according to the business rule "BR130 Determine Student Eligibility to Enroll in a Seminar."

6. The registrar validates the seminar fits into the existing schedule of the student, according to the business rule "BR143 Validate Student Seminar Schedule."

7. The registrar calculates the fees for the seminar, based on the fee published in the course catalog, applicable student fees, and applicable taxes. Apply business rules "BR 180 Calculate Student Fees" and "BR45 Calculate Taxes for Seminar."

8. The registrar informs the student of the fees.

9. The registrar verifies the student still wants to enroll in the seminar.

10. The student indicates she wants to enroll in the seminar.

11. The registrar enrolls the student in the seminar.

12. The registrar adds the appropriate fees to the student's bill according to business rule "BR100 Bill Student for Seminar."

13. The registrar provides the student with a confirmation that she is enrolled.

14. The use case ends.

Alternate Course A: The Student is Not Eligible to Enroll in Seminars.

A.3. The registrar determines the student is not eligible to enroll in seminars.

A.4. The registrar informs the student she is not eligible to enroll.

A.5. The use case ends.

Alternate Course B: The Student Does Not Have the Prerequisites

B.5. The registrar determines the student is not eligible to enroll in the seminar she chose.

B.6. The registrar informs the student she does not have the prerequisites.

B.7. The registrar informs the student of the prerequisites she needs.

B.8. The use case continues at Step 4 in the Basic Course of Action.

Alternate Course C: The Student Decides Not to Enroll in an Available Seminar

C.4. The student views the list of seminars and does not see one in which she wants to enroll.

C.5. The use case ends.

starts with the letter of the alternate course, followed by the number of the step in the basic course of the use case it replaces. For example, the first step of the first alternate course (*A*) replaces Step 3 in the Basic Course of Action. Finally, the last step in each alternate course should indicate either that the use case ends, using the same terminology you would for the last step of the Basic Course of Action, or that the use case continues at another step. Alternate courses *A* and *C* both resulted in the use case ending—the error condition was too grave a problem to continue—whereas for alternate course *B* it was possible to continue.

My experience is that alternate courses are easier to write when your use case statements do one thing and one thing only. Notice how alternate course *A* in Figure 3-11 was easy to write: The step in the Basic Course of Action that it branched from did one thing and one thing only, making it straightforward to define the error condition. Alternate courses *B* and *C* are another matter. Step 4 describes two actions, first that the system presents a list of available seminars to the student and the student picks from this list. It affects alternate course *B* because this is the step that *B* returns to. Do you really need to display the list again? I doubt it. It affects *C* because this is the step *C* branches from, the fact that the student does not see a seminar in which she is interested. The impact is not that large in this case, but it could have been. The point is it simplifies your life if a use case step does one thing and one thing only. Furthermore, imagine trying to add alternate courses to the prose-style use case of Figure 3-7. I doubt you could do it effectively.

A use case step should describe one and only one action.

3.4 Essential User Interface Prototyping

The user interface (UI) is the portion of software with which a user directly interacts. An essential user interface prototype (Constantine and Lockwood, 1999) is a low-fidelity model, or prototype, of the UI for your system. It represents the general ideas behind the UI, but not the exact details. Essential UI prototypes represent user interface requirements in a technology-independent manner, just as essential use case models do for

Essential user interface (UI) models represent the UI requirements for your software in a technology-independent manner.

TIP

Focus on Business Issues, Not Technical Ones

The conditions described in the alternate courses of Figure 3-11 focus on business issues, not technical ones, such as the student not having the right prerequisites. Yes, database errors, network errors, and operating system errors still occur, but those are technical design issues, not behavioral requirements issues. For now, assume these types of things are handled by the system, although if you have not already done so, then you should consider identifying reliability issues such as this as nonfunctional requirements (see Section 3.6.2).

behavioral requirements. An essential user interface prototype is effectively the initial state—the beginning point—of the user interface prototype for your system. It models user interface requirements, requirements that are evolved through analysis (Chapter 6) and design (Chapter 7) to result in the final user interface design for your system.

Essential UI prototyping enables you to understand the problem before you attempt to solve it through UI design.

Two basic differences differentiate essential user interface prototyping and traditional UI prototyping. First, your goal is to focus on your users and their usage of the system, not system features. This is one of the reasons you want to perform essential use case modeling and essential user-interface prototyping in tandem: they each focus on usage. Second, your prototyping tools are simple, including whiteboards, flip-chart paper, and sticky notes. The minute you introduce electronic technology to your prototyping efforts, you have made a design decision about the implementation technology. If you use an HTML development tool to build a user interface prototype, then you immediately narrow your design space to the functionality supported within browsers. If you choose a Java development environment, then you narrow your design space to Java, and if you choose a Windows-based prototyping tool, you narrow your design space to whatever is supported on the Windows platform. Right now, you should focus on requirements, not design; therefore, you don't currently want to use technology-based prototyping tools. Understand the problem first, and then solve it.

So how do you use sticky notes and flip-chart paper to create an essential user interface prototype? Let's start by defining several terms. A major user interface element represents a large-grained item, potentially a screen, HTML page, or report. A minor user interface element represents a small-grained item, typically widgets, such as user input fields, menu items, lists, or static text fields such as labels. When a team is creating an essential user interface prototype, it typically iterates the following tasks:

1. **Explore system usage.** Your team will explore system usage via several means. First, you will likely work together on a whiteboard to discuss ideas, work on initial drawings together, and generally take advantage of the dynamic nature of whiteboards to come to an understanding quickly of the portion of the system you are discussing. For example, with the university system, you may gather around a whiteboard to make an initial drawing of what a university transcript would contain or what a seminar enrollment submission would contain. Second, as you have seen, essential use case modeling (Section 3.3) is an effective technique for understanding the behavioral requirements for your system. You will see that CRC models (Section 3.3) is an effective technique for under-

standing the domain concepts your system must support. As you saw in Figure 3-1, you iteratively work between essential use case modeling, CRC modeling, and essential user interface modeling.

2. **Model major user interface elements.** Major user interface elements, such as potential screens and reports, can be modeled using flip-chart paper. I say potential because whether something is a screen or printed report is a design decision—a university transcript could be implemented as an HTML page your users view in a browser, as a paper report that is printed and mailed to students, or as an application screen. Each piece of flip-chart paper is given a name, such as "Student Transcript" or "Seminar Enrollment Request," and has the appropriate minor user interface elements added to it as needed. Pieces of flip-chart paper have several advantages: they can be taped to a wall; they are good for working in groups because they make it easier for everyone to see and interact; they are large enough so you can put many smaller items such as sticky notes on them; you can draw on them; and they can be stored away between modeling sessions.

3. **Model minor user interface elements.** Minor UI elements, such as input fields, lists, and containers (minor UI elements that aggregate other minor UI elements) are modeled using sticky notes. Constantine and Lockwood (1999) suggest using different color notes for different types of components—for example, bright colors (yellow or red) for active user interface elements such as input fields versus subdued colors (white or tan) for passive interface elements such as containers. Figure 3-12 depicts examples of several minor UI elements modeled using sticky notes. The "Student name" sticky is a container that includes four active elements: "First name," "Surname," "Initial(s)," and "Title." The other sticky represents a list of the seminars a student has taken or is currently enrolled in. Notice how each sticky has a name that describes its purpose, but not how it is implemented. You can look at the sticky and immediately know how it is used. On the bottom part of each sticky is a description of the UI element, indicating the type of UI element but, once again, not implying any given technology. For example, I have used terms such as "input field" and not "javax.swing.JtextArea." Even the Student name container is described as a bounding box although, in practice, I typically don't bother to label containers. Different sizes of sticky notes are used, indicating the relative size of each UI element. Also notice how the relative order of the UI elements are indicated by the order of the sticky notes: A stu-

dent's title comes before his first name, and then come his initials and his surname. This ordering may change during design but, for now, it's close enough.

Whenever you realize you may need a minor user interface element, you simply take a sticky note, label it appropriately, and place it in the general area on a major user interface element where you believe it belongs. Sometimes you identify a minor UI element that may not have a major UI element on which to place it. Don't worry. This is an iterative process, so attempt to identify an appropriate major UI element and continue. The very fact that sticky notes do not look like a real GUI widget is a constant visual reminder to your team that you are building an abstract model of the user interface and not the real thing. Each sticky note is, effectively, a placeholder that says you need something there, but you don't yet know yet the best way to implement it, so for now, you want to leave it open.

4. **Explore the usability of your user interface.** Highly usable systems are learnable, they enable user productivity, their use is easy to remember, and they are supportable. Ensuring system usability is discussed in Section 3.4.2.

5. **Explore the relationships between user interface elements.** The technique you employ to do this is called user interface-flow diagramming, the topic of the following Section 3.4.3.

Figure 3-11.

Examples of minor user interface elements

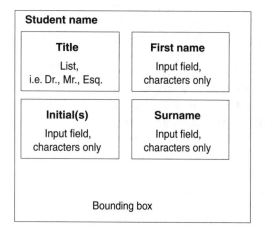

DEFINITIONS

Major user interface element. A large-grained item such as a screen, HTML page, or report.

Minor user interface element. A small-grained item such as a user input field, menu item, list, or static text field.

Sticky note. A small piece of paper, often a few inches on a side, that has glue on one side, so it can be stuck easily onto things. Sticky notes are produced by several manufacturers and come in a wide variety of sizes and colors.

Usability. Highly usable systems are easy for people to learn how to use and easy for people to use productively, they make it easy to remember from one use to another how to use them, and they help people make fewer mistakes.

User interface (UI). The user interface of software is the portion the user interacts with directly, including the screens, reports, documentation, and software support (via telephone, electronic mail, and so on).

Utility. A system has utility if it does something worthwhile, something that is of sufficient value to justify the investment in it.

3.4.1 An Example Essential User-Interface Model

Let's work through an example. Figure 3-12 depicts an essential user interface prototype for enrolling in a seminar. The outside box represents the flip-chart paper; you typically use one piece of flip-chart paper per major user interface element. The name of the major UI element, in this case "Enroll Student in Seminar," is typically written in one of the corners of the flip-chart paper. Notice how there are three containers, the three largest rectangles, none of which are marked as containers. Also notice how some minor UI elements are input fields, such as "Student Number" and "Student Name," whereas others are display only. "Student Name" is interesting because it is a bit of a cheat, listing four separate data elements on the one sticky note (compare this with the approach taken in Figure 3-11. I will often do this when I know some thing always come in a group and when I think I will need the room, which, as you can see in Figure 3-12, I do. The "Professor" and "Enrollment Requester" hang off the edge of their container, something I did on purpose to show you that you do not have to get your essential user interface prototypes perfect. Several "Requester" UI elements exist—for example, "Help Requester" and "Search Requester"—indicating user interface elements that are often implemented as push buttons, function keys, or "hot key" combinations, such as Ctrl+Shift+S. Many of the minor UI elements include detailed notes for how they are used, particularly the elements that support input

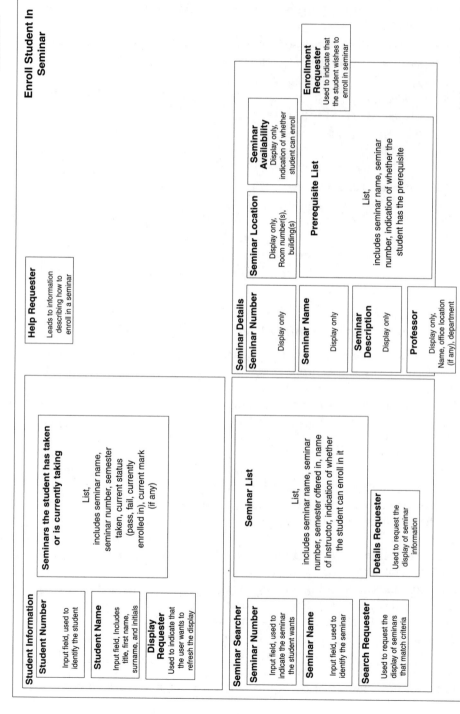

Figure 3-12.
An essential user
interface prototype
to enroll a student
in a seminar

Enroll Student In Seminar

Help Requester
Leads to information
describing how to
enroll in a seminar

Seminar Details

Seminar Number
Display only

Seminar Name
Display only

Seminar Description
Display only

Professor
Display only,
Name, office location
(if any), department

Seminar Location
Display only,
Room number(s),
building(s)

Seminar Availability
Display only,
indication of whether
student can enroll

Prerequisite List
List,
includes seminar name, seminar
number, indication of whether the
student has the prerequisite

Enrollment Requester
Used to indicate that
the student wishes to
enroll in seminar

Student Information

Student Number
Input field, used to
identify the student

Student Name
Input field, Includes
title, first name,
surname, and initials

Display Requester
Used to indicate that
the user wants to
refresh the display

Seminars the student has taken or is currently taking
List,
includes seminar name,
seminar number, semester
taken, current status
(pass, fail, currently
enrolled in), current mark
(if any)

Seminar Searcher

Seminar Number
Input field, used to
indicate the seminar
the student wants

Seminar Name
Input field, used to
identify the seminar

Search Requester
Used to request the
display of seminars
that match criteria

Seminar List
List,
includes seminar name, seminar
number, semester offered in, name
of instructor, indication of whether
the student can enroll in it

Details Requester
Used to request the
display of seminar
information

and the requesters. All of the lists support selection of the information within them; for lists that don't support selection, you should indicate this information.

Figure 3-13 depicts a second example of an essential user interface prototype of a major UI element, in this case the student transcript. It is comprised of several display-only minor UI elements, such as the name and address of the student. It also contains several elements pertaining to the current status of the student, including basic financial information, which could have been grouped together had the SMEs felt it necessary. Normally, when you build the actual transcript, perhaps as a printed report, you would use all the space available to you, although significant whitespace is left on the prototype. For example, the list of seminars could horizontally span the entire printed page, whereas this is not indicated in Figure 3-13. Sticky notes only come in certain sizes and are only meant to model the relative size and positioning of the minor UI elements. In short, I got it close enough, which was exactly my goal. Notice how the seminar list in Figure 3-12 contains different information than the seminar list in Figure 3-13. This is because each list is used for a different purpose: in Figure 3-12, to determine which seminars are available, and in Figure 3-13, to indicate which seminars have been taken by a student. Occasionally, the result will be different informational content and a different purpose.

The informational message UI element in Figure 3-13 is a common feature; in fact, I would argue that it hints at an analysis pattern. This occurs when developing primary communication vehicles with the customers of an organization (a transcript is a critical piece of information the university provides to students). The message is likely something like "Register before September 4th and receive a 5 percent discount on your tuition" or "The Vulcan Science Academy hopes you live long and prosper." The next time you receive a credit card, phone, or utility bill, look for the marketing message(s) printed on it and notice how the messages change monthly to promote new services and products available to you.

Most primary communications with customers include marketing messages.

You should strive to ensure that your models are consistent. For example, every major UI element should support one or more use cases. If a major UI element exists that is not needed by a use case, then either the UI element should be discarded or you are missing one or more use cases. Furthermore, the minor UI elements should support the behavior described within the use cases. Whenever a discrepancy exists, you should consider whether missing or extraneous behavior is described by the use case or missing or extraneous minor UI elements are within the prototypes.

The information modeled by your essential use cases should reflect the information modeled by your essential user interface prototypes.

You should also strive to ensure that your models are accurate. One way to do this is to ask yourself questions about how your essential user-interface prototypes would be used. For example, what should happen if

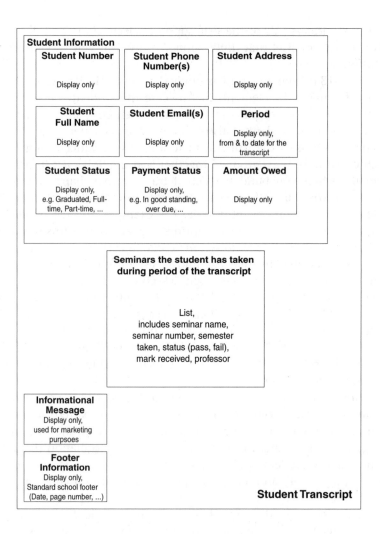

Student Information		
Student Number Display only	**Student Phone Number(s)** Display only	**Student Address** Display only
Student Full Name Display only	**Student Email(s)** Display only	**Period** Display only, from & to date for the transcript
Student Status Display only, e.g. Graduated, Full-time, Part-time, ...	**Payment Status** Display only, e.g. In good standing, over due, ...	**Amount Owed** Display only

Seminars the student has taken during period of the transcript

List, includes seminar name, seminar number, semester taken, status (pass, fail), mark received, professor

Informational Message
Display only, used for marketing purpsoes

Footer Information
Display only, Standard school footer (Date, page number, ...)

Student Transcript

Figure 3-13.
An essential user interface prototype for a student transcript

By asking how your users will work with your user interface, you are able to identify missing features, although you run the risk of goldplating your system if you don't verify the need for these new features.

a student really wants to enroll in a seminar that is currently full? Should she be given the opportunity to add herself to a waiting list? If so, how does that affect the user interface? You likely need to support the capability to indicate that a waiting list of X number of people already exists, as well as a way to request being added to, or removed from, the waiting list. Should obtaining detailed information about the professor teaching a seminar be possible? Should obtaining detailed information about the seminars in the prerequisite list be possible? In Figure 3-12, you see it is possible to search for a seminar by inputting its number or name. Should searching by the department that offers the seminar be possible? Or by day of the week on which it is offered? (When I was a student I had a

1.5- hour commute, so I tried to enroll in seminars that were all held on the same days.) Or, by the name of the instructor teaching it? Interesting questions, the answers for which will affect your models. A significant danger of this approach is *goldplating*, the addition of extraneous features, although this is one you can easily counteract by validating new features with your SMEs.

Meanwhile, Back in Reality

I am jumping through hoops not indicating implementation decisions for the major user interface elements. The reality is you well know that the seminar enrollment prototype of Figure 3-12 is going to be implemented as either a screen or a browser page, so why not admit it? Furthermore, you know the student transcript prototype modeled in Figure 3-13 will be some sort of report because all the information is display only. Granted, it could be implemented as a printed report, as an electronic file, as a browser page, as a screen, or several of these. When a major user interface element contains one or more minor user interface elements that permit editing, then you know it's going to be a screen or a page. When it contains no editable elements, then it will be a report. If you are expending a lot of "unnatural" effort to make your major user interface elements independent of implementation technology, then you may want to loosen up a bit and distinguish between reports and screens/pages.

3.4.2 Ensuring System Usability

An important issue to consider when developing an essential user interface prototype, or any user interface prototype for that matter, is usability. Constantine and Lockwood (1999) suggest that five factors affect the usability of your software:

1. **Access.** Your system should be usable, without help or instruction, by a user who has knowledge and experience in the application domain, but no prior experience with the system.

DEFINITIONS

Analysis pattern. A pattern that describes a solution to a common business/analysis issue.

Goldplating. The addition of extraneous features to a system.

Pattern. A pattern is a solution to a common problem taking relevant forces into account, effectively supporting the reuse of proven techniques and approaches of other developers.

2. **Efficacy.** Your system should not interfere with or impede use by a skilled user who has substantial experience with the system.

3. **Progression.** Your system should facilitate continuous advancement in knowledge, skill, and facility, and accommodate progressive change in use as the user gains experience with the system.

4. **Support.** Your system should support the real work users are trying to accomplish by making it easier, simpler, faster, or more fun by making new things possible.

5. **Context.** Your system should be suited to the real conditions and actual environment of the operational context in which it will be used and deployed.

In today's world, usability is not an option, it's a fundamental requirement.

Why is usability important? First, by focusing first on use and usability instead of on features or functionality, on your users and their usage more than on user interfaces, your system can be turned into a better tool for the job that is smaller, simpler, and ultimately less expensive (Constantine and Lockwood, 1999). Second, the best systems give pleasure and satisfaction, they make people feel good about using them and, in short, they are usable. Third, the harder a system is to use, the harder and more expensive it is to learn how to use and to support. Unusable features that are difficult to master lead to requests for changes, increasing future maintenance costs. Fourth, as users have grown accustomed to using computer applications, they have also grown less patient with them and, in particular, less patient with poorly designed software. The bar has been raised.

3.4.3 User Interface-Flow Diagramming

User interface-flow diagrams show the relationships between the major user interface elements (screens, reports, and so forth) that compose your application.

To your users, the user interface is the system. It is as simple as that. Doesn't it make sense that you should have some sort of diagram to help you model the user interface for your system? Essential user interface prototypes are an excellent means of documenting the requirements for your user interface. You can see in Chapters 6 and 7 that user interface prototypes are great artifacts to develop your user interface design. The problem with both of these techniques is you can quickly bog down in the details of the user interface and not see the bigger picture. Consequently, you often miss high-level relationships and interactions between the user interface elements of your application. User interface-flow diagrams, also called interface-flow diagrams (Ambler, 1998a; Ambler, 1998b), windows navigation diagrams (Page-Jones, 2000), and context-navigation maps (Constantine and Lockwood, 1999), enable you to model the high-level relationships between major user interface elements.

In Figure 3-14, you see the start at a user interface-flow diagram for the university system. Although the Unified Modeling Language (UML) does not yet support user interface-flow diagrams, I have applied a combination of the notations for UML activity diagrams and UML collaboration diagrams in the example. The boxes represent major user interface elements, modeled as you would objects, and the arrows represent the possible flow between them, modeled as you would transitions in activity diagrams. For example, when you are on the main menu screen, you can use the "Enrollment Requestor" to take you to the "Enroll in Seminar" UI element. Once you are there, you can either go back to the main menu (going back is always assumed), go to the "Professor Information" UI element, or go to the "Seminar Information" UI element. The addition of these two major UI elements was the result of the SMEs decision to enable students to learn more information about the instructors teaching a seminar and the detailed information regarding prerequisites to a seminar.

User interface-flow diagrams use a notation that is a combination of the notations for UML activity diagrams and UML collaboration diagrams.

User interface-flow diagrams are typically used for one of two purposes. First, they are used to model the interactions that users have with your software, as defined in a single use case. For example, the use case described in Figure 3-15, refers to several user interface elements and provides insight into how they are used. Based on this information, you can develop a user

User interface-flow diagrams are used to model the behavioral view of a single use case or an architectural view that models the UI aspects of all use cases for your system.

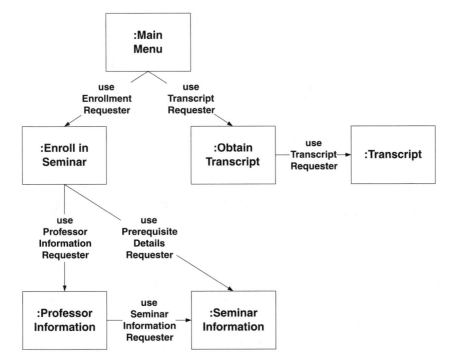

Figure 3-14.
Initial user interface-flow diagram for the university system

interface-flow diagram that reflects the behavioral view of the single use case. Second, as you see in Figure 3-14, they enable you to gain a high-level overview of the user interface for your application. This overview is effectively the combination of all the behavioral views derived from your use cases, the result being called the architectural view of your user interface (Constantine and Lockwood, 1999). I prefer to take the high-level overview approach, also referred to as the architectural approach, because it enables me to understand the complete user interface for a system.

User interface-flow diagrams enable you to validate that your essential user interface prototype is complete.

Because user interface-flow diagrams offer a high-level view of the interface of a system, you can quickly gain an understanding of how the system is expected to work. It puts you in a position where you can validate the overall flow of your application's user interface. For example, does the flow make sense? I am not so sure. Why can't I get from "Seminar Information" to "Instructor Information?" When you are viewing the information for a seminar, isn't it possible you might want to view the information for the instructor of that seminar? Furthermore, user interface-flow diagrams can be used to determine if the user interface will be usable. If there are many boxes and many connections, it may be a signal to you that your system is too large for people to learn and understand.

3.5 Domain Modeling with Class Responsibility Collaborator (CRC) Cards

Domain models represent fundamental business concepts that are pertinent to your problem space.

Domain modeling is the task of discovering the classes that represent the things and concepts pertinent to your problem space (Rosenberg and Scott, 1999). For example, your domain model for a university would include concepts such as student, instructor, tenured professor, seminar, transcript, and registrar. As you can imagine, nouns and noun phrases within your essential use case model are good candidates for concepts that should be included in your domain model. Your domain model serves as a basis for your glossary of terms, an important document that is often either delivered separately or as part of your user documentation.

DEFINITIONS

Activity diagram. A UML diagram that is used to model high-level business processes or the transitions between states of a class (in this respect, activity diagrams are effectively specializations of state chart diagrams).

Collaboration diagram. A UML diagram that shows instances of classes, their interrelationships, and the message flow between them. Collaboration diagrams typically focus on the structural organization of objects that send and receive messages.

Class Name	
Responsibilities	**Collaborators**

Figure 3-15.
The layout of a CRC card

A *CRC model* (Beck and Cunningham, 1989; Wirfs-Brock, Wilkerson, and Wiener, 1990; Wilkinson, 1995; Ambler 1998a) is a collection of standard index cards that have been divided into three sections, as depicted in Figure 3-1. A *class* represents a collection of similar objects, a *responsibility* is something that a class knows or does, and a *collaborator* is another class that a class interacts with to fulfill its responsibilities.

Although CRC cards were originally introduced as a technique for teaching object-oriented concepts, they have also been successfully used by both developers and users to understand an OO application throughout its entire system development lifecycle. My experience is that CRC models are an incredibly effective tool for domain modeling, the modeling of fundamental concepts within your domain, so this is the context in which I discuss them. Using CRC models for design purposes is possible; for example, they are one of the fundamental techniques employed for design in the eXtreme programming (XP) software process (Beck, 2000). However, my experience is that CRC models are effective tools for working with your users and SMEs while you are gathering requirements, whereas UML class diagrams are a better choice for domain modeling during analysis, as you see in Chapter 6.

CRC models are well suited for domain modeling during requirements gathering.

A *class* represents a collection of similar objects. An *object* is a person, place, thing, event, or concept that is relevant to the system at hand. For example, in a university system, classes would represent students, tenured professors, and seminars. The name of the class appears across the top of a CRC card and is typically a singular noun or singular noun phrase, such as "Student," "Tenured Professor," and "Seminar." You use singular names because each class represents a generalized version of a singular object. Although there may be the student "Miles O'Brien," you would model the class "Student." The information about a student describes a single person, not a group of people. Therefore, it makes sense

Class names are a singular noun or a singular noun phrase.

*A class's
responsibilities are
the things it
knows and does.*
to use the name "Student" and not "Students." Class names should also be simple. For example, which name is better: "Student" or "Person who takes seminars"?

A *responsibility* is anything that a class knows or does. For example, students have names, addresses, and phone numbers. These are the things a student knows. Students also enroll in seminars, drop seminars, and request transcripts. These are the things a student does. The things a class knows and does constitute its responsibilities. Important: A class is able to change the values of the things it knows, but it is unable to change the values of what other classes know. In other words, classes update their own attributes and nobody else's.

Sometimes a class has a responsibility to fulfill, but not have enough information to do it. For example, as you see in Figure 3-16, students enroll in seminars. To do this, a student needs to know if a spot is available in the seminar and, if so, he then needs to be added to the seminar. However, students only have information about themselves (their names, and so forth), and not about seminars. What the student needs to do is collaborate/interact with the card labeled "Seminar" to sign up for a seminar. Therefore, "Seminar" is included in the list of collaborators of "Student."

Collaboration takes one of two forms: A request for information or a request to do something. For example, the card "Student" requests an indication from the card "Seminar" whether space is available, a request for information. Furthermore, "Student" then requests to be added to the "Seminar" if a seat is available, a request to do something. Another way to perform this logic, however, would have been to have "Student" simply request "Seminar" to enroll himself into itself. Then have "Seminar" do the work of seeing if a seat is available and, if so, then enrolling the student and, if not, then informing the student that he was not enrolled.

Figure 3-16.
An example CRC
card

Student	
Student number **Name** **Address** **Phone number** **Enroll in a seminar** **Drop a seminar** **Request transcripts**	**Seminar**

So how do you go about domain modeling using CRC models? Perform the following steps:

1. Prepare to CRC model:
   - Put together a modeling group of SMEs
   - Brainstorm
   - Explain the CRC modeling technique

2. Iteratively CRC model:
   - Find classes
   - Find responsibilities
   - Define collaborators
   - Define use cases
   - Move the cards around
   - Prototype

3.5.1 Preparing to CRC Model

The first two steps, putting together a modeling group ofSMEs and brainstorming, were described in detail in Sections 3.1.2 and 3.2.2, respectively. In fact, you are likely to have already performed these two steps as part of your essential use case modeling and essential user interface prototyping efforts. The third step is to explain the CRC modeling technique, information described in the following sections.

3.5.2 Finding Classes

Again, an *object* is any person, place, thing, event, concept, screen, or report that is applicable to your system. A *class* represents a collection of similar objects. For example, although "Gary Mitchell," "Benjamin Finney," and "Janice Lester" are all examples of students, we model the class "Student" and not each individual person. Finding classes is fundamentally an analysis task because it deals with identifying the building blocks for your application. Employ the following strategies to find potential classes:

1. **Actors are potential classes.** Create a card for each actor in your use case model. In fact, you see later that you need to create two cards for most actors: one representing the actor in the real world and one representing the actor as it is stored in your system. For example, there are real-world people who are students

at a university and, at the same time, there are business objects within your system that represent those real-world people.

2. **Identify the customer.** Some sort of customer card will exist 99 times out of 100. Universities have students, banks have clients, network operating systems have users, and airlines have passengers. Students, clients, users, and passengers are all examples of customers.

3. **Follow the money.** Ask yourself where the money comes from (usually customers), how it is earned (through the sale of products or services), and what it is spent on. By following the money, you can identify many of the core classes for the system (the customer(s), the products and/or services being sold, and the components that make up the product/service being sold).

4. **Concepts are potential classes.** Your SMEs will often use business terms they take for granted, terms that are often candidate classes for your domain model. For example, in a university, your SMEs would use business terms such as seminar, course, room, building, and textbook. Each one of these concepts is potentially a class in your system.

5. **Events are potential classes.** Critical events occur within most problem domains. For example, in a university important events include graduation and commencement. Each event is potentially a class within your system because it will have responsibilities (for example "Graduation" would maintain a list of students graduating, would know its date and location, and so on).

6. **Major user interface elements are potential classes.** Create a card for major UI element in your essential user interface model. Real-world actors work with these classes to use your system. Note that these are not domain classes, they are UI classes, so by including them in our CRC model, we are no longer modeling just the domain. Yes, this is not academically pure. However, it is practical because the real-world actors will collaborate with these classes, as you will see in the following.

7. **Look for three to five main classes right away.** These classes are the core of your system and, if you cannot describe the core, then you probably don't understand the business. For example, "Passenger," "Flight," "Staff," and "Airport" would be the main classes for an airline reservation system. "Student," "Professor," "Course," "Seminar," and "Room" would be the main classes for a university information system.

8. **When you think you have identified a class, create a new card for it immediately.** You are using a stack of standard index cards that are available for one or two dollars per hundred. Go wild and spend the penny or two and use up a card. At the end of the modeling session, you will find you have either identified some responsibilities for that card (therefore, it is a valid class) or you haven't (so throw it away). Think of it like this: the time you spend trying to determine whether you have identified a class costs far more than the card itself.

9. **You are interested in several types of classes.** These types include actor classes, UI classes, and business classes. These types are described in detail in Section 3.5.2.1.

3.5.2.1 The Three Types of Classes

Three different types of classes exist: actor classes, user interface classes, and business classes. While distinguishing between these classes in your CRC model is optional, it is still good to understand that you need to be looking for several types of classes.

1. **Actor classes.** Actor classes represent the actors that appear in your use case model. Actors are people and/or organizations in the real world who interact with the system. Examples of people who interact with a university information system include students and professors. For example, students enroll in seminars and instructors teach seminars. An example of an organization that interacts with a university would be a bank. A university would process student payments and loans with a local bank, and would probably need to create summary reports for the bank.

2. **Business classes.** Business classes are places, things, concepts, and events that describe what the business is all about. For example, "Course," "Seminar," and "Room" are all examples of busi-

---

DEFINITIONS

Actor class. A representation of an actor that appears in your use case model.

Business class. Business classes are places, things, concepts, and events that are pertinent to your problem domain. They are often referred to as *domain classes* or *analysis classes*.

User interface class. A screen, menu, or report that is part of the user interface for your system.

ness classes. A course is a concept (well, I suppose you could argue it is a thing), a seminar is an event, and a room is a place.

3. **User interface classes.** User interface classes are the screens, menus, and reports that make up the user interface for your system. With respect to essential user interface modeling, they are the major UI elements. Examples would include a student editing screen, a seminar enrollment HTML page, and a student transcript. Additionally, there would also be one or more menus tying your screens and reports together into one application. For example, there may be "Registrar Workbench" and "Professor Workbench" classes that tie together all the registrar UI classes (the student editing screen, the seminar enrollment screen, and so on) and the professor UI classes (the marks input screen, the course description screen, and so on), respectively.

Let's consider an example. In Figure 3-17, you see several of the classes that would be identified during the analysis of a university information system. There are several actor classes, such as "Instructor" and "Student," and several user interface classes, such as "Enroll in Seminar" and "Transcript." Notice how the actor and user interface classes are marked with the UML stereotypes <<Actor>> and <<UI>>, respectively. The business classes, in this case "Student," "Professor," "Course," "Seminar," and "Room," are not given stereotypes, the common practice when CRC modeling.

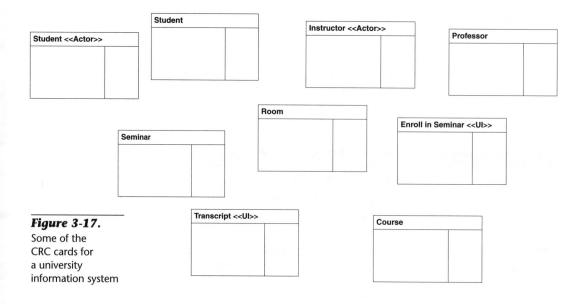

Figure 3-17.
Some of the CRC cards for a university information system

> ### DEFINITION
>
> **Stereotype.** A stereotype denotes a common use of a modeling element. Stereotypes are used to extend the UML in a consistent manner.

In a real CRC modeling session, your SMEs would have talked about each one of these classes, probably in the context of "what this system is all about." If they hadn't realized they identified a new class, then the facilitator should have piped in with something like, "Hey, it sounds like 'Professor' should be a class. What do you think?" The important thing is that your SMEs, often users, are the ones doing the work, not the facilitator. The facilitator provides input and ensures that things run smoothly.

Understanding the difference between actor classes and business classes is important. In Figure 3-18, you see two CRC cards are labeled "Student": one an actor class and one a business class. The actor class represents the real-world students—the actual, physical human beings. The business class, on the other hand, represents the student object within the system, the source code and data that you will develop to support the necessary behaviors. Later in this chapter, you will see the responsibilities of the actor class are typically the high-level interactions it has with your system, more often than not the titles of the use cases with which the actor is associated. The collaborators of the actor class will be the UI classes that it works with to fulfill those responsibilities; actors can only interact with your system via the interfaces you develop and give them access to. You will also see that the business classes, because they are internal to your system, collaborate with one another and have responsibilities that reflect the requests they receive from UI classes and from other business classes. Also interesting to note is that, although an actor class exists called "Instructor," a similarly named business class does not exist. Instead, a class exists called "Professor." Remember, actors model roles, not positions. Professors take on the role of instructor sometimes, but they may also take on the role of grade administrator, researcher, or mentor, as needed. A one-to-one mapping does not only occur between actor classes and the business classes that represent them in the system.

Actor classes represent the real-world actors. Often corresponding business class(es) represent the actors within the system.

The reason we have a class for each major UI element is because significant functionality is often associated with each one (for example, the seminar enrollment screen works with information from "Student," "Seminar," and "Course"). By having a CRC card representing each major UI element, you will have a mapping from your prototype to your domain model, supporting traceability between your models. Furthermore, by putting all the functionality for any given major UI element in

> **DEFINITIONS**
>
> *Maintenance burden.* The need for software organizations to invest money in the support, operation, and enhancement of existing hardware.
>
> *Traceability.* The ease of which the features of one artifact—perhaps a document, model, or source code—may be related/traced to the features of another.

one class, you can change the implementation of that class (add new features or modify existing features) in one place and one place only—the appropriate UI class. This helps to reduce the maintenance burden.

3.5.3 Finding Responsibilities

The responsibilities of a class are the things it knows and does. Finding responsibilities is a requirements and analysis task, because it deals with defining what a class is all about without going into how to do it. The object paradigm is based on combining data and functionality in the form of a class, which is why CRC modeling fits in well with object-oriented development: the things a class knows is its data, and the things it does is its functionality. Identifying classes and their responsibilities is a big part of what object-orientation is all about.

Your use cases describe the initial behaviors required of your user interface classes, which, in turn, can be used to identify the responsibilities of your business classes.

You should ask yourself what a class does. In other words, ask yourself what functionality the class must perform. This is straightforward for actor and UI classes. For actor classes, simply identify the way in which the actor interacts with your system, information that likely already exists within your use cases. For example, in the use case of Figure 3-5, you see that the "Student" actor provides information about himself and requests to enroll in a seminar. UI classes have simpler behavior: they accept input from users, retrieve business objects from the system, display business objects, enable users to manipulate the business objects, and often support the creation, update, deletion, and saving of business objects into the system. For example, the UI class "Enroll in Seminar" would have the responsibility to accept identifying information about a student, for allowing a student to search for available seminars, to display lists of seminars, to enable students to indicate the seminars they want to enroll in, and to display the fees associated with enrolling in a given seminar. The tasks that business classes do are often driven by the behaviors of UI classes and other business classes. For example, the "Seminar" class would need to support the addition of a new student enrolling in it. Also, remember the context of your domain. Yes, students like to watch television, but you don't care in the context of a university.

Another way to identify responsibilities is to ask yourself what information you need to record about a class. This is straightforward for business classes, but not so for actor and UI classes. For example, consider the business class "Student." For students, you want to keep track of their names, addresses, student numbers, and phone numbers. The actor class "Student," however, is a different story. Because actor classes are effectively placeholders for the actors modeled in your use case diagrams, and because they are represented by corresponding business classes in your system, you don't need to identify information they know about themselves. Instead, this belongs on the appropriate business class card(s). Now consider the user interface class "Transcript." There should be a prototype, at this point, an essential user interface prototype (Section 3.4), describing the details of the information that appears on a student transcript. Why record this information again? I might add a comment on the card, perhaps "**See the prototype**" and leave it at that. Figure 3-18 depicts a collection of CRC cards for the university with responsibilities added to them.

Ask yourself what information must be stored about a class.

Figure 3-18 denotes an interesting stylistic issue. The "Student" card includes responsibilies such as "Name" and "Phone number," whereas "Seminar" has responsibilities, such as "Know name" and "Know fees." In other words, "Student" indicates data responsibilities as nouns, whereas "Seminar" shows them as verb phrases. Although both techniques are valid, throughout this book, I use the approach taken with "Student" and show data responsibilities as nouns and functional responsibilities as verbs. The important point is to choose one style and stick to it to ensure consistency within your model.

A consistently followed imperfect standard is far superior to an inconsistently followed perfect standard.

Sometimes you find a responsibility and you are not sure to what class it belongs. This means you are in one of two situations: Either the class it belongs to has already been identified or it hasn't. If the group of SMEs is having problems deciding where the responsibility belongs, the facilitator should mention that perhaps they have overlooked a class. Another possibility is that the responsibility is shared by several classes that collaborate with one another. In this situation, ask yourself what class would initiate the process. The answer may tell you where to put the responsibility. You then need to determine what classes it must collaborate with to fulfill the responsibility and how that collaboration works (which I describe in the next section).

How do you differentiate between a class and a responsibility to know something? For example, why isn't *student name* a class with responsibilities such as "First name," "Surname," and "Middle initials"? Well, depending on your domain, "Person Name" might be a valid class, but for a university system, it likely isn't. A good rule of thumb is that a possessive noun, such as the noun *student* in "Student name," is a likely indicator that "Student" is a class, but "Student name" is a responsibility of that class.

TIP

Possessive Nouns Indicate Responsibilities

Student	
Name Address Phone number Email address Student number	

Enroll in Seminar <<UI>>	
See the prototype Request identifying info for student Enable seminar search Display seminar list Display seminar fees Display professor info	

Student <<Actor>>	

Provide information
    about self
Request to enroll in
    seminar	

Transcript <<UI>>	

See the prototype
Get student info
Get seminars student
    took
Determine average
    mark
Output self	

Seminar	
Know name Know seminar number Know fees Know waiting list Know enrolled students Add student Drop student	

Figure 3-18.

Example CRC cards with responsiblities identified for them

Defining responsibilities and collaborators is a highly iterative process.

You must always remember two issues when identifying responsibilities. First, sometimes you identify responsibilities you will not implement. For example, you might identify that students drive to school. While this is something students do, you likely won't be implementing this feature because it is out of scope for the system. However, selling parking passes to students might be something you will want to do, so knowing that students drive could be valuable information. Second, classes will collaborate to fulfill many of their responsibilities. Finding that a class is unable to fulfil a responsibility by itself is quite common. In other words, it will have to collaborate. Note that when a class needs to collaborate with another class, this means the second class now has the responsibility to fulfill that collaboration. In other words, as you find responsibilities, you need to define collaborations, and as you define col-

> ### DEFINITION
>
> *Project scope.* The definition of the functionality that will, and will not, be implemented by a project.

laborations, you will often find new responsibilities. This is one of the factors that makes CRC modeling an iterative process.

3.5.4 Defining Collaborators

A class often does not have sufficient information to fulfill its responsibilities. Therefore, it must collaborate (work) with other classes to get the job done. Collaboration will be in one of two forms: a request for information or a request to perform a task.

A class collaborates when it does not have sufficient information to fulfill a responsibility.

An important concept to understand is that collaboration must occur when a class needs information it doesn't have. Each class has certain things it knows, and that's it. Very often, a class needs information it does not know. This means it needs to request the information from another class. For example, when a student wants to enroll in a seminar, he needs to find out if any room is left for him in the seminar. This means the card "Student" must collaborate with the card "Seminar" ("Student" will ask for the number of seats still available in the "Seminar").

This is a completely different mindset than in structured development. In the object-oriented world, you have to be polite and ask for information, whereas in the structured world if you want information, you just take it. For example, in structured development, to determine if a space was available in a class, the student program module would read from the "Seminar" data table and count the number of seats left. In other words, it would take the information from the "Seminar" table. While this approach is straightforward, it leads to code that is hard to maintain—when the structure of the "Seminar" table changes, any program that accesses it will be affected. In an OO program, if the structure of a class changes, the effects of that change are localized to the definition of only that class. Nothing else is affected.

Similarly, collaboration occurs when a class needs to modify information it doesn't have because any given class can update only the information it

> ### TIP
>
> A good rule of thumb is, if you need more than one card, you likely need to reconsider the class (Wilkinson, 1995).
>
> *A Busy Card Often Indicates the Need for Several Classes*

A class must
collaborate
to change
information it
does not own.

knows. This implies that if it needs to have information updated in another class, then it must ask that class to update it. For example, if there is room for a student in the seminar, then she needs to be signed up to it. A seminar maintains a list of students who are enrolled in it, which means only the class "Seminar" can modify it. Therefore, a student must ask the seminar to be enrolled in it. Remember, only a class can change its own data. To enroll a student, she needs to be added to the list of students for the seminar, which means the student list changes. Therefore, to enroll in a course, the "Student" card must collaborate with the "Seminar" card.

There are several issues to consider when identifying collaborators:

1. **There will always be at least one initiator of any given collaboration.** In other words, a collaboration always starts somewhere.

2. **Sometimes the collaborator does the bulk of the work.** Just because a class initiates a collaboration, this doesn't mean it is going to do a lot of work. For example, consider enrolling a student in a seminar. "Student" collaborates with "Seminar" to see if any seats are left and, if so, then asks to be added to the seminar list. "Seminar" is doing all the work. "Seminar" has to determine how many seats are left, as well as update the list of students in the given seminar. On the other hand, "Student" merely manages (directs) the entire process.

3. **Don't pass the buck.** To fulfill a collaboration, a class may have to collaborate with other classes. If this is the case, then the class should do something to value to the process. If Class *A* collaborates with Class *B*, who then passes the buck to *C*, consider cutting out the middleman (class *B*) and have *A* collaborate directly with *C*. This is usually more efficient.

4. **New responsibilities may be created to fulfill the collaboration.** When a class is asked for information or asked to do anything, this means it now has the responsibility to fulfill that collaboration. For example, "Student" asks "Seminar" how many seats are left. This means "Seminar" now has the responsibility to fulfill the collaboration (it would need to know the number of available seats).

Figure 3-19 depicts the result of identifying the collaborators for the CRC cards originally depicted in Figure 3-18. First, a style issue: I generally prefer to list a collaborator once on a card. For example, although the "Seminar" class likely collaborates several times with "Student," it only has this collaborator listed once. Another approach you can take is to list all the collaborators for each responsibility adjacent to the responsibility, as

Student

Name Address Phone number Email address Student number Average mark received Validate identifying info Provide list of seminars taken	Enrollment Record

Student   <<Actor>>

Provide information about self Request to enroll in seminar Request Transcript	Enroll in Seminar Transcript

Seminar

Name Seminar number Fees Waiting list Enrolled students Instructor Add student Drop student	Student Professor

Enroll in Seminar   <<UI>>

See the prototype Request identifying info for student Enable seminar search Display seminar list Display seminar fees Display professor info	Student Seminar Seminar, Professor Student Professor

Transcript   <<UI>>

***See the prototype** Get student info Get seminars student took Determine average mark Output self	Student Seminar Professor Enrollment Record

Professor

Name Address Phone number Email address Salary Provide information Seminars instructing	Seminar

Enrollment Record

Mark(s) received Average to date Final grade Student Seminar	

Figure 3-19.
CRC cards with collaborators and new responsibilities added

you see with the "Enroll in Seminar" card. This seems like a lot of needless busy work to me. To record each actual collaboration, have your scribe record in his notes that "Seminar" collaborates with "Student" for each individual responsibility that needs to do so, but don't clutter your cards with this information. Again, pick the approach that works best for you and stick to it. The approach I like might not be the one your SMEs like.

A second stylistic issue pertains to how cards collaborate with one another to obtain information. For example, "Transcript" collaborates with "Professor," "Student," and "Enrollment Record" to obtain information, such as the name of the professor, the name and address of the student, and the final grade a student received in a given seminar. Although "Professor" includes a responsibility called "Provide Information," frankly, it is redundant. For the purpose of CRC modeling, I prefer to assume that if a class knows something, then it is also willing to provide that information to whomever requests it. Yes, there are security access control issues to consider; for example, not everyone should be allowed to access a professor's salary information, but these are issues that should be recorded in your notes about each class, and then taken into account during design (Chapter 7).

While identifying collaborators of the existing cards, I had to introduce two new cards, "Professor" and "Enrollment Record." "Professor" was introduced as the result of several existing responsibilities, particularly the "Provide professor info" responsibility of "Enroll in Seminar" and the "Output self" responsibility of "Transcript" (the name of the instructor is listed for each seminar the student took). The card "Enrollment Record" was introduced because of the need to record the fact that a student is enrolled in a seminar, the mark(s) he receive in the seminar need to be recorded, and the final mark he receives is output on their transcript.

Class A is shown as a collaborator of Class B only if A does something for B.

Sometimes the set of collaborations between two classes is two-way, and sometimes only one-way. For example, the collaboration between "Transcript" and "Seminar" is a one-way street. "Transcript" requests information from "Seminar"; however, "Seminar" asks nothing of "Transcript." Therefore, I listed "Seminar" as a collaborator of "Transcript," but not the other way around. The general rule is "Class *A* is listed as a collaborator of

---

TIP

Your Scribe Should Take Notes for Each Class

CRC cards are small, which is both good and bad. This is good because it makes the cards portable and easy to handle; this is bad because it limits the information you can record on them (which, frankly, is also a good thing). Consequently, your scribe needs to record the information you cannot record on a CRC card, such as the logic of a responsibility of the list of the collaborators required for that responsibility.

Class *B* if and only if *A* does something for *B*." On the other hand, the collaboration between "Seminar" and "Professor" is a two-way street. The class "Professor" knows what seminars it instructs (it likely needs to know this for scheduling purposes), while "Seminar" needs to know who is instructing it. Therefore, "Seminar" is shown as a collaborator of "Professor," and "Professor" is shown as a collaborator of "Seminar."

3.5.5 Arranging the CRC Cards

CRC modeling is typically performed by a group of SMEs around a large desk. As the CRC cards are created, they are placed on the desk, so everyone can see them. To improve everyone's understanding of the system, the cards should be placed on the table in an intelligent manner. Two cards that collaborate with one another should be placed close together on the table, whereas two cards that don't collaborate should be placed far apart. Furthermore, the more two cards collaborate, the closer they should be on the desk. Not only can you have an understanding of what classes are related to each other, you can also get a sense for how much they are related.

By having cards that collaborate with one another close together, it's easier to understand the relationships between classes. For example, the "Student" card collaborates with the "Enrollment Record" card. A business relationship exists between these two cards: students have enrollment records. Because they work together to fulfill common responsibilities—in this case "Enrollment Record" provides the basic information (the final grade) that "Student" needs to calculate its average mark—it makes a lot of sense to have them close together. Think of it like this: In the real world, the more you work with someone else, generally the easier that work becomes when you are close together. The main advantage is when you look at the cards from above (which is exactly the viewpoint your SMEs have standing around the table), you can get an overall view of the system, seeing how each class interacts with the others. Furthermore, you can concentrate on any given section of the system and know you will have all the cards involved with that section right there in front of you.

Cards that collaborate with one another should be close to each other on the table.

Here are a few tips I have learned over the years when CRC modeling:

1. **Expect to move the cards around a lot at the beginning.** Typically, at the beginning of a CRC modeling session, you quickly identify several cards. As you define the initial responsibilities and collaborators for each card, you are moving them around a lot. However, because people have a tendency to identify the most obvious responsibilities first, and because these responsibilities tend to lead to the main collaborations, you will find that you can determine the "right" position for your cards fairly quickly.

2. **Put "busy" cards toward the center of the table.** The busiest cards are often the core of the system, so it makes sense to have the core at the center. One good rule of thumb is to put the customer at or near the center of the table (the customer often has the most important responsibilities within the system and is usually involved in itiating many collaborations).

3. **Actually move the cards around.** The benefits of intelligently moving the cards around on the desk are subtle, yet still important. People tend to fill the cards out, and then put them down on the table wherever there is room. CRC facilitators must keep an eye on the SMEs/users and make sure they move the cards around intelligently. Do not underestimate the value of moving the cards around.

4. **People will identify associations between classes as they move them around.** Typically, one person will pick up a card and say she wants to put it beside another because they collaborate. Somebody else will then say the card should go somewhere else because it is related to another card. The scribe should listen closely to this conversation and record any associations or important business rules (business rules are discussed in Section 3.6.1), that come out of it.

To simplify the example, the CRC model of Figure 3-20 does not include the responsibilities for the classes (to move cards around, you are only concerned about the collaborators). Although the class "Transcript" collaborates with "Professor," I wasn't able to get it anywhere close to the "Professor" card. Moving the "Professor" card into the center would help, but then I would get the same type of problem with either the "Student" or "Seminar" cards. This happens.

Moving your CRC cards around on the table increases the understandability of your CRC model.

The advantage to following these strategies for moving cards around is that you can quickly look at any CRC model and get a good understanding of what it is all about—in other words, your model becomes more readable, which makes modeling that much easier. Second, when one of the SMEs wants to move a card, it will often engender a discussion along the lines of "you can't move that card there because XYZ over here collaborates with it." Conversations such as this help you to grow the model. You are likely to find new responsibilities and to help your SMEs understand the nuances of the model. Another big advantage is that when you convert your CRC model into a class model (class modeling is described in Chapters 6 and 7) the cards on the table are in reasonably good positions for transcribing them onto the class model. Just take my word on this for now (it will become obvious when I cover class modeling).

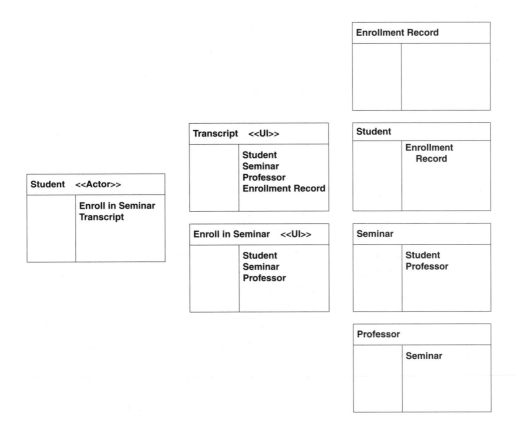

3.5.6 The Advantages and Disadvantages of CRC Modeling

Figure 3-20.
CRC cards after being arranged on the table

CRC modeling is an exciting new analysis technique. As with anything, certain advantages and disadvantages exist. On the one hand, CRC modeling leads to improved analysis quality. This is because, for the most part, CRC modeling is performed by SMEs/users, the people who are the experts, not by technical staff, the people who think they are the experts. On the other hand, many systems professionals find CRC modeling threatening because it represents a completely different modeling mindset. Many systems people fear losing control of the modeling process and, as a result, are leery of trying a new method.

3.5.6.1 The Advantages

The experts do the analysis. The people who understand the business are the ones defining the requirements. Although this is completely different than the current approach taken by many systems departments, if you stop and think about it, having the real experts model the system makes a lot of sense. I have always believed that it is inappropriate for systems people to do analysis. First, unless the person can sit down and do the job of his users, then he obviously doesn't know the business as well as the person who does that job. Second, while techies often have technical skills that are second to none, they might not have the communication skills necessary to obtain user requirements effectively. Third, and most important, when techies are interviewing users, they are usually thinking about how they are going to build the system, not what the system needs to do. I know whenever I am interviewing a user, I constantly find myself thinking about how I am going to design the database or about how the class structure is going to look. I can't help it. I'm sure this also happens to many other systems professionals.

Although having users perform analysis is a radical idea for many organizations, it is an idea whose time has come

1. **User participation in system development is increased.** Numerous studies have shown that the more users who are involved in the development of a system, the greater the chance of success, and CRC modeling increases the participation of users in systems development.

2. **CRC modeling improves communications between users and developers.** By providing users with a technique that actively involves them in system analysis, you increase the opportunities for improving the communication between developers and users. Remember, it doesn't matter how proficient you are technically, you cannot build a system that will meet the needs of your users if you don't know what those needs are.

3. **CRC cards are simple and inexpensive.** As you have seen, CRC modeling is straightforward. Furthermore, the cost of materials to perform CRC modeling is trivial: A few dollars for a package of index cards.

4. **CRC modeling is nonthreatening to users.** In short, nobody is afraid of losing his or her job to a stack of cards. When people are afraid of losing their jobs, they are not willing to work with systems. By using a nonthreatening analysis technique, you lessen the probability of having to deal with recalcitrant users.

5. **CRC cards are quick and portable.** You simply throw a package of index cards and a pen in your briefcase and go.

6. **CRC modeling goes hand in hand with essential use case modeling and essential UI prototyping.** All three techniques are iterative requirements engineering methods. During a modeling session, you find the group will transparently move back and

forth among the three techniques in the effort of recording the requirements for the system.

7. **CRC modeling gives you a good overview of a system.** Users transfer their knowledge of the business onto the CRC cards and into the prototype sketches of the screens and reports.

8. **CRC modeling leads directly into class modeling.** As you see in Chapters 6 and 7, CRC modeling is an excellent start at class modeling. While the CRC model may not be optimal from a design point-of-view, it is still pretty darn close to what you want. Class models are the mainstay of OO analysis and design.

9. **CRC modeling enables you to deal with system complexity one class at a time.** One of the first questions people ask is, "With a 'real' system, wouldn't you get lots of cards?" The answer is yes. This is because systems are complex. One of the advantages of CRC modeling is you can concentrate on one card at a time, which means you don't get bogged down worrying about everything at once. CRC cards emphasize division of responsibility; the physical nature of cards makes it obvious to the modelers which class performs which behavior (Wilkinson, 1995). Think of it like this: If you think dealing with 50 or 60 cards is hard, it is orders of magnitude easier than trying to handle that much detail all at once.

10. **CRC modeling promotes a common project vocabulary.** Wilkinson (1995) points out that CRC modeling is an excellent method for ensuring that key terms within your business domain are explored and defined as your team identifies classes and responsibilities.

3.5.6.2 The Disadvantages
Unfortunately, nothing is perfect, and even something as simple as CRC modeling has a few challenges.

1. **CRC modeling is threatening to systems developers.** CRC modeling is often completely different than the developer-dominated approaches many systems professionals prefer. Users documenting their own requirements? Preposterous. Developers have always documented engineering requirements, not users. It could never work.

2. **It can be difficult to get your SMEs together.** Users have their own jobs to do. Although user involvement is key to systems

development, still one of the hardest tasks facing a modeling facilitator is that of convincing users it is worth their while to be involved in the requirements process. It isn't that SMEs aren't interested, it's just that the past performance of systems developers doesn't exactly motivate users to get involved anymore. Why should users spend their valuable time working with systems developers just to have a system delivered to them that isn't what they need, is late, and is over budget?

3. **CRC cards are limited.** You cannot record detailed business logic on CRC cards (this is why the scribe is there). You cannot record screen/report designs on the cards (this is why you have essential user interface modeling). As you see in Chapter 5, several object-oriented concepts exist, such as inheritance, aggregation, and associations, which you really cannot model using CRC cards. On the other hand, however, CRC cards are effective because they are simple.

4. **You still need to do class modeling.** You cannot hand a stack of index cards to your manager and claim it represents your model, your manager isn't likely to accept it and frankly shouldn't because, as you saw previously, CRC models aren't complete anyway. You need to take your completed CRC model and convert it into a class model. You can then use the class model for your system documentation. UML class models are a more traditional form of model. They show a bunch of bubbles connected by lines.

5. **You need management support.** You are finished if either information systems management or user management do not fully support CRC modeling.

Meanwhile, Back in Reality
Although "inheritance" is a big word, in a way it is a straightforward concept. If you haven't yet read ahead to Chapter 5, the main idea is that inheritance is a mechanism that lets you model similarities between classes. The

TIP *Do Not Make CRC Modeling Complex*	If you have read ahead in the book, you have come across concepts like aggregation and inheritance. Confusing at first, aren't they? Your users don't need to be burdened with these issues during CRC modeling, so do not mention them. CRC modeling works because it is simple and straightforward. Don't complicate it.

DEFINITIONS

Inheritance. The representation of an *is a, is like,* or *is kind of* relationship between two classes. Inheritance promotes reuse by enabling a subclass to benefit automatically from all the behavior it inherits from its superclass(es).

Subclass. If Class *B* inherits from Class *A,* we say *B* is a subclass of *A.*

Superclass. If Class *B* inherits from Class *A,* we say *A* is a superclass of *B.*

---

bottom line is people aren't stupid—whenever similarities exist between cards, the SMEs are tempted to write something like "all the stuff on XYZ plus...." The main point here is the SMEs should come up with this "quasi-inheritance" on their own, and shouldn't be forced into it by the facilitator.

3.6 Developing a Supplementary Specification

A Supplementary Specification is an artifact where all requirements not contained in your use case model, user interface model, or domain model are documented. In many ways, a Supplementary Specification is simply a catch-all for your requirements that don't fit elsewhere. These requirements include constraints, business rules, and nonfunctional requirements, and, in this section, I describe each of these types of requirements in detail. Supplementary Specifications, also called Supplementary Business Specifications, are a key part of your requirements model in the Unified Process (Kruchten 1999; Ambler and Constantine 2000a–c).

3.6.1 Identifying Business Rules

A business rule is effectively an operating principle or policy your software must satisfy. Business rules often focus on access control issues; for example, professors are allowed to input and modify the marks of the students taking the seminars they instruct, but not the marks of students in other seminars. Business rules may also pertain to business calcula-

Business rules often pertain to access control issues, business calculations, or operating policies and principles of your organization.

DEFINITIONS

Supplementary Specification. An artifact where all requirements not contained in your use case model, user interface model, or domain model are documented.

Business rule. A policy your software must satisfy. Business rules are what a functional requirement "knows," the controls and guidelines that are fulfilled by the functional requirement. An operating principle or policy of your organization.

Constraint. A global requirement, such as limited development resources or a decision by senior management, that restricts the way you develop a system.

tions—for example, how to convert a percentage mark (for example, 76 percent) that a student receives in a seminar into a letter grade (for example, A–). Some business rules focus on the policies of your organization— for example, perhaps the university policy is to expel for one year anyone who fails more than two courses in the same semester.

Figure 3-22 summarizes several examples of business rules. Notice how each business rule has a unique identifier; my convention is to use the format of BR#, but you are free to set your own numbering approach. The unique identifier enables you to refer easily to business rules in other development artifacts, such as class models and use cases. You saw an example of this in the use case of Figure 3-5. Figure 3-22 presents a fully documented version of BR123. Notice how the name gives you a good idea about the topic of the business rule, but the description exactly defines the rule. An example of the rule is presented to help clarify it, and the source of the rule is indicated so it may be verified (it is quite common that the source of a rule is a person, often one of your SMEs, or a team of people). A list of related business rules, if any, is provided to support traceability between rules. A revision history of the business rule is also presented, indicating the date a change was made, the person who made the change, and a description of the change.

Business rules are identified in the normal course of requirements gathering and analysis. While you are use case and domain modeling, you will often identify business rules. A rule of thumb is, if something defines a calculation or operating principle of your organization, then it is likely a good candidate to be documented as a business rule. You want to separate business rules out of your other requirements artifacts because they may be referred to within those artifacts several times. For example, BR129 was referenced by the "Enroll Student In Seminar" use case of Figure 3-5 and likely would be referenced in the notes taken by the scribe regarding the CRC cards depicted in Figure 3-20.

A good business rule is cohesive: in other words, it describes one, and only one, concept. By ensuring that business rules are cohesive, you make them easier to define and increase the likelihood they will be reused (every time one of your artifacts refers to a business rule, even other business rules, it is effectively being reused). Unfortunately, because business rules should focus on one issue, you often identify a plethora of rules.

Figure 3-21.
Example business
rules (summarized)

BR123 Tenured professors may administer student grades.

BR124 Teaching assistants who have been granted authority by a tenured professor may administer student grades.

BR177 Table to convert between numeric grades and letter grades.

BR245 All master's degree programs must include the development of a thesis.

Name:	Tenured professors may administer student grades.	*Figure 3-22.* A fully documented business rule
Identifier:	BR123	
Description:	Only tenured professors are granted the ability to initially input, modify, and delete grades students receive in the seminars that they and they only instruct. They may do so only during the period a seminar is active.	
Example:	Dr. Bruce Banner, instructor of "Biology 301: Advanced Uses of Gamma Radiation," may administer the marks of all students enrolled in that seminar, but not those enrolled in "Biology 302: Effects of Radiation on Arachnids," which is taught by Dr. Peter Parker.	
Source:	University Policies and Procedures Doc ID: U1701 Publication date: August 14, 2000	
Related rules:	BR12 Qualifying for Tenure BR65 Active Period for Seminars BR200 Modifying Final Student Grades	
Revision History:	Defined March 2, 2001 by Diana Prince Updated October 10, 2001 by Gwen Stacy to reference-related rule BR200.	

3.6.2 Identifying Nonfunctional Requirements and Constraints

A nonfunctional requirement pertains to the technical aspects your system must fulfill, such as performance-related issues, reliability issues, and availability issues. Nonfunctional requirements are often referred to as technical requirements. Examples of nonfunctional requirements are presented in Figure 3-23. As you can see, technical requirements are summarized in a similar manner as business rules: They have a name and a unique identifier (my convention is to use the format TR#, where TR stands for technical requirement). You document nonfunctional requirements in the same manner as business rules, including a description, an example, a source, references to related technical requirements, and a revision history.

Business rules should be cohesive.

A constraint is a restriction on the degree of freedom you have in providing a solution (Leffingwell and Widrig, 2000). Constraints are effectively global requirements, such as limited development resources or a decision by senior management that restricts the way you develop a system. Constraints can be economic, political, technical, or environmental,

Figure 3-23.
Potential nonfunctional requirements for the university system

TR34 The system shall be unavailable for no less than two minutes in a 24-hour period.

TR78 A seminar search will occur within less than three seconds 95 percent of the time and no more than ten seconds 99 percent of the time.

TIP *Minimize the Number of Purely Technical Requirements*	Technology changes quickly and often requirements based on technology change just as quickly. An example of a pure technical requirement is that an application be written in Java or must run on the XYZ computer. Whenever you have a requirement based purely on technology, try to determine the real underlying business needs being expressed. To do this, keep asking why your application must meet a requirement. For example, when asked why your application must be written in Java, the reply was it has to run on the Internet. When asked why it must run on the Internet, the reply was your organization wants to take orders for its products and services on the Internet. The real requirement is to sell things on the Internet; one technical solution to this need (and a good one) is to write that component in Java. A big difference exists between having to write the entire application in Java and having to support the sales of some products and services over the Internet.

and pertain to your project resources, schedule, target environment, or to the system itself. Figure 3-24 presents several potential constraints for the university system. Like business rules and nonfunctional requirements, constraints are documented in a similar manner.

As with business rules, you identify and reference nonfunctional requirements and constraints as you are developing other artifacts, such as your use case model and user interface model. You treat business rules, nonfunctional requirements, and constraints in similar ways during development. The only real difference in the three types of requirements is their focus.

3.7 Identifying Change Cases

Software is extensible because you design it that way.

Change happens. Any successful software product needs to change and evolve over its lifetime; that is, changes are motivated by new and/or modified requirements. Extensibility, the responsiveness of software to change, has been touted as one of the great benefits of object orienta-

Figure 3-24.
Potential constraints for the university system

C23 The user interface will work on browsers that support HTML v2.0 or better.
C24 The system will work on Sun Solaris servers.
C52 The system will be written using J2EE technologies.
C56 The system will use the data contained the existing Oracle database.
C73 The system will be delivered before June 1, 2002.
C76 The system will be developed by unionized software professionals.

tion, of component-based development, and of virtually any development environment with which you have ever worked. The reality is that software is extensible because it is designed that way, not because you implemented objects, not because you implemented components, and certainly not because you used the latest version of product XYZ.

Change cases (Bennett, 1997) are used to describe new potential requirements for a system or modifications to existing requirements. Change cases are similar in concept to use cases: where use cases describe behavioral requirements for your system, change cases describe a potential requirement your system may need to support in the future. Important to note is that change cases can be defined pertaining to both behavioral and nonbehavioral requirements.

Change cases enable you to document requirements your system may need to fulfill in the future.

Change cases should be developed as part of your overall modeling efforts, particularly during requirements gathering, but also during analysis and design. Change cases are often the result of brainstorming by your SMEs, where questions such as "How can the business change," "What technology can change," "What legislation can change," "What is your competition doing," "What systems will we need to interact with," and "Who else might use the system and how," are explored. In many ways, the change cases for a system is a well-documented risk assessment for changing requirements.

3.7.1 Documenting Change Cases

Change cases are documented in a simple manner. You describe the potential change to your existing requirements, indicate the likeliness of that change occurring, and indicate the potential impact of that change. Figure 3-25 presents two change cases, one potential change that is motivated by technical innovation—in this case the use of the Internet—and a second by a change in your business environment. Notice how both change cases are short and to the point, making them easy to understand. The name of a change case should describe the potential change itself, as you can see in the figure.

The professionals who operate and support your system will be concerned about issues such as the backup and archival of data, the electronic and physical security of your system, the reliability and availability of the system, and the capability of your system to log and recover from errors. Although the previous list is not exhaustive, it should motivate you to invest the time to work with your operations and support staff early in your project to identify their needs. Those needs probably will become nonfunctional requirements and/or constraints on your system.

TIP

Remember the Needs of Operations

Change case: Registration will occur completely via the Internet.

Likelihood: Medium likelihood within two to three years, very likely within ten years.

Impact: Unknown. Although registration will be available online starting in September, we currently expect less than one quarter of registrations to be made via the Internet this year. Response time will be an issue during the peak use periods, which are the two weeks prior to the beginning of classes each term, as well as the first week of classes.

Change case: The university will open a new campus.

Likelihood: Certain. It has been announced that a new campus will be opened in two years across town.

Impact: Large. Students will be able to register in classes at either campus. Some instructors will teach at both campuses. Some departments, such as Computer Science and Philosophy, are slated to move their entire programs to the new campus. The likelihood is great that most students will want to schedule courses at only one of the two campuses, so we will need to make this easy to support.

3.7.2 The Advantages of Change Cases

Change cases have several advantages:

1. **Change cases enable you to consider and document likely changes to your software.** This, in turn, enables you to justify the effort for you to develop a more robust solution to your existing problem to meet those potential changes.

2. **Change cases enable you to consider long-term issues.** Change cases can be used to take your team out of the short-term mentality, which is common to most software development efforts. This mentality generally leads to eventual project failure.

3. **Change cases support architectural efforts.** One of the fundamental precepts of software engineering is you should start with requirements. This is particularly true of the development of system architecture, just as it is of a business application. Because system architectures should balance the needs of today with the likely needs of the future, change cases that document potential future requirements are an excellent approach for defining architectural requirements.

4. **Change cases increase the likeliness of developing extensible software.** By including change cases in your software process, you ensure that the people involved with your project consider, and then document, potential modifications to your system. If your team does not consider potential extensions, it is likely the

---

DEFINITIONS

Extensibility. A measure of how easy it is to add new features to a system. The easier it is to add new features, the more extensible we say the system is.

Scalability. A measure of how easy it is to support increased load on a system. The easier it is to increase the number of users working with a system and/or the number of transactions the system can support, the more scalable we say the system is.

---

software develops will not be easy to extend. Change cases lead you to develop software that is more maintainable, portable, modular, extensible, usable, and robust.

5. **Change cases provide significant payback.** Change cases are fairly simple to document, making them relatively inexpensive, yet they enable you to understand the "big picture" of what it is you are trying to solve and, hence, make better decisions as a result. On one project I was involved with, we invested several hours identifying change cases. I believe this effort saved us months of effort later in the project because, during design, the change cases pointed us away from a technology that would not have scaled sufficiently to meet our needs over the long term.

Change is an inevitable, fundamental aspect of our industry. Everybody recognizes this fact yet, for some reason, the vast majority of us choose not to manage change, not to plan for it in our designs. We have always had excuses: "the users keep changing their minds," "the users don't know what they want," "the people in the marketing department are insane" (okay, that's likely a valid excuse), and "new legislation was introduced" for being caught off-guard by change. Depending on the design of the current software, it is typical that a few changes result in "easy fixes," the majority require significant rework to existing software, and a few simply cannot be supported in an economical manner. Change cases are a simple technique for minimizing the impact of change by preparing for it long before it happens.

3.8 Tips for Organizing a Modeling Room

Several considerations must be taken into account when you are organizing a modeling room:

1. **Reserve a meeting room that has something to write on.** You need a flip-chart and, ideally, a whiteboard to write on to brain-

storm, to draw use case diagrams, and to develop your essential user interface prototype. My advice: The more whiteboard space, the better.

2. **Bring modeling supplies.** You need a few packages of index cards, some sticky notes, some notepads, and some whiteboard markers.

3. **Have a large modeling table.** Provide a large table on which people can CRC model.

4. **Have chairs and desks for the scribe(s).** Your scribes need something to write on. Put them to the back or sides of the room where they are out of the way, but can still see what's happening.

5. **Have enough chairs for everyone.** People will want to sit down during the session, so make sure you have enough chairs.

6. **Put observers at the back of the room.** Observers are not there to participate, so it is valid to put them at the back of the room, where they are out of the way.

3.9 Requirements Tips and Techniques

You can increase your project team's chances of success by following the advice presented in this section.

1. **Prominently display definitions.** As you explain the requirements gathering process and the various techniques described in this chapter to your SMEs, summarize the critical points on a piece of flip-chart paper and post it on the wall. Then your SMEs can refer to the paper during their modeling efforts as needed.

2. **Expect to gather requirements throughout the entire software process.** As you saw in Chapter 2, and will see again in Chapter 10, requirements are identified throughout most of your project. Although the majority of your requirements efforts are performed at the beginning, they often continue until just before your code freeze.

3. **Explain the techniques.** The facilitator should begin a modeling session describing the modeling techniques, and how they fit together, to be used by the group. This usually takes between 10 and 15 minutes and, because people learn best by doing, having the facilitator lead the SMEs through the creation of several examples is a good idea.

4. **Allow observers.** For training purposes, your organization may want to have one or more people sit in on the modeling session as observers. These people should be seated at the back of the room and should not participate in the session.

5. **Use several techniques simultaneously.** As you saw at the beginning of this chapter in Figure 3-1, requirements gathering is an iterative process. Each of the techniques described in this chapter feed off each other, so expect to actively apply several techniques simultaneously.

6. **Use the terminology of your users.** Don't force artificial, technical jargon onto your SMEs. They are the ones doing the modeling and they are the ones the system is being built for; therefore, you should use their terminology to model the system. As Constantine and Lockwood (1999) say, avoid geek-speak.

   Avoid geek speak.

7. **Keep it low-tech.** CRC modeling, essential use cases, and essential user interface prototypes are inherently low-tech methods, which is one of the reasons they work well. Keep it that way.

8. **Keep it fun.** Modeling doesn't have to be an arduous task. In fact, you can always have fun doing it. Tell a few jokes and keep your modeling session light. People will not only have a better time, they will also be more productive in a "fun" environment.

9. **Obtain management support.** Investing the effort to identify and document requirements, and, in particular, the usage-centered design techniques presented in this chapter, are new concepts to many organizations. One of the issues is that your users are now doing modeling, not developing and, when you stop to think about it, this is fundamentally a change in the development culture of most organizations. As with any culture change, without the support of upper management, you most likely won't be successful. You need support from both the managers within your IS (information system) department and within the user area.

DEFINITIONS

Baseline. A tested and certified version of a deliverable representing a conceptual milestone that, thereafter, serves as the basis for further development and that can be modified only through formal change control procedures. A particular version becomes a baseline when a responsible group decides to designate it as such.

Code freeze. A milestone in your project where your code is baselined for submission to your final testing efforts.

10. **Send an agenda ahead a few days before a modeling session.** So people know what to expect, you should send ahead an agenda for your modeling session. The agenda should include the following: a description of the system being analyzed; a one- or two-paragraph description of why they are attending (after all, these people are experts about one or more aspects of the business); a description of anything they are asked to bring (for example, copies of reports or screens currently in use, procedure manuals, and so forth); a description of the modeling process (I'd give them a copy of this book and ask them to read this chapter); and a list of names of the people who will be attending, including contact information so people know how to contact each other. By sending ahead an agenda, you give the SMEs time to prepare for your modeling session(s). While creating an agenda takes some time, it dramatically helps to increase the productivity within the modeling session. In short, a lot of bang for your buck is here.

11. **Don't be afraid to iterate.** You don't need to and, realistically, cannot, develop one requirements model completely, then another, and then another. Instead, you should work a little on your essential use cases, a little on your essential user interface prototype, a little on your CRC cards, some more on your use cases, and so on to evolve your models iteratively in parallel.

12. **Take a breadth-first approach.** My experience is it is better to paint a wide swath at first—to try to get a feel for the bigger picture—than it is to focus narrowly on one small aspect of your system. By taking a breadth-first approach, you quickly gain an overall understanding of your system and you can still dive into the details when appropriate.

13. **Technical support people are good sources of user requirements.** Support professionals work with the users of your systems day-in and day-out. They intimately understand the problems that users face and often understand the issues that are not addressed with your current system(s).

14. **Existing documents are a good source of requirements.** Existing documentation, such as policy manuals, government legislation, and even college textbooks can be an excellent source of requirements. I once worked on an electronic commerce system and the first thing I did was pick up a book about electronic commerce to identify the fundamental requirements (such as supporting secure credit card transactions) that my system would have to fulfill.

DEFINITIONS

Commercial package. Software that is developed for sale.

Open-source software (OSS). Fully functioning software whose source code is available free of charge. Changes, often new features or bug fixes, are often made to open-source software by its users, changes that are then made available (usually) free of charge to the entire user community.

3.10 What You Have Learned

The first step of software development is to gather user requirements because you cannot successfully build a system if you don't know what it should do. Requirements models are complex and typically developed in an iterative manner, as indicated in Figure 3-1. Essential modeling, particularly essential use case modeling and essential user interface prototyping, is a usage-centered design technique in which you focus on the essential characteristics of a system in a technology-independent manner. Technology-dependent requirements, which you should attempt to minimize, are documented in the form of constraints and nonfunctional requirements.

In addition to understanding the technical aspects of requirements gathering, the philosophical aspects are also critical. You saw that users have rights and responsibilities when it comes to requirements, and that they are the best source of requirements because they are the experts. In short, you want to work with your users, not against them.

3.10.1 The ABC Bank Case Study

The Archon Bank of Cardassia (ABC) would like to develop an information system for handling accounts. The following is a summary of interviews with employees and customers of the bank.

> *Scenario* The bank has many different types of accounts. The basic type of account is called a savings account. Savings account customers don't get a monthly account statement. Instead, they have a passbook, which gets updated when they come in. Each passbook page has enough room to have up to ten transactions and, every time the book is updated, the next transaction immediately after the last one is printed in the book. The bank already has the passbook printers and printing software in place (purchased from a third-party vendor).
>
> Customers are able to open and close accounts. They can withdraw or deposit money, or get the current balance. The current balance is dis-

played on an account update screen, which will be part of the teller's information system. This screen displays the account number, the customer's name, and the current balance of the account. An account is associated with a specific branch. Although we now support multibranch banking, every account is still assumed to have a "home" branch.

A checking account is just like a savings account, except customers can also write checks on it. The bank sells checks for $30 for a box of 100. Once a customer uses 75 checks, or check #90 comes in, the bank sends them a notice in the mail asking them if they want to purchase more checks. Account statements are sent out every month. Checking accounts do not have passbooks, and savings accounts do not have account statements.

The bank charges $1,200 a year for private banking accounts (PBAs). PBAs are just like checking accounts. PBAs entitle customers to investment counselling services, as well as other services unavailable to other clients. A PBA account can be held by only one customer, although a customer may have more than one PBA account. This is exactly like savings accounts. Checking accounts, however, can be joint. This means a checking account can be accessed by one or more customers (perhaps a husband and a wife).

A current account is for our corporate customers. It works like a checking account, with a few extra features. For example, a quarterly account statement (which is exactly the same as a monthly account statement, except it is done for an entire quarter) is sent out, in addition to the regular monthly statements. The quarterly statement is sent in the same envelope as the statement for that month. Corporate customers also get to choose the number of checks they are sent (100, 250, 500, or 1,000) at a time. Current accounts are not joint and they cannot be accessed through an Automated Teller Machine (ATM). Furthermore, because of the different service needs of corporate customers, the bank deals with them at special branches called "corporate branches." Corporate branches serve only corporate customers. They don't serve retail (normal) customers. Corporate customers can be served at "retail branches," although they rarely are because the tellers in a retail branch don't have the necessary background to meet their special needs.

More than one account can be accessible from a bank card. The bank currently gives cards out to any customer who wants them. Customers access their accounts using two different methods: At an ATM or at a bank branch. ATMs enable customers to deposit to, withdraw from, and get balances from their accounts. They can also pay bills (this is basically a withdrawal) and transfer money between accounts (this is basically withdrawing from one account and depositing into another).

Everything that can be done at a bank machine can also be done by a real live teller in a branch. The teller will have an information system that provides the screens to perform all of these functions. In addition, tellers can also help customers to open and close their accounts, as well as print out account statements for the customer. The account statements are just like the monthly/quarterly statements, except they can be for any time period. For example, a customer could request a statement from the 15th of August to the 23rd of September, and the bank should be able to print that out on the spot.

Monthly and quarterly account statements are normally printed out on the first Saturday of the following month. This is done by an auto-mated batch job.

Because the bank has started to put ATMs into variety stores and restaurants (in the past, the bank has only had ATMs in branches), it now considers every ATM, including those in its "brick and mortar" branches, to be a branch as well. This means ATMs have branch IDs and addresses, just as a normal branch does.

To manage the bank effectively, it is split up into collections of branches called "areas." An area is a group of 10 to 30 branches. A branch is part of only one area, and all branches are in an area. Each area has a unique name and is managed by an "area manager." Area managers receive weekly transaction summary reports every Monday before 9:00 in the morning. This report summarizes the number and total amounts of all withdrawals, deposits, and bill payments per-formed at each branch (including ATMs) for the previous week. For brick-and-mortar branches, there is also an indication of how many accounts in total were at that branch at the beginning of the week, how many accounts were opened during the week, how many accounts were closed during the week, and how many accounts now exist. Finally, all these figures are summarized and output for the entire area.

3.11 Review Questions

1. Develop essential use cases for the use case diagram of Figure 3-3. Identify potential major user interface elements needed to support these use cases, as well as potential business rules.

2. Develop essential user interface prototypes for each of the major user interface elements identified in Question 1 and a user interface flow diagram. Update your essential use cases from Question 1 to reflect your improved understanding of the system based on your essential user interface prototyping efforts.

3. Develop a CRC model that reflects the information contained in your essential use cases and user interface prototypes developed for Question 1 and Question 2. Update these models as you develop your CRC model.

4. What were the benefits of developing the three models of Questions 1 through 3 in parallel? Discuss from the point-of-view of the quality of the requirements, their consistency, and their reliability.

5. How are use cases, user interface prototypes, and CRC cards interrelated? Discuss from the point-of-view of the changes you made to the three models from Questions 1 through 3. Provide examples of business rules, constraints, and nonfunctional requirements that could potentially be pertinent to two or even three of the models.

6. Compare and contrast small modeling groups of three or four people versus larger modeling groups of 10 to 20 people. Take into consideration management issues, communication issues, logistical issues, decision-making ability, group dynamics, skills, and knowledge. What do you believe is the ideal size for a modeling group? Why?

7. With several other people, brainstorm nonfunctional requirements and constraints for the university system. Identify potential sources for these requirements, such as roles within the organization (the Dean, an instructor, a registrar, and so on) and documents.

8. Develop a requirements model, including all the types of artifacts discussed in this chapter, for the bank case study described in Section 3.10.1.

9. Identify the categories of tools, such as requirements management systems and computer-aided software engineering (CASE) tools, that you could potentially use during requirements gathering. For each category, present three examples of them in the marketplace: one should be an open-source software (OSS) tool and one should be a commercial package. Identify how each category is used and the potential skills required of the people using them.

*The errors that cost us the most are the ones we make
early in development.*

Chapter 4

Ensuring Your Requirements Are Correct: Requirements Validation Techniques

What You Will Learn in This Chapter

*Why you need to test early and often
How to reduce the cost of defects dramatically
How to increase system quality dramatically
How to perform use case scenario testing
How to hold user interface walkthroughs
How to hold requirements reviews*

Why You Need to Read This Chapter

*Most defects are introduced in the early stages of development, particularly
during requirements elicitation. You can find defects in your requirements in
several ways, including use case scenario testing, reviews, and walkthroughs.
Successful developers test early and often; unsuccessful developers leave testing
to the end, when it is often too late.*

If you can build something, you can test it, including your requirements model.

It isn't enough to gather requirements; you also need to verify that they are correct. This is where systems professionals have traditionally fallen down—until now. You can gather requirements until you are blue in the face, but unless you can be sure those requirements are correct, what good are they? The most common errors made in the development of a system are analysis errors—user requirements that are either missing or misunderstood. In many ways, developers are good at building systems correctly and we are very good at the technical aspects of software development. We are just not that good at building the right system because we are not as good at the nontechnical aspects of software development, such as requirements gathering and analysis. Use case scenario testing, requirements reviews, and prototype walkthroughs are simple and effective techniques to detect potential analysis errors when they are the least expensive to fix—during requirements gathering and analysis when they are initially made.

What is the implication of analysis errors for object-oriented development artifacts? With respect to a Class Responsibility Collaborator (CRC) model, you would be missing user requirements if you were missing a few responsibilities for a class, an entire class, or one or more collaborations. For your essential user interface prototype, you would have incomplete screens and reports, or even be missing some. Similarly, your essential use case model may be missing use cases or actors, or may not have described them accurately.

DEFINITIONS

Analysis error. An analysis error occurs when a requirement is missing, a requirement is misunderstood, or an unnecessary requirement is included.

Class Responsibility Collaborator (CRC) card. A standard index card that has been divided into three sections: one indicating the name of the class the card represents, one listing the responsibilities of the class, and the third listing the names of the other classes this one collaborates with to fulfill its responsibilities.

Class Responsibility Collaborator (CRC) model. A collection of CRC cards that model all or part of a system.

Essential use case model. A use case model comprised of essential use cases.

Essential use case. A simplified, abstract, generalized use case that captures the intentions of a user in a technology- and implementation-independent manner.

Essential user interface prototype. A low-fidelity prototype of a system's user interface that models the fundamental, abstract characteristics of a user interface.

Subject matter expert (SME). A person who is responsible for providing pertinent information about the problem and/or technical domain either from personal knowledge or from research.

Misunderstood user requirements are also a serious issue. Requirements can be misunderstood in three ways: by the user, by the analyst, or by the designer. The most serious problem is when users misunderstand a requirement. This is why, when you build a requirements team, you want subject matter experts (SMEs) from a variety of backgrounds, so you reduce the chance of this sort of misunderstanding. The wider the ranges of user experience, the greater the chance the requirements team will get the requirements right. You can reduce the risk of both analysts and designers misunderstanding requirements by producing a model that is simple and unambiguous.

A wide range of experience, combined with unambiguous models, reduces the chance of misunderstood requirements.

In the past, unnecessary requirements were often included in requirements models, something that would not be discovered until field testing. One goal of the testing techniques described in this chapter is to identify unnecessary requirements so they can be removed long before the system is actually built. The addition of unnecessary requirements or features is often referred to as *goldplating*.

Beware of goldplating.

4.1 Testing Early and Often

Why should you test your requirements? First, the most significant mistakes are often those made during requirements and analysis. This is because these types of errors guarantee that your project will not be a complete success. If you overlook or misunderstand a user requirement, you automatically ensure the system will not completely meet the needs of your users: either it is missing a feature or a feature will be implemented incorrectly. Remember, a successful project is on time, on budget, and meets the needs of its users. Analysis errors by definition imply that your system does not fully meet your users' needs, therefore, your system cannot be a complete success.

Successful projects meet the needs of their users, but if you have an analysis error, you won't fully meet their needs.

Second, developers are most likely to make mistakes during the early stages of development, during requirements and analysis modeling (Ambler 1998a; Ambler 1998b). Technical people are very good at technical things such as design and coding—that is why they are technical people. Unfortunately, technical people are often not as good at nontechnical tasks, such as gathering requirements and performing analysis—probably another reason why they are technical people. The end result, as depicted in Figure 4-1, is that developers have a tendency to make more errors during requirements definition and analysis than during design and coding.

DEFINITION

Project success. A project is considered a success when it is on time, on budget, and meets the needs of its users.

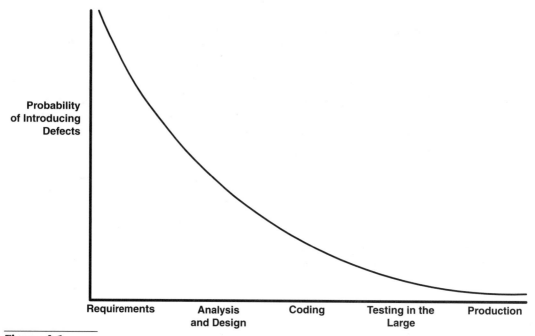

Probability of Introducing Defects

Requirements   Analysis   Coding   Testing in the   Production
                    and Design   Large

Figure 4-1.
The probability of
where errors are
introduced during
development

I don't claim that developers only make analysis errors; mistakes also get made during design and programming, too. What I do claim is that developers are very good at dealing with technical issues, those that arise during design and programming. Because developers are technically competent, they are usually able to find and deal with design and programming problems, which is what they are good at doing. What they are not good at is finding and fixing analysis errors.

Third, Figure 4-2 shows that the cost of fixing errors increases the later they are detected in the development lifecycle. The cost of fixing an error snowballs the longer it takes to detect it (McConnell 1996; Ambler 1998a; Ambler 1998b). If you make an analysis error and find it during requirements, it is inexpensive to fix. You merely change a portion of your requirements model. A change of this scope is on the order of $1 (you do a little bit of retyping/remodeling). If you do not find it until the design stage, it is more expensive to fix. Not only do you have to change your analysis, you also have to reevaluate and potentially modify the sections of your design based on the faulty analysis. This change is on the order of $10 (you do a little more retyping/remodeling). If you do not find the problem until programming, you need to update your analysis, design, and potentially scrap

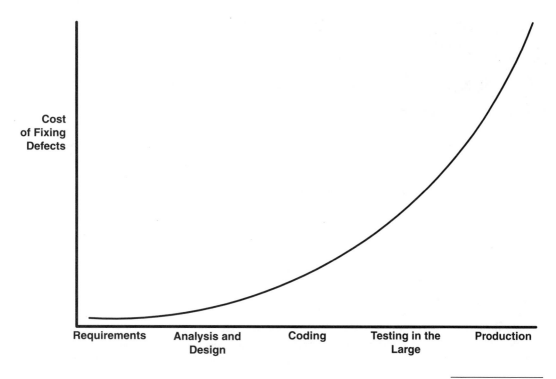

Cost of Fixing Defects

| Requirements | Analysis and Design | Coding | Testing in the Large | Production |

Figure 4-2.
The exponential cost of fixing defects

portions of your code, all because of a missed or misunderstood user requirement. This error is on the order of $100, because of all the wasted development time based on the faulty requirement. Furthermore, if you find the error during the traditional testing stage, it is on the order of $1,000 to fix (you need to update your documentation and scrap/rewrite large portions of code). Finally, if the error gets past you into production, you are looking at a repair cost on the order of $10,000+ to fix (you need to send out update disks, fix the database, restore old data, and rewrite/reprint manuals). Wouldn't it be wonderful if there were a way to find analysis errors when you make them, early in development?

Fourth, by testing your artifacts as you build them, you increase your confidence that your work is correct, that you are building the right system. Testing as you build your system is a fundamental principle of Xtreme Programming (XP) for exactly this reason (Beck, 2000). Moreover, testing as you develop is also an essential best practice of both the Unified Process (Kruchten, 1999; Ambler and Constantine, 2000a–c) and the Object-Oriented Software Process (Ambler, 1998b; Ambler, 1999). Simply put, testing early and often, as opposed to waiting to the end of development to test, is quickly becoming the standard approach within the software industry.

Testing early and often is the norm for object development, not the exception.

TIP

This is Just the Tip of the Testing Iceberg

Use case scenario testing, user interface walkthroughs, and requirements reviews are only three of the testing techniques of the Full Lifecycle Object-Oriented Testing (FLOOT) methodology (Ambler, 1998a). FLOOT is covered in detail in Chapter 9.

So how can you test your requirements model? You can apply one or more of the following techniques:

- Use case scenario testing
- User interface walkthroughs
- Requirements reviews

4.2 Use Case Scenario Testing

Use case scenario testing validates your domain model.

Use case scenario testing is an integral part of the object-oriented development lifecycle. It is a technique that you can use to test your domain model, either a CRC model or a class model (class models are discussed in detail in Chapters 6 and 7). The basic idea is that using a collection of scenarios, you walk through your domain model and validate that it is able to support those scenarios. If it does not, you update your model appropriately. It can and should be performed in parallel with your domain modeling efforts by the same team that created your domain model and, in fact, many people consider use case scenario testing as simply an extension of CRC modeling. Fundamentally, use case scenario testing is a technique that helps to ensure that your domain, in this case your CRC model, accurately reflects the aspect of the business that you are modeling.

4.2.1 The Steps of the Use Case Scenario Testing Process

The steps of the use case scenario testing process are straightforward. They are as follows:

1. **Perform domain modeling.** Create either a CRC model or an analysis class model (presented in Chapter 6), representing the critical domain concepts and their interrelationships. Use case scenario testing is performed as either a part of your CRC modeling efforts, described in detail in Chapter 3, or is performed as a separate task immediately following CRC modeling.

2. **Create the use case scenarios.** A use case scenario describes a particular situation that your system may or may not be expected to handle. How to create use case scenarios is described in Section 4.2.2.

3. **Assign classes to your SMEs.** Each SME should be assigned one or more classes, in our case one or more CRC cards. Ideally, the CRC cards should be distributed evenly; therefore, each SME should have roughly the same number of responsibilities assigned. This means some SMEs will have one or two busy cards, while others may have numerous not-so-busy cards. The main goal here is to spread the functionality of the system evenly among SMEs. In addition, it is important not to give two cards that collaborate to the same person (sometimes you can't avoid this, but you should try). The reason for this will become apparent when you see how to act out scenarios.

4. **Describe how to act out a scenario.** The majority of work with use case scenario testing is the acting out of scenarios. Just as you needed to explain CRC modeling to your SMEs, you must also describe how to act out scenarios. The best way to do this is first to describe the process and then to work through one or two scenarios initially with them. The goal of your initial "practice runs" is to teach the process methodically to the SMEs.

5. **Act out the scenarios.** As a group, the facilitator leads the SMEs through the process of acting out the scenarios. The basic idea is the SMEs take on the roles of the cards they were given, describing the business logic of the responsibilities that support each use case scenario. To indicate which card is currently "processing," a soft, spongy ball is held by the person with that card. Whenever a card has to collaborate with another one, the user holding the card throws the ball to the holder of the second card. The ball helps the group keep track of who is currently describing the business logic and also helps to make the entire process a little more interesting. You want to act the scenarios out so you gain a better understanding of the business rules/logic of the system (the scribes write this information down as the SMEs describe it) and find missing or misunderstood responsibilities and classes.

Throwing a ball around makes it obvious which card is currently doing the work, as well as making this fun for the participants.

6. **Update the domain model.** As the SMEs are working through the scenarios, they will discover they are missing some responsibilities

---

DEFINITION

Domain model. A representation of the business/domain concepts and their interrelationships, applicable to your system. A domain model helps to establish the vocabulary for your project.

and, sometimes, even some classes. Great, this is why they are acting out the scenarios in the first place. When the group discovers
the CRC model is missing some information, it should be updated
immediately. Once all the scenarios have been acted out, the
group ends up with a bulletproof model. Now little chance exists
of missing information (assuming you generated a complete set of
use case scenarios) and little chance exists of misunderstood information (the group has acted out the scenarios, describing the
exact business logic in detail).

7. **Save the scenarios.** Don't throw the scenarios away once you
finish acting them out. The scenarios are a good start at your
user acceptance test plan and you'll want them when you are
documenting the requirements for the next release of your system. User acceptance testing is described in Chapter 9.

4.2.2 Creating Use Case Scenarios

Use case scenarios, also called *usage scenarios*, are conceptually similar to
use cases, although they are still different. A use case describes the logic,
including the basic and alternate courses of action, for a single cohesive
task providing value to a user. On the other hand, a use case scenario
describes a single path of logic through one or more use cases. A use case
scenario could represent the basic course of action, the *happy path*,
through a single use case, a combination of portions of the happy path
replaced by the steps of one or more alternate paths through a single use
case, or a path spanning several use cases.

Use case scenarios describe a single logic path through one or more use cases.

For example, consider the "Enroll in Seminar" and "Pay Tuition" use
cases for the university. One use case scenario would be that a student
enrolls in a seminar without any difficulties. This would be an example
of a use case scenario that follows the basic course of action for a single
use case. Another scenario would be that a student attempts to enroll in a
seminar, but is unable to because he or she doesn't have the proper prerequisites. This is an example of a use case scenario that follows a portion
of the basic course of action, as well as an alternate course of action for a
single use case. A third use case scenario would be a student that enrolls
in several seminars at once, and then immediately pays a portion of his
or her tuition for those seminars, a scenario that spans several use cases.

Use case scenarios have names, brief descriptions, and lists of actions to take.

When you describe a use case scenario, you want to give it a name, a
short description (likely one or two sentences), and then a description of
the steps to take to fulfill the scenario. You should then document the
appropriate actions to follow—short-form is fine—and refer to the use
cases (if any) you are working through.

An example of a use case scenario is shown in Figure 4-3. Notice how it is written in the same sort of style as the essential use cases explained in Chapter 3: It is technology-independent, effectively making it an "essential use case scenario." The point to be made is the level of your use case scenario's text should match the level of detail of the model you are testing. In this case, we are testing a CRC model, one that does not imply our implementation strategy. Had our model been further along—perhaps if we had evolved our CRC model into a class model (something you learn how to do in Chapter 6) and were testing it instead—then the use case scenario may have included implementation details. For example, I could have indicated that the student uses an Internet-based registration application (in this case, the registrar would be a system instead of a person) to enroll in the seminars and that they pay by credit card via a secure link.

A student successfully enrolls in several seminars and pays partial tuition for them.

Description:

A student decides to register in three seminars, which the student has the prerequisites for and which still have seats available in them, and pays half the tuition at the time of registration.

Steps:

The student prepares to register:

The student determines the three seminars she wants to enroll in.

The student looks up the prerequisites for the seminars to verify she is qualified to enroll in them.

The student verifies spots are available in each seminar.

The student determines the seminars fit into her schedule.

The student contacts the registrar to enroll in the seminars.

The student enrolls in the seminars:

The student indicates to the registrar she wants to enroll in the seminars.

For each seminar:

The registrar verifies a spot is available in it.

The registrar verifies the student is qualified to take the seminar.

The registrar registers the student in the seminar.

A total bill for the registration is calculated and added to the student's outstanding balance (there is none).

The outstanding balance is presented to the student.

The student decides to pay half the balance immediately, and does so.

The registrar accepts the payment.

The payment is recorded.

The outstanding balance for the student is calculated and presented to the student.

Figure 4-3.

An example use case scenario

Consider unusual things that could happen when your system is being used.

In Chapter 3, you saw that use cases and use case scenarios are an important part of identifying classes, responsibilities, and collaborations. During CRC modeling, you also saw the SMEs often identify use case scenarios that describe the way actors interact with the system. While these scenarios are an effective way to gather user requirements, they may not be sufficient to verify that the requirements fully describe the system. The main issue here is, while your current requirements model may handle "common" scenarios, they most likely have missed a few unusual ones. For example, consider enrolling a student in a seminar. You have probably identified scenarios such as a student trying to enroll in a seminar that still has seats available and one that does not. While on the surface, these scenarios appear adequate, they probably are not. What happens when the seminar is full, but has nobody on the waiting list yet (for example, there are 30 students enrolled in a seminar that has 30 spots available in it). Is the 31st student put on a waiting list? Is there a waiting list? How long is it? Or is student #31 enrolled into the course with the knowledge that one or two people will likely drop out of it, thereby opening a spot for him or her? What happens with student #32, or #33? At what point do you start putting them on the waiting list? The point to be made here is these are all interesting issues that need to be explored *before* you start building your system. You don't want to get into the position where you are just about to deliver the system and one of your users says, "Oh, by the way, does the system handle this...?" and not be able to answer "Yes, and this is how it does it...."

Scenarios may describe logic that is currently out of scope for your system.

You can identify new scenarios in several ways. First, consider tasks the system should and shouldn't be able to handle. Remember, a good requirements definition describes both what is in and what is out of scope. This means not only do you want to identify scenarios the system should be able to handle, but also ones it should not. Identifying what the system won't do helps to prevent scope creep. When you identify a scenario the system shouldn't handle or perhaps will handle in a future version, you want to document your reasons why (therefore, you can cover yourself).

Create scenarios that invoke one or more business rules.

Second, explore business rules. If your users have told you about a business rule, create a scenario for it. For example, if students can take a maximum of five courses, create a scenario for someone trying to enroll in six. By doing this, you will bring into question the validity of existing business rules that may or may not make sense anymore. Perhaps the reason people are only allowed to enroll in five courses per term is because that's how much room was on the paper form when it was originally designed in the sixties. Do we still want our system to conform to this business rule?

Third, do some more brainstorming. To create "testing" use case scenarios, the facilitator should make the SMEs aware of the issues previously described, and then lead them through another short brainstorming session.

Meanwhile, Back in Reality

Finding that you are missing more than one or two "testing" use case scenarios is rare. The fact is that your SMEs will probably have identified and included pertinent business rules in the existing scenarios, and they will have identified scenarios they later decided the system wasn't going to handle after all.

4.2.3 Acting Out Scenarios

Once all the use case scenarios have been defined, or at least an initial collection of scenarios have been, you want to ensure that your system has the capability to deal with them. As shown in Figure 4-4, the SMEs should act out each scenario one at a time and update the CRC cards as they go along. The following describes the steps of acting out scenarios:

1. **Call out a new scenario.** The facilitator reads the scenario description to the group. The group must decide if this scenario is reasonable (remember, the system cannot handle some scenarios) and, if it is, which card is initially responsible for handling the scenario. The facilitator starts out with the ball and throws it to the person holding that card. When the scenario is completely acted out, the ball will be thrown back to the facilitator.

2. **Determine which card should handle the responsibility.** When a scenario has been described, or when the need for collaboration has been identified, the group should decide what CRC card should handle the responsibility. Very often, a card already has the responsibility identified. If this is not the case, update the appropriate card. Once the update is complete (if necessary),

---

DEFINITIONS

Business rule. A policy your software must satisfy. Business rules are what a functional requirement "knows," the controls and guidelines that are fulfilled by the functional requirement. An operating principle or policy of your organization.

Feature creep. The addition, as development proceeds, of new features to a system that are beyond what the original specification called for. This is also called *scope creep*.

Use case scenario. A single path of logic through one or more use cases. A use case scenario could represent the basic course of action through a single use case, a combination of portions of the basic course replaced by the steps of one or more alternate paths through a single use case, or a logic path spanning several use cases. Use case scenarios are also called *usage scenarios*.

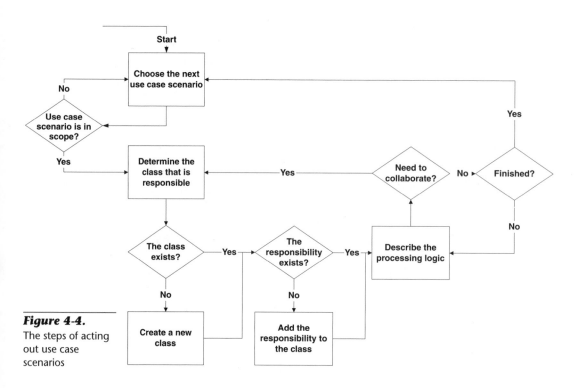

Figure 4-4.
The steps of acting out use case scenarios

whoever has the ball should throw it to the person with the card who has the responsibility.

You may need to update your prototype as you update your domain model.

3. **Update the cards whenever necessary.** If a card needs to be updated, one of two situations has arisen: The responsibility needs to be added to an existing card or a new card needs to be created with that responsibility. If a responsibility needs to be added to an existing card, ask yourself which card logically should have it, and then have the SME with that card update it. If a new card needs to be created, the facilitator should hand a blank CRC card to one of the SMEs and ask him or her to complete it. At the same time, you may also find you need to update your prototype drawings as well (if a user interface or report class changes, then the prototype may need to change as well).

4. **Describe the processing logic.** When the ball is thrown to someone, he or she should describe the business logic for the responsibility step by step. Think of it like this: the SMEs are effectively describing pseudo-code (high-level program code) for the responsibility. This is often the most difficult part of use case scenario testing, as some of your SMEs might not be used to doc-

umenting processes step by step. If this is the case with some of your SMEs, then the facilitator needs to help them through the logic. You will find that, after running through the first few scenarios, the SMEs will quickly get the hang of describing processing logic. As the SME describes the processing logic, the scribe should be writing it down (remember, the job of the scribe is to record the business logic/rules for the system, which is exactly what the SME is currently describing). You may also find you need to update your scenario logic as you work through it, and steps may be missing, out of order, or even unnecessary.

5. **Collaborate if necessary.** As the SME describes the business logic of the responsibility, he will often describe a step where he needs to collaborate with another card to complete. This is good. This is what use case scenario testing is all about. If this is the case, go back to Step 2.

6. **Pass the ball back when done.** Eventually, the SME will finish describing the responsibility. When this happens, he should throw the ball back to whomever originally threw the ball to him. This will be another SME (remember, every time you need to collaborate, you throw the ball to the person holding the card with whom you need to collaborate) or to the facilitator (the facilitator starts with the ball, and then throws it to the person holding the card who initially handles the scenario).

The critical thing to note is that the role of the facilitator is to ensure the processing logic is being described thoroughly, the SMEs update the cards, and he throws the ball whenever he needs to collaborate. The ball is important because it indicates who currently has "processing control" (who's doing something). Furthermore, using a tape or video recorder to take down the business logic is often tempting. The cost of transcription, between two and six hours per hour of tape, and the knowledge that people don't like to be recorded, should make you think twice about this. You should also keep your eyes open for classes or responsibilities you never used, as this is a sure sign something is wrong: either you have identified "useless" classes and/or responsibilities or you've missed some scenarios that would test those classes/responsibilities. Finally, expect to identify new scenarios occasionally when you are working through another one. Acting out scenarios often gets the "intellectual juices" flowing and gets people thinking about new potential scenarios.

Keep it simple, have fun throwing the ball around, and think twice about tape recording your efforts.

In the next section, I walk you through, in detail, the acting out of a simple use case scenario. You should pay attention to how the facilitator keeps things flowing smoothly, and at the same time has the SMEs describe the business logic in exacting detail.

T I P *Flag "Questionable" Scenarios as Risks*	During the use case scenario testing, you should strive to determine which scenarios are going to be hard to achieve or rely on nonexistent or questionable resources/technologies. These scenarios increase the project's risk and should either be dropped from the project or flagged for special attention later. You often have a good idea at the beginning of a project what things might go wrong, and it is better to deal with them sooner than later.

4.2.3.1 Acting Out a Scenario: An Example

The following example should help give you a better idea of what acting out a scenario is like.

Scenario The facilitator, Dixon Hill, says "Okay, here's the next scenario: A student wants to enroll in a seminar and has the correct prerequisites. What card should handle this?"

Madeline, one of the SMEs, says: "Well, to enroll in a course the student needs to go to the registrar's office and hand in the appropriate forms. The registrar would check the form to verify it is filled in correctly, and then input the information into the system. I guess this means the registrar's screen needs to be able to handle that feature. I think Felix has that card."

"Wait a minute," says Jessica. "I don't get it. Isn't it the registrar who enrolls students in courses, not the system?"

"Yes, the registrar uses the system to do this," answers Dixon. "But we're modeling the system and not the person, so even though the student goes to the registrar, for the purpose of this model, the only thing we're interested in is the system used to do the job. Although, there isn't anything stopping us from creating a new card representing the registrar to represent his role in the registration process."

Felix says "Hey, I have the registrar's screen card, and I have the responsibility to enroll students in seminars." The facilitator throws the ball to Felix.

"This is an easy one for me," says Felix. "I display an input dialog box to enter the student's name. I have that card, too. Once it is entered, the student editing screen is displayed, which includes a list of all the courses the student either has taken or is enrolled in currently. Who has that card?"

"I do," says Cyrus. "Throw me the ball." Felix does, and Cyrus continues. "I display myself and wait for the registrar to hit a function key. If he presses the 'Enroll' key, the seminar enrollment dialog box is displayed. Madeline has that card." Cyrus throws the ball to Madeline.

Speaking quickly, Madeline blurts, "The enrollment screen basically enables the registrar to input up to seven course numbers the student wants to enroll in. When the number is input, the name of the course should be displayed to the right of the input field. In addition to the course number, the registrar must also input the section number of the specific seminar the student wants. Many of our courses have more than one seminar running in a term. When the section number is input, the date, time, and room number for the seminar is also displayed on the screen. Once all the course numbers are input, the registrar presses the Enter key and the student is enrolled in all the courses. I'm done, here's the ball back, Cyrus."

"Hey, hold on!" says the facilitator. "I think you've missed a few details."

"Like what?"

"Well, first of all, Madeline, how do you get the name of the course, as well as the date, time, and room number?"

"Oh, that's easy, I get the course name from the course card, and the date, time, and room number from the seminar card. Does that mean I need to throw the ball to the people with those cards?"

"Yes it does," answers the facilitator. "Whenever you need to get information from another card or you have another card to do something for you, you need to collaborate with it. To collaborate, you have to throw the ball to the person holding that card."

"Okay. I guess that means to get the name of the course, I need to throw the ball to the person with the course card. Who has it?"

"I do, Madeline," says Cyrus. Madeline throws the ball to Cyrus. Cyrus says he already has the responsibility to give the name of the course to whoever asks for it. He says he does that, and then he asks, "Okay. I've given Madeline the name of the course, so now what do I do with this stupid ball?"

"Madeline was the person who initially threw it to you, so give it back to her," says the facilitator. Cyrus does so.

"Okay, I display the name, and then I collaborate with the 'Seminar' card to get the date, time, and room." Madeline throws the ball to Jessica, who holds the seminar card.

"Okay, I know the date, time, and room number. I'll just give them to Madeline," says Jessica.

"Hold on. Jessica, do you have the responsibilities to give the date, time, and room number?" asks the facilitator.

"No I don't. I guess I'd better add them to the card." Jessica does so and throws the ball back to Madeline.

"Okay, all the information is displayed on the screen, the registrar presses the Enter key, and the student gets enrolled. I'm finally done."

"No you're not." answers the facilitator. "What happens when the student doesn't have the prerequisites for the course?"

"But that would never happen," says Madeline. "The registrar wouldn't enter the course number if the student didn't have the prerequisites."

"Yes, he would. Registrars are always enrolling students in courses accidentally. Eventually, we figure it out, but often it's too late. Seems to me the system should be able to figure out whether a student should be allowed in a course," says Cyrus.

Thinking about it, Madeline answers, "I guess that's right. I guess the system could display a screen that says the student doesn't have the correct prerequisites. It could ask if the student wanted to go through the special enrollment process where the professor teaching the course has to sign-off on enrolling the student. Hey, we could even email the professor and cut out having the student to fill out a form and then submit it."

"That's a great idea, Madeline. I guess this means we need to add a new CRC card to represent this new screen. Jessica, could you handle that?" asks the facilitator. "We need to prototype both the screen and how to implement this email message thing. For now, though, let's finish this scenario, and then we can discuss these new changes immediately afterwards. Let's assume the student has all the prerequisites."

"Okay, I guess that means I need to collaborate with the 'Seminar' card to add the student to the seminars," says Madeline, as she throws the ball to Jessica, who has the seminar card. Jessica says she knows how to enroll the student, describes how to do it, and throws the ball back to Madeline.

"I'm done, so I guess I finally throw the ball back to Cyrus now," says Madeline, doing so. Cyrus says he's done, so he throws the ball back to Felix, who originally threw him the ball. Felix is also finished, so he throws the ball back to the facilitator.

"Okay, that worked out well. We identified a few missing responsibilities, as well as a missing class," says the facilitator. "Now let's do a scenario where a students tries to sign up for a seminar for which she doesn't have the prerequisites."

4.2.3.2 Note-taking by the Scribe: An Example

While the SMEs act out the scenarios, the scribe(s) should be writing down a detailed explanation of each scenario in some sort of pseudo-code. The following text is an example:

Enrolling a student with the correct prerequisites into a seminar:

1. The student enters the registrar's office and submits the necessary forms.

2. The registrar verifies the forms are completed properly and uses the enrollment screen to input the information into the system.

3. The student search dialog box is displayed and is used by the registrar to find the student's information.

4. The student information screen for this person is displayed and the registrar presses the "Enroll" key to add the student to a seminar.

5. The registrar inputs the course number into the enrollment screen, as well as the section number for the seminar the student wants.

6. The course name is retrieved for the appropriate course and is displayed on the screen. Similarly, room, date, time, and location information is obtained for the appropriate seminar and is displayed on the screen.

7. If there is room in the seminar, the student is enrolled in it. If not, the system displays a list of other sections the student may want to enroll in instead.

TIP	Get the food and drinks off the table and close all windows and doors. I've lost track of the number of times I've seen full cups of coffee knocked over, the balls never seem to go anywhere near the empty cups, or a ball bounces out an open window.
Don't Forget You Are Throwing a Ball Around	

Some people like to create one use case scenario for each alternative, while others like to create one really big scenario. For example, when a student enrolls in a seminar, he or she may or may not have the prerequisites for it, and there may or may not be room in the seminar. Some people would create four (two times two) simple scenarios (one where the student has the prerequisites and there's room, one where the student has the prerequisites but there's no room, and so on). Other people would create one scenario, which describes "if logic" for each alternative, as we saw previously in Step 7. Both styles work well, you just need to pick the one that's best for you.

4.2.4 The Advantages of Use Case Scenario Testing

Several advantages exist to this approach:

1. **Use case scenario testing helps you to find and fix analysis errors inexpensively.** It enables you to detect errors where they are inexpensive to fix, when you make them, instead of after the fact, when it is usually too late to deal with them.

2. **Use case scenario testing provides you with a detailed description of the business logic of the system.** Acting through each scenario provides the scribe(s) with enough information to describe the business logic of the system fully. During use case scenario testing, discovering that you are missing classes, responsibilities, and/or collaborations is common. Conversely, you may also find you have identified some classes, responsibilities, and/or collaborations that never get used.

3. **Use case scenario testing is simple and it works.** Use case scenario testing is low-tech, making it easy to understand. Furthermore, it fosters the development of a detailed and correct description of the system, which is exactly what you are striving for.

4. **Scenarios help to define how people interact with the system.** Use case scenarios help you to flesh out the human-

> **DEFINITION**
>
> ***Human-computer interaction (HCI) boundary.*** The point at which people work with a system. The HCI boundary consists of the user interface elements, such as screens and reports, that people work with, as well as they way in which they work with them.

computer interaction (HCI) boundary, basically the definition of how and when people interact with the system and, hence, the interface and report classes of the system. The HCI boundary is represented on a CRC model as the collection of interactions between actor classes and interface/report classes and on use case models by the associations between human actors and use cases.

4.2.5 The Disadvantages of Use Case Scenario Testing

As you would expect, this approach also has some disadvantages:

1. **Your SMEs must make the time to do the testing.** As previously discussed with respect to the requirements definition in Chapter 3, one of the most difficult parts of the entire process is to get the people together to do it.

2. **Managers often feel "real" work isn't being accomplished.** A bunch of people gathered together in a room throwing a ball back and forth to one another? You call that systems development? Some people just aren't happy unless you go though a complex, time-consuming process that generates mounds of documentation that no one ever reads. Go figure.

3. **Developers are often skeptical.** Use case scenario testing is low-tech and, frankly, looks much too simple. Throwing a ball around will help you to test an electronic information system? My reply to this is the proof is always in the pudding: Give it a try; you will probably like it.

Use case scenario testing should be performed as part of your CRC modeling efforts. The best way to think about it is CRC modeling and use case scenario testing are really one process, not two.

TIP

Test Your Requirements as You Model Them

4.3 User Interface Walkthroughs

User interface walkthroughs are similar to use case scenario testing sessions, the only difference being your system's user interface is being tested instead of your domain model.

User interface walkthroughs are performed in the same manner as use case scenario testing sessions, the only difference being that another type of artifact is being validated, in this case, the user interface of your system. User interface walkthroughs may be performed on an essential user interface prototype, a working user interface prototype, or even the user interface of the actual system itself. At the present moment, you would use this technique to test your essential user interface prototype.

During a user interface walkthrough when you act out a scenario, you first want to identify which major user interface element—perhaps an HTML page, a screen, or a report—is responsible for initially handling it. The SMEs describe how they would use the user interface element or work with another user interface element as needed, to work through the scenario. As before, the major user interface elements are assigned to SMEs before they begin acting out a scenario, and when they work through a scenario, they can throw a ball back and forth to one another. Furthermore, it is common to validate both your domain model and your user interface model at the same time.

4.4 Requirements Reviews

Requirement reviews are used to verify that your application will meet the needs of your users and to define the scope of your project.

A requirements review (Ambler, 1998b) is a formal process in which a review facilitator gathers together a group of users who have the authority to confirm and prioritize the user requirements documented by a development team. Requirement reviews typically take from several hours to several days, depending on the size of your project. They are often used in addition to use case scenario testing and user interface walkthroughs. Requirements reviews follow the steps of the solution to the Technical Review process pattern (Ambler, 1999), as shown in Figure 4-5.

The steps of a requirements review:

1. **The requirements team prepares for review.** The artifacts, such as your use case model and your supplementary specifications that are to be reviewed are gathered, organized appropriately, and packaged so they can be presented to the reviewers.

2. **The team indicates it is ready for review.** The requirements team must inform the review facilitator (often a member of your quality assurance department, if you have one) or another project manager when it is ready to have its work reviewed as well as what the team intends to have reviewed.

3. **The review facilitator performs a cursory review.** The first job the review facilitator must do is determine if the requirements

Figure 4-5.
The solution to the
Technical Review
process pattern

team has produced work that is ready to be reviewed. The manager will probably discuss the requirements team's work with the team leader and do a quick rundown of what it has produced. The main goal is to ensure the work to be reviewed is good enough to warrant getting a review team together.

4. **The review facilitator plans and organizes the review.** The review facilitator must schedule a review room, any equipment needed for the review, invite the proper people, and distribute any materials ahead of time that are needed for the review. This includes an agenda for the review, as well as the artifacts to be reviewed. The review package may also contain supporting artifacts—artifacts the reviewers may need handy to understand the artifacts they are reviewing. Supporting artifacts are not meant to be reviewed; they are only used as supplementary resources. The review often includes the standards and guidelines your team is following in the package, so the reviewers can understand the development environment of your team.

5. **The reviewers review the package prior to the review.** This enables the reviewers to become familiar with the material and prepare for the review. Reviewers should note any defects, issues, or questions before the review takes place. During the review, they should be raising previously noted issues, not reading the material for the first time.

6. **The review takes place.** Requirements reviews can take anywhere from several hours to several days, depending on the amount of material being reviewed. The best reviews are less than two hours long, so as not to overwhelm the people involved. The entire requirements team should attend, or at least the people responsible for what is being reviewed, to answer questions and to explain/clarify their work. There are typically between three to five reviewers, as well as the review facilitator, all of whom are responsible for the review. All material must be reviewed because it is too easy to look at something quickly and assume it is correct. The job of the review facilitator is to ensure everything is

TIPS

How to Hold Successful Requirements Reviews

1. **Understand that quality comes from more than just reviews.** Reviews are one of many ways to achieve quality, but when used alone, they result in little or no quality improvement over the long run. In application development, quality comes from developers who understand how to build software properly, developers who have learned from experience, and/or have gained these skills from training and education. Reviews help you to identify quality deficits, but they will not help you build quality into your application from the outset. Reviews should be only a small portion of your overall testing and quality strategy.

2. **Set expectations ahead of time.** Art Staden, an experienced developer and a friend of mine, likes to provide guidance to review teams before the review to help set their expectations, as well as to help make the review run smoother. Some of the words of advice Art provides are

   - The more detail a document has, the easier it is to find fault.
   - The more clearly defined a position on an issue, the easier it is to find fault.
   - Finding many faults may often imply a good, not a bad, job has been performed.
   - The goal is to find gaps in the work, so they can be addressed appropriately.

3. **Understand you cannot review everything.** Karl Wiegers (1999) advises that if you do not have time to inspect everything, and you rarely do, then you should prioritize your artifacts on a risk basis and review the ones that present the highest risk to your project if they contain serious defects. The implication is you need to distinguish between the critical portions of your requirements model that must be formally reviewed and the portions that can be informally reviewed, most likely by use case scenario testing or an informal walkthrough.

looked at and everything is questioned. The review scribe should record each defect or issue raised by the reviewers. Note that most reviews focus on the high-priority items identified by the reviewers. Low-priority defects are written down and handed to the authors during the review and are not even discussed during the review. The authors then address these less critical defects without taking up review time. At the end of the review, the artifacts are judged, the typical outcome being one of: passed, passed with exceptions, or failed. For reviews where several artifacts were looked at—perhaps you reviewed your use case model and user-interface prototype simultaneously—the outcome may be broken down by artifact, so the model may pass, but the prototype fail.

7. **The review results are acted on.** A document is produced during the review describing both the strengths and weaknesses of the work being reviewed. This document should provide a description of any weakness, why it is a weakness, and provide an indication of what needs to be addressed to fix the weakness. This document is then given to the requirements team, so it can act on it, and to the review facilitator to be used in follow-up reviews. The work is inspected again in follow-up reviews to verify the weaknesses were addressed.

4.5 What You Have Learned

The cost to fix a defect increases exponentially the later you discover it. Furthermore, most defects are introduced early in a project, during requirements gathering and analysis (the topic of Chapter 6). In this chapter, you learned that use case scenario testing is a simple, low-tech approach to validating your domain model. You also discovered that user interface walkthroughs, similar conceptually to use case scenario testing, can be used to validate your user interface model. Finally, other artifacts, such as your use case model and supplementary specification can be validated in a requirements review. By testing early and often, you are able to find and fix defects early in the lifecycle, simultaneously increasing the quality of your system while decreasing your developments costs.

4.6 Review Questions

1. Test and update your requirements model for the bank case study presented in Section 3.10.1. This is a multipart task, the steps for which you can perform either serially or iteratively:

   • Identify use case scenarios for the bank case study.

   • Perform use case scenario testing on your CRC model, ideally in a group setting.

   • Walk through your essential user interface using the scenarios, updating it as appropriate.

   • Update your two models as appropriate.

2. Identify what you have learned. What worked well during your use case scenario testing and user interface walkthrough? What didn't work well? Why?

3. [Optional] Review your use case model. In a group setting, hold a requirements review for your use case model. The tasks you should

perform are:

- Identify who the reviewers will be.
- Justify the presence of each reviewer.
- Write an agenda for the walkthrough.
- Identify the artifact(s) to be reviewed, as well as any necessary supporting artifacts.
- Put the review package together.
- Distribute the package.
- Hold the review.
- Update the artifact(s) as appropriate.

4. Compare and contrast the techniques of use case scenario testing, user interface walkthroughs, and requirements reviews. When would you use one technique over the other? Why? What factors would lead you to chose one technique over the other? Why?

5. For each of the requirements artifacts described in Chapter 3, such as essential use case models and business rule definitions, identify which of the three testing techniques presented in this chapter could be used to validate the artifact. Where more than one technique is valid, indicate which technique is preferable and justify why.

6. Discuss how the approach to organizing your CRC cards, presented in Chapter 3, helps your effort to distribute the cards evenly among the SMEs when you are use case scenario testing.

Object-oriented concepts seem simple.

Don't be deceived.

Chapter 5

Understanding the Basics: Object-Oriented Concepts

What You Will Learn in This Chapter

You will explore the following object-oriented concepts:

Object	Cohesion
Class	Inheritance
Method/Operation	Association
Attribute	Aggregation
Abstraction	Collaboration
Encapsulation	Messaging
Information Hiding	Polymorphism
Coupling	Persistence

Why You Need to Read This Chapter

You need to understand the underlying concepts of object orientation, as well as the standard Unified Modeling Language (UML) notation to represent them, before you can learn how to apply them in object-oriented modeling.

You are able to gather requirements with little knowledge of object orientation.

You need to understand object-oriented (OO) concepts before you can successfully apply them to systems development. As OO techniques grew, in part, out of the disciplines of software engineering and information modeling, many of them will seem familiar to you. Don't let this make you complacent—you also need to understand several new concepts.

Although I have discussed two object-oriented modeling techniques, Class Responsibility Collaborator (CRC) modeling and use case modeling, in previous chapters, you didn't need to understand object-oriented concepts to do them. That's one of the strengths of those two techniques: you don't need a degree in software engineering to be able to work with your users. One of the many strengths of CRC modeling and use case modeling is they are based on a few simple concepts. That enables your users to be involved in system development to a greater extent than in the past with structured techniques.

The problem with use case and CRC modeling is they are not sufficient to describe an application completely. While they are a fantastic start, you still need to do class modeling; and to do class modeling, you need to understand the basic underlying concepts of OO.

5.1 New and Old Concepts Together

OO and good design go hand in hand. Doing good design doesn't mean you're doing OO, however, and doing OO doesn't mean you're doing good design.

This chapter discusses the concepts that make up the foundation of OO modeling techniques. Some of these concepts you have seen before, and some of them you haven't. Many OO concepts, such as encapsulation, coupling, and cohesion, come from software engineering. These concepts are important because they underpin good OO design. The main point to be made here is you don't want to deceive yourself—just because you have seen some of these concepts before, it doesn't mean you were doing OO, it just means you were doing good design. While good design is a big part of object orientation, there's still a lot more to it than that.

TIP

It Is Harder Than It Looks

OO concepts appear deceptively simple. Don't be fooled. The underlying concepts of structured techniques also seemed simple, yet we all know structured development was actually quite difficult. For example, consider the definition for top-down design. Sounds simple, doesn't it? I'm surprised our users didn't just go out and develop systems all by themselves by doing top-down design. Just as there was more to the structured paradigm than a few simple concepts, there is also more to the OO paradigm. Just as it took time to get truly good at structured development, it also takes time to get good at OO development. To give you a taste for what this chapter is about, the concepts and the terms I describe are briefly summarized in Table 5-1.

Table 5-1. A summary of object-oriented concepts and terms

Object-Oriented Concepts and Terms: A Quick Summary

Abstract class	A class that doesn't have objects instantiated from it
Abstraction	The essential characteristics of an item, such as a class or operation
Aggregation	Represents "is part of" relationships between two classes or components
Aggregation hierarchy	A set of classes that are related through aggregation
Association	Objects are related (associated) to other objects
Attribute	Something a class knows (data/information)
Cardinality	Represents the concept "how many?"
Class	A software abstraction of similar objects, a template from which objects are created
Cohesion	The degree of relatedness of an encapsulated unit (such as a component or a class)
Collaboration	Classes work together (collaborate) to fulfill their responsibilities
Component	A cohesive unit of functionality that can be independently developed, delivered, and composed with other components to build a larger unit.
Composition	A strong form of aggregation in which the "whole" is completely responsible for its parts and each "part" object is only associated to the one "whole" object
Concrete class	A class that has objects instantiated from it
Coupling	The degree of dependence between two items
Encapsulation	The grouping of related concepts into one item, such as a class or a component
Information hiding	The restriction of external access to attributes
Inheritance	Represents "is a" and "is like" relationships
Inheritance hierarchy	A set of classes that are related through inheritance
Instance	An object is an instance of a class
Instantiate	We instantiate (create) objects from classes
Interface	The definition of a collection of one or more operation signatures that defines a cohesive set of behaviors
Message	A message is either a request for information or a request to perform an action
Messaging	To collaborate, classes send messages to each other
Method	Something a class does (similar to a function in structured programming)
Multiple inheritance	When a class directly inherits from more than one class
Object	A person, place, thing, event, concept, screen, or report
Object space	Main memory, plus all available storage space on the network

Optionality	Represents the concept "do you need to have it?"
Override	Sometimes you need to override (redefine) attributes and/or methods in subclasses
Pattern	A reusable solution to a common problem taking relevant forces into account
Persistence	The issue of how objects are permanently stored
Persistent object	An object that is saved to permanent storage
Polymorphism	Different objects can respond to the same message in different ways, enabling objects to interact with one another without knowing their exact type
Single inheritance	When a class directly inherits from only one class
Stereotype	Denotes a common usage of a modeling element
Subclass	If Class B inherits from Class A, we say B is a subclass of A
Superclass	If Class B inherits from Class A, we say A is a superclass of B
Transitory object	An object that is not saved to permanent storage

Meanwhile, Back in Reality

Don't get me wrong. You can still do good design using structural/procedural techniques, it's just that object orientation offer more opportunities to do so.

5.2 OO Concepts from a Structured Point-of-View

Raise your hand if you were overwhelmed by the list of concepts presented in Table 5-1. Okay, everyone put down your hands. If you are studying for a test, I suppose the list will be useful to you. Most of us are looking for a way to learn OO concepts easily. Before I get into detailed explanations, I want to describe the four basic OO concepts quickly, in structured terminology, which is likely to be familiar to you.

1. **Class.** A *class* is a software abstraction of an object, effectively, a template from which objects are created. If you have database experience, start thinking of a class as a table. The definition of a table describes the layout of the records to be stored in it. The

---

DEFINITION

Top-down design. When you have a problem you cannot easily deal with, break it down into small problems. Break those problems down, until you are finally left with a collection of small problems that you can deal with, one at a time.

> You should consider making a photocopy of Table 5-1 and keeping it at your side while you are learning object orientation, particularly if you are attending a class on this topic. You are being inundated with new ideas and techniques, and it certainly wouldn't hurt to have a "cheat sheet" close at hand to help you understand OO concepts.
>
> **TIP**
>
> *Keep a List of Common Terms at Hand*

definition of a class describes the layout, including both the data and the functionality, of the objects that are going to be created from it. Notice how I said both data and functionality. Unlike a table, which defines only data, a class defines both data (attributes) and code (operations/methods). For now, a good way to think about a class is that it is the combination of a table definition and the definition of the source code that accesses the data.

2. **Object.** An *object* is a person, place, thing, event, concept, screen, or report. If a class can be thought of as a table, an object can be thought of as a record occurrence. For example, consider customers. In a structured application, each customer would be represented as a record in the customer data table. In an object-oriented application, each customer would be represented as an object in memory. The main difference is that where customer records have only data, customer objects have both data (attributes) and functionality (methods). More on this later.

3. **Attribute.** An *attribute* is equivalent to a data element in a record. From a programming point-of-view, it also makes sense to think of an attribute as a local variable that is applicable only to a single object.

4. **Method.**[1] A *method* can be thought of as either a function or procedure. Methods access and modify the attributes of an object. Some methods return a value (like a function), whereas other methods don't (like a procedure).

---

[1] The term *method* comes from the Smalltalk language. Methods are commonly referred to as *member functions* in C++ and *operations* in Java. The Unified Modeling Language (UML) takes it one step further to define a method as the logic, the code, of an operation. In UML, an operation is the combination of its signature (its name, the definition of the parameters passed to it, and what it returns) and its method (the code). This is an interesting distinction to make if you're an academic or CASE tool builder, but not of much interest if you're an everyday developer. Because I come from a Smalltalk background, throughout this book I use the terms *method*, *operation*, and *member function* to represent what the UML considers to be an operation.

To understand the concepts of OO, expect to reread this chapter several times. This is hard stuff.

While you read this book, you may find the need to come back to these definitions occasionally. Don't worry, that's normal. Object orientation introduces several new concepts and terms that can easily overwhelm you. So take your time and reread this chapter a few times. That's the only way you're going to learn this stuff.

5.3 Objects and Classes

The OO paradigm is based on building systems from reusable items called classes. An object is any person, place, thing, event, concept, screen, or report. A class generalizes or represents a collection of similar objects and is effectively a template from which to create objects.

An object is any person, place, event, thing, screen, report, or concept that is applicable to the system. In a university system, Christopher Pike is a student object, he attends several class objects, and he is working on a degree object. In a banking system, Pike is a customer object. He has a checking account object from which he bounces rubber-check objects. In an inventory control system, every inventory item is an object, every delivery is an object, and every customer is an object.

A class represents a collection of similar objects

In the real world, you have objects; therefore, you need that as a concept to reflect your problem space accurately. However, in the real world, objects are often similar to other kinds of objects. Students share similar qualities (they do the same sort of things, they are described in the same sort of way), courses share similar qualities, inventory items share similar qualities, bank accounts share similar qualities, and so on. While you could model (and program) every object, that is a lot of work. I prefer to define what it is to be a student once, define course once, define inventory item once, define bank account once, and so on. That is why you need the concept of a class.

Figure 5-1 depicts how, in the real world, we have student objects and how we model the class "Student." It also shows the standard notations to model a class using the Unified Modeling Language. Classes are modeled in one of two ways: as either a rectangle that lists its attributes and

TIP

How to Name Classes

1. Class names are typically nouns. The name of a class should be one or two words, usually a noun, and should accurately describe the class. If you are having trouble naming the class, either you need to understand it better or it might be several classes you have mistakenly combined.
2. Class names are usually singular. You should model classes with names such as "Student," "Professor," and "Course," not "Students," "Professors," and "Courses." Think of it like this: in the real world, you would say "I am a student," not "I am a students."

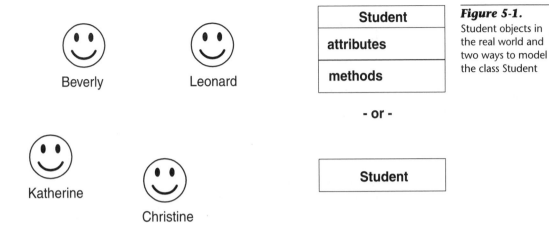

Figure 5-1.
Student objects in the real world and two ways to model the class Student

Beverly   Leonard

Katherine

Christine

Some Student Objects   **The Student Class**

methods, or as just a rectangle. There are reasons for modeling classes either way. On the one hand, listing the attributes and methods is nice. This enables readers of your class models to gain a better understanding of your design while, on the other hand, listing the attributes and methods can clutter your diagrams. In this book, I use both techniques, listing the methods and attributes only where appropriate.

Objects are instances of a class.

DEFINITIONS

Class. A template from which objects are created (instantiated). Although, in the real world, Doug, Wayne, John, and Bill are all "student objects," we would model the class "Student" instead.

Instance. Just as we say a data record is an occurrence of a data entity, we say an object is an instance of a class.

Instantiate. When we create a student object, we say we instantiate it from the class "Student."

Object. A person, place, thing, concept, event, screen, or report. Objects both know things (that is, they have data) and they do things (that is, they have functionality).

Unified Modeling Language (UML). The definition of a standard modeling language for object-oriented software, including the definition of a modeling notation and the semantics for applying it as defined by the Object Management Group (OMG).

Attributes are the things classes know. Methods are the things classes do.

When object-oriented software is running, objects are instantiated (created/defined) from classes. We say an object is an instance of a class and that we instantiate objects from classes.

5.4 Attributes and Methods

Attributes and methods are the responsibilities of classes.

In Chapter 3, you saw that classes have responsibilities, the things they know and do. Attributes are the things classes know; methods are the things classes do. The object-oriented paradigm is based on the concepts that systems should be built out of objects, and that objects have both data and functionality. Attributes define the data, while methods define the functionality.

In CRC modeling, one goal was to identify the responsibilities of a class: the things it knows and does. When we get right down to it, we are really looking for the attributes and the methods of the class. The reason I talked about finding responsibilities instead of finding attributes and methods is that attributes and methods are technical concepts, whereas responsibilities are straightforward business concepts. Remember, when you are working with your users, you want to use terminology they are comfortable with, not technical jargon.

When you define a class, you must define the attributes it has, as well as its methods. The definition of an attribute is straightforward. You define its name, perhaps its type (whether it is a number, a string, or a date, and so forth). Weakly typed languages such as Smalltalk enable you to use attributes any way you want and, therefore, don't require you to define their type. Strongly typed languages such as Java and C++, however, insist you define the type of an attribute before you actually use it. You may also choose to indicate any business rules or constraints that are applicable to the attribute, such as the valid values the attribute may have.

The definition of a method is simpler: you define the logic for it, just as you would code for a function or a procedure. At a minimum, you should describe the method in a sentence or two, indicate the parameters

---

DEFINITIONS

Attribute. Something a class or object knows. An attribute is fundamentally a single piece of data or information.

Method. Something a class or object does. A method is similar to a function or procedure in structured programming and is often referred to as an operation or member function in object development.

Responsibility. A responsibility is an obligation a class must fulfill, such as knowing something or doing something.

> **DEFINITIONS**
>
> **Business rule.** A policy your software must satisfy. Business rules are what a functional requirement "knows," the controls and guidelines fulfilled by the functional requirement.
>
> **Constraint.** A global requirement, such as limited development resources or a decision by senior management, that restricts the way you develop a system.

(if any) that must be passed to it, and what the method returns (if anything). In Chapters 7 and 8, I elaborate on object-oriented design and object-oriented programming; moreover, I go into further detail regarding the specification of methods.

Methods either return a value and/or they do something of value.

Remember how in CRC Modeling we said collaborations are of one of two types, either a request for information or a request to do something? Also remember how whenever you defined a collaboration that the second class had a new responsibility to fulfill that collaboration? When I cover the concept of collaboration, you will see that collaborations are fulfilled by methods. For now, an important implication is that methods do one of two things: either they return a value and/or they do something of value.

In Figure 5-2, you see two different types of objects: a student and a seminar. Both objects know and do certain things, and you want to make sure you record this in your models, as you see in Figure 5-3. Note how a class is divided into three sections: the top section for its name, the middle section to list its attributes, and the bottom section to list its methods. As indicated previously, it is optional in UML to show the attributes and

I am a student. I know my name, my student number, and my birth date. I enroll in seminars and pay tuition.

I am a seminar. I know when and where I am held and keep track of the students that are enrolled in me. I also enable students to enroll in me or drop me from their schedules.

Computer Science 100 Section 3

Figure 5-2.
Objects in the "real world"

methods of a class—classes can also be shown as just a rectangle with the name of the class as its label. This is commonly done to simplify class diagrams. With this style, although you don't show the attributes and methods within the "class bubble," you must still document them elsewhere.

An instance attribute stores a value pertaining to a single object, whereas a static attribute stores a value pertaining to all instances of a class.

Figure 5-3 indicates two types of attributes: instance attributes that are applicable to a single object and static attributes that are applicable to all instances of a single class. Static attributes are underlined, instance attributes are not. For example, "name" is an instance attribute of the class "Student." Each individual student has a name; for example, one student may have the name "Allen, Barry," whereas another student may have the name "Jordan, Hal." It could even happen that two individual students may have the same name, such as "Smith, John" although they are, in fact, two different people. On the other hand, "nextStudentNumber" is a static attribute that is applicable to the class "Student," not specifically to individual instances. This attribute is used to store the value of the next student number to be assigned to a student: when a new student joins the school, his or her student number is set to the current value of "nextStudentNumber," which is then incremented to ensure all students have unique student numbers.

The scope of an instance method is a single object, whereas the scope of a static method is a single class.

Similarly, there is the concept of instance methods and static methods: Instance methods operate on a single instance, whereas static methods operate potentially on all instances of a single class. In Figure 5-3 you see that "Student" has instance methods called "enrollInSeminar" and "dropSeminar," things an individual student would do. It also has the static method "findByName," which supports the behavior of searching for students whose names meet specified search criteria, a method that operates on all instances of the class.

Student
name phoneNumber studentNumber
enrollInSeminar dropSeminar payTuition requestTranscript

Seminar
instructors location listOfStudents
addStudent removeStudent

Figure 5-3.
The Student and Seminar classes

> ### DEFINITIONS
>
> *Instance attribute.* An attribute that is applicable to a single instance (object) of a class. Each object will have its own value for an instance attribute.
>
> *Instance method.* A method that operates on a single instance (object) of a class.
>
> *Static attribute.* An attribute whose value is all instances of a class. Each instance of a class will share the single value of a static attribute.
>
> *Static method.* A method that operates at the class level, potentially on all instances of that class.

5.5 Abstraction, Encapsulation, and Information Hiding

Instead of saying we determined what a class knows and does, we say we *abstracted* the class. Instead of saying we designed how the class will accomplish these things, we say we *encapsulated* them. Instead of saying we designed the class well by restricting access to its attributes, we say we have *hidden* the information.

5.5.1 Abstraction

The world is a complicated place. To deal with that complexity, we form generalizations, or abstractions, of the things in it. For example, consider the abstraction of a person. From the point-of-view of a university, it needs to know the person's name, address, telephone number, social security number, and educational background. From the point-of-view of the police, they need to know a person's name, address, phone number, weight, height, hair color, eye color, and so on. It's still the same person, just a different abstraction, depending on the application at hand.

The abstraction of an item depends on the context in which you define the abstraction.

Abstraction is an analysis issue that deals with what a class knows or does. Your abstraction should include the features, attributes, and methods that are of interest to your application and ignore the rest. That's why the abstraction of a student would include the person's name and address, but probably not his or her height and weight. People often say

Abstraction is the art of painting a clear box around an item.

> ### DEFINITIONS
>
> *Abstraction.* The essential characteristics of an item, such as a class or operation.
>
> *Encapsulation.* The grouping of related concepts into one item, such as a class or component.
>
> *Information hiding.* The restriction of external access to attributes.

abstraction is the act of painting a clear box around something or they say abstraction is the act of defining the interface of something. Either way, you are defining what the class knows and does.

5.5.2 Encapsulation

Although the act of abstraction tells us that we need to store a student's name and address, as well as be able to enroll students in seminars, it doesn't tell us how we are going to do this. Encapsulation deals with the issue of how you intend to modularize the features of a system. In the object-oriented world, you modularize systems into classes, which, in turn, are modularized into methods and attributes. We say that we encapsulate behavior into a class or we encapsulate functionality into a method.

Encapsulation addresses the issue of how functionality is compartmentalized within your system.

Encapsulation is a design issue that deals with how functionality is compartmentalized within a system. You shouldn't have to know how something is implemented to be able to use it. The implication of encapsulation is that you can build anything anyway you want, and then you can later change the implementation and it will not affect other components within the system (as long as the interface to that component does not change).

Encapsulation is the art of painting the box black.

People often say encapsulation is the act of painting the box black: You are defining how something is going to be done, but you are not telling the rest of the world how you're going to do it. For example, consider your bank. How does it keep track of your account information, on a mainframe, a mini, or a PC? What database does it use? What operating system? It doesn't matter, because it has encapsulated the way in which it performs account services. You just walk up to a teller and do whatever transactions you want. By hiding the details of the way it has implemented accounts, your bank is free to change that implementation at any time, and it shouldn't affect the way services are provided to you.

5.5.3 Information Hiding

To make your applications maintainable, you want to restrict access to data attributes and some methods. The basic idea is this: If one class wants information about another class, it should have to ask for it, instead of taking it. When you think about it, this is exactly the way the real world works. If you want to learn somebody's name, what would you do? Would you ask the person for his name, or would you steal his wallet and look at his ID? By restricting access to attributes, you prevent programmers from writing highly coupled code. When code is highly coupled, a change in one part of the code forces you to make a change in another, and then another, and so on. Coupling is described in detail in Section 5.1.2.

DEFINITION

Coupling. The degree of dependence between two items. In general, it is better to reduce coupling wherever possible.

5.5.4 An Example

In Figure 5-4 the abstraction is how you work with the wheel, pedals, and gearshift to drive a car. Encapsulation enables various car makers to provide a consistent interface, although each brand of car is built differently. Information hiding is represented by the fact that, although the oil is kept at a specific pressure within the engine, the driver doesn't know what the exact pressure is. In other words, information about the oil is hidden from the user.

5.5.5 Why This Is Important

Remember how I said it was up to you how you implement things and that you should be able to change the way you implemented it at any time? This was called encapsulation. Encapsulation requires information hiding. For example, say the programmer for class "Student" knows the attribute "listOfStudents" in the class "Seminar" was implemented as an array. The programmer decides to have the instance of "Student" add itself in the first available array element. A few months later, somebody else comes along and decides to reimplement "listOfStudents" as a linked list to use memory more efficiently. This is a reasonable and likely change. Unfortunately, the second programmer doesn't know the first programmer was directly updating the array of students; consequently, the university information system crashes.

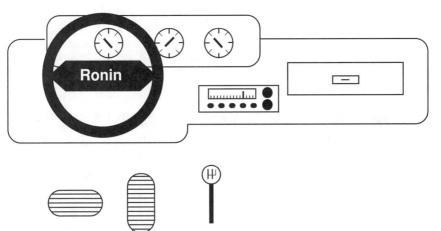

Figure 5-4.
The driver's
interface for a car

*Abstraction,
encapsulation,
and hiding
information
lead to more
maintainable
systems.*

Had access to the attribute "listOfStudents" been restricted, the programmer of "Student" wouldn't have been able to update its value directly. Therefore, the programmer would have had to write code to ask seminar objects to add a student object into its list. If this had been the case, when "listOfStudents" was changed into a linked list, a problem would not have occurred (when the second programmer changed the implementation of the attribute, she would also have modified any methods of "Seminar" that accessed it). By hiding the information (the seminar list) and encapsulating how students are enrolled in courses, you are able to keep the abstraction the same.

5.6 Inheritance

Similarities often exist between different classes. Two or more classes often share the same attributes and/or the same methods. Because you don't want to have to write the same code repeatedly, you want a mechanism that takes advantage of these similarities. Inheritance is that mechanism. Inheritance models "is a" and "is like" relationships, enabling you to reuse existing data and code easily.

*Inheritance
enables you to
reuse existing
work by taking
advantage of
similarities
between classes.*

For example, students have names, addresses, and telephone numbers, and they drive vehicles. At the same time, professors also have names, addresses, and telephone numbers, and they drive vehicles. Without a doubt, you could develop the classes for student and professor, and get them both running. In fact, you could even develop the class "Student" first and, once it is running, make a copy of it, call it "Professor," and make the necessary modifications. While this is straightforward to do, it is not perfect. What if there were an error in the original code for student? Now you have to fix the error in two places, which is twice the work. What would happen if you needed to change the way you handled names (say, you go from a length of 30 to a length of 40)? Now you would have to make the same change in two places again, which is a lot of dull, boring, tedious work. Wouldn't it be nice if you had only one copy of the code to develop and maintain?

DEFINITIONS

Inheritance. The representation of an *is a, is like,* or *is kind of* relationship between two classes. Inheritance promotes reuse by enabling a subclass to benefit automatically from all the behavior it inherits from its superclass(es).

Subclass. If Class *B* inherits from Class *A,* we say B is a subclass of *A*.

Superclass. If Class *B* inherits from Class *A,* we say that *A* is a superclass of *B*.

This is exactly what inheritance is all about. With inheritance, you define a new class that encapsulates the similarities between students and professors. This new class would have the attributes "name," "address," and "phone Number," and the method "driveVehicle." Because you need to name all the classes, you need to ask yourself what this collection of data and functionality describes. In this case, I think the name "Person" is fitting.

Once you have the class "Person" defined, you then make "Student" and "Professor" inherit from it. You would say "Person" is the superclass of both "Student" and "Professor," and "Student" and "Professor" are the subclasses of "Person." Everything that a superclass knows or does, the subclass knows or does free. Actually, for this example, you would need to write two lines of code, one saying "Student" is a subclass of "Person," and another saying "Professor" is a subclass of "Person"; therefore, it's almost free. Because "Person" has a name, address, and telephone number, both "Student" and "Professor" also have those attributes. Because "Person" has the ability to drive a vehicle, so do the classes "Student" and "Professor."

5.6.1 Modeling Inheritance

Figure 5-5 depicts the UML modeling notation for inheritance, which is a line with a closed arrowhead. The way you would read the diagram is B inherits from A. In other words, B is a direct subclass of A and A is the direct superclass of B (I discuss the concept of indirect subclasses and superclasses later in this chapter).

The arrow always points from the subclass to the superclass.

Figure 5-6 presents how you would model the "Person" inheritance class hierarchy, often simply called a class hierarchy. Notice how the name of the "Person" class is in italics, indicating it is *abstract*, whereas "Professor" and "Student" are *concrete* classes. Abstract and concrete

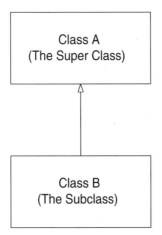

Figure 5-5.
The UML modeling notation for inheritance

classes are discussed in Section 5.6.4. For now, simply take note of the way to indicate classes in the UML.

5.6.2 Inheritance Tips and Techniques

The following tips and techniques should help you apply inheritance effectively:

1. **Look for similarities.** Whenever you have similarities between two or more classes, either similar attributes or similar methods, then you probably have an opportunity for inheritance.

2. **Look for existing classes.** When you identify a new class, you might already have an existing class to which it is similar. Sometimes you can directly inherit from an existing class, and just code the differences of the new class. For example, assume your university information system also needed to support university administrators. The "Person" class already has many of the features an "Administrator" class needs, so you should consider having "Administrator" inherit from "Person."

3. **Follow the sentence rule.** One of the following sentences should make sense: "A subclass IS A superclass," "A subclass IS A KIND OF superclass," or "A subclass IS LIKE A superclass." For example, it makes sense to say a student is a person and a dragon is like a bird. It does not make sense to say a student is a vehicle or is like a vehicle, so the class "Student" likely should not inherit from "Vehicle." If one of the sentences does not make sense, then you have likely found either an aggregation relationship or an association (I describe both of these concepts later in this chapter).

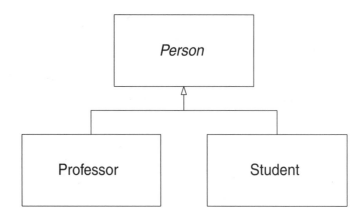

Figure 5-6.
Modeling the concept that "Professor" and "Student" inherit from "Person"

4. **Avoid implementation inheritance.** Developers new to object orientation have a tendency to misapply inheritance, often in an effort to reuse as much as they possibly can (a good motive). Inheritance often is arguably the most exciting concept in their object repertoire, so they want to use it as much as possible. Usually the problem is something called implementation or convenience inheritance: the application of inheritance when the sentence rule does not apply and the only justification is that the subclass needed one or more of the features of the superclass, the application of inheritance being more convenient than refactoring your classes. A good rule of thumb is to reconsider "is like a" applications of inheritance because this is a weaker justification.

5. **Inherit everything.** The subclass should inherit everything from the superclass, a concept called pure inheritance. If it does not, the code becomes harder to understand and maintain. For example, say Class *B* inherits from *A*. To understand *B*, you need to understand what *A* is all about, plus all the features *B* adds on. If you start removing functionality, you also need to understand what *B* isn't. This is a lot of work. Besides, if you need to start removing functionality, the sentence probably didn't make sense. You wouldn't have been able to say "a *B* IS AN *A*," instead you would have said "a *B* IS AN *A*, except for...." This is a sign that inheritance might not be appropriate.

DEFINITIONS

Inheritance hierarchy. A set of classes related through inheritance. Also referred to as a class hierarchy.

Abstract class. A class that doesn't have objects instantiated from it.

Concrete class. A class that has objects instantiated from it.

DEFINITIONS

Implementation inheritance. When inheritance is applied simply for convenience, even though it doesn't make sense to say the subclass "IS A" superclass. Also known as convenience inheritance.

Override. When you redefine an attribute or method in a subclass, we say you override it.

Pure inheritance. Inheritance in which the subclass doesn't override any behavior implemented by its superclass(es). The subclass is free to add new behavior.

5.6.3 Single and Multiple Inheritance

When a class inherits from only one other class, we call this *single inheritance*. When a class inherits from two or more other classes, we call this *multiple inheritance*. Remember this: The subclass inherits all the attributes and methods of its superclass(es).

5.6.3.1 Single Inheritance

In Figure 5-7, you see several similarities between airplanes and cars. They both have a number of passengers, a maximum fuel level, and they can either increase or decrease their speed. To take advantage of these similarities, you could create a new class called "Vehicle" and have "Airplane" and "Car" inherit from it. We say the classes "Vehicle," "Airplane," and "Car" form an inheritance hierarchy, also called a class hierarchy. The topmost class in a class hierarchy (in this case "Person") is called the root or root class.

Notice how there is the method "Turn" for "Car" and "Bank" for "Airplane." Turning and banking are exactly the same thing. You could have defined a "Turn" method in "Vehicle," and had "Airplane" and "Car" inherit it (then you would remove "Bank" and "Turn" from the subclasses). This would imply that you require users of airplanes (probably pilots) to change their lingo. Realistically, this wouldn't work. A better solution would be to define "Turn" in "Vehicle" and have the method "Bank" invoke it as needed.

DEFINITIONS

Multiple inheritance. When a class directly inherits from more than one class.

Single inheritance. When a class directly inherits from only one class.

Before:

After:

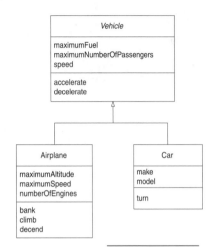

Airplane

maximumAltitude
maximumFuel
maximumNumberOfPassengers
maximumSpeed
numberOfEngines
speed

accelerate
bank
climb
decelerate
decend

Car

make
maximumFuel
maximumNumberOfPassengers
model
speed

accelerate
decelerate
turn

Figure 5-7.
Creating the vehicle class hierarchy

5.6.3.2 Multiple Inheritance

In the "before picture" of Figure 5-8, you want to create a new class called "Dragon." You already have the classes "Bird" and "Lizard." A dragon is like a bird because they both fly. A dragon is also like a lizard because they both have claws and scales. Because dragons have the features of both birds and lizards, in the "after picture" I have the class "Dragon" inheriting from both "Bird" and "Lizard." This is an example of an "is like" relationship: a dragon IS LIKE a bird and a dragon IS (also) LIKE a lizard.

Notice how I listed the method "eat" for dragon. Although all three types of creatures eat, they all eat in different ways. Birds eat bird seed, lizards eat bugs, and dragons eat knights in shining armor. Because the way dragons eat is different from the way either birds or lizards eat, I needed to redefine, or override, the definition of the "eat" method. The general idea is a subclass will need to override the definition of either an attribute (occasionally) or a method whenever it uses that data, or performs that method in a different manner than its superclass.

C++ is one of the few languages that supports the concept of multiple inheritance, whereas languages such as Java, Smalltalk, and Objective-C do not. The point to be made is if your target implementation language doesn't support multiple inheritance, then you shouldn't use it when you are modeling.

TIP

Many Languages Don't Support Multiple Inheritance

<table>
<tr><td>TIP

You Don't Need to Indicate Inherited Things</td><td>Notice how the attributes and methods of the superclass are not listed in the subclasses (they have been inherited). The only time you would model an attribute or method in both a subclass and a superclass is when the subclass overrides its definition.</td></tr>
</table>

5.6.4 Abstract and Concrete Classes

Abstract classes are introduced into your model to implement behaviors common to several classes.

In Figure 5-7, the class "Vehicle" has its name in italics, whereas "Airplane" and "Car" do not. This is because we say "Vehicle" is an abstract class, whereas "Airplane" and "Car" are both concrete classes. The main difference between abstract classes and concrete classes is that objects are instantiated (created) from concrete classes, but not from abstract classes. For example, in your problem domain, you have airplanes and cars, but you don't have anything that is just a vehicle (if something is not an airplane or a car, you are not interested in it). This means your software will instantiate airplane and car objects, but will never create vehicle objects. Abstract classes are modeled when you need to create a class that implements common features from two or more classes.

5.7 Association

Associations exist between objects.

In the real world, objects have relationships, associations, to other objects. The relationships between objects are important because they help us to define how they interact with each other. For example, students TAKE

Before: **After:**

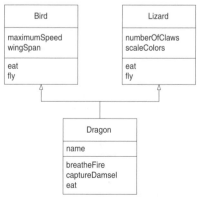

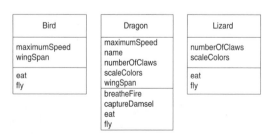

Figure 5-8.
An example
of multiple
inheritance

> Unless you're a game designer, the example in Figure 5-8 likely does not apply to your problem domain. In fact, it is one of the few nonbusiness examples in this book for the simple reason that, in my experience, multiple inheritance rarely occurs in the real world. In over ten years of object development I have only seen one example where the use of multiple inheritance was truly required (granted, I have seen many times where it was incredibly convenient). In the early 1990s, there was a great debate regarding the value of multiple inheritance. I suspect this debate still rages on occasionally at local pubs after work, although the designers of Java, interestingly enough, choose not to include it in the language (and still don't) although it was a well-understood concept at the time.
>
> **T I P**
>
> *Multiple Inheritance Rarely Occurs In the Real World*

courses, professors TEACH courses, criminals ROB banks, politicians KISS babies, and captains COMMAND starships. Take, teach, rob, kiss, and command are all verbs that define associations between objects. You want to identify and document these relationships, therefore, you can gain a better understanding as to how objects interact with one another.

Not only must you identify what the relationship(s) are between classes, you must also describe the relationship. For example, it's not enough to know that students take seminars. How many seminars do students take? None, one, or several? Furthermore, relationships are two-way streets: Not only do students take seminars, but seminars are taken by students. This leads to questions such as: how many students can be enrolled in any given seminar and is it possible to have a seminar with no one in it? The implication is you also need to identify the cardinality and optionality of an association. *Cardinality* represents the concept of "how many," whereas *optionality* represents the concept of "whether you must have something." Important to note is that UML chooses to combine the concepts of optionality and cardinality into the single concept of *multiplicity*.

Cardinality represents "how many." Optionality represents "may or must."

5.7.1 Modeling Associations

When you model associations in UML class diagrams, you show them as a thin line connecting two classes, as you see in Figure 5-9. Associations can

---

DEFINITIONS

Root class. The topmost class in an inheritance hierarchy.

Invoke. Object *A* sends message X to object *B* by invoking (calling) the X method implemented by object *B*.

TIP	My experience is that significant value exists in considering the two concepts of optionality and cardinality in isolation: For each direction of an association there is value in asking whether the association must exist (optionality) and how many could possibly exist (cardinality). For example, consider the association between professors and seminars. I would ask:
Consider Optionality and Cardinality Separately	• Must a professor teach a seminar or is it possible that some professors don't do any teaching? • How many seminars could a single professor teach? • Must a seminar be taught by a professor or is it possible that someone who isn't a professor could teach a course? • How many professors are potentially needed to teach a single seminar?

become quite complex; consequently, you can depict two things about them on your diagrams. Figure 5-9 shows the common items to model for an association. You may want to refer to *The Unified Modeling Language Reference Manual* (Rumbaugh, Jacobson, and Booch, 1999) for a detailed discussion, including the role and cardinality on each end of the association, as well as a label for the association. The label, which is optional, is typically one or two words describing the association. The multiplicity of the association is labeled on either end of the line, one multiplicity indicator for each direction (Table 5-2 summarizes the potential multiplicity indicators you can use). At each end of the association, the role—the context that an object takes within the association—may also be indicated.

Consider the class diagram depicted in Figure 5-10, which shows several classes and the associations between them. First, here is how you would read the associations:

- A student takes one or more seminars

- A seminar is taken by zero or more students

- A student, as a teaching assistant, may assist in one or more seminars

- A seminar may have one student who acts as a teaching assistant

DEFINITIONS

Cardinality. Represents the concept "how many?" in associations.

Optionality. Represents the concept "do you need to have it?" in associations.

Multiplicity. The UML combines the concepts of cardinality and optionality into the single concept of multiplicity.

Class A	cardinality A	label	cardinality B	Class B
	role A		role B	

Figure 5-9.
Notation overview for modeling associations on UML class diagrams

- A seminar is a section of one course

- A course has zero or more sections

- An employee holds one position

- A position may be held by one employee (some positions go unfilled)

- An employee may be managed by one other employee, his or her manager (the company president is the only one without a manager)

- An employee manages zero or more employees (some employees don't have any staff members)

Second, several important lessons are contained in Figure 5-10. First, you see it is possible to have more than one association between two classes: The classes "Student" and "Seminar" have the "takes" and "assists" associations between them. Two relationships exist between these two classes in the real world that you are interested in for your university information system; therefore, you need to model both associations. Second, it is valid that the same class may be involved with both ends of an association, something called a *recursive association*. A perfect example of this is the "manages" association that the "Employee" class has with itself. The way you read this association is that any given

Table 5-2. UML multiplicity indicators

Indicator	Meaning
0..1	Zero or one
1	One only
0..*	Zero or more
1..*	One or more
n	Only n (where n > 1)
0..n	Zero to n (where n > 1)
1..n	One to n (where n > 1)

DEFINITIONS

Bidirectional association. An association that may be traversed in both directions.

Recursive association. An association in which the objects involved in it are instances of the same class. For example, people marry people.

Role. The context that an object takes within an association. For example, a person can have the role of "husband" within a family.

Unidirectional association. An association that may be traversed in only one direction.

employee may have several other employees he or she manages, and that one other employee may, in turn, manage them.

Third, sometimes the direction of an association is one-way, as you see in Figure 5-10 with the "holds" association between "Employee" and "Position." The implication is employee objects know the position object they hold, but the position object doesn't need to know what employee holds it. This is called a *unidirectional association*, an association that is traversed in only one direction. You indicate unidirectional associations with an open arrowhead (so it is not confused with inheritance) pointing in the direction the association may be traversed. Bidirectional associations, ones that can be traversed in both directions, have no arrowheads. Therefore, you never see an association with two arrowheads. Furthermore, if there are no arrowheads, then you automatically assume the association is bidirectional. If you don't have a requirement to traverse an association in both directions, for example, Position objects don't have a need to collaborate with employee objects; then you should use a

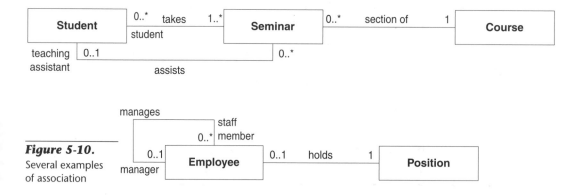

Figure 5-10.
Several examples
of association

> No matter how good a job you did during CRC Modeling, you are almost guaranteed to have missed the full details about object relationships. So, what do you do, make something up and hope for the best? Of course not. You would go back to your users and ask them what the real situation is, wouldn't you? The problem is remembering to go back to your users. The solution: Mark it as "currently unknown" by putting a question mark beside the part of the relationship of which you are unsure. For example, in Figure 5-10 you believe zero or more employees hold a position. You know it is possible for a position not to be currently filled, but what you aren't sure of is whether you can have one or several persons holding the same position. Is job sharing going on in the organization? Are there generic positions, such as "Janitor," that are held by many people? Or, is it really one person to one position, as we currently show now? Because you don't know for sure yet, you mark the relationship with a question mark, indicating you must go back later and verify your "educated guess." Note, the UML does not include question marks as part of the notation, yet it is a technique I have found to work well in practice.

TIP

Indicate What You Don't Yet Know

unidirectional association. You will see in Chapter 8 that unidirectional associations require less work to implement.

5.7.2 How Associations Are Implemented

Associations are maintained through the combination of attributes and methods. The attributes store the information necessary to maintain the relationship and methods keep the attributes current. For example, the "Student" class of Figure 5-10 would potentially have an attribute called "takes," perhaps an array, which is used to keep track of the "Seminar" objects the student is currently taking. The "Student" class might also have methods such as "addSeminar" and "removeSeminar" to add and remove seminar objects into the array. The "Seminar" class would have a corresponding attribute called "students" and methods called "addStudent" and "removeStudent" to maintain the association in the opposite direction. All of this has a significant implication: Because attributes and methods are inherited, associations are, too. You will see why this is important in Chapters 6 and 7.

In Figure 5-10, the unidirectional association "holds" between "Employee" and "Position" would be easier to implement because you only need to traverse it in one direction: from "Employee" to "Position." Therefore, "Employee" would have an attribute called "position" and methods, called something like "setPosition" and "getPosition" to maintain the association. There would be nothing added to "Position" because there is no need for Position objects to collaborate with

Associations are implemented as a combination of attributes and methods. As a result, associations are inherited.

Figure 5-11.
Indicating the
unknown

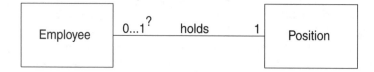

Employee objects, therefore, there is no added code to maintain the association in that direction.

5.8 Aggregation

Aggregation models "is part of" associations.

Sometimes an object is made up of other objects. For example, an airplane is made up of a fuselage, wings, engines, landing gear, flaps, and so on. A delivery shipment contains one or more packages. A team consists of two or more employees. These are all examples of the concept of aggregation, which represents "is part of" relationships. An engine is part of a plane, a package is part of a shipment, and an employee is part of a team.

5.8.1 Modeling Aggregation

Because examples of aggregation appear so frequently, the concept has its own notation within the UML, the diamond, depicted in Figure 5-12. The diamond is connected to the "whole" class. Aggregation is simply a type of association, therefore, you still need to model the multiplicity and roles, just as you would with associations. Not indicating the multiplicity of the "whole" end of an aggregation association is permissible. For example, in Figure 5-12, multiplicity is not indicated for either shipments or airplanes; in these cases it is assumed the multiplicity is 1.

Just as associations are two-way streets, so is aggregation. Furthermore, the aggregation associations depicted in Figure 5-12 are read in a similar manner:

T I P *Don't Show the Attributes and Methods to Maintain Associations*	Common style is to assume the attributes and methods exist to maintain associations (you don't need to show them on your diagrams). You should consider setting naming conventions for these attributes and methods. I typically use the role name or the class name for the attribute name and method names, such as "addAttributeName" and "removeAttributeName" for many associations, and "setAttributeName" and "getAttributeName" for single associations when I'm writing the source code, the topic of Chapter 8.

> **DEFINITIONS**
>
> **Aggregation.** The representation of "is part of" associations.
>
> **Composition.** A strong form of aggregation in which the "whole" is completely responsible for its parts and each "part" object is only associated with the one "whole" object.

- An item is part of one and only one shipment
- A shipment is composed of one or more items
- An engine is part of one and only one airplane
- An airplane has one or more engines
- An employee may be part of one or more teams
- A team is made up of one or more employees
- Any given team may be part of a larger team
- A team may be made up of smaller subteams

As you see in Figure 5-12, there are two flavors of aggregation: the first one modeled with a hollow diamond and the second one modeled with a solid diamond. The solid diamond indicates composition, a strong form of aggregation in which the "whole" is completely responsible for its parts and each "part" object is only associated to the one "whole" object. For example, at any given time, an engine is part of one and only one airplane

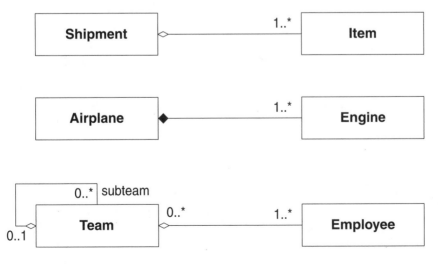

Figure 5-12.
Several examples of aggregation

(otherwise, you have a serious problem). Furthermore, no object other than the airplane will directly collaborate with an engine object; for example, passenger objects on the airplane cannot directly request that an engine increase its speed.

5.8.2 Aggregation Tips and Techniques

The following tips and techniques should help you to model aggregation effectively:

1. **Apply the sentence rule.** It should make sense to say "the part IS PART OF the whole." For example, it makes sense to say an engine is part of an airplane and an employee is part of a team. However, it doesn't make sense to say an employee is part of a position or a position is part of an employee, which is why association is appropriate in the example depicted in Figure 5-10. If the sentence doesn't make sense, then aggregation is most likely not appropriate. Either inheritance or association is what you need.

2. **It should be a part in the real world.** The part should actually be a part in the real world and should have its own set of responsibilities (attributes and methods).

3. **You should be interested in the part.** An object may actually be a part in the real world, but if you are not interested in keeping track of it, then don't model it. For example, an airplane maintenance system would be interested in keeping track of engines because it needs to record maintenance information about each engine. On the other hand, an air-traffic control system is not interested in tracking engines, just airplanes. Therefore, an engine would not appear as a class in an air-traffic control system.

4. **Show multiplicity and roles.** Aggregation relationships are a very common type of association. Just as you show the multiplicity and roles for an association, you need to do the same for an aggregation relationship.

5. **Aggregation is inherited.** Aggregation associations, like ordinary associations, are maintained by a combination of attributes and methods. Therefore, aggregation associations are also inherited.

5.9 Collaboration

In Chapter 3, in the discussion about Class Responsibility Collaborator (CRC) modeling, you saw that classes often need to work together to fulfill their responsibilities. Actually, it is the objects, the instances of the classes, that are working together. Collaboration occurs between objects when one object asks another for information or to do something. For example, an airplane collaborates with its engines to fly. For the plane to go faster, the engines must go faster. When the plane needs to slow down, the engines must slow down. If the airplane didn't collaborate with its engines, it would be unable to fly.

5.9.1 Messages

Objects collaborate with one another by sending each other messages. A message is either a request to do something or a request for information. Messages are modeled in UML sequence diagrams and UML collaboration diagrams. Figure 5-13 depicts a simple sequence diagram (see Chapter 6 for a detailed description of sequence diagrams and their use). You see how a student object requests to be enrolled in a seminar, the seminar object, in turn, sends a message to the course object to which it is associated because it needs to know whether the student object is qualified to enroll in the course (for example, the student has the prerequisites for the course). Figure 5-14 shows the same example as a collaboration diagram. Collaboration diagrams are described in detail in Chapter 7.

    Although sequence diagrams are described in detail in Chapter 6, I'll take this opportunity to present a quick overview of them. The boxes across the top of the diagram represent objects. The dashed lines hanging from them are called lifelines, which represent the life span of the object during the scenario being modeled. Objects have labels in the format "<u>name: class</u>"

Objects collaborate with one another via messages.

Figure 5-13.
A UML sequence diagram depicting messaging

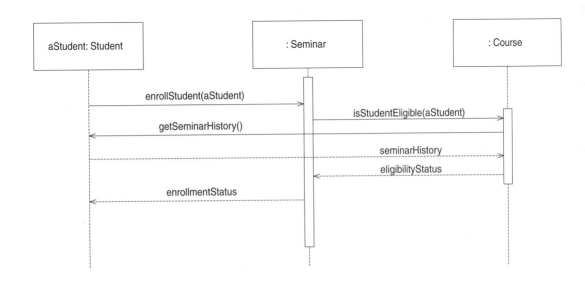

DEFINITIONS

Anonymous object. An object appearing on the diagram that has not been given a name; instead, the label is simply an indication of the class, such as "*: Invoice.*"

Lifeline. Represents, in a sequence diagram, the life span of an object during an iteration.

Signature. The combination of the name, parameter names (in order), and name of the return value (if any) of a method.

where "name" is optional (objects that haven't been given a name on the diagram are called anonymous objects). The instance of "Student" was given a name because it is used as a parameter in a message, whereas the instances of "Seminar" and "Course" didn't need to be referenced anywhere else in the diagram and, thus, could be anonymous. Messages are indicated as labeled arrows, the label being the signature of the method. Return values are optionally indicated using a dashed arrow with a label indicating the return value. Return values were indicated in Figure 5-13, but not in Figure 5-15. The sequencing of the messages is implied by the order of the messages themselves, starting at the top-left corner of the diagram.

Collaboration diagrams, described in detail in Chapter 7, have a similar notation to sequence diagrams. Objects are indicated in the same sort of manner, although they are connected via unlabelled association lines unlike sequence diagrams. Messages are indicated with arrows again, although they are not connected to the objects (no lifelines exist on collaboration diagrams). The sequence of the messages is optionally indicated by

Figure 5-14.
A UML collaboration diagram depicting messaging

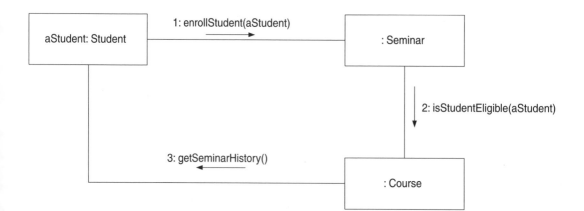

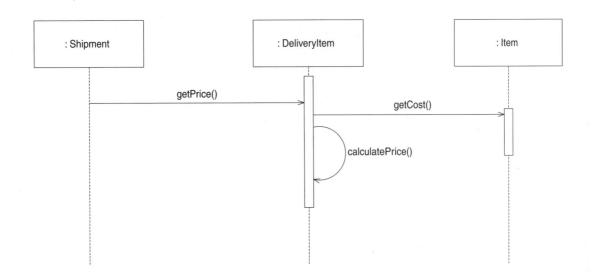

Figure 5-15.
Objects collaborating to calculate the total cost of a shipment

putting a number in front of the message name. In Figure 5-14, the same messaging sequence is indicated as in the sequence diagram of Figure 5-13.

5.9.2 Collaboration Tips and Techniques

The following tips and techniques should help you to model collaborations effectively:

1. **Some sort of association must exist.** The only way an object can send a message to another object is if it knows about it in the first place. In the real world, you cannot ask anyone for help unless you know how to get in contact with them. The same principle applies to objects. There must be an association, or an aggregation association, between the two classes for their instances (objects) to be able to collaborate.

2. **A corresponding method must exist in the target object.** Collaborations are implemented as method invocations, implying that the method must exist in the target for it to be invoked. If an object is asked for information, it must have a method that returns this information. For example, in Figure 5-13, the message "isStudentEligible()" is sent to the course object; therefore, a corresponding method must be implemented in the "Course" class called "isStudentEligible()." If an object is asked to do something, it must have a method to do it. Similarly, in Figure 5-13, you see

the message "enrollStudent()" is sent to seminar objects; therefore, the "Seminar" class must have a method "enrollStudent()."

3. **There might be a return value.** If the collaboration is a request for information, then there must be a return value (the requested information). This fact should be included in the documentation for the method and will, optionally, be indicated on the sequence diagram as a dashed line. Return values typically are not modeled on collaboration diagrams because they tend to clutter the diagrams.

4. **There may or may not be parameters.** Some messages have parameters and some do not. Remember, a message is effectively a method (function) call. Just as functions may take parameters, so do methods. For example, in Figure 5-13, a student object passes itself as a parameter when it invokes the "enrollStudent()" message on the seminar object. In Figure 5-15, the shipment object does not need to pass any parameters when it asks the item object for its cost.

5. **Messages show collaboration, not data flows.** Messages are requests. That is it. They are not data flows. Process diagrams (data flow diagrams) from the structured world show data flows, which are movements of data from one part of the system to another.

6. **Sometimes the target needs to collaborate.** The receiver of a message may be unable to fulfill the request by itself completely and may need to collaborate with other objects to fulfill its responsibility. For example, in Figure 5-13, the seminar object needed to interact with the course object of which it is a section to enroll a student into itself. That's perfectly fine.

7. **Each method should do something.** It is important that each object being collaborated with should always do something—

> **DEFINITIONS**
>
> *Object database (ODB).* A permanent storage mechanism, also known as an objectbase or an object-oriented database management system (OODBMS), which natively supports the persistence of objects.
>
> *Permanent storage.* Any physical medium to which data may be saved, retrieved, and deleted. Potential permanent storage mechanisms for objects include relational databases, files, and object databases.
>
> *Persistence layer.* Software, also known as a persistence framework, which encapsulates permanent storage mechanisms such as relational databases so application developers don't have knowledge of how or where objects are stored. Persistence layers automate significant portions of the efforts required to persist objects.
>
> *Persistence.* The issue of how objects are permanently stored.
>
> *Persistent object.* An object saved to permanent storage.
>
> *Relational database (RDB).* A permanent storage mechanism in which data is stored as rows in tables. RDBs don't natively support the persistence of objects, requiring the additional work on the part of developers and/or the use of a persistence layer.
>
> *Transitory object.* An object that is not saved to permanent storage.

not just forward the message to another object, something called a *pass through*. Pass throughs often results in "spaghetti code," which can be difficult to maintain.

8. **An object can collaborate with itself.** Objects will often send themselves messages to obtain information and/or to have themselves get something done. This is the same as a function calling another function in a procedural language such as C. In Figure 5-15, the "DeliveryItem" object sends itself a message to calculate the price (presumably the cost of the "Item" object multiplied by the number of items to be delivered).

5.10 Persistence

Persistence focuses on the issue of how to make objects available for future use of your software—in other words, how to save objects to permanent storage. To make an object persistent, you must save the values of its attributes to permanent storage (such as a relational database or a file), as well as any information needed to maintain the relationships (aggregation, inheritance, and association) with which it is involved. In addition to saving objects, persistence is also concerned with their retrieval and deletion.

Persistence focuses on how to save, retrieve, and delete objects to/from permanent storage.

From a development point-of-view, two types of objects exist: persistent objects that stick around and transient objects that don't. For example, a customer is a persistent object. You want to save customer objects into some sort of permanent storage so you can work with them again in the future. A customer editing screen, however, is a transient object. Your application creates the customer-editing screen object, displays it, then gets rid of it once the user is done editing the data for the customer with whom he or she is currently dealing.

5.10.1 Persistence Tips and Techniques

The following tips and techniques should help you to understand and apply persistence concepts better:

1. **Business/domain classes are usually persistent.** You are naturally going to need to keep a permanent (persistent) record of the instances of real-world classes such as "Student," "Professor," and "Course."

2. **User interface classes are usually transitory.** User interface classes (screens and reports) are usually transitory. Screens are created and displayed when needed, and then, once they are no longer in use, they are destroyed (removed from memory). Report classes are created, they gather the data they need, manipulate the data, and then output the data. Once this is done, the report object is usually destroyed as well. Note that sometimes you might need to maintain a log of when you printed a report and who/what you sent it to, making the report log persistent.

DEFINITIONS

Business/domain class. A class that models a concept in the problem domain of your system, for example, "Customer" and "Account" in a banking environment. Business/domain classes are usually found during requirements and/or analysis.

Hypertext Markup Language (HTML). Industry-standard definition of a platform-independent file format for sharing information HTML pages are the de facto standard approach for user interfaces on the World Wide Web (WWW).

User interface class. A class that provides the capability for users to interact with the system. User interface classes typically define a graphical user interface for an application, although other interface styles, such as voice command or HTML, are also implemented via user interface classes.

3. **You need to store both attributes and associations.** When an object is written to disk, you obviously need to store the value of its attributes. However, you must also store information about any relationships/associations with which the object is involved. For example, the student Alyssa Ogawa is taking the courses Bio-Medicine 101 and Nursing 301, so you want to ensure that when you store the "Alyssa" object to disk that the software records the information that she's enrolled in those two courses.

5.10.2 Persistent Memory: The Object Space

In the structured world, we had the concept of "virtual memory," which was where structured applications run. Virtual memory is the combination of main memory, plus any drive space on your computer. Figure 5-16 depicts the concept of persistent memory, also called the *object space*, which is where object-oriented applications run. Persistent memory is the combination of the main memory on your computer, plus all the available permanent storage on your network. One way to look at it is the object space is simply distributed virtual memory. In short, the object space is where objects exist and interact with one another.

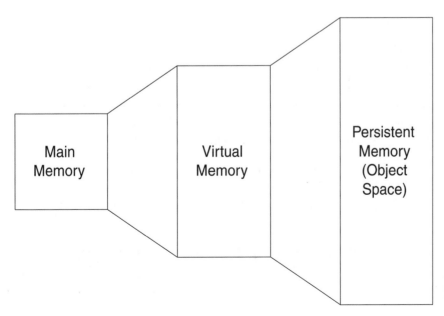

Figure 5-16.
The object space

DEFINITION

Object space. The memory space, including all accessible permanent storage, in which objects exist and interact with one another.

5.10.3 Object Databases (ODBs)

Relational databases (RDBs) are good at storing straightforward, simple objects, but are often not good at storing objects that are involved in complex relationships. Object databases (ODBs), on the other hand, are good at storing both variable and fixed-length data (pictures and sound bites, as well as strings and numbers), and at maintaining complex relationships between objects. You need to be able to traverse these relationships quickly (to get to other objects to which the current object is related) and that is exactly what ODBs are tuned for. ODBs are what make persistent memory persistent: Although objects interact with each other in the object space (persistent memory), they are stored in an OODB. Think of it like this: In the structured world, you store data in databases and read it into virtual memory to work with it. In the object-oriented world, you store objects in ODBs and retrieve them into persistent memory so they can interact/collaborate with each other.

Another advantage of ODBs over RDBs is that a true ODB not only stores data, but also the method code. Remember, an object is made up of both data and functionality (programming). Therefore, to make an object persistent (to save it to permanent storage), you should be saving both the data and the methods.

Meanwhile, Back in Reality

Understanding that RDBs have a significantly larger marketshare than object databases is important, as is the fact that ODBs, at best, are niche products that will likely never garner a large portion of the database market. Because relational databases have a large market share, significantly more people have experience working with them, which, in turn, makes it easier for your organization to find people with expertise in RDB technologies. This advantage, in combination with other strengths of RDBs such as tool support, typically make relational databases more attractive than object databases as a long-term solution for most organizations.

5.11 Persistent versus Transitory Associations

Two types of object relationships exist: persistent and transitory. The main difference is persistent associations must be saved, whereas transitory rela-

---

DEFINITIONS

Dependency relationship. A dependency relationship exists between Class A and B when instances of Class A interact with instances of Class B. Dependency relationships are used when no direct relationship (inheritance, aggregation, or association) exists between the two classes.

Persistent association. An association that is permanent or, at least semipermanent, in nature, which must be saved in permanent storage (that is it must be persisted).

Transitory association. An association that is not permanent and is not saved to permanent storage. Transitory associations are modeled in the UML as dependency relationships.

---

tionships are only temporary in nature and, thus, are not saved. Persistent associations and persistent aggregation associations are modeled, as shown previously in Sections 5.7 and 5.8, respectively. Transitory associations, however, are modeled in UML as dependencies between classes.

5.11.1 Persistent Associations

Persistent associations are those that are permanent or, at least semipermanent, in nature. An object relationship is persistent if information to maintain it is saved to permanent storage. For example, the TAKE relationship between students and courses is persistent. This is important business information that must be stored to disk. The TEACH relationship between professors and courses is persistent for the same reason. All of the associations we have dealt with so far in this book have been persistent.

5.11.2 Transitory Associations: Dependencies

Transitory associations are temporary in nature. They are not saved to permanent storage. Transitory relationships usually (but not always) involve at least one transitory object, such as a screen or report. The reason for this is simple: If you are not persisting the object, then you likely are not going to be persisting any of the associations it was involved with either. Transitory associations can also occur between two persistent objects. For example, in Figure 5-13, an implied transitory association[1] exists between the student object and the course object (student is passed as a parameter to the course, which then asks it for its prerequisites).

Transitory associations almost always involve at least one transitory object.

---

[1] This association was not modeled in Figure 5-13 because the concept had not been introduced at that point. For consistency purposes, however, it normally would have been introduced.

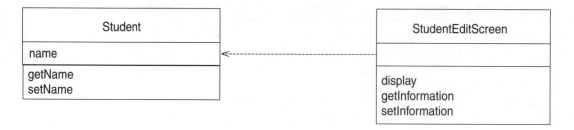

Figure 5-17.
A transitory
relationship
between two
classes.

Transitory relationships exist between objects for one reason only—so they may collaborate with one another. For an object to collaborate with another object it needs to know about it. This means there must be either an object relationship or a part-of relationship between the two objects. When a persistent association does not exist between two objects, but they need to collaborate with one another, you model a dependency relationship between the two classes.

In Figure 5-17, you see there is a dependency relationship—modeled as a dashed line with an open arrowhead—between the classes "Student" and "Student Editing Screen," representing the transitory relationship between a student-editing screen object as it edits the information of a student object. The editing screen obtains the current information from the student object, displays it in editing mode, and then updates the student object with the new information once it is finished. The transitory association between the editing screen object and the student object exists for as long as the student information is displayed on the screen. Once the screen is closed, the association no longer exists.

5.12 Coupling

Coupling is a measure of how much two items, such as classes or methods, are interrelated. When one class depends on another class, we say they are coupled. When one class interacts with another class, but doesn't know any of the implementation details of the other class, we say they are loosely coupled. When one class relies on the implementation (that is, it directly accesses the data attributes of the other), we say they are highly coupled.

Loose coupling is usually very good. High coupling is usually very bad.

Previously, I discussed the example of how the class "Student" could implement the "enroll" function: It could directly access the attribute "listOfStudents" in "Seminar," or it could send "Seminar" objects a message asking it to enroll the student in the seminar. Directly accessing and updating the attribute "listOfStudents" might save a few CPU cycles and

> ### DEFINITION
>
> *Maintenance burden.* The need for software organizations to invest money in the support, operation, and enhancement of existing hardware.

run a little quicker, but as soon as the implementation of that attribute changes, you would need to modify the code in "Student." As you saw, this was not very good. The basic problem is when two classes are highly coupled, a change in one often requires a change in the other. This, in turn, could require a change in another class, and then another, and then another, and so on. High coupling is one of the main reasons such a large maintenance burden exists. What should be a simple maintenance change can often create months of work, if it can be done at all. It is amazing how much code is out there that nobody is willing to touch because they're afraid of breaking it.

Every so often, developers are seduced by the dark side of the force and decide to write code that is highly coupled. This approach only makes sense when you are truly desperate to cut down on the processing overhead in your system. For example, database drivers are often highly coupled to the file system of the operating system on which the database runs. If you can save a few milliseconds accessing data, it quickly adds up when you are accessing hundreds of thousands of objects.

Increasing the coupling between two items may make sense for performance reasons.

5.12.1 Coupling Tips and Techniques

If you are in a position where you think you need to write highly coupled code, here is my advice:

1. **Avoid high coupling if you can.** High coupling leads to higher maintenance costs and, very often, the cost of the processing time you save is not as much as the increased cost to maintain the system. Furthermore, faster/bigger hardware might be the solution. Why spend an extra $50,000 maintaining a system when all you need is a faster CPU with more memory that costs $5,000?

2. **Document high coupling thoroughly.** The higher the coupling, the better the documentation has to be. You need to document thoroughly how and why two classes are coupled. Maintenance programmers need to know how the classes are coupled so they know how the classes will be affected when they make a change. They also need to know why the classes are highly coupled because they might be tempted to "fix" the problem—code that is highly coupled often looks like it was poorly designed.

DEFINITION
Cohesion. The degree of relatedness within an encapsulated unit (such as a component or a class).

5.13 Cohesion

You generally want to define highly cohesive classes and methods.

Cohesion is a measure of how much an item, such as a class or method, makes sense. A good measure of the cohesiveness of something is how long it takes to describe in one sentence; the longer it takes, the less cohesive it likely is. You want to design methods and classes that are highly cohesive. In other words, it should be very clear what a method or class is all about.

Small, cohesive methods that do one thing, and one thing only, are easier to understand and maintain.

A method is highly cohesive if it does one thing and one thing only. For example, in the class "Student" you would have methods to enroll a student in a seminar and to drop a student from a seminar. Both of these methods do one thing and one thing only. You could write one method to do both these functions, perhaps called "changeSeminarStatus." The problem with this solution is the code for this method would be more complex than the code for the separate "enrollInSeminar" or "dropSeminar" methods. This means your software would be harder to understand and, hence, harder to maintain. Remember, you want to reduce the maintenance burden, not increase it.

A highly cohesive class represents one type of object and only one type of object. For example, for the university information system we model professors, not employees. While a professor is, indeed, an employee, they are very different from other kinds of employees. For example, professors do different things than janitors, who do different things than secretaries, who do different things than registrars, and so on. We could easily write a generic "Employee" class that is able to handle all the functionality performed by every type of employee working for the university. However, this class would quickly become cumbersome and difficult to maintain. A better solution would be to define an inheritance hierarchy made up of

TIP

Method Names Often Indicate Their Cohesiveness

The name of a method often indicates how cohesive it is. Whenever you see a strong verb/noun combination used for the name of the method, very often it is highly cohesive. For example, consider methods such as "getName," "printName," "enrollInSeminar," and "dropSeminar." Verbs such as *get*, *print*, *enroll*, and *drop* are all very strong. Now consider "changeSeminarStatus." Is change as strong or as explicit as the words *enroll* and *drop*? I don't think so.

the classes "Professor," "Janitor," "Secretary," "Registrar," and so on. Because many similarities exist between these classes, you would create a new abstract class called "Employee," which would inherit from "Person." The other classes, including "Professor," would now inherit from "Employee." The advantage of this is each class represents one type of object. If there are ever any changes that need to be made with respect to janitors, you can go right to the class "Janitor" and make them. You don't need to worry about affecting the code for professors. In fact, you don't even need to know anything about professors at all.

5.14 Polymorphism

An individual object may be one of several types. For example, a "Gregory Quinn" object may be a student, a registrar, or even a professor. Should it matter to other objects in the system what type of person Greg is? It would significantly reduce the development effort if other objects in the system could treat people objects the same way and not need to have separate sections of code for each type. The concept of "polymorphism" says you can treat instances of various classes the same way within your system. The implication is you can send a message to an object without first knowing what type it is and the object will still do "the right thing," at least from its point-of-view.

5.14.1 An Example: The Poker Game

Consider an example. A poker game had been going on for hours, and it was Slick Scotty's turn to deal. One of the players turns to him and asks, "So what'll it be, partner?" Thinking about it, Slick Scotty replies "draw." Suddenly, everyone goes wild. The artist who was sitting across the table from Slick Scotty suddenly pulls out a pad of paper and a pencil and starts drawing. The professional card player to Scotty's right starts playing draw poker. To Scotty's alarm, the gunfighter to his left goes for his guns. *This always happens whenever I say "draw"—darn polymorphism,* thinks Slick Scotty to himself.

You can learn several interesting lessons from this experience. First, the polymorphism is in the way the dealer interacts with the players. The dealer didn't care what types of people objects he had at the table, he

Polymorphism enables objects to collaborate with other objects without knowing their type in advance.

DEFINITION

Polymorphism. Different objects can respond to the same message in different ways; enables objects to interact with one another without knowing their exact type.

treated them all the same way, even though the message "draw" meant one thing to an artist, another thing to a poker player, and yet another thing to a gun slinger. As far as the dealer is concerned, they're only people. Polymorphism is the concept that permits this to happen.

Polymorphism enables you to implement consistent and appropriate method names.

Second, the different objects responded to the message in their own way. In this scenario, Slick Scotty sends out the "draw" message to each person at the table. The artist object responded to the message by drawing a picture. The professional card player object responded to the message by starting to play draw poker. The gunfighter object responded to the message by drawing his guns. The same message went out to different objects and each one did something different (actually, a better way to look at it is that, from their point-of-view, they each did the appropriate thing). The interesting thing to note is that Slick Scotty didn't have to send different messages to each object (for example, "drawPicture," "playDrawPoker," and "drawYourGuns"), he just had to send the "draw" message.

Third, there is still work to be done. Although each type of object responds to "draw" in an appropriate manner, somebody still has to implement each version of that method.

5.14.2 Polymorphism at the University

Consider a slightly more realistic example of polymorphism by exploring the design of how the university handles the hiring of new staff, depicted in Figure 5-18. The university has a standard process for hiring staff: Once a person is hired, she is added to the university pension plan and an employee card is created for her. When a professor is hired at the university, the same process is followed, with the addition of a parking space assigned to her (if there is no parking space, the professor is added to the waiting list).

If the "hire" method has been implemented in the "Employee" class, it would implement the behavior needed to add the person into the university pension plan and print an employee card for them. The "hire" method has been overridden in the "Professor" class. Presumably, it would invoke the "hire" method in the "Employee" class because that behavior is still applicable for professors, plus it would add the functionality needed to reserve a parking space.

Polymorphism enables the reduction of coupling within object-oriented software, reducing your overall maintenance burden.

By being able to send the message "hire" to any kind of employee, there isn't the need for a complicated set of IF or CASE statements in the "hireNewEmployee" method of the screen object. This method doesn't need to send a "hireProfessor" message to professor objects, "hireJanitor" to janitor objects, and so on. It just sends "hire" to any type of employee and the object will do the right thing. As a result, you can add new types of employees (perhaps "Registrar") and you don't need to change the screen object at all. In other words, the class is loosely coupled to the employee class hierarchy, enabling you to extend your system easily.

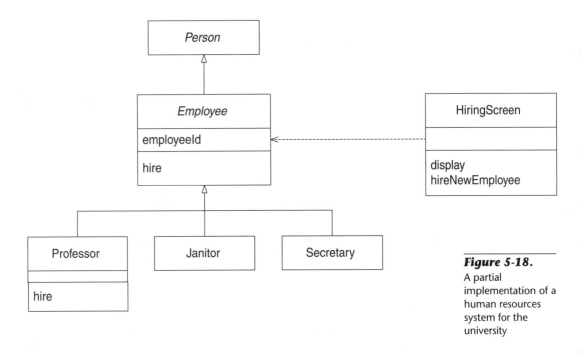

Figure 5-18.
A partial
implementation of a
human resources
system for the
university

5.15 Interfaces

An interface is the definition of a collection of one or more operation signatures, and zero or more attributes, ideally one that defines a cohesive set of behaviors. Interfaces are implemented by classes and components. To implement an interface, a class or component must include methods that have the operation signatures defined by the interface. For example, Figure 5-19 indicates that the class "Student" implements the "Serializable" interface and the "Searchable" interface. To implement the "Searchable" interface, "Student" would include a method called "find," which takes criteria as a parameter. In Chapters 6 and 7, I describe operation signatures in greater detail. Any given class or component may implement zero or more interfaces, and one or more classes or components can implement any given interface. Interfaces are used to promote consistency within your models and source code (Java has built-in support for interfaces).

Interfaces define a set of operation signatures that can be implemented by a class or component.

Also notice in Figure 5-19, that there are two ways to indicate that something implements an interface: the lollipop notation used for the "Serializable" interface and the box notation used for the "Searchable" interface. The lollipop notation has the advantage that it is visually compact, whereas the box notation provides details about the interface itself. The "Searchable" interface box is the same notation as a class, with the addition of the stereotype of "interface." Stereotypes are a mechanism to define common and consistent extensions to the UML notation. In

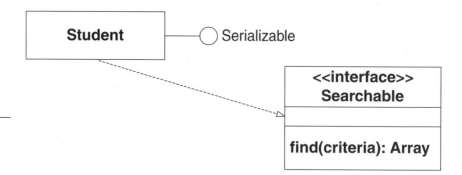

Figure 5-19.
The two UML
notations for
interfaces

Chapter 3, you saw how to apply the stereotypes of "extend" and
"include" to use case models. The dashed arrow from "Student" to
"Searchable" is a "realizes" relationship in the UML, indicating that "Student" implements (realizes) the "Searchable" interface.

5.16 Components

*Components are
modular, well-
encapsulated
units that can be
independently
deployed.*

A component is a modular, extensible unit of independent deployment
that has contractually specified interface(s) and explicitly defined dependencies, if any. Ideally, components should be modular, extensible, and
open. *Modularity* implies a component contains everything it needs to
fulfill its responsibilities, *extensibility* implies that a component can be
enhanced to fulfill more responsibilities than it was originally intended
to, and *open* implies it can operate on several platforms and interact with
other components through a single programming interface.

*Component
diagrams show
software
components,
their interfaces,
and their
interrelationships.*

   Component diagrams (Ambler, 1998a; Rumbaugh, Jacobson, and
Booch, 1999) show the software components that make up a larger piece
of software, their interfaces, and their interrelationships. For the sake of
our discussion, a component may be any large-grain item—such as a

---

DEFINITIONS

Interface. The definition of a collection of one or more operation signatures
and, optionally, attribute definitions that comprises a cohesive set of behaviors.
Some object languages support the capability for classes and/or components to
implement interfaces.

Realizes relationship. A type of relationship where an item implements (realizes) a concept or type, such as a standard or an interface.

Stereotype. A stereotype denotes a common use of a modeling element.
Stereotypes are used to extend the UML in a consistent manner.

common subsystem, a commercial off-the-shelf (COTS) system, an OO application, or a wrapped legacy application—that is used in the daily operations of your business. In many ways, a component diagram is simply a class diagram at a larger, albeit less-detailed, scale. Figure 5-20 shows an example of a component diagram being used to model the business architecture, a simple telecommunications company. The boxes represent components, in this case either applications or internal subsystems, and the dotted lines represent dependency relationships between the components.

Components, like classes, implement interfaces. A component's interfaces define its access points. Components are typically implemented as collections of classes, ideally classes that form a cohesive subset of your overall systems. Components are typically heavyweights and could even be thought of as large classes or even subsystems. For example, a database could be a component, or the collection of business/domain classes that implement the behaviors required to implement people within your application could be a component. Common component technologies include Microsoft's Component Object Model (COM) and COM and Sun Microsystems' Enterprise JavaBeans, two topics discussed in Chapter 11.

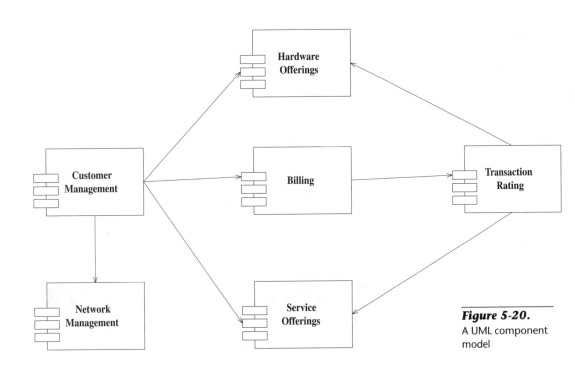

Figure 5-20.
A UML component model

<table>
<tr><td>

TIP

*The UML
Notation Is
Consistent*

</td><td>

You may notice the consistency of the notation between class diagrams and component diagrams: they use exactly the same notation for dependency relationships, as you saw in Figure 5-17. This is a good feature of the Unified Modeling Language: its notation is consistent. Yes, a few nitpicky details of UML aren't consistent but, for the most part, each concept is modeled the same way across the various diagrams of UML.

</td></tr>
</table>

5.17 Patterns

*Patterns are
reusable solutions
to common
problems.*

Doesn't it always seem as if you are solving the same problems repeatedly? If you personally haven't solved a given problem before, then chances are pretty good you could hunt somebody down who had tackled the same or, at least, a similar problem in the past. Sometimes the problem you are working on is simple, sometimes it is complex, but usually it has been worked on before. Wouldn't it be nice to be able to find a solution easily, or at least a partial solution, to your problem? Think how much time and effort you could save if you had access to a library of solutions to common system-development problems. This is what patterns are all about.

*Many types of
patterns exist,
including analysis
patterns, design
patterns, and
process patterns.*

A *pattern* is a solution to a common problem taking relevant forces into account, effectively supporting the reuse of proven techniques and approaches of other developers. Several flavors of patterns exist, including analysis patterns, design patterns, and process patterns. Analysis patterns describe a solution to common problems found in the analysis/business domain of an application. Design patterns describe a solution to common problems found in the design of systems. And process patterns address software process-related issues. Analysis patterns are discussed in Chapter 6, design patterns in Chapter 7, and process patterns in Chapter 10.

For example, it is common to discover classes in your application that should only have one instance. Perhaps there should only be one instance of a certain editing screen open at any given time, perhaps you have configuration information you want to store in one place only, or perhaps you have one or more constant values you need to maintain somewhere. In all these examples, you need to have a single instance of the class in

---

DEFINITION

Component. A modular, extensible unit of independent deployment that has contractually specified interface(s) and explicitly defined dependencies, if any.

DEFINITIONS

Pattern. A solution to a common problem taking relevant forces into account, effectively supporting the reuse of proven techniques and approaches of other developers.

Analysis pattern. A pattern that describes a solution to a common business/analysis issue.

Design pattern. A pattern that describes a solution to a common design issue.

Process pattern. A collection of general techniques, actions, and/or tasks (activities) that address a specific software process problem taking the relevant forces/factors into account.

---

question—a single instance of the dialog box, a single instance of the configuration information, and a single instance of the constants. This problem is resolved by the Singleton pattern (Gamma, Helm, Johnson, and Vlissides, 1995), a design pattern that shows how to ensure that only one single instance of a class exists at any one time. In Figure 5-21, you see a class diagram describing the Singleton design pattern. Note that a static attribute exists that keeps track of the single instance and a static method that creates the instance if it does not already exist. Although Singleton is a simple pattern, I suspect it is one you will use over and over again when developing OO applications.

The Singleton pattern ensures that only one instance of a class exists at any one time.

5.18 What You Have Learned

In this chapter, you discovered the main concepts of the object-oriented paradigm and were presented with the basic Unified Modeling Language (UML) notations to model them. Refer to Table 5-1 for a summary.

Singleton
singleInstance
create()

Figure 5-21.
The Singleton design pattern

5.19 Review Questions

1. Discuss the difference between inheritance and aggregation. What are the advantages and disadvantages of each?

2. Discuss the difference between association and aggregation. What are the advantages and disadvantages of each?

3. When would you apply inheritance? When wouldn't you? Provide examples of when inheritance is appropriate and when it is not, discussing each.

4. Discuss the concepts of coupling and cohesion. How do they relate, if at all, to one another?

Your requirements define what is requested to be built.

Your analysis defines what will be built.

Chapter 6

Determining What to Build: Object-Oriented Analysis

What You Will Learn In This Chapter

How to develop a system use case model from an essential use case model
How to develop sequence diagrams
How to develop a conceptual class model from a domain model
How to develop activity diagrams
How to develop a user interface prototype
How to evolve your supplementary specification
How to apply the Object Constraint Language (OCL)
How to apply analysis patterns
How to write user documentation
How to apply packages on your diagrams

Why You Need to Read This Chapter

Your requirements model, although effective for understanding what your users want to have built, is not as effective at understanding what will be built. Object-oriented analysis techniques, such as system use case modeling, sequence diagramming, class modeling, activity diagramming, and user interface prototyping are used to bridge the gap between requirements and system design.

*Requirements
engineering
focuses on
understanding
users and their
usage, whereas
analysis focuses
on understanding
what needs to be
built.*

The purpose of analysis is to understand what will be built. This is similar to requirements gathering, described in Chapter 3, the purpose of which is to determine what your users want to have built. The main difference is that the focus of requirements gathering is on understanding your users and their potential usage of the system, whereas the focus of analysis shifts to understanding the system itself.

Figure 6-1 depicts the main artifacts of your analysis efforts and the relationships between them. The solid boxes indicate major analysis artifacts, whereas the dashed boxes represent your major requirements artifacts. As with the previous Figure 3-1, the arrows represent "drives" relationships; for example, you see that information contained in your CRC model affects information in your class model and vice versa. Figure 6-1 has three important implications. First, analysis is an iterative process.

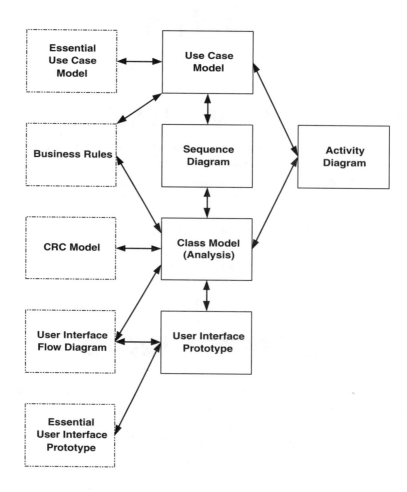

Figure 6-1.
Overview of analysis artifacts and their relationships

Second, taken together, requirements gathering and analysis are highly interrelated and iterative. As you see in Chapter 7, which describes object-oriented design techniques, analysis and design are similarly interrelated and iterative. Third, the "essential" models, your essential use case model and your essential user interface prototype, evolve into corresponding analysis artifacts—respectively, your use case model and user interface prototype. What isn't as obvious is that your Class Responsibility Collaborator (CRC) model evolves into your analysis class model.

Your use case model describes how your users work with your system, reflecting the business rules pertinent to your system, as well as aspects of your user interface model. You can use either Unified Modeling Language (UML) sequence diagrams or UML activity diagrams to flesh out and verify the logic contained in your use cases. Furthermore, you see that sequence diagrams act as a bridge to your class model, which depicts the static structure of the classes from which your system will be built. Your user interface model, including your user interface prototype and your user interface flow diagram (see Chapter 3), also drives changes to your class model.

An important concept to note about Figure 6-1, and similarly Figures 7-1 and 8-1, is that every possible "drives" relationship is not shown. For example, as you are developing your use case model, most likely you will realize you are missing a feature in your user interface, yet a relationship doesn't exist between these two artifacts. From a pure/academic point of view, when you realize your use case model conflicts with your user-interface model, you should first consider what the problem is, update your use case model appropriately, propagate the change to your essential use case model, and then to your essential user interface model, and, finally, into your user interface model. Yes, you may, in fact, take this route. Just as likely, and probably more so, is that you will, instead, update both your use case model and user interface model together, and then propagate the changes to the corresponding requirements artifacts. This is an important aspect of iterative development. You don't necessarily work in a defined order; instead, your work reflects the relationships between the artifacts you evolve over time.

Analysis is an iterative process.

A second important concept is the difference between a model and a diagram. A diagram is a picture—typically consisting of bubbles connected by lines documented with labels—that depicts an abstraction of a portion or an aspect of a system. A model is also an abstraction, although it is more robust because it consists of zero or more diagrams, plus associated documentation. For example, a class model is composed of a UML class diagram and the specifications of the classes and associations depicted on that diagram, whereas a CRC model is a collection of CRC cards.

DEFINITIONS

Activity diagram. A UML diagram used to model high-level business processes or the transitions between states of a class (in this respect, activity diagrams are effectively specializations of state chart diagrams).

Class diagram. Shows the classes of a system and the associations between them.

Class model. A class diagram and its associated documentation.

Class Responsibility Collaborator (CRC) card. A standard index card that has been divided into three sections: one indicating the name of the class the card represents, one listing the responsibilities of the class, and the third listing the names of the other classes with which this one collaborates to fulfill its responsibilities.

Class Responsibility Collaborator (CRC) model. A collection of CRC cards that model all or part of a system.

Diagram. A visual representation of a problem or solution to a problem.

Essential use case. A simplified, abstract, generalized use case that captures the intentions of a user in a technology and implementation independent manner.

Essential use case model. A use case model comprised of essential use cases.

Essential user interface prototype. A low-fidelity prototype of a system's user interface that models the fundamental, abstract characteristics of a user interface.

Model. An abstraction describing a problem domain and/or a solution to a problem domain. Traditionally models are thought of as diagrams plus their corresponding documentation, although non-diagrams, such as interview results and collections of CRC cards, are also considered to be models.

Project stakeholder. Anyone who could be materially affected by the implementation of a new system or application.

Prototype. A simulation of an item, such as a user interface or a system architecture, the purpose of which is to communicate your approach to others before significant resources are invested in the approach.

Sequence diagram. A diagram that models the sequential logic, in effect, the time ordering of messages.

Use case. A sequence of actions that provide a measurable value to an actor.

Use case diagram. A diagram that shows use cases, actors, and their interrelationships.

Use case model. A model comprised of a use case diagram, use case definitions, and actor definitions. Use case models are used to document the behavior requirements of a system.

User interface (UI). The user interface of software is the portion the user directly interacts with, including the screens, reports, documentation, and software support (via telephone, electronic mail, and so on).

User interface flow diagram. A diagram that models the interface objects of your system and the relationships between them. Also know as an interface-flow diagram, a windows navigation diagram, or an interface navigation diagram.

User interface prototype. A prototype of the user interface (UI) of a system. User interface prototypes could be as simple as a hand-drawn picture or a collection of programmed screens, pages, or reports.

6.1 System Use Case Modeling

During analysis, your main goal is to evolve your essential use cases into system use cases. The main difference between an essential use case and a system use case is, in the system use case, you include high-level implementation decisions. For example, a system use case refers to specific user-interface components—such as screens, HTML pages, or reports—something you wouldn't do in an essential use case. During analysis, you make decisions regarding what will be built, information reflected in your use cases, and, arguably, even how it will be built (effectively design). Because your use cases refer to user interface components, and because your user interface is worked on during design, inevitably design issues will creep into your use cases. For example, a design decision is whether your user interface is implemented using browser-based technology, such as HTML pages or graphical user interface (GUI) technology such as Windows. Because your user interface will work differently depending on the implementation technology, the logic of your system use cases, which reflect the flow of your user interface, will also be affected.

System use cases reflect analysis decisions and, arguably, even design decisions.

What is a system use case model? Similar to essential use case models described in Chapter 3, a system use case model is composed of a use case diagram (Rumbaugh, Jacobson, and Booch, 1999) and the accompanying documentation describing the use cases, actors, and associations. Figure 6-4, which provides an example of a use case diagram, depicts a collection of use cases, actors, their associations, a system boundary box (optional), and packages (optional). A use case describes a sequence of actions that provide a measurable value to an actor and is drawn as a horizontal ellipse. An actor is a person, organization, or external system that plays a role in one or more interactions with your system. Actors are drawn as stick figures. Associations between actors and classes are indicated in use case diagrams, a relationship exists whenever an actor is involved with an interaction described by a use case. Associations also exist between use cases in system use case models, a topic discussed in the following section, something that didn't occur in essential use case models. Associations are modeled as lines connecting use cases and actors to one another, with an optional arrowhead on one end of the line indicating the direction of the initial invocation of the relationship. The rectangle around the use cases is called the system boundary box and, as the name suggests, it delimits the scope of your system—the use cases inside the rectangle represent the functionality you intend to implement. Finally, packages are UML constructs that enable you to organize model elements (such as use cases) into groups. Packages are depicted as file folders that can be used on any of the UML diagrams, including both use case diagrams and class diagrams. Section 6.9 presents strategies to apply packages effectively in your UML models.

6.1.1 Writing System Use Cases

Writing system use cases is fairly straightforward. You begin with your essential use cases and modify them to reflect the information captured within your UML sequence diagrams (Section 6-2), your UML activity diagrams (Section 6-7), your user interface prototype (Section 6-5), and the contents of your evolved supplementary specification (Section 6-6). You will also rework your use cases to reflect opportunities for reuse, applying the UML stereotypes of <<extend>> and <<include>>, as well as the object-oriented concept of inheritance, techniques covered next in Section 6.1.2.

Consider the system use case presented in Figure 6-4. Notice how it is similar to the essential use cases of Chapter 3, with the main exceptions being the references to user interface elements and references to other use cases. The use case has a basic course of action, which is the main start-to-finish path the user will follow. It also has three alternate courses of action, representing infrequently used paths through the use case, exceptions, or error conditions. Notice how I have added an identifier, something I could have done for the essential use cases depicted in Chapter 3. It also has sections labeled "Extends," "Includes," and "Inherits From" indicating the use cases, if any, with which this use case is associated. I discuss what you need to put here in Section 6.1.1.

Two common styles exist for writing use cases: narrative style and action-response style. Choose one style and stick to it.

Until now, I have presented use cases in what is called narrative style—the use case of Figure 6-2 is written this way—where the basic and alternate courses of action are written one step at a time. A second style, called the action-response style, presents use case steps in columns, one column for each actor and a second column for the system. Figure 6-3 presents the basic course of action for Figure 6-4 rewritten using this style. For the sake of brevity, I didn't include rewritten versions of the alternate courses. Of the two columns, one is for the Student actor and one for the system, because only one actor is involved in this use case.

DEFINITIONS

Extend association. A generalization relationship where an extending use case continues the behavior of a base use case. The extending use case accomplishes this by inserting additional action sequences into the base use case sequence. This is modeled using a use case association with the <<extend>> stereotype.

Include association. A generalization relationship denoting the inclusion of the behavior described by a use case within another use case. This is modeled using a use case association with the <<include>> stereotype Also known as a "uses" or a "has-a" relationship.

Name: Enroll in Seminar

Identifier: UC 17

Description: Enroll an existing student in a seminar for which he is eligible.

Preconditions: The Student is registered at the University.

Postconditions: The Student will be enrolled in the course he wants if he is eligible and room is available.

Extends: —

Includes: —

Inherits From: ——

Basic Course of Action:

1. The student wants to enroll in a seminar.

2. The student inputs his name and student number into the system via "UI23 Security Login Screen."

3. The system verifies the student is eligible to enroll in seminars at the university, according to business rule "BR129 Determine Eligibility to Enroll."

4. The system displays "UI32 Seminar Selection Screen," which indicates the list of available seminars.

5. The student indicates the seminar in which he wants to enroll.

6. The system validates the student is eligible to enroll in the seminar, according to the business rule "BR130 Determine Student Eligibility to Enroll in a Seminar."

7. The system validates the seminar fits into the existing schedule of the student, according to the business rule "BR143 Validate Student Seminar Schedule."

8. The system calculates the fees for the seminar based on the fee published in the course catalog, applicable student fees, and applicable taxes. Apply business rules "BR 180 Calculate Student Fees" and "BR45 Calculate Taxes for Seminar."

9. The system displays the fees via "UI33 Display Seminar Fees Screen."

10. The system asks the student whether he still wants to enroll in the seminar.

11. The student indicates he wants to enroll in the seminar.

12. The system enrolls the student in the seminar.

13. The system informs the student the enrollment was successful via "UI88 Seminar Enrollment Summary Screen."

14. The system bills the student for the seminar, according to business rule 'BR100 Bill Student for Seminar."

15. The system asks the student if he wants a printed statement of the enrollment.

16. The student indicates he wants a printed statement.

17. The system prints the enrollment statement "UI89 Enrollment Summary Report."

18. The use case ends when the student takes the printed statement.

Figure 6-2.
"Enroll in seminar" written in narrative style

continued on page 90

Alternate Course A: The Student is Not Eligible to Enroll in Seminars

A.3. The system determines the student is not eligible to enroll in seminars.

A.4. The system informs the student he is not eligible to enroll.

A.5. The use case ends.

Alternate Course B: The Student Does Not Have the Prerequisites

B.6. The system determines the student is not eligible to enroll in the seminar he has chosen.

B.7. The system informs the student he does not have the prerequisites.

B.8. The system informs the student of the prerequisites he needs.

B.9. The use case continues at Step 4 in the basic course of action.

Alternate Course C: The Student Decides Not to Enroll in an Available Seminar

C.4. The student views the list of seminars and doesn't see one in which he wants to enroll.

C.5. The use case ends.

The advantage of the action-response style is it is easier to see how actors interact with the system and how the system responds. The disadvantage is, in my opinion, it is a little harder to understand the flow of logic of the use case. This is particularly true for alternate courses and their references to other courses of action. The style you choose is a matter of preference. What's important is that your team and, ideally, your organization selects one style and sticks to it.

I want to point out an important style issue pertaining to Steps 2 and 3 of the use case of Figure 6-2. I could just as easily have defined a precondition that the student has already logged in to the system and has been verified as an eligible student. Actually, this should be two preconditions: one for being logged in and one for being eligible (this way, the preconditions are cohesive). To support the first precondition, being logged in, I would be tempted to write a "Log Into System" use case that would describe the process of logging in and validating the user, perhaps including alternate courses for obtaining a login identifier. This use case would be a candidate for inclusion in your common, enterprise model because it is a feature that should belong to your organization's shared technical architecture. Cross-project issues such as this are among the topics I cover in *Process Patterns* (Ambler, 1998b) and *More Process Patterns* (Ambler, 1999), the third and fourth books in this series. The second precondition, the one for being eligible to enroll, likely doesn't need its own use case, but I would still reference the appropriate business rule.

Student

1. The student wants to enroll in a seminar.

2. The student inputs his name and student number into the system via "UI23 Security Login Screen."

5. The student indicates the seminar in which she wants to enroll.

11. The student indicates she wants to enroll in the seminar.

16. The student indicates she wants a printed statement.

18. The use case ends when the student takes the printed statement.

System

3. The system verifies the student is eligible to enroll in seminars at the university, according to business rule "BR129 Determine Eligibility to Enroll."

4. The system displays "UI32 Seminar Selection Screen," which indicates the list of available seminars.

6. The system validates the student is eligible to enroll in the seminar, according to the business rule "BR130 Determine Student Eligibility to Enroll in a Seminar."

7. The system validates the seminar fits into the existing schedule of the student, according to the business rule "BR143 Validate Student Seminar Schedule."

8. The system calculates the fees for the seminar based on the fee published in the course catalog, applicable student fees, and applicable taxes. Apply business rules "BR 180 Calculate Student Fees" and "BR45 Calculate Taxes for Seminar."

9. The system displays the fees via "UI33 Display Seminar Fees Screen."

10. The system asks the student whether she still wants to enroll in the seminar.

12. The system enrolls the student in the seminar.

13. The system informs the student the enrollment was successful via "UI88 Seminar Enrollment Summary Screen."

14. The system bills the student for the seminar, according to business rule "BR100 Bill Student for Seminar."

15. The system asks the student if she wants a printed statement of the enrollment.

17. The system prints the enrollment statement "UI89 Enrollment Summary Report."

Figure 6-3.
Basic course of action for "Enroll in Seminar" written in action-response style

6.1.2 Reuse in Use Case Models: <<extend>>, <<include>>, and Inheritance

You can indicate potential opportunities for reuse on your use case models

One of your goals during analysis is to identify potential opportunities for reuse, a goal you can work toward as you are developing your use case model. Potential reuse can be modeled through four generalization relationships supported by the UML use case models: extend relationships between use cases, include relationships between use cases, inheritance between use cases, and inheritance between actors.

6.1.2.1 Extend Associations Between Use Cases

The <<extend>> stereotype is used to indicate an extend association.

An extend association, formerly called an extends relationship in the UML v1.2 and earlier, is a generalization relationship where an extending use case continues the behavior of a base use case. The extending use case accomplishes this by conceptually inserting additional action sequences into the base use case sequence. This enables an extending use case to continue the activity sequence of a base use case when the appropriate extension point is reached in the base use case and the extension condition is fulfilled. When the extending use case activity sequence is completed, the base use case continues. In Figure 6-4, you see that the use case "Enroll International Student in University" extends the use case "Enroll in University;" the notation for doing so is simply a normal use case association with the stereotype of <<extend>>. In this case, "Enroll in University" is the base use case and "Enroll International Student in University" is the extending use case.

Extending use cases are often introduced to resolve complexities of alternate courses.

An extending use case is, effectively, an alternate course of the base use case. In fact, a good rule of thumb is you should introduce an extending use case whenever the logic for an alternate course of action is at a complexity level similar to that of your basic course of action. I also like to introduce an extending use case whenever I need an alternate course for an alternate course; in this case, the extending use case would encapsulate both alternate courses. Many use case modelers avoid the use of extend associations as this technique has a tendency to make use case diagrams difficult to understand. My preference is to use extend associations sparingly. Note that the extending use case—in this case "Enroll International Student in University"—would list "UC33 Enroll in University," the base use case, in its "Extends" list.

Extension points are placed in base use cases to indicate where the logic of the extending use case replaces that of the base use case.

Just as you indicate the point at which the logic of an alternate course replaces the logic of a portion of the basic course of action for a use case, you need to be able to do the same thing for an extending use case. This is accomplished through the use of an extension point, which is simply a marker in the logic of a base use case indicating where extension is allowed. Figure 6-5 presents an example of how an extension point would be indicated in the basic course of action of the "Enroll in University" use

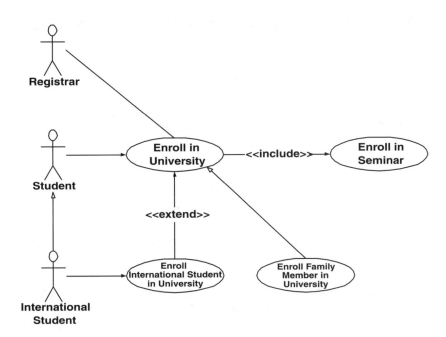

Figure 6-4.
The opportunities for reuse in use case models

case. Notice how the identifier and the name of the use case is indicated. If several use cases extended this one from the same point, then each one would need to be listed. A condition statement, such as "Condition: Enrollee is an international student," could have been indicated immediately following the name of the use but, in this example, it was fairly obvious what was happening.

6.1.2.2 Include Associations Between Use Cases

A second way to indicate potential reuse within use case models exists in the form of include associations. An include association, formerly known as a uses relationship in the UML v1.2 and earlier, is a generalization relationship denoting the inclusion of the behavior described by another use case. The best way to think of an include association is that it is the invocation of a use case by another one. In Figure 6-4, notice that the use case

An include association is the equivalent of a function call.

4. The system displays "UI43 Student Information Entry." [Extension Point: UC34 Enroll International Student In University.]
5. The student...

Figure 6-5.
Documenting an extension point within a use case

DEFINITIONS

Base use case. A use case extended by another via an extend association.

Extending use case. A use case that extends another use case via an extend association.

Extension point. A marker in a use case where extension is allowed.

"Enroll in University" includes the use case "Enroll in Seminar"; the notation for doing so is simply a normal use case association with the stereotype of <<include>>. Figure 6-6 presents an example of how you would indicate where the use case is included in the logic of the including use case. Similar to calling a function or invoking an operation within source code, isn't it? Object-oriented programming is covered in Chapter 8.

You use include associations whenever one use case needs the behavior of another. Introducing a new use case that encapsulates similar logic that occurs in several use cases is quite common. For example, you may discover that several use cases need the behavior to search for and then update information about students, indicating the potential need for an "Update Student Record" use case included by the other use cases.

As you would expect, the use case "Enroll in University" should list "UC17 Enroll in Seminar" in its "Includes" list. Why should you bother maintaining an "Includes" and an "Extends" list in your use cases? The answer is simple: Your use cases should stand on their own; you shouldn't expect people to have your use case diagram in front of them. Yes, it would be nice if everyone has access to the use case diagram because it also contains this information, but the reality is that sometimes you use different tools to document each part of your model. For example, your diagrams could be drawn using a drawing package and your use cases documented in a word processor. Some of your project stakeholders may have access to the word processor you are using, but not the drawing package. The main disadvantage of this approach is you need to maintain these two lists in parallel with the diagram, the danger being they may become unsynchronized.

Figure 6-6.
Indicating the
inclusion of a
use case

8. The student indicates the seminar(s) she wants to take via the use case UC 17 Enroll in Seminar.

9. The student…

6.1.2.3 Inheritance

Use cases can inherit from other use cases, offering a third opportunity to indicate potential reuse. Figure 6-4 depicts an example of this, showing that "Enroll Family Member in University" inherits from the "Enroll In University" use case. Inheritance between use cases is not as common as either the use of extend or include associations, but it is still possible. The inheriting use case would completely replace one or more of the courses of action of the inherited use case. In this case, the basic course of action is completely rewritten to reflect that new business rules are applied when the family member of a professor is enrolling at the university. Family members are allowed to enroll in the school, regardless of the marks they earned in high school; they don't have to pay any enrollment fees, and they are given top priority for enrollment in the university.

Use cases may inherit from other use cases.

Inheritance between use cases should be applied whenever a single condition, in this case, the student is a family member of a professor, would result in the definition of several alternate courses. Without the option to define an inheriting use case, you need to introduce an alternate course to rework the check of the student's high-school marks, the charging of enrollment fees, and for prioritization of who is allowed to enroll in the given semester.

Apply inheritance between use cases when a single condition would result in several alternate courses.

The inheriting use case is much simpler than the use case from which it inherits. It should have a name, description, and identifier, and it should also indicate from which use case it inherits in the "Inherits From" section. In sections that you replace, you may need to rewrite the preconditions, postconditions, or courses of action. If something is not replaced, then leave that section blank, assuming it is inherited from the parent use case (you might want to put text, such as "see parent use case," in the section).

The fourth opportunity for indicating potential reuse within use case models occurs between actors: An actor on a use case diagram can inherit from another actor. An example of this is shown in Figure 6-4, where the "International Student" actor inherits from "Student." An international student is a student, the only difference being he or she is subject to different rules and policies (for instance, the international student pays more in tuition). The standard UML notation for inheritance, the open-headed arrow, is used and the advice presented about the appropriate use of inheritance still applies: It should make sense to say the inheriting actor is or is like the inherited actor.

Actors may inherit from other actors.

6.1.3 Good Things to Know About Use Case Modeling

An important thing to understand about use case models is that the associations between actors and use cases indicate the need for interfaces. When the actor is a person, then to support the association, you need to develop user interface components, such as screens and reports. When

Associations between actors and use cases imply the need for interfaces.

the actor is an external system, then you need to develop a system interface, perhaps a data file transfer or a real-time online link to the external system. For example, in the "Enroll in Seminar" use case of Figure 6-2, the Student actor interacts with the system via several major UI components, particularly "UI23 Security Login Screen," "UI32 Seminar Selection Screen," "UI33 Display Seminar Fees Screen," "UI88 Seminar Enrollment Summary Screen," and "UI89 Enrollment Summary Report."

You should be able to exit from a use case at any time.

Second, use cases are often written under the assumption that you can exit at any time. For example, in the middle of the "Enroll in Seminar" use case, the student may decide to give up and try again later or the system may crash because the load on it is too great. The description of the use case doesn't include these as alternate courses because it would greatly increase the complexity of the use case without adding much value. Instead, it is assumed, if one of these events occurs, that the use case simply ends and the right thing will happen. However, your subject matter experts (SMEs) may want to define nonfunctional requirements that describe how situations such as this should be handled.

Beware of the "use case driven" hype of consultants and tool vendors.

Third, in my opinion, use case modeling has received far more attention than it actually deserves. Yes, it is a useful technique but no, it isn't the be-all-and-end-all of requirements and analysis modeling. You saw in Chapter 3 that essential use case modeling is one technique of several you can use to gather requirements and, as you see in this chapter, it is also one of several techniques to perform object-oriented analysis. Don't let the marketing hype of CASE tool vendors and object-oriented consultants deceive you into thinking everything should be "use case driven." Use case modeling is merely one of many important techniques you should have in your modeling toolkit.

Include, extend, and inheritance associations between use cases can lead to functional decomposition if you are not careful.

Fourth, although the reuse techniques—extend associations, include associations, and inheritance—are useful, don't overuse them. Include associations and, to a lesser degree, extend associations, lead to functional decomposition within your use case model. The problem is use cases are not meant to describe functions within your source code; they are meant to describe series of actions that offer value to actors. A good rule of thumb to use is if you are able to describe a use case with a single sentence, then you have likely decomposed it too much, something that occurs when you apply include associations too often. Another rule of thumb is, if you have more than two levels of include associations, for example, if use case *A* includes use case *B*, which includes use case *C*, then two levels of include exist, and then you are in danger of functional decomposition. The same can be said of extend associations between use cases, as well as inheritance.

6.1.4 Use Case Modeling Tips and Techniques

In this section, I want to share a collection of tips and techniques I have found useful over the years to improve the quality of my system use case models.

1. **Write from the point-of-view of the actor in the active voice.** Use cases should be written in the active voice: "The student indicates the seminar," instead of in the passive voice, "The seminar is indicated by the student." Furthermore, use cases should be written from the point-of-view of the actor. After all, the purpose of use cases is to understand how your users will work with your system.

2. **Write scenario text, not functional requirements.** A use case describes a series of actions that provide value to an actor; it doesn't describe a collection of features. For example, the use case of Figure 6-2 describes how a student interacts with the system to enroll in a seminar. It doesn't describe what the user interface looks like or how it works. You have other models to describe this important information, such as your user interface model and your supplementary specifications. Object-oriented analysis is complex, which is why you have several models to work with, and you should apply each model appropriately.

3. **A use case is neither a class specification nor a data specification.** This is the sort of information that should be captured by your conceptual model, described in Section 6.3, which in the object world is modeled via a UML class model. You are likely to refer to classes described in your conceptual model; for example, the "Enroll in Seminar" use case includes concepts, such as seminars and students, both of which would be described by your conceptual model. Once again, use each model appropriately.

4. **Don't forget the user interface.** System use cases often refer to major user interface (UI) elements, often called boundary or simply user interface items, and sometimes minor UI elements as appropriate.

5. **Create a use case template.** As you can see in Figure 6-2, use cases include a fair amount of information, information that can easily be documented in a common format. You should consider either developing your own template based on what you have learned in this book or adopting an existing one you have either purchased with an object modeling tool or downloaded from the Internet.

6. **Organize your use case diagrams consistently.** Common practice is to draw inheritance and extend associations vertically, with the inheriting/extending use case drawn below the parent/base use case. Similarly, include associations are typically drawn horizontally. Note that these are simple rules of thumb, rules that, when followed consistently, result in diagrams that are easier to read.

7. **Don't forget the system responses to the actions of actors.** Your use cases should describe both how your actors interact with your system and how your system responds to those interactions. With the "Enroll in Seminar" use case, had the system not responded when the student indicated she wanted to enroll in a seminar, I suspect the student would soon become discouraged and walk away. The system wasn't doing anything to help the student fulfill her goals.

8. **Alternate courses of action are important.** Start with the happy path, the basic course of action, but don't forget the alternate courses as well. Alternates courses will be introduced to describe potential usage errors, as well as business logic errors and exceptions. This important information is needed to drive the design of your system, so don't forget to model it in your use cases.

9. **Don't get hung up on <<include>> and <<extend>> associations.** I'm not quite sure what happened, but I've always thought the proper use of include and extend associations, as well as uses and extends associations in older versions of the Unified Modeling Language (UML), were never described well. As a result, use case modeling teams had a tendency to argue about the proper application of these associations, wasting an incredible amount of time on an interesting, but minor, portion of the overall modeling technique. I even worked at one organization that went so far as to outlaw the use of the <<include>> and <<extend>> stereotypes, an extreme solution that had to be reversed after a few weeks when the organization realized it still needed these concepts, even though the organization hadn't come to a full agreement as to their proper use. Anyway, I believe Section 6.1.2 does a good job explaining how to apply these associations effectively.

10. **Use cases drive user documentation.** The purpose of user documentation is to describe how to work with your system. Each use case describes a series of actions taken by actors using your system. In short, use cases contain the information from which you can start writing your user documentation. For example, the

"how to enroll in a seminar" section of your system's user documentation could be written using the "Enroll in Seminar" use case as its base.

11. **Use cases drive presentations.** Part of software development is communicating your work efforts with project stakeholders, resulting in the occasional need to give presentations. Because use cases are written from the point-of-view of your users, they contain valuable insight into the type of things your users are likely to want to hear about in your presentations. In other words, use cases often contain the logic from which to develop presentation scripts.

6.2 Sequence Diagrams: From Use Cases to Classes

Sequence diagrams (Rumbaugh, Jacobson, and Booch, 1999) are used to model the logic of usage scenarios. A usage scenario is exactly what its name indicates—the description of a potential way your system is used. The logic of a usage scenario may be part of a use case, perhaps an alternate course. It may also be one entire pass through a use case, such as the logic described by the basic course of action or a portion of the basic course of action, plus one or more alternate scenarios. The logic of a usage scenario may also be a pass through the logic contained in several use cases. For example, a student enrolls in the university, and then immediately enrolls in three seminars. Figure 6-7 models the basic course of action for the "Enroll in Seminar" use case. Sequence diagrams model the flow of logic within your system in a visual manner, enabling you both to document and validate your logic, and are commonly used for both analysis and design purposes.

Sequence diagrams enable you to visually model the logic of your system.

The boxes across the top of the diagram represent classifiers or their instances, typically use cases, objects, classes, or actors. Because you can send messages to both objects and classes, objects respond to messages through the invocation of an operation, and classes do so through the invocation of static operations, it makes sense to include both on

Objects, classes, and actors are depicted in sequence diagrams.

DEFINITIONS

Major user interface element. A large-grained item, such as a screen, HTML page, or report.

Minor user interface element. A small-grained item, such as a user input field, menu item, list, or static text field.

Supplementary specification. An artifact where all requirements not contained in your use case model, user interface model, or domain model are documented.

sequence diagrams. Because actors initiate and take an active part in usage scenarios, they are also included in sequence diagrams. Objects have labels in the standard UML format "name: ClassName," where "name" is optional (objects that haven't been given a name on the diagram are called anonymous objects). Classes have labels in the format "ClassName," and actors have names in the format "Actor Name"—both UML standards as well. For example, in Figure 6-7, you see the Student actor has the name "A Student" and is labeled with the stereotype <<actor>>. The instance of the major UI element representing "UI32 Seminar Selection Screen," is an anonymous object with the name ":SeminarSelector" and the stereotype <<UI>>. The "Student" class is indicated on the diagram, the box with the name "Student," because the static message "isEligible(name, studentNumber)" is sent to it. More on this later. The instance of "Student" was given a name "theStudent" because it is used in several places as a parameter in a message, whereas the instance of the "StudentsFees" class didn't need to be referenced anywhere else in the diagram and, thus, could be anonymous.

The dashed lines hanging from the boxes are called object lifelines, representing the life span of the object during the scenario being modeled. The long, thin boxes on the lifelines are method-invocation boxes indicating that processing is being performed by the target object/class to fulfill a message. The X at the bottom of a method-invocation box is a UML convention to indicate that an object has been removed from memory, typically the result of receiving a message with the stereotype of <<destroy>>.

Messages are indicated by labeled arrows, and return values by dashed and labeled arrows.

Messages are indicated as labeled arrows, when the source and target of a message is an object or class the label is the signature of the method invoked in response to the message. However, if either the source or target is a human actor, then the message is labeled with brief text describing the information being communicated. For example, the ":EnrollInSeminar" object sends the message "isEligibleToEnroll(theStudent)" to the instance of "Seminar." Notice how I include both the method's name and the name of the parameters, if any, passed into it. Figure 6-7 also indicates that the Student actor provides information to the ":SecurityLogon" object via the messages labeled "name" and "student number" (these really aren't messages; they are actually user interactions). Return values are optionally indicated as using a dashed arrow with a label indicating the return value. For example, the return value "theStudent" is indicated coming back from the "Student" class as the result of invoking a message, whereas no return value is indicated as the result of sending the message "isEligibleToEnroll(theStudent)" to "seminar." My style is not to indicate the return values when it's obvious what is being returned, so I don't clutter my sequence diagrams (as you can see, sequence diagrams get complicated fairly quickly).

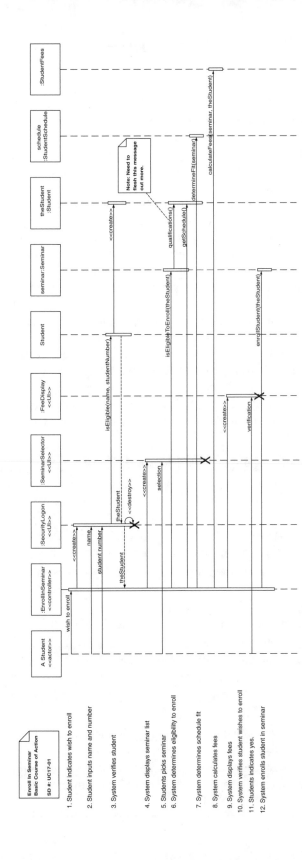

Figure 6-7.

A UML sequence diagram for the basic course of action for Figure 6-2

Messages fulfill the logic of the steps of the use case, summarized down the left-hand side of the diagram. Notice how the exact wording of the use case steps isn't used because the steps are often too wordy to fit nicely on a diagram. What is critical is that the step numbers correspond to those in the use case and that the general idea of the step is apparent to the reader of the diagram.

Stereotypes may be applied to actors, objects, classes, and messages on sequence diagrams.

Notice the use of stereotypes throughout the diagram. For the boxes, I applied the stereotypes <<actor>>, <<controller>>, and <<UI>> indicating that they represent an actor, a controller class, or a user interface (UI) class, respectively. For now, a controller class is a placeholder for one or more classes that would be fleshed out during design (Chapter 7) to implement the business logic of your system. As you see in Chapter 7, you want to layer your system, separating your user interface logic, business logic, system logic, and persistence logic away from each other. Stereotypes are also used on messages. Common practice on UML diagrams is to indicate creation and destruction messages with the stereotypes of <<create>> and <<destroy>>, respectively. For example, you see that the ":SecurityLogon" object is created in this manner (actually, this message would likely be sent to the class that would then result in a return value of the created object, so I cheated a bit). This object later

---

DEFINITIONS

Anonymous object. An object appearing on the diagram that hasn't been given a name; instead, the label is simply an indication of the class, such as ": Invoice."

Classifier. A mechanism that describes behavioral or structural features. Classifiers include use cases, classes, interfaces, and components.

Lifeline. Represents, in a sequence diagram, the life span of an object during an interaction.

Method. Something a class or object does. A method is similar to a function or procedure in structured programming and is often referred to as an operation or member function in object development.

Message-invocation box. The long, thin, vertical boxes that appear on sequence diagrams, which represent invocation of an operation on an object or class.

Signature. The combination of the name, parameter names (in order), and name of the return value (if any) of a method.

Static method. A method that operates at the class level, potentially on all instances of that class.

Stereotype. A stereotype denotes a common usage of a modeling element. Stereotypes are used to extend the UML in a consistent manner.

destroys itself in a similar manner, presumably when the window is closed. In Java and C++, methods that create objects are called *constructors*, and in C++, methods that destroy objects are called *destructors* (Java automatically manages memory, whereas C++ doesn't, so Java doesn't require destructor methods).

I used a UML note; notes are basically free-form text that can be placed on any UML diagram, to provide a header for the diagram, indicating its title and identifier (as you may have noticed, I give unique identifiers to everything). Notes are depicted as a piece of paper with the top-right corner folded over. I also used a note to indicate future work that needs to be done, either during analysis or design; in this diagram, the "qualifications()" message likely represents a series of messages sent to the student object. Common UML practice is to anchor a note to another model element with a dashed line when appropriate, as you see in Figure 6-7, with the note attached to the message.

Notes can be used to add free-form text to any UML diagram.

When I developed the sequence diagram of Figure 6-7, I made several decisions that could potentially affect my other models. For example, as I modeled Step 10, I made the assumption (arguably, a design decision) that the fee display screen also handled the verification by the student that the fees were acceptable. This decision should be reflected by the user interface prototype, the topic of Section 6.5, and verified by my SMEs. Sequence diagramming is something you should be doing together with your SMEs, particularly sophisticated ones who understand how to develop models such as this. Also, as I was modeling Steps 2 and 3, I came to the realization that students should probably have passwords to get into the system. I brought this concept up with my SMEs and discovered I was wrong: the combination of name and student number is unique enough for our purposes and the university didn't want the added complexity of password management. This is an interesting decision that would be documented in the supplementary specification, likely as a business rule, because it is an operating policy of the university. By verifying this idea with my SMEs, instead of assuming I knew better than everyone else, I avoided an opportunity for goldplating and, thus, reduced the work my team would need to do to develop this system.

Verify modeling decisions with your SMEs.

Regarding style issues for sequence diagramming, I prefer to draw messages going from left-to-right and return values from right-to-left, although that doesn't always work with complex objects/classes. I justify the label on messages and return values, so they are closest to the arrowhead. As mentioned earlier, I prefer not to indicate return values on sequence diagrams to simplify the diagrams whenever possible. However, equally valid is to decide always to indicate return values, particularly when your sequence diagram is used for design instead of analysis (I like my analysis diagrams to be as simple as possible and my design diagrams

Understand the basic logic during analysis, flesh out the details during design.

DEFINITIONS

C++. A hybrid object-oriented programming language that adds object-oriented features to the C programming language.

Constructor. A method, typically a static one, whose purpose is to instantiate and, optionally, initialize an object.

Controller. A class that implements business/domain logic, coordinating several objects to perform a task.

Destructor. A method whose purpose is to remove an object completely from memory.

Goldplating. The addition of extraneous features to a system.

Java. An object-oriented programming language based on the concept of "write once, run anywhere."

Note. A modeling construct for adding free-form text to the UML diagrams.

---

to be as thorough as possible). During analysis, my goal is to understand the logic and to ensure I have it right. During design, I then flesh out the exact details, as the note reminds me to do with the "qualifications()" message in Figure 6-7. I also prefer to layer the sequence diagrams from left-to-right. I indicate the actors, then the controller class(es), and then the user interface class(es), and, finally, the business class(es). During design, you probably need to add system and persistence classes, which I usually put on the right-most side of sequence diagrams. Laying your sequence diagrams in this manner often makes them easier to read and also makes it easier to find layering logic problems, such as user interface classes directly accessing persistence classes (more on this in Chapter 7).

Interesting to note is the style of logic changed part way through the sequence diagram of Figure 6-7. The user interface was handling some of the basic logic at first—particularly the login—yet for selecting the seminar, and then verifying it, the controller class did the work. This is actually a design issue. I wouldn't get too worked up over this but, as always, I suggest choosing one style for now and sticking to it.

Although Figure 6-7 models the logic, the basic course of action for the "Enroll in Seminar" use case, how would you go about modeling alternate courses? The most common way to do so is to create a single sequence diagram for each alternate course, as you see depicted in Figure 6-8. This diagram models only the logic of the alternate course, as you can tell by the numbering of the steps on the left-hand side of the diagram. The header note for the diagram indicates that it is an alternate course of action. Also notice how the ID of this diagram includes that this is alternate course *B*, yet another modeling rule of thumb I have found useful over the years.

You may have heard terms such as *dynamic modeling* and *static modeling* bantered about by other developers familiar with object-oriented modeling techniques. You may even have heard arguments about the merits of each style. Dynamic modeling techniques focus on identifying the behavior within your system. These techniques include sequence diagramming and activity diagramming (both of which are described in this chapter) and collaboration diagramming, described in Chapter 7. Static modeling focuses on the static aspects of your system, including the classes, their attributes, and the associations between classes. Class models, described in this chapter, are the main artifact of static modeling, as are persistence models, which are described in Chapter 7. Both dynamic and static modeling techniques are required to specify an object-oriented system adequately, which makes the "dynamic modeling versus static modeling" debates questionable at best.

TIP

Sequence Diagrams Are Dynamic

The sequence diagram of Figure 6-8 is simpler than that of Figure 6-7; this is generally the case of alternate courses. I modeled the return value from the "isEligibleToEnroll(theStudent)" message because this is what causes the alternate course to occur in the first place. This arguably points to the need always to model return values in your sequence diagrams. I still prefer to keep my diagrams as simple as possible, though, so I model them only when the information is vital to my understanding of the logic. I also chose to show the ineligibility notice as its own user- interface element, once again bordering on a design decision that would need to be reflected in the user interface prototype. I also modeled that the prerequisites list is displayed as part of the seminar details user interface element, which is more than the use case currently calls for. This implies that I should verify the change with my SMEs because I have effectively increased the requirements although, by doing so, I have likely indicated an opportunity for both reuse and an overall simplification of the poten-

Figure 6-8.
A UML sequence diagram for an alternate course

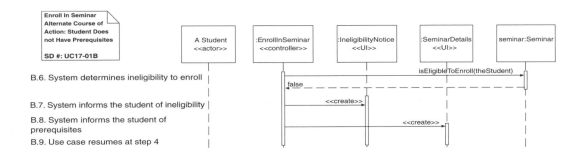

tial design. As you can see with this example, the line between analysis and design is fuzzy with object-oriented development; experienced developers new to objects can take time to get used to this. Finally, I left the "Student" actor in the diagram, even though no direct interaction occurs at this point because this actor is referred to in the steps of the use case.

6.2.1 *How to Draw Sequence Diagrams*

The following steps describe the fundamental tasks of sequence diagramming, tasks you perform in an iterative manner.

1. **Identify the scope of the sequence diagram.** Begin by identifying what you are modeling. Is it the basic course of action for a single use case? A single alternate course? The combination of the basic course of action and one or more alternate courses? Logic from several use cases? Once you identify the scope of your diagram, you should add a label at the top, using a note, indicating an appropriate title for the diagram and a unique identifier for it. You may also want to include the date and also the names of the authors of the diagram.

2. **List the use case steps down the left-hand side.** I like to start a sequence diagram by writing a summary of the original use case text in the left-hand margin, as you saw in Figure 6-7 and Figure 6-8. This logic is what you are modeling, so you might as well have it on your diagram from the start. Rosenberg and Scott (1999) point out this also provides valuable traceability information between your use cases and sequence diagrams.

3. **Introduce boxes for each actor.** Introduce a box for each actor across the top of your diagram. I prefer to put actors that represent humans and organizations on the left-hand side and those that represent external systems on the right-hand side. Label each box with the <<actor>> stereotype.

4. **Introduce controller class(es).** My style is to introduce at least one controller class whose purpose is to mediate the logic described by the use case steps. This business logic typically doesn't belong in your user interface classes. Instead, it should be encapsulated by business classes (a controller class is a type of business class). Later, during design, you will likely refactor this logic into one or more classes to reflect issues with your chosen implementation technologies. Label each box with the <<controller>> stereotype.

5. **Introduce a box for each major UI element.** Major user interface elements, and minor ones for that matter, are implemented as classes in object-oriented systems. Therefore, they should be modeled as a box in a sequence diagram. My style is to list the UI elements to the immediate right of the controller class(es). Label each box with the <<UI>> stereotype.[1]

6. **Introduce a box for each included use case.** Although I didn't include this in an example, included use cases are treated just like objects. Mark them with the stereotype <<use case>> and give them a name in the format "id:Use case name," such as "UC17:Enroll in Seminar." To indicate that the use case is being invoked by a step, I simply send it a message with the stereotype of <<uses>>.

7. **Identify appropriate messages for each use case step.** Going one step at a time, walk through the process logic for the scenario, identifying each message that needs to be sent and its destination. The sequencing of the messages is implied on the diagram by the order of the messages themselves, starting at the top-left corner of the diagram. When you are drawing sequence diagrams, the important task is to get the logic right; you effectively flesh out your logic as you identify messages for each step. Also, don't forget that an object or class can send a message to itself, as you saw in Figure 6-7.

8. **Add a method-invocation box for each invocation of a method.** Every time an object or class receives a message, a method is invoked. To represent this, you should include a method-invocation box to the lifeline of the target. The incoming message will be received at the top of the box and, to fulfill the logic of the step, you may find the target needs to send messages to other objects and classes, which, in turn, invoke methods on those new targets. From the box, messages may be sent to other objects that, in turn, invoke methods within those targets. Eventually, this method will complete; therefore, the method invocation box "stops" and, possibly, a value is returned to the original sender of the message.

---

[1] Stereotypes in the UML typically begin with a lowercase letter. However, because I am using the term "UI" for the stereotype label, instead of "user interface," I have chosen to capitalize it. Also, in Chapter 3, I was using the stereotype <<Actor>> instead of <<actor>> on the Class Responsibility Collaborator (CRC) cards. I did this for two reasons. First, CRC models are not part of the UML and, therefore, don't have comply with UML practices. Second, I did it to show you the world won't end if you break the rules a bit. I've lot track of the amount of time, easily in the hundreds of hours, that I've wasted in conversations during modeling sessions over nitpicky issues such as this. Your goal is to model your system accurately in a way that is understandable to the people involved; whether you use <<Actor>> or <<actor>> as a stereotype is barely relevant when the big picture is taken into consideration.

9. **Add destruction messages where appropriate.** At the end of a method invocation, the target object may be destroyed. This is common for transitory objects such as user interface elements and for business objects deleted as the result of an operation. Therefore, a message with the stereotype <<destroy>> should be sent to the object and the method-invocation box labeled with an *X* at its bottom. Sometimes an object will destroy itself, as you saw in Figure 6-7.

10. **Add your business classes and objects.** As you identify messages you also need to identify targets for those messages, targets that will inevitably be classes or objects. The appropriate classes (objects are instances of classes) should be in your conceptual model (if not, then you need to add them). Use the class names from your conceptual model for the names of the classes in your sequence diagrams (any business class that appears on a sequence diagram should also appear in your conceptual model). For now, don't worry too much whether an object or a class should be the target of a message. You can always rework your diagram if you get it wrong at first. The important thing is to get the fundamental idea correct, and then you can go back to perfect it later. Remember to layer your classes and objects as described in previous steps. Also, you may find you need several instances of the same class on a single sequence diagram. For example, had I modeled a scenario in which a student enrolled in three different seminars, then I would have included three seminar objects in the diagram.

11. **Update your class model.** Because you are sequence diagramming, you will identify new responsibilities for classes and objects, and, sometimes, even for new classes. Remember, each message sent to a class invokes a static method/operation on that class, an operation that should appear on your class model. Similarly, each message sent to an object invokes an operation on that object, an operation that should also appear on your class model. Sequence diagramming is a significant source for identifying behavior to be modeled on your class model, the subject of Section 6.3.

12. **Update your user interface model.** As you work through the logic of each scenario, you may discover you are missing features in your user interface or you have modeled some features inappropriately. When you discover this, you should work together with your SMEs to identify the proper way for your user interface to work, the topic of Section 6.5.

13. **Update your use case model.** As you are sequence diagramming, you may find errors in your original use case logic, errors that need to be fixed on both your sequence diagram(s) and in your use case(s). As always, validate any use case changes with your SMEs first.

6.2.2 Why and When Should You Draw Sequence Diagrams?

You want to draw sequence diagrams for several reasons. First and foremost, sequence diagrams are a great way to validate and flesh out your logic (not that this should stop you from use case scenario testing, as described in Chapter 4). Second, sequence diagrams are a great way to document your design, at least from the point-of-view of use cases. Third, sequence diagrams are a great mechanism for detecting bottlenecks in your design. By looking at what messages are being sent to an object, and by looking at roughly how long it takes to run the invoked method, you quickly get an understanding of where you need to change your design to distribute the load within your system. In fact, some CASE tools even enable you to simulate this aspect of your software. Finally, sequence diagrams often give you a feel for which classes in your application are going to be complex, which, in turn, is an indication you may need to draw state chart diagrams for those classes (UML state chart diagrams are described in Chapter 8).

Sequence diagrams are used to test your design and to document use cases.

6.2.3 How to Document Sequence Diagrams

I generally don't develop documentation specific to sequence diagrams. Sequence diagrams provide a bridge between your use cases and your class model. Everything that is shown in a sequence diagram is documented in these models. For example, the steps depicted by the sequence diagram are documented by your use cases. The boxes across the top of the diagram are documented.

6.2.4 A Good Thing to Know About Sequence Diagrams

You need to do at least one sequence diagram for each use case and, often, you will create several for each use case. Because the diagram should match the narrative flow of the use case, Rosenberg and Scott

---

DEFINITION

Transitory object. An object that is not saved to permanent storage.

DEFINITION

Computer-aided system engineering (CASE) tool. Software that supports the creation of models of software-oriented systems.

(1999) point out that if you are having problems getting started drawing sequence diagrams for a use case, then you likely wrote the use case incorrectly and should reconsider its logic. They also point out that sequence diagramming is the primary vehicle for allocating behavior.

During analysis, you will begin to add solution-space objects to the problem-domain objects (from your CRC model), including controller and user interface objects. Furthermore, during design, Rosenberg and Scott (1999) also point out that you will infrastructure objects such as system and persistence objects, scaffolding, and other helper objects into your models.

6.3 Conceptual Modeling: Class Diagrams

Class models (Rumbaugh, Jacobson, and Booch, 1999) are the mainstay of object-oriented analysis and design. Before the UML, most methodologies called them object models instead of class models.[2] Class models are created by using many of the modeling concepts and notations discussed in Chapter 5. Class models show the classes of the system, their interrelationships (including inheritance, aggregation, and association), and the operations and attributes of the classes. During analysis, you use class models to represent your conceptual model, an expansion of the domain model described in Chapter 3, because it shows greater detail and a wider range of detail. Conceptual models are used to depict your detailed understanding of the problem space for your system. During design, this model is evolved further to include classes that address the solution space, as well as the problem space.

The easiest way to begin conceptual modeling is to use your domain model as a base. In this case, you will take your Class Responsibility Collaborator (CRC) model (Beck and Cunningham, 1989) and convert it directly into a UML class diagram. CRC models show the initial classes of a system, their responsibilities, and the basic relationships (in the form of a list of collaborators) between those classes. While a CRC model provides an excellent overview of a system, it doesn't provide the details

---

[2] In the original edition of this book, written in 1995, I argued for, and then used, the term "class model," instead of "object model," for the simple reason that you use them to model classes and their relationships, not objects.

DEFINITIONS
Problem space. The scope of your business domain being addressed by your system.
Solution space. The problem space being addressed by your system plus the nondomain functionality required to implement your system.

needed to actually build it. Luckily, those details have been captured in the notes taken down by the scribe(s) during CRC modeling. Figure 6-9 depicts the CRC model we developed in Chapter 3, the "SecurityLogon" class identified in the sequence diagrams earlier has been introduced to CRC model, and Figure 6-10 depicts the UML class diagram that would be created based on that CRC model.

For each card in the CRC model, you create a concrete class in the class diagram, with the exception of cards that represent actors (actors exist in the real world). Notice how the names stayed the same (spaces were removed

Figure 6-9.
A CRC model for the university

Student <<Actor>>	
Provide information about self Request to enroll in seminar Request Transcript	Enroll in Seminar Transcript

Transcript <<UI>>	
See the prototype Get student info Get seminars student took Determine average mark Output self	Student Seminar Professor Enrollment Record

Enroll in Seminar <<UI>>	
See the prototype Enable seminar search Display seminar list Display seminar fees Display professor info	Seminar Professor

SecurityLogon <<UI>>	
See the prototype Request identifying info for student	Student

Professor	
Name Address Phone number Email address Salary Provide information Seminars instructing	Seminar

Seminar	
Name Seminar number Fees Waiting list Enrolled students Instructor Add student Drop student	Student Professor

Student	
Name Address Phone number Email address Student number Average mark received Validate identifying info Provide list of seminars taken	Enrollment Record

Enrollment Record	
Mark(s) received Average to date Final grade Student Seminar	Seminar

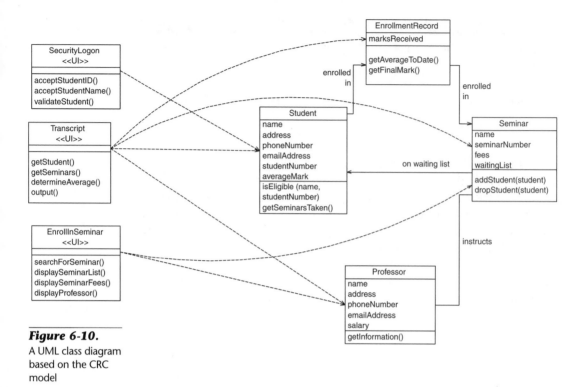

Figure 6-10.
A UML class diagram
based on the CRC
model

from the names to follow the naming convention of ClassName). Next, the
collaborators on CRC cards indicate the need for an association, aggregation
association, or dependency between classes. I modeled dependencies
between user interface classes and the business classes with which they col-

*Collaborations from
a user interface
class implies a
dependency, whereas
collaborations
from business/
domain classes
imply either
association or
aggregation
between the classes.*

laborate because user interface classes are transitory in nature, implying the
associations they are involved with are transitory and, hence, should be
modeled as dependencies. Whenever a collaboration occurred between two
business classes, I modeled an association for now. As you see later, these
associations may, in fact, prove to be aggregation associations but, for now, it
is good enough simply to have modeled the line.

Consider the associations modeled in Figure 6-10. The "waiting list"
association between "Seminar" and "Student" was added, modeling the
similarly named responsibility on the "Seminar" CRC card. I could have
added an attribute in the "Seminar" class called "waitingList" but,
instead, chose to model it as an association because that is what it actually represents: that seminar objects maintain a waiting list of zero or
more student objects. In Chapter 5, I showed that associations are implemented as a combination of attributes and operations so, frankly, you
may as well add the attribute to the model now and get it over with. The
"waiting list" association is unidirectional because there was neither a

corresponding collaborator indicated by the "Student" card nor did a responsibility indicate that the "Student" card had knowledge of being on a waiting list. I modeled an "enrolled in" association between the "Student" and "EnrollmentRecord" classes to support the similarly named responsibility on the "Student" CRC card. For this association, it appears student objects know what enrollment records they are involved with, recording the seminars they have taken in the past, as well as the seminars in which they are currently involved. This association would be traversed to calculate their student object's average mark and to provide information about seminars taken. There is also an "enrolled in" association between "EnrollmentRecord" and "Seminar" to support the capability for student objects to produce a list of seminars taken. The "instructs" association between the "Professor" class and the "Seminar" class is bidirectional because professor objects know what seminars they instruct (the Seminar's instructing responsibility) and seminar objects know who instructs them (the Instructor responsibility).

Associations are bidirectional only if they need to be traversed in both directions.

Other than the previously noted exceptions, the responsibilities on the CRC cards were modeled either as attributes or methods of the corresponding classes. The "Student" class is interesting because I chose to model the "Average mark received" responsibility as an attribute and not a method. How this responsibility is actually implemented is a design decision, one I don't need to make now. I have made a good guess as to how to implement this responsibility and moved on to other issues. It is too early in the modeling process to worry about nitpicky issues like this: The "Student" class could go away, based on another design decision (unlikely, but…), so why invest a lot of effort getting the details right when close enough works just as well? My style is to name attributes and methods using the formats attributeName and methodName(parameterName), respectively, which happen to be the common naming conventions for both Java (Vermeulen et al., 2000) and C++.

Responsibilities are usually modeled as attributes or methods.

Also notice, in Figure 6-10, how I haven't modeled the visibility of the attributes and methods to any great extent. Visibility is an important issue during design but, for now, it can be ignored. Also notice, I haven't defined the full method signatures for the classes. Yes, I have indicated the parameters, but not their type. And I haven't indicated the return value from each method either, another task I typically leave to design.

Now consider the user interface classes. I didn't bother to list the attributes because they are modeled well enough by the prototype and

Modeling user interface classes on class diagrams often adds a lot of clutter without adding much useful information.

eventual user interface design. The purpose of models is to describe your system adequately, rarely to describe it thoroughly. Yes, I could create detailed classes for each UI class in my model, but what value would that be? It sounds like a lot of work for little return, particularly when more than enough details are in the user interface model already. Also, as you can see in Figure 6-10, the UI classes have made quite a mess of the diagram, requiring the modeling of a lot of dependencies that add significant clutter without communicating much valuable information. This information could be better recorded as part of your user interface model; a simple spreadsheet listing each major UI element and the business classes on which they are dependent should be sufficient.

Figure 6-11 presents a revised version of Figure 6-10; the user interface classes have been removed and the multiplicity of the associations have been modeled. Based on what the SMEs tell you and on the information contained in the notes your scribe(s) took as part of requirements gathering, you should be able to make educated guesses at the multiplicities of each association. In Figure 6-11, I was able to determine with certainty, based on this information, the multiplicities for all but one association and, for that one, I marked it with a note to myself. Notice my use of question marks in the note. As mentioned in Chapter 5, my style is to mark unknown information on my diagrams this way to remind myself that I need to look into it.

Model complex or important concepts on your UML diagrams using OCL.

In Figure 6-11, I also modeled a UML constraint, in this case "{ordered FIFO}," on the association between "Seminar" and "Student." The basic idea is that students are put on the waiting list on a first-come, first-out (FIFO) basis. In other words, the students are put on the waiting list in order. UML constraints are used to model complex and/or important information accurately in your UML diagrams. UML constraints are modeled using the format "{constraint description}" format, where the constraint description may be in any format, including predicate calculus. Fowler and Scott (1997) suggest that you focus on readability and understandability and, therefore, suggest using an informal description. Constraints are described in further detail in Section 6.6.1.

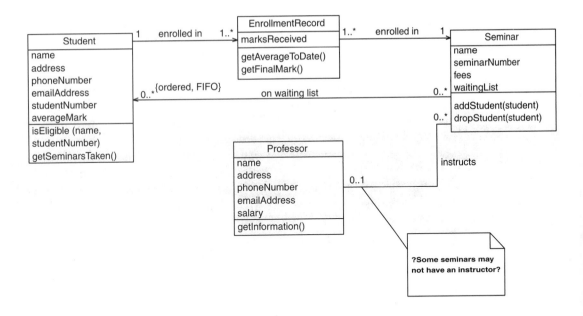

Figure 6-11.
The revised class diagram

Once you have converted the information contained in your CRC model into an initial UML class model, you are then ready to continue fleshing out your model with added detail. Class models contain a wealth of information and can be used for both the analysis and design of systems. To create and evolve a class model, you need to model:

- Classes
- Methods
- Attributes
- Associations
- Dependencies
- Inheritance relationships
- Aggregation associations
- Association classes

6.3.1 Modeling Classes, Attributes, and Methods

An object, as defined previously, is any person, place, thing, concept, event, screen, or report applicable to your system. Objects both know things (they have attributes) and they do things (they have methods). A class is a representation of an object and, in many ways, it is simply a template from which objects are created. Classes form the main building blocks of an object-oriented application. Two of the steps of CRC modeling included the finding of classes and the finding of responsibilities. Classes represent a collection of similar objects. For example, although thousands of students attend the university, you would only model one class, called "Student," which would represent the entire collection of students.

Classes are modeled as rectangles with three sections: the top section for the name of the class, the middle section for the attributes of the class, and the bottom section for the methods of the class. The initial classes of your model will be identified when you convert from your CRC model, as will the initial attributes and methods. To describe a class, you define its attributes and methods. Attributes are the information stored about an object (or at least information temporarily maintained about an object), while methods are the things an object or class does. For example, students have student numbers, names, addresses, and phone numbers. Those are all examples of the attributes of a student. Students also enroll in courses, drop courses, and request transcripts. Those are all examples of the things a student does, which get implemented (coded) as methods. You should think of methods as the object-oriented equivalent of functions and procedures.

An important aspect of analysis is to model your classes to the appropriate level of detail. Consider the "Student" class modeled in Figure 6-11, which has an attribute called "address." When you stop and think about it, addresses are complicated things. They have complex data, containing street and city information for example, and they potentially have behavior. An arguably better way to model this is depicted in Figure 6-12. Notice how the "Address" class has been modeled to include an attribute for each piece of data it comprises and two methods have been added: one to verify it is a valid address and one to output it as a label (perhaps for an envelope). By introducing the "Address" class, the "Student" class has become more cohesive. It no longer contains logic (such as validation) that is pertinent to addresses. The "Address" class could now be reused in other places, such as the "Professor" class, reducing your overall development costs. Furthermore, if the need arises to support students with several addresses—during the school term, a student may live in a different location than his permanent mailing address, such as a dorm—this is information the system may

<table>
<tr>
<td>

TIP

Use the Terminology of Your Users

</td>
<td>

Use the terminology of your users in all your models. The purpose of analysis is to understand the world of your users, not to foist your artificial, technical terms on them. Remember, they're the experts, not you. In short, avoid geek-speak.

</td>
</tr>
</table>

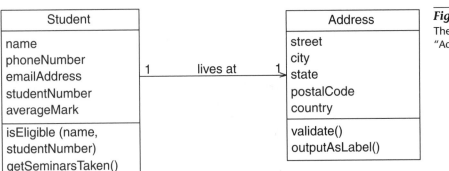

Figure 6-12.
The "Student" and "Address" classes

need to track. Having a separate class to implement addresses should make the addition of this behavior easier to implement.

Similarly, the "Seminar" class of Figure 6-11 is refactored into the classes depicted in Figure 6-13. Refactoring such as this is called *class normalization* (Ambler, 1998a), a process in which you refactor the behavior of classes to increase their cohesion and/or to reduce the coupling between classes. A seminar is an offering of a course; for example, there could be five seminar offerings of the course "CSC 148 Introduction to Computer Science." The attributes "name" and "fees" were moved to the "Course" class and "courseNumber" was introduced. The "getFullName()" method concatenates the course number, "CSC 148," and the course name, "Introduction to Computer Science," to give the full name of the course. This is called a *getter* method, an operation that returns a data value pertinent to an object. Although getter methods, and the corresponding *setter* methods, need to be developed for a class, they are typically assumed to exist and are therefore not modeled (particularly on conceptual class diagrams) so they do not clutter your models. Figure 6-14 depicts "Course" from Figure 6-13 as it would appear with its getter and setter methods modeled. Setters and getters are described in detail in Chapter 7.

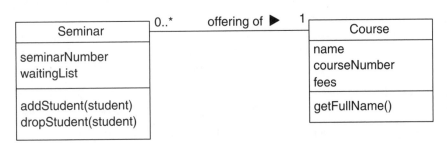

Figure 6-13.
Normalizing the "Seminar" class

Course
name courseNumber fees
getFullName() getCourseNumber() setCourseNumber(number) getFees() setFees(amount) getName() setName(name)

Figure 6-15 presents the class diagram that results[3] when Figures 6-11, 6-12, and 6-13 are combined. Notice how "Professor""now references the "Address" class, taking advantage of the work we did to improve the "Student" class.

6.3.2 Modeling Associations

Objects are often associated with, or related to, other objects. For example, as you see in Figure 6-15, several associations are between objects: Students are on waiting list for seminars, professors instruct seminars, seminars are an offering of courses, a professor lives at an address, and so on. Associations are modeled as lines connecting the two classes whose instances (objects) are involved in the relationship.

Identifying the multiplicities of an association is an important part of modeling it.

When you model associations in UML class diagrams, you show them as a thin line connecting two classes, which was illustrated in Figure 5-9. Associations can become quite complex; consequently, you can depict some things about them on your diagrams. Figure 5-9 demonstrated the common items to model for an association. You may want to refer to *The Unified Modeling Language Reference Manual* (Rumbaugh, Jacobson, and Booch, 1999) for a detailed discussion, including the role and cardinality on each end of the association, as well as a label for the association. The label, which is optional, although highly recommended, is typically one or two words describing the association. For example, in Figure 6-15, you see professors instruct seminars. However, it is not enough simply to know professors instruct seminars. How many seminars do professors instruct? None, one, or several? Furthermore,

---

[3] I have cheated a little and added the method "purchaseParkingPass()" to the "Professor" and "Student" classes, even though I didn't have requirements for this. You'll see why I added this method later in Section 6.3.4 when I discuss inheritance.

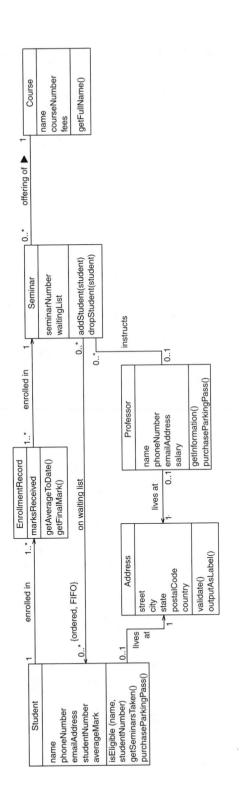

Figure 6-15.
Combined class
diagram

DEFINITIONS

Class normalization. The process by which you refactor the behavior within a class diagram in such a way as to increase the cohesion of classes while minimizing the coupling between them.

Cohesion. The degree of relatedness within an encapsulated unit (such as a component or a class).

Coupling. The degree of dependence between two items. In general, it is better to reduce coupling wherever possible.

Getter. A method to obtain the value of a data attribute, or to calculate the value, of an object or class.

Setter. A method that sets the value of a data attribute of an object or class. Also known as a *mutator*.

associations are often two-way streets: not only do professors instruct seminars, but also seminars are instructed by professors. This leads to questions such as: how many professors can instruct any given seminar and is it possible to have a seminar with no one instructing it? The implication is you also need to identify the cardinality and optionality of an association. Cardinality represents the concept of "how many," and optionality represents the concept of "whether you must have something." Important to note is the UML chooses to combine the concepts of optionality and cardinality into the single concept of multiplicity. The multiplicity of the association is labeled on either end of the line, one multiplicity indicator for each direction (Table 6-1 summarizes the potential multiplicity indicators you can use).

Another option for associations is to indicate the direction in which the label should be read. This is depicted using a filled triangle, an example of which is shown on the "offering of" association between the "Seminar" and "Course" classes of Figure 6-15. This marker indicates that the association should be read "a seminar is an offering of a course," instead

TIP

Always Indicate the Multiplicity

For each class involved in an association, there is always a multiplicity for it. When the multiplicity is one and one only (for example, one and one only person may be President of the United States at any given time), then it is common practice not to indicate the multiplicity and, instead, to assume it is "1." I believe this is a mistake. If the multiplicity is "1," then indicate it as such. When something is left off a diagram, I can't tell if that is what is meant or if the modeler simply hasn't gotten around to working on that aspect of the model yet. I always assume the modeler hasn't done the work yet.

Table 6-1. UML multiplicity indicators

Indicator	Meaning
0..1	Zero or one
1	One only
0..*	Zero or more
1..*	One or more
n	Only n (where n > 1)
0..n	Zero to n (where n > 1)
1..n	One to n (where n > 1)

of "a course is an offering of a seminar." Direction markers should be used whenever it isn't clear which way a label should be read. My advice, however, is if your label is not clear, then you should consider rewording it. Refer to Figure 5-9 for an overview of modeling associations in UML class diagrams.

At each end of the association, the role, the context an object takes within the association, may also be indicated. My style is to model the role only when the information adds value, for example, knowing the role of the "Student" class is "enrolled student" in the "enrolled in" association doesn't add anything to the model. I indicate roles when it isn't clear from the association label what the roles are, if there is a recursive association, or if there are several associations between two classes. In Figure 6-16, I have evolved our class diagram to include two associations between "Professor" and "Seminar." Not only do professors instruct seminars, they also assist in them. When several associations exist between two classes, something that is relatively common, you often find you need to indicate the roles to understand the associations fully. In this case, I indicated the roles professors take, but not seminars, because the role of the seminar objects weren't very interesting. Both roles are modeled for the "mentors" recursive association that the "Professor" class has because it is interesting to know that the mentoring professor is called an advisor and the mentored professor is called an associate.

Model roles when an association is recursive or when several associations exist between two classes.

Figure 6-16 is also interesting because it uses a UML contraint to indicate that a professor may instruct a given seminar, may assist with a seminar, or may not be involved in the seminar, but wouldn't be both an assistant and an instructor for the same seminar. The contraint description "NAND" represents the logical concept of "not and."

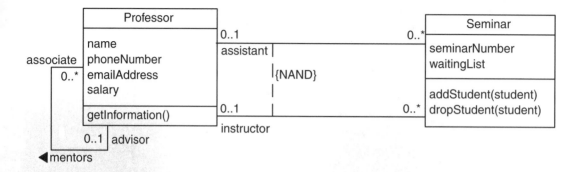

Figure 6-16.
Modeling roles in
associations

6.3.3 Modeling Dependencies

Dependency relationships are used to model transitory associations between
two classes. Transitory associations occur when one or both of the classes are
not persistent, in other words, their instances are not saved to permanent
storage. User interface classes are typically not persistent: you create the
screen or report object, work with it, and then discard/destroy it when you
no longer need it. Because these objects collaborate with other objects to fulfill their responsibilities, and because the only way an object can collaborate
with another is if it knows about it, then some sort of relationship must exist
between the two classes. In this case, you model this fact with a dependency
relationship, which, as you see in Figure 6-17, is depicted as a dashed arrow.
In this diagram, I chose to model the classes simply as boxes, instead of the
usual three-sectioned boxes indicating the name of the class, its attributes,
and its methods. As you saw in Chapter 5, both notations are acceptable
within the UML.

6.3.4 Introducing Reuse Between Classes via Inheritance

Similarities often exist between different classes. Very often two or more
classes will share the same attributes and/or the same methods. Because you

---

DEFINITIONS

Cardinality. Represents the concept "how many?" in associations.

Optionality. Represents the concept "do you need to have it?" in associations.

Multiplicity. The UML combines the concepts of cardinality and optionality
into the single concept of multiplicity.

Recursive association. An association in which the objects involved in it are
instances of the same class. For example, people marry people.

Figure 6-17.
Modeling
dependencies
between classes

don't want to have to write the same code repeatedly, you want a mechanism that takes advantage of these similarities. Inheritance is that mechanism. Inheritance models "is a" and "is like" relationships, enabling you to reuse existing data and code easily. When *A* inherits from *B*, we say *A* is the subclass of *B* and *B* is the superclass of *A*. Furthermore, we say we have "pure inheritance" when *A* inherits all the attributes and methods of *B*. The UML modeling notation for inheritance is a line with a closed arrowhead pointing from the subclass to the superclass.

In Figure 6-15, many similarities occur between the "Student" and "Professor" classes. Not only do they have similar attributes, but they also have similar methods. To take advantage of these similarities, I created a new class called "Person" and had both "Student" and "Professor" inherit from it, as you see in Figure 6-18. This structure would be called the "Person" inheritance hierarchy because "Person" is its root class. The "Person" class is abstract: Objects are not created directly from it, and it captures the similarities between the students and professors. Abstract classes are modeled with their names in italics, as opposed to concrete classes, classes from which objects are instantiated, whose names are in normal text. Both classes had a name, email address, and phone number, so these attributes were moved into "Person." The "purchaseParkingPass()" method was also common between the two classes, so that was also moved into parent class. By introducing this inheritance relationship to the model, I reduced the amount of work to be performed. Instead of implementing these responsibilities twice, they are implemented once, in the "Person" class, and reused by "Student" and "Professor."

An interesting aspect of Figure 6-18 is the association between "Person" and "Address." First, this association was pushed up to "Person" because both "Professor" and "Student" had a "lives at" association with

*Associations are
inherited.*

DEFINITIONS

Dependency relationship. A dependency relationship exists between Class *A* and *B* when instances of Class *A* interact with instances of Class *B*. Dependency relationships are used when no direct relationship (inheritance, aggregation, or association) exists between the two classes.

Persistence. The issue of how objects are permanently stored.

DEFINITIONS

Abstract class. A class that doesn't have objects instantiated from it.

Concrete class. A class that has objects instantiated from it.

Inheritance hierarchy. A set of classes related through inheritance. Also referred to as a *class hierarchy.*

Inheritance. The representation of an *is a, is like,* or *is kind of* relationship between two classes. Inheritance promotes reuse by enabling a subclass to benefit automatically from all the behavior it inherits from its superclass(es).

Root class. The top-most class in an inheritance hierarchy.

Subclass. If Class *B* inherits from Class *A,* we say *B* is a subclass of *A.*

Superclass. If Class *B* inherits from Class *A,* we say *A* is a superclass of *B.*

"Address." I could do this because, as I described in Chapter 5, associations are implemented by the combination of attributes and methods. Because attributes and methods can be inherited, any association they implemented can also be inherited by implication. It made sense to apply inheritance here because the associations represented the same concept: a person lives at an address (I was also lucky because the direction of the associations, as well as their multiplicities, were identical).

Another interesting aspect of Figure 6-18 is that although both "Professor" and "Student" had associations with "Seminar," I didn't choose to push this association up into "Person." The issue is that the semantics of the two associations are different. First, one association is unidirectional whereas the other is bidirectional, a good indication that they are significantly different. Second, the multiplicities are different, another good indication that the associations are different. Third, and most important, the two associations are completely different from one another. One represents the fact that professors instruct seminars, whereas the other one represents that students are on waiting lists to enroll in a seminar.

6.3.5 Modeling Aggregation Associations

Aggregation models "is part of" associations.

Sometimes an object is made up of other objects. For example, an airplane is made up of a fuselage, wings, engines, landing gear, flaps, and so on. A delivery shipment contains one or more packages. A team consists of two or more employees. These are all examples of the concept of aggregation, which represents "is part of" relationships. An engine is part of a plane, a package is part of a shipment, and an employee is part of a team.

Modeling aggregation associations, or composition associations that are simply stronger forms of aggregation, is similar conceptually to modeling

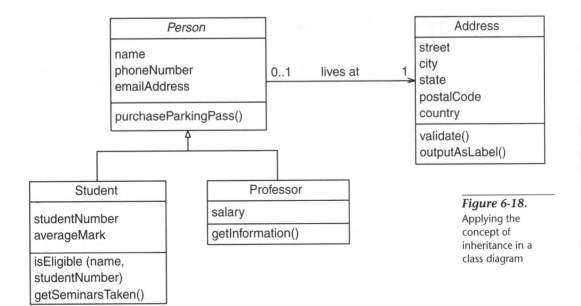

Figure 6-18.
Applying the concept of inheritance in a class diagram

associations. In Figure 6-19, you see a simple class model depicting the relationships between "Program," (a program is a collection of courses that lead to a degree) and the "Course" class. A course may be part of one or more programs—some courses such as "ARC 305 Medieval Gardening Tools" are for general interest only and are not part of a program—and any given program has one or more courses in it. Also notice how an association exists between "Program" and "Course" representing that some courses are recommended for a program, but are not officially offered as part of them (my SMEs told me this). For example, the course "CSC 148 Introduction to Computer Science" is recommended for the engineering, business, and physics programs within the university. It made sense to model this relationship with an association instead of an aggregation because it isn't true that a recommended course is part of a program.

| In the class diagram of Figure 6-15, I was lucky because I used similar names for these attributes in both classes: "name," "emailAddress," and "phoneNumber," respectively. However, you will often find situations where one class has an attribute called "name," whereas another one has "firstName," "middleInitial," and "lastName." You then need to decide whether these are, in fact, the same thing and, if they are, be prepared to refactor your existing model, and perhaps even code to reflect whichever approach to storing a person's name you accept. A similar issue can also occur with methods and associations. | **T I P**

Sometimes Opportunities for Inheritance Are Not So Obvious |

DEFINITIONS

Aggregation. The representation of "is part of" associations.

Composition. A strong form of aggregation in which the "whole" is completely responsible for its parts and each "part" object is only associated with the one "whole" object.

In Figure 6-20, I present an example using composition, modeling the fact that a product is composed of one or more components, and then, in turn, that a component may be composed of several subcomponents (you can have recursive aggregation and composition associations). Composition makes sense in both these cases because whatever you do to an instance of the whole, you are likely to also do to its parts. For example, if I sell a product by implication, I am selling its components. A good rule of thumb is that the composition form of aggregation is generally applicable whenever both classes represent physical items and aggregation makes sense.

6.3.6 *Modeling Association Classes*

Association classes may be useful during analysis, but need to be resolved during design.

Association classes, also called *link classes*, are used to model associations that have methods and attributes. "EnrollmentRecord" is modeled as an associative class in Figure 6-21, instead of being modeled as a "normal" class as in Figure 6-15. Associative classes are typically modeled during analysis, as you see in Figure 6-21, and then refactored into the original approach you see in Figure 6-15 during design. The reason this occurs is,

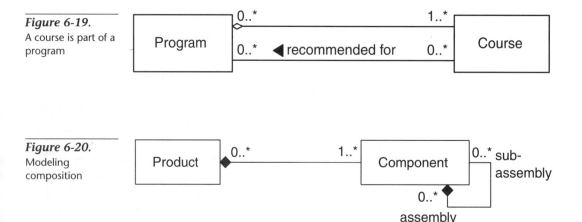

Figure 6-19.
A course is part of a program

Figure 6-20.
Modeling composition

> One of the following sentences should make sense: "A subclass IS A superclass" or "A subclass IS LIKE A superclass." For example, it makes sense to say a student *is a* person and a dragon *is like a* bird. It doesn't make sense to say a student is a vehicle or is like a vehicle, so the class "Student" likely shouldn't inherit from "Vehicle."
>
> **T I P**
>
> *Apply the*
> *Sentence Rule*

to date, at least to my knowledge, no mainstream programming language exists that supports the notion of associations that have responsibilities. Because you can directly build your software in this manner, I have a tendency to stay away from using association classes and, instead, resolve them during analysis, as you saw with my original approach. Yes, this is not a purist way to model, but it is programmatic. Nothing is wrong with using associative classes. I apply this concept on occasion; I just don't find many situations where it makes sense.

I want to take a minute to point out a potential problem with the "enrolled in" associations in both Figure 6-15 and Figure 6-21. I doubt they are truly unidirectional. In Chapter 3, a use case indicates that lists of students enrolled in a seminar are produced for professors. This tells me a need exists to traverse from "Seminar" objects to "Student" objects, indicating that these associations should be modeled bidirectionally.

6.3.7 Documenting Class Models

It isn't enough to draw a class diagram; it also needs to be documented. The bulk of the documentation work is documenting the details about a class, as well as the reasoning behind any trade-offs you have made. Here's what to do:

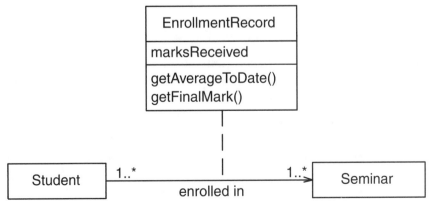

Figure 6-21.

An example of an associative class

TIP

If In Doubt,
Leave It Out

When deciding whether to use aggregation or composition over association, Craig Larman (1998) says it best: If in doubt, leave it out. The reality is that many modelers will agonize over when to use aggregation even though little difference exists among association, aggregation, and composition at the coding level, something you see in Chapter 8.

1. **Classes.** A class is documented by a sentence or two describing its purpose. You should also indicate whether the class is persistent or transitory, and if it has any aliases (other names it is called) for the class. Documenting the potential alias for a class is important because different people in an organization can call the same thing by different names. For example, do banks serve clients or customers? Do truckers drive trucks, vehicles, or lorries? Do children eat sweets, candies, or goodies? You want to ensure that everyone is using the same terminology. Also, include references to any applicable business rules or constraints contained in the supplementary specification.

2. **Attributes.** An attribute is best described with one or two sentences, its type should be indicated if appropriate, an example should be given if not unclear how the attribute is to be used, and a range of values should be defined, if appropriate. Also, include references to any applicable business rules or constraints contained in the supplementary specification.

3. **Methods.** Methods are documented with pseudo-code, also known as structured English, describing its logic. The parameters (if any) and the return value (if any) should be documented in a manner similar to attributes. The preconditions and postconditions for the method should be indicated so developers understand what the method does. Also, include references to any applicable business rules or constraints contained in the supplementary specification.

4. **Inheritance.** I generally don't document inheritance relationships. My belief is if you need to document why you have applied inheritance, then you probably shouldn't have applied it to start.

5. **Associations.** The most important information about associations—the label, multiplicities, and roles—already appear on the diagram. I typically also include a few sentences describing the association, as well as reference any applicable business rules or constraints contained in the supplementary specification.

6. **Aggregation and composition**. These are both documented exactly as you would associations.

6.3.8 Conceptual Class Modeling Tips

In this section, I want to share a collection of tips and techniques that I have found useful over the years to improve the quality of my conceptual class models.

1. **You don't have to get it perfect at the start.** I started the conceptual model by converting my Class Responsibility Collaborator (CRC) model into a UML class model. This was a good start, but I quickly found I needed to evolve the model as my analysis of the system moved forward. The point is I didn't get the model right at the start and that was okay. I didn't get the multiplicities on associations at the beginning, and I didn't even get all the classes to start. Many modelers will waste a lot of time at the beginning of conceptual modeling by focusing on one small aspect of the model and trying to get it right at first. It's also common to see modeling teams argue for hours about whether to use association, aggregation, or composition in a certain spot when little difference actually exists among the three options. I would rather pick one, move forward, and trust that, at some point in the future, it will become clearer which option to use as I understand the problem domain better.

2. **Start at your domain model.** Your CRC model contains important information that is relevant to your conceptual model, providing an excellent starting point.

3. **Evolve your class diagram via sequence diagrams.** Your sequence diagrams model the logic of your use cases, in particular, the critical business logic your system must support. As you develop your sequence diagrams, the topic of Section 6.2, you quickly flesh out the behaviors required of your classes.

DEFINITIONS

Postcondition. An expression of the properties of the state of an operation or use case after it has been invoked successfully.

Precondition. An expression of the constraints under which an operation or use case will operate properly.

4. **Focus on the problem space.** The purpose of analysis is to understand and model the problem space of your system, not the solution space. Optimization and technology issues shouldn't yet be taken into account within your models; this is what design is all about.

5. **Focus on fulfilling the requirements first.** Many modelers make the mistake of focusing on the application of inheritance relationships or an analysis pattern they have read about, instead of on analyzing their requirements model. Inheritance and analysis patterns are good things but, if your model doesn't reflect your problem space, then it doesn't really matter what fancy techniques you have applied, does it?

6. **Use meaningful names.** Your model elements should all have names that describe what they represent. Use full words. I prefer to see method names, such as "calculateInvoiceTotal()" as opposed to "calcInvTot()." Yes, the second name is easier to type because it's shorter, but is it easier to understand? Even worse are names such as "param1" and "x" because you have no idea what they represent.

7. **Perform object-oriented analysis.** Throughout this chapter, I describe proven techniques for performing object-oriented analysis (OOA), yet nowhere do you see me advise you to look at the existing database schema and create your models based on that design. This is a data-driven approach to development, not an object-oriented one, an approach that rarely results in high-quality software (Ambler, 1998b). Many organizations flounder with objects because they refuse to give up their old data-driven ways and/or they seek to recover their huge investment in existing legacy data models. Data modeling, more accurately called persistence modeling, is described in Chapter 7. Another related issue you run into, luckily one that is easier to overcome, is SMEs who describe requirements in terms of tables. Don't worry about it; just convert the concept to classes and move forward.

8. **Understand and effectively apply analysis patterns.** This is the topic of Section 6.7, so the only thing I say now is analysis patterns are good things.

9. **Class model in parallel with user interface prototyping.** As you develop your user interface prototype, you quickly discover that detailed attributes and operations need to be implemented by your classes. Never forget that object-oriented development is iterative—you will typically work on several models in parallel, working on each one a bit at a time.

6.4 Activity Diagramming

UML activity diagrams (Rumbaugh, Jacobson, and Booch, 1999) are used to document the logic of a single operation/method, a single use case, or the flow of logic of a business process. In many ways, activity diagrams are the object-oriented equivalent of flow charts and data-flow diagrams (DFDs) from structured development (Gane and Sarson, 1978). The activity diagram of Figure 6-22 depicts the business logic for how someone new to the university would enroll for the first time.

Activity diagrams are used to model the logic of a business process, use case, or method.

The filled circle represents the starting point of the activity diagram—effectively a placeholder—and the filled circle with a border represents the ending point. The rounded rectangles represent processes or activities that are performed. For the diagram of Figure 6-22, the activities map reasonably closely to use cases, although you will notice the "Enroll in Seminar(s)" activity would be the invocation of the "Enroll in Seminar" use case several times. Activities can also be much more finely grained, particularly if I had chosen to document the logic of a method instead of a high-level business process. The diamond represents decision points. In this example, the decision point had only two possible outcomes, but it could just as easily have had many more. The arrows represent transitions between activities, modeling the flow order between the various activities. The text on the arrows represent conditions that must be fulfilled to proceed along the transition and are always described using the format "[condition]."[4] The thick bars represent the start and end of potentially parallel processes—after you are successfully enrolled in the university, you must attend the mandatory overview presentation, as well as enroll in at least one seminar and pay at least some of your tuition.

Exiting from an activity is possible in several ways, as you see with the "Fill out Enrollment Forms" activity. If your forms are correctly filled out, then you can proceed to enroll in the university. If your forms aren't correct, however, then you need to obtain help, perhaps from a registrar, to fill them out correctly.

This activity diagram is interesting because it cuts across the logic of several of the use cases identified in Chapter 3. It is a good thing that use case models don't communicate the time ordering of processes well. For example, although the use case diagram presented in Figure 3-8 gives you a good idea as to the type of functionality this system performs, it offers no definitive answer as to the order in which these use cases might occur. The activity diagram of Figure 6-22 does, however. Once again, different models have different strengths and weaknesses.

---

[4] I suspect, in future versions of the UML, we will see conditions documented using the UML constraint notation discussed earlier.

Figure 6-22.
A UML activity
diagram for
enrolling in school
for the first time

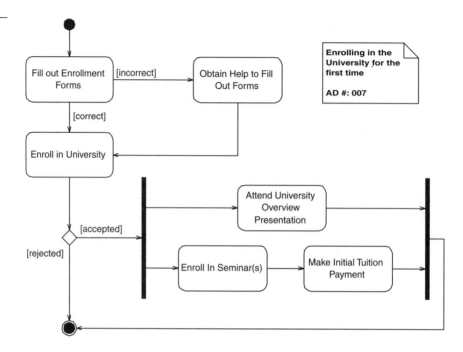

6.4.1 How to Draw Activity Diagrams

The following steps describe the fundamental tasks of activity diagramming, tasks you will perform in an iterative manner.

1. **Identify the scope of the activity diagram.** Begin by identifying what it is you are modeling. Is it a single use case? A portion of a use case? A business process that includes several use cases? A single method of a class? Once you identify the scope of your diagram, you should add a label at the top, using a note, indicating an appropriate title for the diagram and a unique identifier for it. You may also want to include the date and even the names of the authors of the diagram, as well.

2. **Add start and end points.** Every activity diagram has one starting point and one ending point, so you might as well add them right away. Fowler and Scott's (1997) style is to make ending points optional. Sometimes an activity is simply a dead end but, if this is the case, then there is no harm in indicating the only transition is to an ending point. This way, when someone else reads your diagram, he or she knows you have considered how to exit from these activities.

> ### DEFINITIONS
>
> *Activity diagram.* A UML diagram used to model high-level business processes or the transitions between states of a class (in this respect, activity diagrams are effectively specializations of state chart diagrams).
>
> *Data-flow diagram (DFD).* A diagram that shows the movement of data within a system among processes, entities, and data stores. Data-flow diagrams, also called process diagrams, were a primary artifact of structured/procedural modeling.
>
> *Flow chart.* A diagram depicting the logic flow of a single process or method. Flow charts were a primary artifact of structured/procedural modeling.
>
> *State chart diagram.* A UML diagram that describes the states an object may be in, as well as the transitions between states. Formerly referred to as a "state diagram" or "state-transition diagram."

3. **Add activities.** If you are modeling a use case, introduce an activity for each major step initiated by an actor (this activity would include the initial step, plus any steps describing the response of the system to the initial step). If you are modeling a high-level business process, introduce an activity for each major process, often a use case or a package of use cases. Finally, if you are modeling a method, then it is common to have an activity for this step in the code.

4. **Add transitions from the activities.** My style is always to exit from an activity, even if it is simply to an ending point. Whenever there is more than one transition out of an activity, you must label each transition appropriately.

5. **Add decision points.** Sometimes the logic of what you are modeling calls for a decision to be made. Perhaps something needs to be inspected or compared to something else. Important to note is that the use of decision points is optional. For example, in Figure 6-22, I could just as easily have modeled the accepted and rejected transitions straight out of the "Enroll in University" activity.

6. **Identify opportunities for parallel activities.** Two activities can occur in parallel when no direct relationship exists between them and they must both occur before a third activity can. For example, in Figure 6-22, you see it is possible to attend the overview or enroll in seminars in either order; it is just that both activities must occur before you can end the overall process.

T I P *Activities Have* *Entry and Exit* *Transitions*	Every activity has at least one entry transition—otherwise, you would never perform the activity, and at least one exit transition—otherwise you would never stop performing it. For each activity, I always ask myself: From where could I get into this and where can I go from here? By asking this question, it enables you to model the pertinent logic thoroughly.

6.4.2 How to Document Activity Diagrams

Activity diagrams are usually documented with a brief description of the activity and an indication of any actions taken during a process. Often, this is simply a reference to one or more use cases or methods. Also, for complex activities, it is common to document it using an activity diagram. In many ways, activity diagrams are simply a variation of the UML state chart diagrams, described in Chapter 7.

6.5 User Interface Prototyping

User interface prototyping is an iterative analysis technique in which users are actively involved in the mocking-up of the UI for a system. UI prototyping has two purposes: First, it is an analysis technique because it enables you to explore the problem space your system addresses. Second, UI prototyping enables you to explore the solution space of your system, at least from the point-of-view of its users, and provides a vehicle for you to communicate the possible UI design(s) of your system. In this chapter, I discuss the fundamentals of UI prototyping and, in Chapter 7, I present a collection of tips and techniques for designing effective user interfaces for object-oriented software.

As you see in the activity diagram depicted in Figure 6-23, four high-level steps are in the UI prototyping process:

- Determine the needs of your users
- Build the prototype
- Evaluate the prototype
- Determine if you are finished

6.5.1 Determining the Needs of Your Users

User interface modeling moves from requirements definition into analysis at the point you decide to evolve all or part of your essential user interface

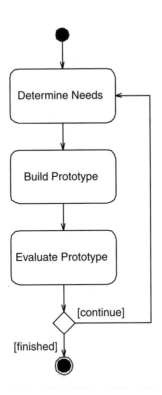

Figure 6-23.
The iterative steps
of prototyping

prototype, described in detail in Chapter 3, into a traditional UI prototype. *You begin by* This implies that you convert your handdrawings, flip-chart paper, and *choosing the* sticky notes into something a little more substantial. You begin this process *user interface* by making platform decisions. For example, do you intend to deploy your *platform.* system so it runs in an Internet browser, as an application with a Windows-based graphical user interface (GUI), as a cross-platform Java application, or as a mainframe-based set of "green screens"? Different platforms lead to different prototyping tools, for a browser-based application, you need to use an HTML-development tool, whereas a Java-based application would require a Java development tool and a different approach to the user interface design. User interface design is discussed in Chapter 7.

As you iterate through UI prototyping, you discover you need to *You discover the* update your defined requirements, including your use case model (Sec- *need to update* tion 6.1) and your essential user interface prototype (Chapter 3). You are *other models as* also likely to discover that information is missing from your domain *your UI prototype* model, a Class Responsibility Collaborator (CRC) model (Chapter 3), as *evolves.* well as from your conceptual model, a UML class model (Section 6.3). These models should be updated, as is appropriate, as you proceed with UI prototyping. Remember, object-oriented software development is an iterative process, so this is normal.

T I P *User Interface Prototyping Is Not a Substitute for Analysis and Design*	Although UI prototyping is an important part of analysis and design, it's not sufficient by itself. UI prototypes depict what will be built, but are unable to communicate adequately how they will be used (that is what use case models are good for). Furthermore, UI prototypes don't provide much indication as to the details of the business logic behind the screens, which is what sequence and activity diagrams are good at. And they aren't good at depicting the static structure of your software, which is where class models excel.

6.5.2 Building the Prototype

Using a prototyping tool or high-level language, you develop the screens, pages, and reports needed by your users. The best advice during this stage of the process is not to invest a lot of time in making the code "good" because chances are high you will scrap large portions of your prototype code when portions or all of your prototype fail the evaluation. With the user interface platform selected, you can begin converting individual aspects of your essential UI prototype into your traditional UI prototype. For example, with a browser-based platform, your major UI elements become HTML pages whereas, with a Windows-based platform, they would become windows or dialog boxes. Minor UI elements would become buttons, list boxes, custom list boxes, radio buttons, and so on as appropriate.

6.5.3 Evaluating the Prototype

After a version of the UI prototype is built, it needs to be evaluated by your SMEs to verify that it meets their needs. I've always found I need to address three basic questions during an evaluation:

- What is good about the UI prototype?
- What is bad about the UI prototype?
- What is missing from the UI prototype?

6.5.4 Determining If You Are Finished

After evaluating the prototype, you may find you need to scrap parts of it, modify parts, and even add brand-new parts. You want to stop the UI prototyping process when you find that the evaluation process is no longer generating any new ideas or it is generating a small number of not-so-important ideas. Otherwise, back to step one.

6.5.5 Good Things to Understand About Prototyping

Constantine and Lockwood (1999) provide valuable insight into the process of user interface prototyping. First, you cannot make everything simple. Sometimes your software will be difficult to use because the problem it addresses is inherently difficult. Your goal is to make your user interface as easy as possible to use, not simplistic. Second, they differentiate between the concepts of WYSIWYG, "What You See Is What You Get," and WYSIWYN, "What You See Is What You Need." Their point is that a good user interface fulfills the needs of the people who work with it. It isn't loaded with a lot of interesting but unnecessary, features. Third, consistency is important in your user interface. Inconsistent user interfaces lead to less usable software, more programming, and greater support and training costs. Fourth, small details can make or break your user interface. Have you ever used some software, and then discarded it for the product of a competitor because you didn't like the way it prints, saves files, or some other feature you simply found too annoying to use? I have. Although the rest of the software may have been great, that vendor lost my business because a portion of its product's user interface was deficient.

6.5.6 Prototyping Tips and Techniques

I have found the following tips and techniques have worked well for me in the past while UI prototyping:

1. **Work with the real users.** The best people to get involved in prototyping are the ones who will actually use the application when it is done. These are the people who have the most to gain from a successful implementation, and these are the people who know their own needs best.

2. **Use a prototyping tool.** Invest the money in a prototyping tool that enables you to put screens together quickly. Because you probably won't want to keep the prototype code you write—code written quickly is rarely worth keeping—you shouldn't be too concerned if your prototyping tool generates a different type of code than what you intend to develop in.

3. **Get your SMEs to work with the prototype.** Just as you want to take a car for a test drive before you buy it, your users should be

---

DEFINITIONS
WYSIWYG. What You See Is What You Get.
WYSIWYN. What You See Is What You Need.

able to take an application for a test drive before it is developed. Furthermore, by working with the prototype hands-on, they can quickly determine whether the system meets their needs. A good approach is to ask them to work through some use case scenarios using the prototype as if it were the real system.

4. **Understand the underlying business.** You need to understand the underlying business before you can develop a prototype that supports it. In other words, you need to base your UI prototype on your requirements. The more you know about the business, the more likely it is you can build a prototype that supports it.

5. **Don't spend a lot of time making the code good.** At the beginning of the prototyping process, you will throw away a lot of your work as you learn more about the business. Therefore, it doesn't make sense to invest a lot of effort in code you probably aren't going to keep anyway.

6. **Only prototype features that you can actually build.** Christmas wish lists are for kids. If you cannot possibly deliver the functionality, don't prototype it.

7. **Get an interface expert to help you design it.** User interface experts understand how to develop easy-to-use interfaces, whereas you probably don't. A general rule of thumb is, if you've never taken a course in human factors, you probably shouldn't be leading a UI prototyping effort.

8. **Explain what a prototype is.** The biggest complaint developers have about UI prototyping is their users say "That's great. Install it this afternoon." Basically, this happens because users don't realize a few months of work are left to do on the system. The reason this happens is simple: From your user's point-of-view, a fully functional application is a bunch of screens and reports tied together by a menu. Unfortunately, this is exactly what a prototype looks like. To avoid this problem, point out that your prototype is like a Styrofoam model that architects build to describe the design of a house. Nobody would expect to live in a Styrofoam model, so why would anyone expect to use a system prototype to get a job done?

9. **Avoid implementation decisions as long as possible.** Be careful about how you name user interface items. Strive to keep the names generic, so you don't imply too much about the implementation technology. For example, in Figure 6-2, I used the name "UI23 Security Login Screen," which implies I intend to use GUI technology to implement this major UI item. Had I

named it "UI23 Security Login," I wouldn't have implied an implementation technology.

6.6 Evolving Your Supplementary Specification

During analysis, you will evolve your understanding of the contents of your supplementary specification. This includes fleshing out the constraints, business rules, and nonfunctional requirements you identified during the requirements definition. As you evolve your other models, such as your activity diagrams and your conceptual class model, you are likely to discover that the information contained in your supplementary specification is not as detailed as it should be and, therefore, needs to be worked on more. Also, you will apply the information contained in your supplementary specification within your models, either on your diagrams using the UML's Object Constraint Language (OCL) or as references within the model documentation.

You will apply the information contained in your supplementary specification in your other models.

6.6.1 The Object Constraint Language

OCL (Warner and Kleppe, 1999) is a formal language, similar to structured English, used to express side-effect-free constraints within Unified Modeling Language models. OCL can appear on any UML diagram or in the supporting documentation describing a diagram. OCL can be used for a wide variety of purposes, including specifying the invariants of classes, preconditions and postconditions on operations, and constraints on operations. The reality is that a graphical model, such as a UML class diagram, isn't sufficient for a precise and unambiguous specification. You must describe additional constraints about the objects in the model, constraints that are defined in your supplementary specification. OCL can be used to model actual constraints, described in your supplementary specification, as well as business rules and functional requirements. Although this information is described in your supplementary specification using natural language your users understand, experience shows that natural language often results in ambiguities that, in turn, lead to defects in your software. Hence, the need for OCL.

OCL is used to depict constraints, preconditions, postconditions, and invariants within your UML models.

OCL statements are depicted on UML diagrams in the format "{constraint description}," where the constraint description may be in any format, including predicate calculus. Fowler and Scott (1997) suggest you focus on readability and understandability and, therefore, suggest using an informal description. For example, in Figure 6-11, I modeled the constraint "{ordered FIFO}" on the association between "Seminar" and "Student" and, in Figure 6-16, I modeled the "{NAND}" constraint between two association roles. The basic idea is that students are put on the waiting list on a first-come, first-served basis—in other words, the students are put on the waiting list in order. UML constraint statements are used to model complex and/or important information accurately in your UML diagrams. An important aspect of OCL is it is a modeling language, not a programming language. You will use a language such as OCL to document your object design, and a language such as Java or C++ to implement it.

6.7 Applying Analysis Patterns Effectively

Analysis patterns (Fowler, 1997; Ambler, 1998a) describe solutions to common problems found in the analysis/business domain of a system. Analysis patterns are typically more specific than design patterns, described in Chapter 7, because they describe a solution for a portion of a business domain. This doesn't mean an analysis pattern is applicable only to a single line of business, although it could be. In this section, I overview two analysis patterns I have used in various business domains, patterns I believe you will find useful when you are modeling.

6.7.1 The Business Entity Analysis Pattern

The Business Entity analysis pattern describes the different types of people and organizations with whom you interact.

Every organization has to deal either with other organizations or people, usually both. As a result, you need to keep track of them. The solution for the Business Entity analysis pattern (Ambler, 1998a), similar to Fowler's (1997) Party pattern, is presented in Figure 6-24. This pattern is a specialization of Peter Coad's Roles Played pattern (Coad, 1992; Ambler, 1998a) to model the different types of organizations and people with whom your company interacts.

Figure 6-24.
The Business Entity
analysis pattern

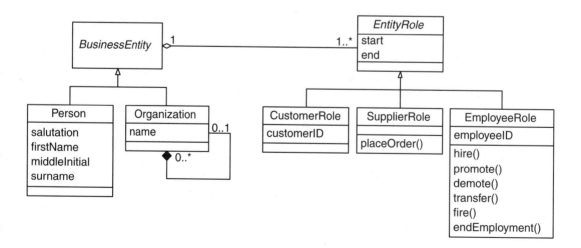

DEFINITIONS

Invariant. A set of assertions about an instance or class that must be true at all "stable" times, where a stable time is the period before a method is invoked on the object/class and immediately after a method is invoked.

Object Constraint Language (OCL). A formal language, similar to structured English, to express side-effect-free constraints within UML models.

The basic idea of this pattern is to separate the concept of a business entity, such as a person or company, from the roles it fulfills. For example, Tony Stark may be a customer of your organization, as well as an employee. Furthermore, one day he may also sell services to your company, also making him a supplier. The person doesn't change, but the role(s) he has with your organization does, so you need to find a way to model this, which is what this pattern does. Each business entity has one or more roles with your organization and each role has a range during which it was applicable (the "start" and "end" attributes). Each role implements the behavior specific to it, such as placing an order with a supplier or the hiring and promotion of an employee.

Note that the use of aggregation between ""BusinessEntity" and "EntityRole" is questionable at best. Is a role really part of a business entity? This sounds like a philosophical question that likely won't have a definitive answer. However, the Roles Played pattern, on which this is based, uses aggregation, so I decided to stay consistent with the source.

6.7.2 The Contact Point Analysis Pattern

The Contact Point analysis pattern (Ambler, 1998a), the solution for which is depicted in Figure 6-25, describes an approach for keeping track of the various means by which you interact with business entities. Your organization most likely sends information and bills to, as well as ships products to, the surface addresses of your customers. Perhaps it emails information to customers and employees, or faxes information to them. It also probably needs to keep track of the contact phone number for anyone with whom it interacts. The Contact Point pattern models an approach to supporting this functionality.

The Contact Point analysis pattern describes an approach for keeping track of the way your organization interacts with business entities.

The basic idea behind this pattern is that surface addresses, email addresses, and phone numbers are really the same sort of thing—a means by which you can contact other business entities. Subclasses of "ContactPoint" need to be able to do at least two tasks: They need to know how things/information can be sent to them and they need to know how to output their "label information." You can send faxes to

TIP

*How to Use Analysis
Patterns Effectively*

The real value of analysis patterns is the thinking behind them. A pattern might not be the total solution to your problem, but it might provide enough insight to help save you several hours or days during development. Consider analysis patterns as a good start at solutions.

phone numbers, email to electronic addresses, and letters and packages to surface addresses. You also need to be able to print contact point information on labels, letterhead, and reports. To do so, contact points collaborate with instances of "ContactPointType" for descriptor information. For example, you want to output "Fax: (416) 555-1212," not just "(416) 555-1212." Furthermore, the "Phone" class should have the capability to be automatically dialed. The different varieties of contact point types would include details such as voice phone line, fax phone line, work address, home address, billing address, and personal email ID.

*You can use
patterns together
to solve difficult
problems.*

I applied the Item-Item Description pattern (Coad, 1992; Ambler, 1998a) when modeling the "ContactPoint" and "ContactPointType" classes. This demonstrates an important principle of object-oriented patterns—they can be used in combination to solve larger problems.

6.7.3 The Advantages and Disadvantages of Patterns

Several advantages and disadvantages exist to working with object-oriented patterns. They are discussed in the following sections.

6.7.3.1 The Potential Advantages of Patterns

1. **Patterns increase developer productivity.** By documenting solutions to common problems, patterns promote reuse of development efforts. Increased reuse within your organization improves your productivity.

2. **Patterns describe proven solutions to common problems.** Patterns are "born" when developers recognize they are applying the same solution to a common problem over and over again. I developed the Contact Point analysis pattern after implementing similar solutions for a variety of computer systems.

3. **Patterns increase the consistency between applications.** By using the same patterns over and over again, you increase the consistency between applications, making them easier to understand and maintain. When your applications are developed in a

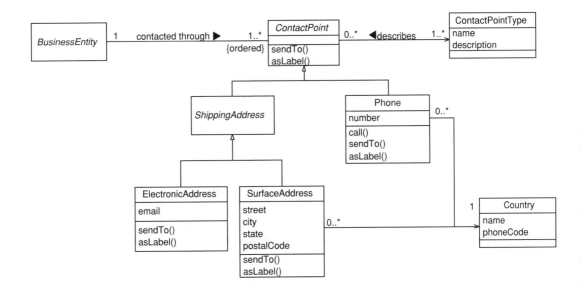

Figure 6-25.
The Contact Point
analysis pattern

consistent manner, it's that much easier to do technical walk-throughs that enable you to improve the quality of your development efforts.

4. **Patterns are potentially better than reusable code.** People can talk about reusable code all they want, but the differences between system platforms makes this dream difficult at best. However, patterns support the reuse of other people's approaches to solving problems (Ambler, 1998b; Ambler, 1999) and, therefore, can be applied in a wide range of environments because they are not environment-specific.

5. **More and more patterns are being developed every day.** A lot of exciting work is going on in patterns, with new patterns being introduced every day. This enables you to take advantage of the development efforts of thousands of people, often for the mere cost of a book, magazine, or telephone call to link you to the Internet.

I maintain a Web page, *http://www.ambysoft.com/processPatternsPage.html,* that provides links and references to printed literature pertaining to patterns and the software process. From this page, I link to the major patterns sites online, including sites specializing in analysis patterns.

T I P

Visit the Process Patterns Resource Page

6.7.3.2 The Potential Disadvantages of Patterns

1. **You need to learn a large number of patterns.** Although there's an advantage to having access to a large number of patterns, the disadvantage is you have to learn a large number of them, or at least know they exist. This can be a lot of work.

2. **The NIH (not-invented-here) syndrome can get in the way.** Many developers are unwilling to accept the work of others: If they didn't create it, then it isn't any good. In addition, if a pattern is not exactly what they need, then they might not be willing to use it. Whenever I run into this attitude, I always like to point out the versatility and widespread acceptance of patterns within the object community and discuss several common patterns such as Singleton (Gamma et al., 1995) and Item-Item Description (Coad, 1992).

3. **Patterns are not code.** Hard-core techies are often unwilling to accept anything as reusable except code. For some reason, they find it hard to accept that you can reuse ideas as well as source code.

4. **"Pattern" is quickly becoming a buzzword.** As more people realize the value of patterns, more marketing people are beginning to exploit it to increase the sales of whatever product or service they are pushing. Just as in the mid-1990s we saw the term "object-oriented" used as an adjective to describe products that had almost nothing to do with objects, I suspect we'll see the same sort of thing happen with the term "pattern."

6.8 User Documentation

User documentation is required for most modern systems. Mayhew (1992) believes the user documentation is part of the user interface for an application and that well-written user documentation is no excuse for a poorly designed user interface. My experience confirms these beliefs—because modern systems are complex, your users often require significant documentation that describes how to use them effectively. Because different types of users have different needs, you also discover you need to develop several kinds of user documentation. Don't worry, it's not as hard as it sounds, particularly if you have developed the models this book recommends.

6.8.1 Types of User Documentation

Weiss (1991) points out the need for different kinds of manuals to support the needs of different types of users. The lesson to be learned is that one manual does not fit all. He suggests a tutorial manual for novice users, a user manual for intermediate users, and a reference manual for expert users. Tourniaire and Farrell (1997) also recommend that you develop a support user's guide describing the support services provided to your user community, a document that is typically less than a page in length.

The user documentation for your application includes a tutorial manual, a reference manual, a user manual, and a support user's guide.

When appropriate, your user documentation should include a description of the skills needed to use your system. For example, your users may require training in your business domain or in basic computer skills, such as using a mouse. This information is needed to develop training plans for users and by support engineers when they are attempting to determine the source of a problem. Quite often, support engineers will receive support calls where the solution is to give the user additional training.

6.8.2 How to Write User Documentation

What were you trying to do the last time you looked at a user manual? You were likely trying to determine how to accomplish a task, a task that probably would be described via a use case or activity diagram in your analysis model. My experience is that the easiest way to write your user documentation is to start with the models that describe how your users work with your system: your use case model and your activity diagrams. Use cases describe how users interact with your system and, as you saw in Section 6.4, UML activity diagrams are often used to describe high-level business logic. This is exactly the type of information your user documentation should reflect.

Your use cases and activity diagrams drive the development of your user documentation.

Start your user manual with a description of the system itself, probably several paragraphs, information you likely have in your supplementary specification. Then, add a section describing any high-level business

---

DEFINITIONS

Reference manual. A document, either paper or electronic, aimed at experts who need quick access to information.

Support user's guide. A brief document, usually a single page, that describes the support services for your application that are available to your user community. This guide includes support phone numbers, fax numbers, and Web site locations, as well as hours of operations and tips for obtaining the best services.

Tutorial. A document, either paper or electronic, aimed at novice users who need to learn the fundamentals of an application.

User manual. A document, either paper or electronic, aimed at intermediate users who understand the basics of an application, but who may not know how to perform all applicable work tasks with the application.

processes, processes you should have documented the logic for using a UML activity diagram. For large systems, you may find you have a section for each UML package within your use case model or even a separate user manual. Then, for each use case, add an appropriate subsection describing it; the use case text will drive the body of that section. You will likely want to combine steps into paragraphs to make your documentation more readable. Wherever you reference a UI element, you may decide to include a relevant picture of that portion of your user interface (my suggestion is to wait until you have baselined your user interface design before investing the time to generate the pictures). You may also decide to replace references to business rules with their descriptions to help increase your user's understanding of how the system actually works. Although many in the industry call this a use case driven approach to writing user documentation, it really is a model-driven approach because your use cases simply aren't sufficient for this purpose.

Your use cases, activity diagrams, and UI prototype drive the development of your user manual and tutorial.

Tutorials are developed in a similar manner to user manuals, although a few differences exist. First, tutorials focus on the most critical uses of the system, whereas a user manual should focus on the entire system. Second, tutorials should have a more explicit focus on learning a product, so they'll include more detailed use instructions than a user manual might. The assumption is that anyone using a tutorial likely knows little about the system and, therefore, needs more help, whereas someone using a user manual is probably familiar with the system itself, but needs help with a specific aspect of it.

Your user interface model often drives the development of your reference manual.

Your reference manual, because it has a slightly different purpose, is generally driven by your user interface model, instead of your use cases and activity diagrams. I generally include an overview of the system, sections for each major portion of your system, and subsections describing the major user interface elements. The subsections should describe the purpose of the relevant screen/report/page and how to work with it.

You will often hear advice within the software industry to write your documentation before you write you code. Although this is a reasonably

<table>
<tr><td>T I P

Hire a Technical Writer</td><td>Writing is hard and writing good user documentation is even harder. It takes a lot of effort and significant skill to do well, the type of skill technical writers have. If possible, hire a technical writer to work with you to produce your user documentation. This will improve the quality of your documentation and, hence, the quality of your overall user interface, Hiring a technical writer will also free you to focus on other development activities, such as modeling, coding, and testing.</td></tr>
</table>

good practice, why do people give this advice? I believe the motivation is that writing user documentation first forces you to think about how your system will be used before you start to build it. My advice is different: invest the time to understand your system by developing requirements for it, analyzing it, and designing it, and then let this understanding drive the development of your source code and your user documentation. I have worked on several systems where we developed the user documentation in parallel with the source code, not before it, and it worked out well.

Model before you write your user documentation and source code.

6.9 Organizing Your Models with Packages

Packages are UML constructs that enable you to organize model elements into groups, making your UML diagrams simpler and easier to understand. Packages are depicted as file folders and can be used on any of the UML diagrams, although they are most common on use case diagrams and class diagrams because these models have a tendency to grow. I use packages only when my diagrams become unwieldy, which generally implies they cannot be printed on a single page, to organize a large diagram into smaller ones. A good rule of thumb is that a diagram should have 7 +/– 2 bubbles on it, a bubble being a use case or class.

So how do you identify packages on use case diagrams? I like to start with use cases that are related to one another via extend and include associations, my rule of thumb being that included and extended use cases belong in the same package as the base/parent use case. This heuristic works well because these use cases typically were introduced by "pulling out" their logic from the base/parent use case to start. I then analyze the use cases with which my main actors are involved. What you find is each actor will interact with your system to fulfill a few main goals; for example, students interact with your system to enroll in the university, manage their schedules, and manage their financial obligations with the university. This suggests the need for an "Enrollment" package, a "Student Schedule Management" package, and a "Student Financial Management" package.

Anything you put into a package should make sense when considered with the rest of the contents of the package. To determine whether a package is cohesive, a good rule of thumb is you should be able to give your package a short, descriptive name. If you can't, then you may have put several unrelated things into the package.

TIP

Packages Should Be Cohesive

With respect to class diagrams, I take a similar approach and, once again, I apply several rules of thumb. First, classes in the same inheritance hierarchy typically belong in the same package. Second, classes related to one another via aggregation or composition often belong in the same package. Third, classes that collaborate with each other a lot—information reflected by your sequence diagrams and collaboration diagrams (Chapter 7)—often belong in the same package. Fourth, the desire to make your packages cohesive will often drive your other decisions to put a class into a package.

6.10 What You Have Learned

This chapter introduced you to the main artifacts of object-oriented analysis (OOA) and their interrelationships, as depicted in Figure 6-1. You learned that the purpose of analysis is to understand what will be built, as opposed to the purpose of requirements gathering (Chapter 3), which is to determine what your users would like to have built. The main difference is that the focus of requirements gathering is on understanding your users and their potential use of the system, whereas the focus of analysis shifts to understanding the system itself.

In this chapter you saw how to apply the key object-oriented analysis techniques: system use case modeling, sequence diagramming, class modeling, activity diagramming, and user interface prototyping. In Chapter 7, you see how your analysis efforts bridge the gap between requirements and system design.

6.11 Review Questions

1. Develop system use cases for the use case diagram of Figure 3-10. Use the essential use cases you developed for Question 1 in Chapter 3 as your starting point.

2. Rework the class diagrams of Figures 6-15, 6-16, and 6-18 to include the fact that professors also enroll in seminars exactly the way students do. For the purpose of this question, focus on the associations

---

DEFINITIONS

Cohesion. The degree of relatedness within an encapsulated unit (such as a component or a class).

Package. A UML construct that enables you to organize model elements into groups.

between classes and the resulting opportunities for applying inheritance, if any. Draw a new class diagram that includes the inheritance hierarchy, assists association between "Professor" and "Seminar," and any new associations. Justify any new applications of inheritance.

3. Your coworker has two classes, *A* and *B,* and she knows some sort of relationship exists between them. However, what she isn't sure of is whether it is an association, an aggregation association, a composition association, or an inheritance relationship. Develop a UML activity diagram to help your coworker decide among the different types of relationships.

4. The "Enroll in Seminar" use case, described in Figure 6-3, states that when a student is not qualified to enroll in a seminar, a list of the prerequisites for that seminar would be displayed. What changes to the conceptual class diagram developed in Section 6.3 would need to be made to support this feature? What association(s) did you need to add? What do you think the multiplicities would be? Why? The role(s)? Why? Is there more than one way to model this? If so, what are the trade-offs?

5. Develop a UML activity model describing the business logic of the "Enroll in Seminar" use case described in Figure 6-2. Be sure to include the alternate courses described in the figure. Are any alternate courses missing? If so, model them in your activity diagram. Is there any opportunity for performing some activities in parallel?

6. Both Figures 6-20 and 6-24 showed a similar use of composition. A component is potentially composed of other components and an organization is potentially composed of other organizations. Discuss why this may or may not indicate the existence of a "composition pattern." Has such a pattern been previously identified? (Do a search of the patterns literature.)

7. Apply the Contact Point and Business Entity analysis patterns to your class model for the university. Discuss how this has improved your model. Has this detracted from your model in any way? If so,

---

DEFINITION

Baseline. A tested and certified version of a deliverable representing a conceptual milestone, which, thereafter, serves as the basis for further development and that can be modified only through formal change control procedures. A particular version becomes a baseline when a responsible group decides to designate it as such.

how? Do you need to verify this change with your SMEs? Why or why not?

8. Develop sequence diagrams for your use cases in Question 1. As you develop the sequence diagrams, update your conceptual class model to reflect new operations or classes you identify. Also, update the logic of your system use cases as appropriate.

9. Develop a conceptual class model for the bank case study, described in Section 3.10.1, following the approach described in this chapter. First, start with your CRC model, and then try to flesh it out as best you can (develop sequence diagrams for the use cases you developed in Chapter 3). When you have done so, baseline your model. You may decide to organize your model using packages, as well as apply common analysis patterns.

10. Compare and contrast the information content of your domain model (your CRC model), and your conceptual class model for the bank case study. What are the strengths and weaknesses of each model? Why?

11. Compare and contrast the narrative style for writing use cases with the action-response style. What are the advantages and disadvantages of each? When would or wouldn't you use each approach?

12. Search the Web for documentation templates for use cases, actors, and user interface specifications. For use case templates, compare and contrast the content they capture with what has been suggested in this book.

13. Search the Web for papers and information about object-oriented analysis. Compare and contrast the various techniques. Formulate a reason why differences exist among the various approaches and discuss the advantages and disadvantages of having different approaches available to you.

Model twice, code once.

Chapter 7

Determining How to Build Your System: Object-Oriented Design

What You Will Learn in This Chapter

How to evolve your analysis model into a design model
How to layer the architecture of your system
How to develop a design class model
How to apply design patterns effectively
How to develop state chart diagrams
How to develop collaboration diagrams
How to develop a component-based design
How to develop a deployment model
How to develop a persistence model for your system
How to evolve your user interface prototype
How to take advantage of common object design tips

Why You Need to Read This Chapter

Your analysis model, although effective for identifying what will be built, doesn't contain sufficient information to define how your system will be built. Object-oriented design techniques—such as class modeling, state chart modeling, collaboration modeling, component modeling, deployment modeling, persistence modeling, and user interface prototyping—are used to bridge the gap between analysis and implementation.

The purpose of design is to determine how you are going to build your system and to obtain the information needed to drive the actual implementation of your system. This is different from analysis, which focuses on understanding what will be built.

Object-oriented design is highly iterative.

As you can see in Figure 7-1, your analysis artifacts, depicted as dashed boxes, drive the development of your design artifacts. As with the previous Figures 3-1 and 6-1, the arrows represent "drives" relationships; information in your analysis (conceptual) class model drives information in your design class model and vice versa. Figure 7-1 has three important implications: First, as with requirements and analysis, design is also an iterative process. Second, taken together, analysis and design are highly interrelated and iterative. As you see in Chapter 8, which describes object-oriented programming techniques, design and programming are similarly interrelated and iterative. Third, your analysis class model evolves into your design class model, as you see in this chapter, to reflect features of your implementation environment, design concepts such as layering, and the application of design patterns.

Are you taking a pure object approach or a component-based approach?

You must decide on several high-level issues at the beginning of design. First, do you intend to take a pure object-oriented approach to design or a component-based approach? With a pure OO approach, your software is built from a collection of classes, whereas with a component-based approach, your software is built from a collection of components. Components, in turn, are built using other components or classes (it is possible to build components from nonobject technology although that is not the topic of this book). Component modeling is the topic of Section 7.6.

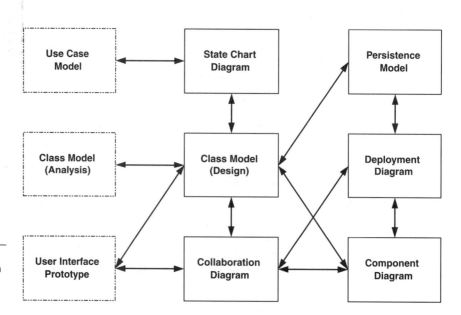

Figure 7-1.
Overview of design artifacts and their relationships

DEFINITIONS

Activity diagram. A UML diagram used to model high-level business processes or the transitions between states of a class (in this respect, activity diagrams are effectively specializations of state chart diagrams).

Class diagram. Show the classes of a system and the associations between them.

Class model. A class diagram and its associated documentation.

Class Responsibility Collaborator (CRC) card. A standard index card divided into three sections: one indicating the name of the class the card represents, one listing the responsibilities of the class, and the third listing the names of the other classes with which this one collaborates to fulfill its responsibilities.

Class Responsibility Collaborator (CRC) model. A collection of CRC cards that model all or part of a system.

Collaboration diagram. A UML diagram that shows instances of classes, their interrelationships, and the message flow between them. Collaboration diagrams typically focus on the structural organization of objects that send and receive messages.

Component diagram. A UML diagram that depicts the software components that compose an application, system, or enterprise. The components, their interrelationships, interactions, and their public interfaces are depicted.

Deployment diagram. A UML diagram showing the hardware, software, and middleware configuration for a system.

Persistence model. A model that describes the persistent data aspects of a software system.

Prototype. A simulation of an item, such as a user interface or a system architecture, the purpose of which is to communicate your approach to others before significant resources are invested in the approach.

State chart diagram. A UML diagram that describes the states an object may be in, as well as the transitions between states. Formerly referred to as a "state diagram" or a "state-transition diagram."

Use case. A sequence of actions that provide a measurable value to an actor.

Use case diagram. A diagram that shows use cases, actors, and their interrelationships.

Use case model. A model comprised of a use case diagram, use case definitions, and actor definitions. Use case models are used to document the behavioral requirements of a system.

User interface (UI). The user interface of software is the portion the user directly interacts with, including the screens, reports, documentation, and software support (via telephone, electronic mail, and so on).

User interface prototype. A prototype of the user interface (UI) of a system. User interface prototypes could be as simple as a hand-drawn picture or as complex a collection of programmed screens, pages, or reports.

    A second major design decision is whether you plan to follow all or a portion of a common business architecture. This architecture may be defined by your organization-specific business/domain architecture model (Ambler, 1998b), sometimes called an enterprise business model, or by a common business architecture promoted within your business community. For example, standard business models exist within the manufacturing, insurance, and banking industries. If you choose to follow a common business architecture, your design models need to reflect this decision, showing how you plan to apply your common business architecture in the implementation of your business classes.

    Third, you must decide whether you plan to take advantage of all or a portion of a common technical infrastructure. Will your system be built using your enterprise's technical infrastructure, perhaps comprised of a collection of components or frameworks, such as those suggested in Table 7-1? Enterprise JavaBeans (EJB), CORBA, and the San Francisco

Table 7-1. Common infrastructure services

Service	Description
Data Sharing	Encapsulates the management of common data formats, such as XML and EDI files.
File Management	Encapsulates and manages access to files.
Inter-Process Communication (IPC)	Implements middleware functionality, including support for messaging between nodes, queuing of services, and other applicable system communication services.
Persistence	Encapsulates and manages access to permanent storage devices, such as relational databases, object databases, and object-relational databases.
Printing	Implements the physical output of your system onto paper.
Security	Implements security access control functionality, such as determining who is entitled to work with certain objects or portions thereof, as well as encryption/decryption and authentication.
System Management	Implements system management features, such as audit logging, real-time monitoring (perhaps via SNMP), error management, and event management.
Transaction Management	Manages transactions, single units of work that either completely succeed or completely fail, across potentially disparate nodes within your system.

Component Framework (*www.ibm.com*) are examples of technical infrastructures on which you may decide to base your system. Perhaps one of the goals of your project is to produce reusable artifacts for future projects. If so, then you want to seriously consider technical architectural modeling. Although beyond the scope of this book, technical architectural modeling is a topic covered in *Process Patterns* (Ambler, 1998b), the third book of this series.

Fourth, you need to decide which nonfunctional requirements and constraints, and to what extent, your system will support. You refined these requirements during analysis (Chapter 6) and, hopefully, resolved any contradictions, but it is during design that you truly begin to take them into account in your models. These requirements typically pertain to many of the services described in Table 7-1. For example, it is common to have nonfunctional requirements describing security access rights, as well as data-sharing approaches. As you try to fulfill these requirements, you may find you are unable to implement them completely; perhaps it

To what extent will you be able to support the nonfunctional requirements and constraints defined for your system?

DEFINITIONS

Common Object Request Broker Architecture (CORBA). An industry-standard, proven approach to distributed object computing, although in practice CORBA has also proven to be a significant force in the middleware arena. CORBA is defined and maintained by the Object Management Group (OMG).

Electronic Data Interchange (EDI). An industry-standard approach to sharing data between two or more systems.

Enterprise Java Beans (EJB). A component architecture, defined by Sun Microsystems, for the development and deployment of component-based distributed business applications.

Extensible Markup Language (XML). An industry-standard approach to data-sharing, an important enabling technology for EAI and e-commerce.

Framework. A reusable set of prefabricated software building blocks that programmers can use, extend, or customize for specific computing solutions.

Middleware. Technology that enables software deployed on disparate computer hardware systems to communicate with one another.

Node. A computer, switch, printer, or other hardware device.

Simple Network Management Protocol (SNMP). A standard protocol that specifies how to communicate status simply, often in near-real time, of system services. SNMP is used to monitor the status of the various software and hardware components of a system.

Transaction. A single unit of work that either completely succeeds or completely fails. A transaction may be one or more updates to an object, one or more reads, one or more deletes, or any combination thereof.

will be too expensive to build your system to support response times of less than a second, whereas a response time of several seconds proves to be affordable. The moral of the story is every system has design trade-offs.

7.1 Layering Your Models—Class Type Architecture

Layering your software increases its robustness.

Layering is the concept of organizing your software design into layers/ collections of classes or components that fulfill a common purpose, such as implementing your user interface or the business logic of your system. A class-type architecture provides a strategy for layering the classes of your software to distribute the functionality of your software among classes. Furthermore, class-type architectures provide guidance as to what other types of classes a given type of class will interact with, and how that interaction will occur. This increases the extensibility, maintainability, and portability of the systems you create.

Good class-type architecture leads to systems that are extensible and portable.

What are the qualities that make up good layers? First, it seems reasonable that you should be able to make modifications to any given layer without affecting any other layers. This will help to make the system easy to extend and to maintain. Second, layers should be modularized. You should be able either to rewrite a layer or simply replace it and, as long as the interface remains the same, the rest of the system should not be affected. This will help to increase the portability of your software.

Figure 7-2 depicts a five-layer class-type architecture for the design of object-oriented software. As the name suggests, a user interface (UI) class implements a major UI element of your system. The business behavior of your system is implemented by two layers: business/domain classes and controller/process classes. Business/domain classes implement the concepts pertinent to your business domain such as "student" or "seminar," focusing on the data aspects of the business objects, plus behaviors specific to individual objects. Controller/process classes, on the other hand, implement business logic that involves collaborating with several business/domain classes or even other controller/process classes. Persistence classes encapsulate the capability to store, retrieve, and delete objects permanently without revealing details of the underlying storage technology. Finally, system classes provide operating-system-specific functionality for your applications, isolating your software from the operating system (OS) by wrapping OS-specific features, increasing the portability of your application.

Collaboration between classes is allowed within a layer. For example, UI classes can send messages to other UI classes and business/domain classes can send messages to other business/domain classes. Collaboration can also occur between classes in layers connected by arrows. As you see in Figure 7-2, user interface classes may send messages to business/

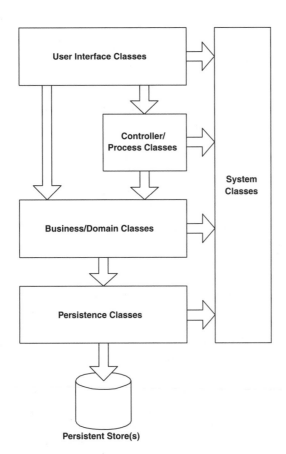

Figure 7-2.
Layering your system based on class types

domain classes, but not to persistence classes. Business/domain classes may send messages to persistence classes, but not to user interface classes. By restricting the flow of messages to only one direction, you dramatically increase the portability of your system by reducing the coupling between classes. For example, the business/domain classes don't rely on the user interface of the system, implying that you can change the interface without affecting the underlying business logic.

All types of classes may interact with system classes. This is because your system layer implements fundamental software features such as inter-process communication (IPC), a service classes use to collaborate with classes on other computers, and audit logging, which classes use to record critical actions taken by the software. For example, if your user-interface classes are running on a personal computer (PC) and your business/domain classes are running on an Enterprise JavaBean (EJB) application server on another machine, then your UI classes will send messages

Restricting message flow between layers increases portability by decreasing the coupling between classes.

to the business/domain classes via the IPC service in the system layer. This service is often implemented via the use of middleware.

7.1.1 The User-Interface Layer

Your system may need to support several user interfaces.

A user interface class contains the code for the user interface part of an application. For example, a graphical user interface (GUI) will be implemented as a collection of menu, editing screen, and report classes. Don't lose sight of the fact that not all applications have GUIs, however. For example, integrated voice response (IVR) systems using telephone technology are common, as are Internet-based approaches. Furthermore, by separating the user interface classes from the business/domain classes, you are now in a position to change the user interface in any way you choose. Consider the university where users currently interact with the system through an existing GUI application. It seems reasonable that people should also be able to interact with the system, perhaps find out information about seminars, or even enroll in seminars, over the phone or the Internet. To support these new access methods, you should only have to add the appropriate user interface classes. Although this is a dramatic change in the way the university interacts with its customers (students), the fundamental business has not changed, therefore, you shouldn't have to change your business/domain classes. The point to be made here is that the user interface for any given system can take on many possible forms, even though the underlying business is still the same. The only change is the way you interact with that business functionality.

User interface classes are often identified as part of your UI prototyping efforts, as well as sequence modeling. Referring back to Figure 6-8, you see the sequence diagram for the basic course of action for the "Enroll in Seminar" use case. Classes that belong to the user interface layer include the three boxes with the stereotype of "<<UI>>": the security logon class, the seminar selector class, and the fee display class.

User interface classes are often referred to as interface classes (Jacobson et al., 1992) or boundary classes (Jacobson, Booch, and Rumbaugh, 1999), so don't be surprised if you see stereotypes of "<<interface class>>" or "<<boundary class>>." As usual, pick one style and stick with it.

7.1.2 The Controller/Process Layer

The purpose of a controller/process class is to implement business logic that pertains to several objects, particularly objects that are instances of different classes. On Figure 7-3, controller classes are given the stereotype of "<<controller>>" although you may also see "<<controller class>>" applied as well (Jacobson, Booch, and Rumbaugh, 1999).

I reworked the analysis version of the sequence diagram, depicted in Figure 6-8, to reflect more closely how the system would actually be built,

DEFINITIONS

Audit logging. The recording of information to identify an action of interest to the system, when the action took place, and who/what took the action.

Business/domain class. Implements the concepts pertinent to your business domain, such as "customer" or "product." Business/domain classes are usually found during the analysis process. Although business/domain classes often focus on the data aspects of your business objects, they will also implement methods specific to the individual business concept.

Class-type architecture. A defined approach to layering the classes that comprise the software of a system. The interaction between classes is often restricted based on the layer to which they belong.

Controller/process class. Implements business logic that involves collaborating with several business/domain classes or even other controller/process classes.

Extensibility. A measure of how easy it is to add new features to, to extend, existing software. If item *A* is easier to change that item *B,* then we say that item *A* is more extensible than item *B.*

Inter-process communication (IPC). The act of having software running on two separate pieces of hardware interact with one another.

Layering. The organization of software collections (layers) of classes or components that fulfill a common purpose.

Maintainability. A measure of how easy it is to add, remove, or modify existing features of a system. The easier a system is to change, the more maintainable we say that system is.

Persistence class. Provides the capability to store objects permanently. By encapsulating the storage and retrieval of objects via persistence classes, you are able to use various storage technologies interchangeably without affecting your applications.

Portability. A measure of how easy it is to move an application to another environment (which may vary by the configuration of either their software and hardware). The easier it is to move an application to another environment, the more portable we say that application is.

System class. Provides operating-system-specific functionality for your applications or wraps functionality provided by other tool/application vendors. System classes isolate your software from the operating system (OS), making your application portable between environments, by wrapping OS-specific features.

User interface class. A class that provides the capability for users to interact with the system. User interface classes typically define a graphical user interface for an application, although other interface styles, such as voice command or HTML, are also implemented via user interface classes.

> **DEFINITIONS**
>
> *Graphical user interface (GUI).* A style of user interface composed of graphical components, such as windows and buttons.
>
> *Major user interface element.* A large-grained item, such as a screen, HTML page, or report.
>
> *Sequence diagram.* A UML diagram that models the sequential logic; in effect, the time ordering of messages between objects.
>
> *Stereotype.* Denotes a common use of a modeling element. Stereotypes are used to extend UML in a consistent manner.
>
> *User interface-flow diagram.* A diagram that models the interface objects of your system and the relationships between them; also known as an interface-flow diagram, a windows navigation diagram, or an interface navigation diagram.

Controller classes collaborate with other controller classes and business classes.

resulting in Figure 7-3. Part of the rework effort was to layer the application appropriately, including the refactoring (Fowler, 1999) of the controller class to interact only with business classes. This refactoring included the introduction of a new user interface class representing the main menu (or front page) of the application, the purpose of which is to manage the user's main interactions with the rest of the system's major user interface items. The second aspect of the refactoring is that the controller class, "EnrollInSeminar," now only manages interactions between business classes. Notice how this refactoring supports the message flow rules, indicated by Figure 7-2. For example, the only types of classes that interact with user interface classes are other user interface classes, whereas in the analysis version of the diagram, the controller class also interacted with UI classes. The problem with the approach in the analysis version is the controller classes, which should just implement business logic, has knowledge of the user interface, reducing its portability and reusability (you couldn't use this controller with a browser-based UI, for example). Now, taking a layered approach, the class is more robust. Interesting to note is that the controller class destroys itself at the end because it is no longer needed—it completes its job, and then removes itself from memory when it is finished.

Classes provide collections of their own instances.

Another interesting aspect of Figure 7-3 is the introduction of the "Seminar" class to support getting a list of available seminar objects via the static method "getAvailableSeminars()." You know it is a static method because the message is being sent to a class. Had it been sent to an object, then it would have been an instance method. Typically, the responsibility of a class is to implement basic searching responsibilities, such as providing a collection of all seminars or, in this case, all seminars that are available to be enrolled in (some seminars may not be offered this term).

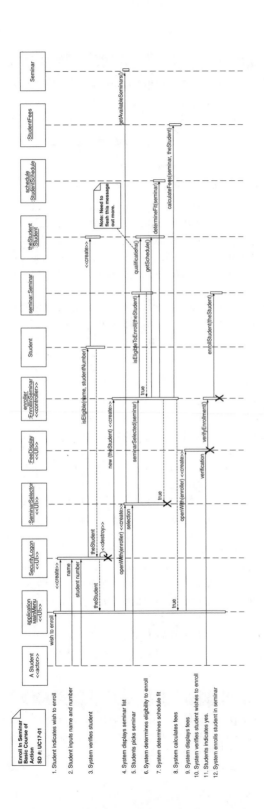

**Enroll In Seminar
Basic Course of
Action

SD #: UC17-01**

1. Student indicates wish to enroll
2. Student inputs name and number
3. System verifies student
4. System displays seminar list
5. Students picks seminar
6. System determines eligibility to enroll
7. System determines schedule fit
8. System calculates fees
9. System displays fees
10. System verifies student wishes to enroll
11. Students indicates yes.
12. System enrolls student in seminar

Figure 7-3.
A reworked
sequence diagram
respecting layering

DEFINITIONS
Instance method. A method that operates on a single instance (object) of a class.
Static method. A method that operates at the class level, potentially on all instances of that class.

7.1.3 The Business/Domain Layer

A business/domain class, also called an analysis or entity class (Jacobson, Booch, and Rumbaugh, 1999), is a class that is usually identified during analysis. Your subject matter experts (SMEs) are often the people who identify these classes or, at least, the concrete business/domain classes. Referring back to Figure 6-16 we see a conceptual class model that contains business/domain classes pertinent to a university information system. The business layer enables you to encapsulate the basic business functionality without having to concern yourself with user interface, data management, or system management issues.

7.1.4 The Persistence Layer

Your business objects should not be affected by changes to your persistence strategy.

The persistence layer provides the infrastructure for the storage and retrieval of objects. This helps to isolate your application from changes to your permanent storage approach. You might decide to install the latest version of your database, change your existing database schema, migrate to a new database vendor, or even change your data storage approach completely (perhaps migrating from a relational database to an object database). Regardless of how your persistence strategy changes, your applications should not be affected. The persistence layer, by encapsulating data management functionality, increases the maintainability, extensibility, and portability of your applications.

The persistence layer encapsulates access to permanent storage, but it is not the storage mechanism itself.

In the layered class-type architecture of Figure 7-2, messages flow from the business/domain class layer to the persistence class layer. These messages take the form of "create a new object," "retrieve this object from the database," "update this object," or "delete this object." These types of messages are referred to as *object-oriented create, retrieve, update, and delete* (OOCRUD). Another essential concept here is that the persistence layer

DEFINITION
Subject matter expert (SME). A person who is responsible for providing pertinent information about the problem and/or technical domain either from personal knowledge or from research.

only provides access to permanent storage; it is not the permanent storage mechanism itself. For example, the persistence layer may encapsulate access to a relational database, but it is not the database itself. The goal of the persistence layer is to reduce the maintenance effort that is required whenever changes are made to your database.

Why do you need a persistence layer? You know your database will be upgraded. You know tables will be moved from one database to another, or from one server to another. You know your data schema will be changed. You know field names will be changed. The implication is clear: because the database is guaranteed to change, we need to encapsulate it to protect ourselves from the change. A persistence layer is the best way to do this because it minimizes the effort required to handle changes to permanent storage.

The persistence layer isolates you from the impact of changes to your storage strategy.

7.1.5 The System Layer

Every operating system offers functionality that we want to be able to access in our applications—file handling, multitasking, multithreading, and network access to name a few. Most operating systems offer these features, albeit in slightly different manners. Although many people find this little fact to be worthy of great debate and, perhaps, it actually is, the real issue is that the differences between operating systems can make it tough if you are writing an application that needs to work on many different platforms. You want to wrap the features of an operating system in such a way that when you port an application, you only need to modify a minimum number of classes. In other words, you need to create classes that wrap specific features of the operating system. Even if you don't intend to port your applications to other operating systems, you still need to consider wrapping system functionality. The reason for this is

The system layer provides access to the operating system and non-OO resources.

DEFINITIONS

Object database (ODB). A permanent storage mechanism, also known as an objectbase or an object-oriented database management system (OODBMS), that natively supports the persistence of objects.

OOCRUD. Object-oriented create, retrieve, update, and delete.

Permanent storage. Any physical medium to which data can be saved, retrieved, and deleted. Potential permanent storage mechanisms for objects include relational databases, files, and object databases.

Relational database (RDB). A permanent storage mechanism in which data is stored as rows in tables. RDBs don't natively support the persistence of objects, requiring the additional work on the part of developers and/or the use of a persistence layer.

simple: Operating systems constantly get upgraded. Every time an upgrade occurs, there are always changes to the way that functionality is currently being offered, including issues such as bug fixes and completely new ways to do things.

System classes encapsulate non-OO functionality by wrapping it with OO code.

The key concept here is wrapping (Ambler, 1998a). System classes for the most part encapsulate non-OO functionality that we need to make accessible to objects within an application. It is quite common to wrap a series of related operating system calls to provide a related set of functionality. A perfect example would be the file stream classes commonly found in Java and C++. When you look into the inner workings of these classes, you find their methods make specific file-handling calls to the operating system. These classes, particularly the Java ones, provide a common way to work with files, regardless of the platform.

Message flow for system classes is greatly restricted. System classes are only allowed to send messages to other system classes, even though each type of class is allowed to send messages to system classes. This is because system classes are the lowest common denominator in software development. This means they don't need to know anything about the business logic or user interface logic to do their job. Actually, it is not completely true that system classes don't interact with nonsystem classes. The use of callbacks, when one object passes itself as a message parameter to another so the receiver can later call it back, is permitted (it is allowed between all layers, but it is most common with system classes). For example, instead of waiting, a business class may request that a printing system class inform it when/if the print request was successful. When the printing is complete, a message would be sent from the system object to the business object informing it of success.

7.2 Class Modeling

Your design class model will reflect the wide variety of technology decisions you make.

The purpose of design is to model how the software will be built. As you would expect, the purpose of design-class modeling is to model the static structure of how your software will be built. The techniques of Chapter 7

DEFINITIONS

Callback. An approach where one object indicates it wants to be sent a message once its request has finished processing; in effect, it wants to be "called back."

Wrapper. A collection of one or more classes that encapsulates access to non-OO technology to make it appear as if it is OO.

Wrapping. The act of encapsulating non-OO functionality within a class, making it look and feel like any other object within the system.

still apply. The only difference is your focus is on the solution domain, instead of on the problem domain. You will introduce changes to your class model based on implementation technologies. And perhaps you will implement business rules using a business rules engine, which means your business/domain classes will invoke the rules, instead of directly implementing them in methods. Perhaps you will apply known design patterns, the topic of Section 7.3, to improve the design quality of your models. Perhaps you will decide to take a component-based approach. Component modeling is discussed in Section 7.6. Or, perhaps you will take advantage of features of your permanent storage mechanism. Persistence modeling is covered in Section 7.8.

In this section, I describe a collection of topics that are important to your design-class modeling efforts. These topics are as follows:

- Inheritance techniques
- Association and dependency techniques
- Aggregation and composition techniques
- Modeling attributes and methods during design
- Modeling interfaces
- Documenting design trade-offs
- Class modeling design tips

7.2.1 Inheritance Techniques

Similarities often exist between different classes. Quite often, two or more classes share the same attributes and/or the same methods. Because you don't want to have to write the same code repeatedly, you want a mechanism that takes advantage of these similarities. Inheritance is that mechanism. Inheritance models "is a," "is like," and "is kind of" relationships, enabling you to reuse existing data and code easily. Over the years, I have

---

An important goal of your architectural and design modeling efforts is to understand where your chosen technology breaks (Ambler, 1998b). This is called *technical prototyping,* an important aspect of the Unified Process's Elaboration phase (Kruchten 1999; Ambler and Constantine, 2000b), the goal of which is to build an end-to-end working prototype of your system earlier in development to validate that your chosen approach actually works. This approach mitigates much of the technical risk of your project, improving your chances of success because you know early on that your design will work as hoped.

TIP

Understand Where the Technology Breaks

DEFINITIONS

Problem space. The scope of your business domain being addressed by your system.

Solution space. The problem space being addressed by your system plus the nondomain functionality required to implement your system.

Technical prototyping. The act of creating a prototype to validate that your proposed solution works. Often called *proof-of-concept prototyping* or *end-to-end prototyping*.

---

found the following techniques, including the ones described in Chapter 6, to be valuable for ensuring that I apply inheritance properly:

1. **The sentence rule works 99.9 percent of the time.** If it does not make sense to say "the subclass is a superclass" or at least "the subclass is like the superclass," then you are likely misapplying inheritance.

2. **Beware of implementation inheritance.** Implementation inheritance, often called *convenience inheritance*, occurs when a class inherits from another class simply to reuse part or the entirety of its behavior, even though the sentence rule failed. Implementation inheritance is particularly common when developers want to take shortcuts and have business classes inherit system or persistence behaviors, instead of accessing these services through collaboration.

3. **Any kind of class can inherit from any other kind.** Both abstract and concrete classes can inherit from either abstract or concrete classes. Remember, you inherit attributes and methods, not whether the class is concrete or abstract.

4. **You should be able to substitute an instance of a subclass for an instance of a superclass.** This advice is effectively a rewording of the Liskov Substition Principle (Liskov, 1988) which is "If for each object o1 of type S there is an object o2 of type T such that for all programs P defined in terms of T, the behavior of P is unchanged when o1 is substituted for o2, then S is a subtype of T." For example, if you have written code that manipulates instances of the "Person" class, the code should also be able to work with instances of the "Professor" class as well if "Professor" inherits from "Person." If you find you are writing code that checks the type of an object, in this case to see if the object is an employee or an executive, then you likely have problems in your design.

5. **Beware of multiple inheritance.** Not only is multiple inheritance, the capability of a class to inherit directly from two or more classes, difficult to understand, it isn't an option for most development languages. For example, C++ supports multiple inheritance, but Java, Smalltalk, and Eiffel do not. C++ has an interesting concept called *mixin classes*, where multiple inheritance is used to obtain behaviors implemented by another class. Uses of mixin classes are typically an indication of implementation inheritance, although, admittedly, their use is convenient at times. Riel (1996) suggests you should assume that multiple inheritance within your model is a mistake and should be able to prove otherwise.

6. **Beware of inheritance based only on common data attributes.** If the only reasons two classes inherit from each other is because they share common data attributes, it indicates one of two things: You have either missed some common behavior (this is likely if the sentence rule applies) or you should have applied association instead of inheritance.

7. **Superclasses should know nothing of their subclasses.** The basic idea is that you should be free to create a class without having to change the code of any classes from which it inherits, either directly or indirectly (Riel, 1996).

8. **Factor commonality as high as possible in your class hierarchy.** The higher in a class hierarchy a method is, the greater its reuse. However, this doesn't mean you should place every single method in the root class. Instead, if Classes B and C both inherit from Class A, and they both need behavior X, then X should be implemented in A. If only Class B needs X, then X belongs in B.

9. **A subclass should inherit everything.** A subclass should inherit all the attributes and methods of its superclass and, therefore, all its relationships as well. When a subclass inherits everything from its superclass, we say we have "pure inheritance." The advantage of pure inheritance is you only have to understand what a subclass inherits and not what it does not inherit. While this sounds trivial, in a deep class hierarchy, life is a lot easier if you only need to understand what each class adds and not what it takes away.

Meanwhile, Back in Reality
I am not saying you cannot override (redefine) attributes and methods. For example, in Chapter 5, you saw how the class "Dragon" inherits everything

from the classes "Bird" and "Lizard," including the method "Eat." However, in the definition of "Dragon," I needed to override "Eat" because dragons eat differently than either birds or lizards (dragons eat knights in shining armor). What I am saying is, if you find your subclasses need to override methods, then perhaps you need to rethink your inheritance hierarchy.

7.2.2 *Association and Dependency Techniques*

In the real world, objects have associations to other objects. The associations between objects are important because they help us to define how they interact with each other. For example, students *take* courses and professors *teach* courses. Associations between objects enable collaboration—an object needs to know about another object to work with it. When a persistent association doesn't exist between two objects, but they need to collaborate with one another, you model a dependency relationship between the two classes. In this section, I present a collection of tips and techniques for modeling associations and dependencies, in addition to the advice presented in Chapters 5 and 6.

1. **Model the scaffolding for your associations.** Some developers will add the necessary attributes and methods needed to maintain associations, whereas others will assume the programmers

---

DEFINITIONS

Implementation inheritance. When inheritance is applied simply for convenience even though it doesn't make sense to say the subclass "is a" superclass.

Inheritance. The representation of an *is a, is like,* or *is kind of* relationship between two classes. Inheritance promotes reuse by enabling a subclass to benefit automatically from all the behavior it inherits from its superclass(es).

Mixin class. A class that implements cohesive behavior, such as printing or persistence, that a wide variety of classes may need. The behaviors of the mixin class are obtained, mixed in, via multiple inheritance.

Multiple inheritance. When a class directly inherits from more than one class.

Override. When you redefine an attribute or method in a subclass, you override it.

Pure inheritance. Inheritance in which the subclass does not override any behavior implemented by its superclass(es). The subclass is free to add new behavior.

Single inheritance. When a class directly inherits from only one class.

Subclass. If Class *B* inherits from Class *A*, we say *B* is a subclass of *A*.

Superclass. If Class *B* inherits from Class *A*, we say *A* is a superclass of *B*.

will handle it and won't bother to document this scaffolding on their class models. Both approaches are fine. I prefer to model the details of the scaffolding during design to reflect the nuances of how I think it should be implemented but, as usual, choose the style that works best for you and stick to it. In Chapter 8, I discuss how to implement associations.

2. **Multiplicity must be shown.** The multiplicities of an association should be modeled, one on each end of the association line. Table 7-2 lists the potential multiplicity indicators you can use on your UML class diagrams.

3. **Question multiplicities involving minimums and maximums.** The problem with minimums and maximums is they change over time. For example, today you may have a business rule that states a student may enroll in no more than five seminars in any given term. Say you build your system to reflect this rule. Perhaps your design relies on a performance trick that works well for collections of five or fewer items and the rule changes, so students can take more than five seminars, then you may quickly find that to support this change you have to rewrite a major portion of your system. My experience is it is interesting to know about any minimums and maximums. They often reflect important business rules at the time, but I don't take advantage of them when I design (unless I have to for exceptionally good reasons) to avoid maintenance complications in the future.

4. **Associations and dependencies are inherited.** Because associations and dependencies are implemented as a combination of attributes and methods, and because attributes and methods are inherited, by implication, associations are also inherited.

Table 7-2. UML multiplicity indicators

Indicator	Meaning
0..1	Zero or one
1	One only
0..*	Zero or more
1..*	One or more
n	Only n (where n > 1)
0..n	Zero to n (where n > 1)
1..n	One to n (where n > 1)

5. **Collaboration goes hand-in-hand with relationships.** You need to have some sort of relationship—an association, dependency, aggregation association, or composition association—between two model elements to enable them to collaborate. Furthermore, if two model elements don't collaborate with one another, then no need exists for a relationship between them. The basic thinking is this: If the classes never take advantage of the relationship, why maintain it?

6. **Model a unidirectional association when collaboration is only one way.** Assume an assocation exists between Class *A* and Class *B*. If instances of *A* send messages to instances of *B*, and instances of *B* send messages to instances of *A*, then you need a bidirectional assocation. If instances of *A* send messages to instances of *B*, but instances of *B* don't send messages to instances of *A*, then you need a unidirectional assocation from *A* to *B*. For example, student objects send messages to instances of "EnrollmentRecord," such as "getFinalMark()," but no need occurs for messages going in the other direction (not yet at least), so a unidirection assocation from "Student" to "EnrollmentRecord" is modeled in Figure 6-16.

7. **Model a dependency when one of the instances is transient.** When one of the classes is transient, it is not saved to permanent storage. It is an indication that you likely have a dependency. For example, user interface classes are transitory, but their instances collaborate with persistent business objects, such as instances of the "Student" and "Seminar" classes.

8. **Model a dependency when an object interacts only with a class, but not the instance.** A perfect example of this is when an object interacts with a factory class (Gamma et al., 1995) whose responsibility is to create instances of other classes (similar conceptually to the idea that, in the real world, cars and trucks are built in factories). In software, an instance of "CarDealership" would collaborate with the "VehicleFactory" class to obtain instances of the "Car" and "Truck" classes, not an instance of "VehicleFactory." The "CarDealership" class would have a dependency on "VehicleFactory" and assocations with "Car" and "Truck."

9. **Do not model implied associations.** An implied association exists between students and seminars: students take seminars. Yet in Figure 6-11, this association is not modeled between these two classes. A mistake? No, the association is implied by the "EnrollmentRecord" class; "Student" is associated to "EnrollmentRecord," which, in turn, is associated to "Seminar." These two

associations, when taken together, implement the implied association that students take (enroll in) seminars. If you model this implied association, then somebody, your programmers, need to implement it.

10. **The Liskov Substitution Principle applies to mirror hierarchies.** In Figure 7-5, you see a UML class diagram representing portions of two class hierarchies and the associations between them. This is an example of what is known as mirror hierarchies, something that happens when two or more class hierarchies take on the same shape because they model highly related concepts. In this case, the type of equipment contained in a laboratory reflects the type of laboratory. Considering each class hierarchy in isolation, they appear to make sense because a nuclear laboratory is a laboratory and nuclear equipment is equipment. Taken together, however, they may not make as much sense. According to the Liskov Substitution Principle, you should be able to substitute instances of a subclass for its superclass, which indicates that you should be able to use nuclear equipment wherever you can use equipment. According to Figure 6-15, you can use equipment in a laboratory; therefore, you can use also nuclear equipment in a laboratory. That is not the intention of the model. Instead, nuclear equipment can only be used in a nuclear laboratory. Figure 7-6 presents a resolution of this issue. I made "Equipment" an abstract class and introduced the class "LaboratoryEquipment." I also introduced "equipped with" aggregation associations between the relevant classes; the fact that they are named the

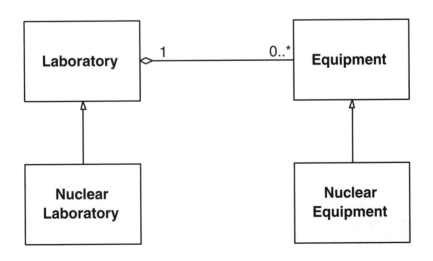

Figure 7-5.
Classrooms and equipment class model

same and have the same multiplicities should let people know what's going on (adding a note wouldn't hurt either). Most of the scaffolding attribute(s) and methods to implement these aggregation associations are likely to be implemented in "Equipment," although "NuclearEquipment" is likely to include code that validates that it is in a laboratory, which is able to contain it.

7.2.3 Aggregation and Composition Techniques

Sometimes an object is made up of other objects. For example, an airplane is made up of a fuselage, wings, engines, landing gear, flaps, and so on. A delivery shipment contains one or more packages. A team consists of two or more employees. These are all examples of the concept of aggregation, which represents "is part of" relationships. Composition is a strong form of aggregation in which the "whole" is completely responsible for its parts and each part is only associated to one whole. During design, several considerations are specific to aggregation and composition as follows:

1. **The advice for associations applies to aggregation and composition.** Aggregation and composition associations are merely specializations of the concept of association and, as a result, the heuristics for associations apply to them.

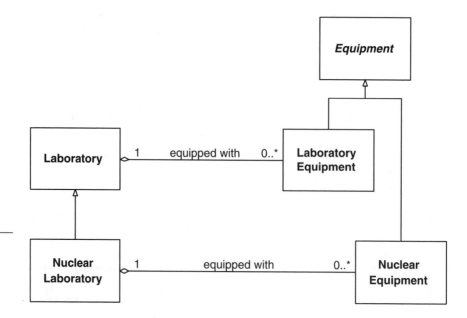

Figure 7-6.
Refactored classrooms and equipment class model

DEFINITIONS

Bidirectional association. An association that may be traversed in both directions.

Dependency relationship. A dependency relationship exists between Class *A* and *B* when instances of Class *A* interact with instances of Class *B*. Dependency relationships are used when there is no direct relationship (inheritance, aggregation, or association) between the two classes.

Mirror hierarchies. Two or more class hierarchies, because they each model concepts that are highly related, take on similar structures to one another.

Multiplicity. The UML combines the concepts of cardinality and optionality into the single concept of multiplicity.

Scaffolding. Additional code, often complete methods and attributes, required to make your design work. Programmers often introduce scaffolding. It is not modeled as part of analysis and often not even as part of design.

Transient class. A class whose instances are not saved to permanent storage.

Unidirectional association. An association that may be traversed in only one direction.

2. **The sentence rule should make sense for aggregation and composition.** It should make sense to say that one object "is part of" or "contained by" another object.

3. **You should be interested in both the whole and the part.** For aggregation and composition associations, you should be interested in both the whole and the part separately. Another way to look at it is this: both the whole and the part should exhibit behavior that is of value to your system. For example, I could model the fact that my watch has hands on it, but if this fact isn't pertinent to my system (perhaps I sell watches, but not watch parts), then no value exists in modeling this fact.

4. **You need to understand how the whole and the parts collaborate with each other.** If the whole and the parts do not collaborate, it is an indication that either a relationship does not exist between the two classes to begin with or you have not yet identified how they collaborate with each other.

5. **The majority of the interaction is from the whole to the part.** An engine is part of an airplane. To fly, an airplane will collaborate with its engines, requesting they shut on or off, as well as increase or decrease their speed. It is unlikely that an engine will initiate much interaction with the airplane, except perhaps to inform it of a malfunction.

DEFINITIONS
Aggregation. The representation of "is part of" associations.
Composition. A strong form of aggregation in which the "whole" is completely responsible for its parts, and each "part" object is only associated with the one "whole" object.

6. **Don't confuse inheritance with aggregation.** It's easy to get confused about when to use inheritance and when to use aggregation. Remember this: Inheritance models "is a" or "is like" relationships, while aggregation models "is part of" relationships. By following the sentence rules (it should make sense to say a subclass *is a* superclass) you should be able to determine when to use each concept appropriately.

7.2.4 Modeling Methods During Design

On design class diagrams, indicate the visibility, name, parameters, return value, and stereotype of methods.

Methods, also called *operations* or *member functions*, are the object-oriented equivalent of functions and procedures. Until now, I have been modeling methods in a simple manner, indicating their names and the names of any parameters passed to them. With the UML, however, it is possible to model far more information about a method's signature than just this, as you can see in Figure 7-7. During design, you should indicate the visibility, the level of access that external objects have to a method, on your class diagrams. Method visibility is described in Section 7.2.4.2. The name of the method is also indicated; strategies for naming methods are described in Section 7.2.4.1. You also see that the names of parameters, as well as their types and default values (if any), should also be indicated for each method. The type of the return value, if any, should be indicated the applicable stereotype[1] should also be indicated. Finally, the scope of a method, whether it is a static method that works on the class or an instance method that works on instances of the class, should also be indicated.

Static methods are underlined, instance methods are not.

Figure 7-8 depicts the "Student" class (refer to Figure 6-16) with its methods fully modeled. I added the accessor methods for the "averageMark" attribute so I had an example of an operation, "setAverageMark()," with a different visibility than the other methods and the constructor "Student(stu-

---

[1] The UML currently states that the stereotype for a method, if any, should be placed at the beginning of its definition. However, from a stylist point of view, this looks rather poor on class models (try it) and, as a result, I prefer to indicate stereotypes as the last item in a method's definition. As usual, pick one approach and stick to it.

visibility name(param1:type1=default1,...): returnType <<stereotype>>

Figure 7-7.
The UML format for
an operation
signature

dentNumber)," so I had an example of a method with a stereotype. The "isEligible(...)" method is interesting for several reasons. First, you know it is a static method because it is underlined (instance methods are not underlined). Second, you know it is a publicly accessible method because its visibility indicator is a "+" sign. Third, its "name" parameter is a simple string, whereas its "studentNumber" is an instance of the class "StudentNumber"—the type of a parameter may be either a primitive type or a class. Both Java and C++ have integers, floats, and strings among its primitive types, but Smalltalk, a typeless language, by definition has no primitive types. Fourth, you see it returns a Boolean value, either true or false.

The other methods depicted in Figure 7-8 are also worth noting. You see the "Student(studentNumber)" method is a constructor, a method that instantiates instances of "Student" (note the return value) and presumably sets the value of the "studentNumber" attribute within the object. Methods that don't take parameters have nothing listed in their parameter list and operations that don't return anything, have no return value indicated. Similarly, the "Student(studentNumber)" method has a stereotype indicated for it, but the other methods don't because no stereotypes are applicable to them. Finally, the accessor methods "getAverageMark()" and "setAverageMark(...)" deal with the same type, in this case "long," implying that the "averageMark" attribute must also be of type long. Attributes are discussed in detail in Section 7.2.5.

*Some methods
have parameters;
some do not. Some
methods have
return values;
some do not.*

7.2.4.1 Naming Methods

Methods should be named using a full description, using mixed case with the first letter of any noninitial word capitalized, using the format "methodName()." Also common practice is for the first word of a member function name to be a strong, active verb. Table 7-3 depicts examples

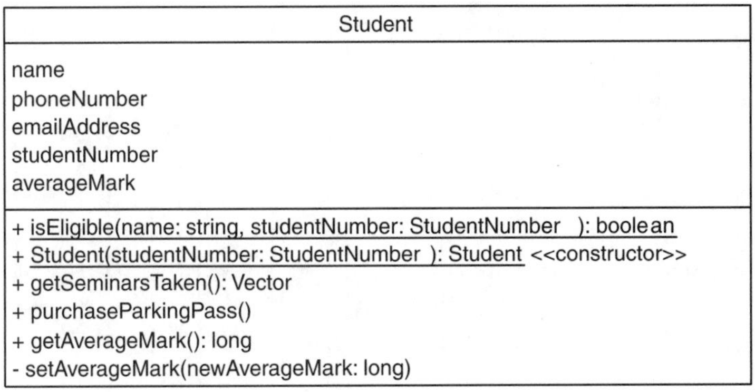

*Name methods
using the format
methodName().*

Figure 7-8.
The "Student" class
with its methods
fully modeled

Table 7-3. Example names for member functions

"Bad" Name	"Good" Name	Issue
openAcc()	openAccount()	An abbreviation was replaced with the full word to make the meaning clear.
mailingLabelPrint()	printMailingLabel()	The verb was moved to the beginning of the name to make it active.
purchaseparkingpass()	purchaseParkingPass()	Mixed case was applied to increase the readability of the name.
saveTheObject()	save()	The name was shortened because the term "TheObject" did not add any value.

of method names that were not ideal, presents an improved version of the name, and describes what changed and why.

A little extra typing can dramatically improve the quality of your design.

These conventions result in methods whose purpose can often be determined just by looking at its name. Although this approach results in a little extra typing by developers—because it often results in longer method names—this is more than made up for by the increased understandability of your code.

7.2.4.2 Method Visibility

Make your methods as visible as they need to be and no more.

How a method is accessed by objects is defined by its visibility. In the Unified Modeling Language (UML), you have your choice of three levels of visibility, defined in Table 7-4: public, protected, and private (Rumbaugh, Jacobson, and Booch, 1999). To reduce the coupling within your system, the general rule of thumb is to be as restrictive as possible when setting the visibility of a method. In other words, if a method doesn't have to be public, then make it protected. If it doesn't have to be protected, then make it private.

TIP

You Need to Choose an Implementation Language

You need to make a decision as to what language you intend to implement a class in to describe a method fully. For example, I have made the decision to implement the "Student" class of Figure 7-8 using Java and, therefore, have modeled it using Java conventions (Vermeulen et al., 2000). Had I chosen Smalltalk as a language, the "name" attribute would have been an instance of the class "String" and the "getAverageMark" method (Smalltalk does not use parenthesis in its methods) would likely have returned an instance of "Float." Furthermore, because Java does not support default values for parameters, I did not model them, whereas a language such as Visual Basic does. Each language has its own unique set of features, features your design model needs to reflect.

Table 7-4. UML method visibilities

Visibility	Symbol	Description	Proper Usage
public	+	A public method can be invoked by any other method in any other object or class.	When the method must be accessible by objects and classes outside of the class hierarchy in which the method is defined.
protected	#	A protected method can be invoked by any method in the class in which it is defined or any subclasses of that class.	When the method provides behavior that is needed internally within the class hierarchy, but not externally.
private	-	A private method can only be invoked by other methods in the class in which it is defined, but not in the subclasses.	When the method provides behavior that is specific to the class. Private methods are often the result of refactoring.

Let's work through the accessibility of each method in Figure 7-9. The method "publicMethod()" can be invoked by instances of all three classes because it is public. However, "protectedMethod()" is invokable only by instances of "Superclass" and "Subclass." Instances of "Superclass" can access this method because it is defined in "Superclass" and it is also invokable by instances of "Subclass" because protected methods are visible all the way down the class hierarchy. Because "privateMethod()" is private, it can only be invoked by instances of "Superclass"—instances of both "OtherClass" and "Subclass" don't even know this method exists.

DEFINITIONS

Accessor. An operation used either to modify or retrieve a single attribute. Also known as *getter* and *setter* operations.

Constructor. A method, typically a static one, whose purpose is to instantiate and, optionally, initialize an object.

Method. Something a class or object does. A method is similar to a function or procedure in structured programming, and is often referred to as an *operation* or *member function* in object development.

Primitive type. A type of attribute built into a computer language.

Signature. The combination of the name, parameter names (in order), and name of the return value (if any) of a method.

Visibility. The level of access that external objects have to an item, such as an object's attributes or methods, or even to a class itself.

As an aside, notice how I have named the classes of Figure 7-9—the word "class" is capitalized in "OtherClass," but not in "Superclass" and "Subclass." This is because superclass and subclass are actual words; therefore, it would not be appropriate to capitalize the *c* in "class." Good class names are typically nouns, two or three words at most, are fully spelled out, and are written in mixed case with the first letter of each word capitalized.

List methods first by scope, then by visibility, and then by type.

As a matter of style, I prefer to list static methods before instance methods in classes, as you can see in Figure 7-8. Furthermore, for each type of method scope, I list public methods first, then protected methods, and then private methods. Finally, for each visibility, I list the business methods before the accessor and scaffolding methods (such as those required to maintain associations). I also take a similar approach to listing attributes within a class.

7.2.4.3 Documenting Methods
Every method should have both header documentation that describes it and internal documentation that describes specific source code.

7.2.4.3.1 Writing Header Documentation for a Method
Every method should include some sort of documentation at the top of the source code that documents all the information critical to understanding it. This information includes, but is not limited to, the following:

1. **What and why the method does what it does.** By documenting what a method does, you make it easier for others to determine if they can reuse your code. Documenting why it does something makes it easier for others to put your code into context. You also make it easier for others to determine whether a new change should actually be made to a piece of code (perhaps the reason for the new change conflicts with the reason why the code was written in the first place).

2. **Known bugs.** Any outstanding problems with a method should be documented so other developers understand the weak-

---

TIP

Visibility Varies Between Languages

Understanding that each major OO language takes its own approach to visibility is important. For example, C++ supports public, protected, and private visibility. Java supports public, protected, private, and default visibility (a cross between private and protected). Smalltalk, on the other hand, does not have the concept of visibility.

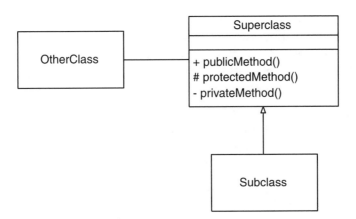

Figure 7-9.
Visibility of methods

nesses/difficulties with the method. If a given bug is applicable to more than one method within a class, then it should be documented for the class instead. Better yet, fix the bug!

3. **Any error conditions and/or exceptions a method throws.** You should document any and all error conditions and/or exceptions a method throws, so other programmers know what their code will need to catch.

4. **Visibility decisions.** If you feel other developers will question your choice of visibility for a method—perhaps you have made a method public even though no other objects invoke the method yet—then you should document your decision. This will help to make your thinking clear to other developers, so they don't waste time worrying about why you did something questionable.

5. **How a method changes the object.** If a method changes an object—for example, the "withdraw()" method of a bank account modifies the account balance—then this fact needs to be indicated. This information is needed so other Java programmers know exactly how a method invocation will affect the target object.

6. **Include a history of any code changes.** Whenever a change is made to a method, you should document when the change was made, who made it, why it was made, who requested the change, who tested the change, and when it was tested and approved to be put into production. This history information is critical for the future maintenance programmers who are responsible for

modifying and enhancing the code. Note: This information really belongs in your software configuration management/version control system, not the source code itself. If you aren't using these sorts of tools (and you should), then put this information into your code.

7. **Examples of how to invoke the method, if appropriate.** One of the easiest ways to determine how a piece of code works is to look at an example. Consider including an example or two of how to invoke a method.

8. **Applicable preconditions and postconditions.** A precondition is a constraint under which a method will function properly. A postcondition is a property or assertion that will be true after a method is finished running (Meyer, 1997). In many ways, preconditions and postconditions describe the assumptions you have made when writing a method (Ambler, 1998a), defining exactly the boundaries of how a method is used.

7.2.4.3.2 Writing Internal Documentation for a Method
Internally, you should always document the following:

1. **Control structures.** Describe what each control structure, such as comparison statements and loops, do and why they do it. You shouldn't have to read all the code in a control structure to determine what it does. Instead, you should only have to look at a one- or two-line comment immediately preceding it.

2. **Why, as well as what, the code does.** You can always look at a piece of code and figure out what it does, but for code that is not obvious, you can rarely determine why it is done that way. For example, you can look at a line of code and easily determine that a 5 percent discount is being applied to the total of an order. That's easy. What isn't easy is figuring out *why* that discount is being applied. Obviously, some sort of business rule says to apply

---

DEFINITIONS

Postcondition. An expression of the properties of the state of an operation or use case after it has been invoked successfully.

Precondition. An expression of the constraints under which an operation or use case will operate properly.

the discount, so that business rule should at least be referred to in your code, and then other developers can understand why your code does what it does.

3. **Local variables.** Each local variable defined in a method should be declared on its own line of code and should usually have an endline comment describing its use.

4. **Difficult or complex code.** If you find you either cannot rewrite it or you don't have the time, then you must thoroughly document any complex code in a method. My rule of thumb is that if your code is not immediately obvious, then you need to document it.

5. **The processing order.** If statements in your code must be executed in a defined order, then you should ensure that this fact gets documented (Ambler, 1998a). There is nothing worse than making a simple modification to a piece of code only to find it no longer works, and then spending hours looking for the problem, only to find you have things out of order.

7.2.4.4 Techniques for Methods

During design, what factors lead to high-quality methods? I find the following guidelines lead to superior methods:

1. **Develop consistent method signatures.** The greater the consistency within your designs, the easier they are to learn and to understand. First, method names should be consistent with one another. Method names such as "getFirstName()" and "fetchLastName()" are not consistent, whereas starting both method names with "get" would make them so. Second, parameter names should also be consistent with one another. For example, parameter names such as "theFirstName," "firstName," and "firstNm" are not consistent with one another, and neither are "firstName," "aPhoneNumber," and "theStudentNumber." Pick one naming style for your parameters and stick to it. Third, the order of parameters should also be consistent. For example, the methods "doSomething(securityToken, startDate)" and "doSomethingElse(studentNumber, securityToken)" could be made more consistent by always passing "securityToken" as either the first or the last parameter.

2. **Define preconditions and postconditions for your methods.** A precondition describes something that must be true before a method may be invoked. A postcondition describes something that will be true once a method has completed (assuming the initial pre-

DEFINITIONS

Endline comment. The use of a line comment to document a line of source code, where the comment immediately follows the code on the same line as the code. Also known as inline comments.

Exception. An indication that an unexpected condition has occurred within some software. In Java, exceptions are "thrown" by methods to indicate potential problems.

Software configuration management (SCM). A collection of engineering procedures for tracking and documenting software and its related artifacts throughout their lifecycles. These ensure that all changes are recorded and the current state of the software is known and reproducible.

Version control tool. A software tool used to check in/out, define, and manage versions of project artifacts.

conditions were met). Preconditions and postconditions are a vital aspect of the definition of a method, even if the answer is "none" for a given method. Other developers need this information to be able to determine whether they should invoke a method.

3. **Preconditions of an overridden method should be weaker.** Meyer (1997) points out that when a subclass overrides (redefines) an existing method, its preconditions must be the same or weaker than that of the method it is overriding. This is because the subclass must still conform to the preconditions of its superclass(es); therefore, the overriding method should at least be able to accept anything the original method can.

4. **Postconditions of an overridden method should be stronger.** Meyer (1997) also points out that when a subclass overrides (redefines) an existing method, its postconditions must be the same or stronger than that of the method it is overriding. This is because the subclass must still conform to the postconditions of its superclass(es); therefore, the overriding method should be as restrictive, or more so, than the original method.

5. **Model the appropriate stereotypes.** The Unified Modeling Language (Rumbaugh, Jacobson, and Booch, 1999) allows for stereotypes to be applied to methods. I often apply stereotypes such as "<<constructor>>" and "<<destructor>>," for constructors and destructors, respectively, to methods, but I stay away from "<<getter>>" and "<<setter>>" for accessor methods because I prefer to name them using a "getAttributeName()" and "setAttributeName()" format.

7.2.5 Modeling Attributes During Design

Attributes are the data aspects of objects. Until now, I have modeled attributes simply, indicating just their names. However, with the UML, it is possible to model far more information about an attribute than just this, as you can see in Figure 7-10. During design, you should indicate each attribute's visibility (the level of access external objects have to an attribute) on your class diagrams. Visibility is described in Section 7.2.5.2. The name of the attribute is also indicated; strategies for naming attributes are described in Section 7.2.5.1. The type and initial value (if any) for each attribute should also be indicated and, if the attribute repeats, it should be indicated with the "[*]" notation. Finally, the scope of an attribute, whether it is a static attribute applicable to the class or an instance attribute applicable to an individual instance of the class, should also be modeled.

On design-class diagrams, indicate the visibility, name, parameters, return value, and stereotype of methods.

Figure 7-11 depicts the "Student" and "StudentNumber" classes with their attributes fully modeled. In the static attribute, "nextStudentNumber," you know it is static because it is underlined. In the "StudentNumber," class is an incremental value. Each time an instance of "StudentNumber" is created, this static attribute is incremented by one, and then its value is assigned to the object (the instance). The instance attribute "averageMark" of the "Student" class is interesting because its type is "long," one of Java's primitive types, which is consistent to the parameter passed to the corresponding setter, as well as the return value of the getter. Primitive types—such as "long," "string," and "int" in Figure 7-11—are typically indicated in lowercase, whereas types that are classes are indicated using the proper mixed case for the name of the class (such as "PhoneNumber" and "StudentNumber" in Figure 7-11).

Primitive types are indicated in lowercase. Types that are classes are indicated in mixed case.

"StudentNumber" is an interesting class because it is an example of what would be called a dependent class in the Enterprise JavaBean (EJB) architecture (Monson-Haefel, 1999; Roman, 1999). A dependent class is a fine-grained class that implements cohesive behavior that is important to your system—in this case, the calculation of the value of a unique student number. Dependent classes are often identified through a process called *class normalization* (Ambler, 1998a), a technique where you refactor your class design to make it easier to maintain and to extend by reducing the coupling in your design and increasing its cohesion. Although it is not modeled in Figure 7-11, the "PhoneNumber" and "EmailAddress" classes (the respective types of the "phoneNumber" and "emailAddress" attributes of "Student") are likely also dependent classes.

Dependent classes implement fine-grained, cohesive behavior.

visibility name: type = initialValue <<stereotype>>
visibility name[*]: type <<stereotype>>

Figure 7-10.
The UML formats for an attribute

> ### DEFINITION
>
> ***Destructor.*** A method whose purpose is to remove an object completely from memory.

7.2.5.1 Naming Attributes

Name attributes using the format "attributeName."

Like classes and methods, you should use full descriptions to name your attributes so it is obvious what the attribute represents, using the format "attributeName." Attributes that are collections, such as arrays or vectors in Java, should be given names that are plural to indicate that they represent multiple values. Furthermore, your attributes should be named in a consistent manner, at least within the definition of a single class, and ideally within all classes you develop. Also, if the name of the field begins with an acronym, such as "sqlDatabase," then the acronym (in this case, "sql") should be completely in lowercase. See Table 7-5 for tips on naming attributes.

7.2.5.2 Attribute Visibility

Table 7-6 describes the three types of attribute visibility supported by the Unified Modeling Language: public, protected, and private. As you can see, the rules and notation for attribute visibility are consistent with those for method visibility. My experience is that all fields should be declared as private for purposes of information hiding and encapsulation. When fields are declared as protected, the possibility exists that methods in subclasses will directly access them, effectively increasing the coupling within a class hierarchy. This makes your classes more difficult to maintain and to enhance; therefore, it should be avoided.

Figure 7-11.
The "Student" and "StudentNumber" classes

Attributes should never be accessed directly; instead, accessors should be used. The proper use of accessor methods is covered in Chapter 8.

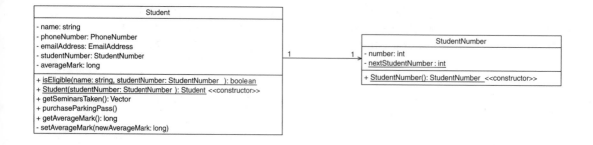

7.2.5.3 Documenting Attributes

Every attribute should be documented well enough so other developers can understand it. To be effective, you need to document the following:

1. **The description of the attribute.** You need to describe an attribute so people know how to use it. For example, the description of the "lastName" attribute might be "The last name, also known as the surname, of the person." Descriptions are usually one or two sentences in length. Long descriptions often indicate the need to refactor an attribute into several smaller and more cohesive attributes or into a dependent class.

2. **All applicable invariants.** The *invariants* of an attribute are the conditions that are always true about it. For example, an invariant about the attribute "day" might be that its value is from 1 to 31 (you could obviously get far more complex with this invariant by referring to the collection of business rules for calculating the number of days in each month). By documenting the restrictions on the value of an attribute you help to relate it to the applicable business rules, ensuring that your class will be developed properly.

Table 7-5. Example names for attributes

"Bad" Name	"Good" Name	Issue
fName	firstName	Don't use abbreviations in attribute names.
firstname	firstName	Capitalizing the second word makes the attribute name easier to read.
personFirstName	firstName	This depends on the context of the attribute, but if this is an attribute of the "Person" class, then including "person" merely lengthens the name without providing any value.
nameLast	lastName	The name "nameLast" was not consistent with "firstName" (and it sounded strange anyway).
hTTPConnection	httpConnection	The abbreviation should be all in lowercase.
firstNameString	firstName	Indicating the type of the attribute—in this case, "string"—couples the attribute name to its type. If the type changes (perhaps you decide to reimplement this attribute as an instance of the class "NameString"), then you would need to rename the attribute.
orderItemCollection	orderItems	The second version of the name is shorter and easier to understand.

DEFINITIONS

Class normalization. A process for refactoring the design of your classes to increase their cohesion and to reduce the overall coupling with a system.

Dependent class. A fine-grained class typically identified through the normalization of an attribute into a full-fledged class.

Getter. A method to obtain the value of a data attribute, or calculate the value, of an object or class.

Setter. A method that sets the value of a data attribute of an object or class. Also known as a *mutator.*

---

3. **Examples.** For attributes that have complex business rules associated with them, you should provide several examples to make them easier to understand. An example is often like a picture—it is worth a thousand words.

4. **Visibility decisions.** If you have declared a field to be anything but private, then you should document why you have done so. You should have a good reason for not declaring a variable as private.

Table 7-6. UML attribute visibilities

Visibility	Symbol	Description	Proper Usage
public	+	A public attribute can be accessed by any other method in any other object or class.	Don't make attributes public.
protected	#	A protected attribute can be accessed by any method in the class in which it is declared or by any method defined in subclasses of that class.	Don't make attributes protected.
private	-	A private attribute can only be accessed by method in the class in which it is declared, but not in the subclasses.	All attributes should be private and accessed by getter and setter methods (accessors).

The public interface of a class is the collection of public methods and public attributes (if any) it either implements or inherits. Riel (1996) suggests you don't clutter the public interface of a class with methods and attributes that don't need to be public. Minimizing the public interface of a class reduces the potential for coupling within your system.

7.2.5.4 Techniques for Attributes

The most important technique for designing and using attributes effectively is not to access them directly in your code. Although I go into greater detail on this topic in Chapter 8, my approach to attributes is to:

- Assign private visibility to all attributes

- Update attributes only in their setter methods[2]

- Directly access attributes only in their getter methods

- Always invoke a setter method for an attribute to update its value, even within the class where it is defined

- Always invoke a getter method for an attribute to obtain its value, even within the class where it is defined

- Implement simple validation logic for an attribute in its setter method

- Implement complex validation logic in separate methods

- Apply lazy initialization in getter methods for attributes that are rarely needed and have high overhead

Simple validation logic for an attribute occurs when you only need to access the value of that single attribute. For example, simple validation logic for "firstName" would include rules such as the first name of a person must be defined and it is in mixed case, beginning with a capital letter. This sort of logic can easily be encapsulated in the setter method for "firstName." Complex validation logic for an attribute, however, occurs when you need to access the value of the attribute in question, as well as the value of other attributes. For example, one part of validating the "day" attribute of a date would be to verify its value is from 1 to 30 when

Simple validation logic should be implemented in setter methods and complex validation logic in separate validation methods.

---

[2] Sometimes you also need to set attributes directly in your constructors as well, although this is often an indication of poor design.

DEFINITIONS

Encapsulation. The grouping of related concepts into one item, such as a class or component.

Information hiding. The restriction of external access to attributes.

Public interface. The collection of methods and attributes of a software element, such as a class or component, that have been assigned public visibility. The public interface includes any inherited methods and attributes.

---

the month is April. In this case, you need to access the values of both "day" and "month" as part of your validation logic. Although this appears simple, it can lead to problems in your validation logic: if the validation logic for the "month" attribute also included verifying that the value was consistent with "day," you could find your code doesn't work correctly. With this validation logic in each setter, you would always have to set the value of "month" after you set the value of "day" (if the date is currently April 30th and you tried to set it to February 28th, you would be unable to change the value of "month" because you would have an invalid date of February 30th). A better approach is to implement the validation logic in a single method, perhaps "validate()," that is invoked after the two attributes are set. An even better approach is not to allow the invocation of the individual setter methods by external objects at all but, instead, to have a bulk setter method that sets the value of all the attributes—in this case the year, month, and day—after validating that their values are consistent.

7.2.6 Introducing Interfaces Into Your Model

Interfaces define a set of operation signatures that can be implemented by a class or component.

An interface is the definition of a collection of one or more operation signatures and zero or more attributes, ideally one that defines a cohesive set of behaviors. Interfaces are implemented by classes and components. To implement an interface, a class or component must include methods that have the operation signatures defined by the interface. For example, Figure 5-19 demonstrated that the class "Student" implements the "Serializable" interface and the "Searchable" interface. You have two ways to indicate something implements an interface: the lollipop notation used for the "Serializable" interface and the box notation used for the "Searchable" interface. The lollipop notation has the advantage that it is visually compact, whereas the box notation provides details about the interface itself. The dashed arrow from "Student" to "Searchable" is a "realizes" relationship in the UML, indicating that the "Student" class implements (realizes) the "Searchable" interface. The "Searchable" interface box is the same

---

DEFINITION

Invariant. A set of assertions about an instance or class that must be true at all "stable" times, where a stable time is the period before a method is invoked on the object/class and immediately after a method is invoked.

---

notation as a class, with the addition of the stereotype of "interface." Any given class or component may implement zero or more interfaces, and one or more classes or components can implement any given interface.

Interfaces are named in the same manner as classes: They have fully described names in the format "InterfaceName." In Java, it is common to have interface names such as "Serializable" that end in "able" or "ible." In COM+ environments, common practice is to prefix interface names with a capital *I,* resulting in names such as "IComponent."

Java and COM+ development environments often include predefined interfaces.

There are two sources of interfaces: existing interfaces you have purchased with your development environment or interfaces you have developed yourself. Java development environments come with predefined interfaces, such as "Serializable" (refer to Figure 5-19), as well as "Observer" and "EnterpriseBean." You will choose to develop interfaces when you realize you need to implement something that needs to work with a wide range of objects in a similar manner. For example, consider how you would build a common facility for printing objects. This service would need to be able to work with instances of "Seminar," "Student," "Professor," "EnrollmentRecord," and so on. It would even need to work with classes you haven't even identified yet. To solve this problem, you could have all these classes either directly or indirectly inherit from a common superclass, which assumes all classes in any given hierarchy would need to support printing. A better approach would be to have any class implement a common interface perhaps named "Printable," that defines the methods it must have to support printing. Your printing facility would then invoke these methods on each object as needed.

DEFINITIONS

Bulk setter. A setter method that updates several interdependent attributes as one transaction. Bulk setter methods will invoke the individual setter methods for each attribute as needed.

Lazy initialization. An approach in which the initial value of an attribute is set in its corresponding getter method the first time the getter is invoked.

Transaction. A single unit of work that either completely succeeds or completely fails. A transaction may be one or more updates to an object, one or more reads, one or more deletes, or any combination thereof.

Interfaces are modeled using the same notation you use for classes.

By definition, the methods and attributes of interfaces are always public. Figure 7-12 depicts two interfaces, "Printable" and "Searchable." Notice the application of the <<interface>> stereotype. Neither of the interfaces has attributes defined for them because this would not only go against the principle of information hiding—any attributes would be public—it would also constrain the classes that implement this interface. Attributes and methods are depicted the same way as they are for classes. When you are developing applications using object technology, it is likely you will need both of these interfaces, thus you will find you need to refactor them to your environment. With respect to searching, *Enterprise Java Beans* (Monson-Haefel, 1999; Roman, 1999) defines a common set of "find" methods, although they are not as sophisticated as the approach implied by the "Searchable" interface—the "RetrieveCriteria" class, described in a white paper posted at *http://www. ambysoft.com/persistenceLayer.html*, supports a generic approach to finding objects that doesn't require the development of specific searching code.

Interfaces increase the flexibility, extensibility, and pluggability within your system by defining polymorphic types that are independent of inheritance.

Why interfaces? Interfaces are used to promote consistency within your models and source code, as well as to define new types for use within your system (classes also define types). Coad and Mayfield (1997) argue that interfaces help to increase the flexibility, extensibility, and pluggability of your designs because your code is no longer hardwired for instances of specific classes. Instead, it is designed to work with objects that implement a common interface. This supports polymorphism within your design. Interfaces are also an alternative to multiple inheritance. Instead of using mixin classes to achieve common behavior, you simply develop common infrastructure components (see Section 7.6) that take as parameters objects that implement defined interfaces.

Develop interfaces to generalize common behavior and/or to support common design patterns.

When would you decide to introduce a new interface? First, whenever you discover common behavior exhibited by several dissimilar classes, such as the need to support searching and printing capabilities throughout your business classes, you should attempt to generalize the common behaviors into the definition of an interface. Second, it is common to develop interfaces that support common design patterns, such as "Singleton" and "Façade," as described in the following Section 7.3. This is actually a specific, albeit common, instance of the first case.

Important to note is that interfaces are not explicitly supported by all programming languages. For example, Java has built-in support for interfaces

Figure 7-12.
The "Printable" and "Searchable" interfaces

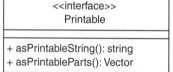

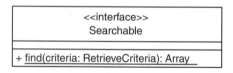

> My style is not to model the methods of an interface in the classes that implement them. The convention is that it is assumed the methods defined by the interface are implemented by that class (or at least by itself or by its subclasses if the class is abstract).
>
> **TIP**
>
> *Don't Model the Methods of an Interface In Your Classes*

whereas languages, such as C++ and Smalltalk, don't. If the language you are using doesn't support interfaces, you may instead develop a set of programming *idioms* for naming methods and attributes within your classes. Your language won't enforce the conformance of your class to a specific interface, but your coding guidelines can.

Use idioms in place of interfaces in languages that don't explicitly support interfaces.

What factors make a good interface? First, interfaces should be cohesive; they should fulfill one well-defined purpose. Second, the methods and attributes should be well defined, exactly as you would for a class. For methods, this includes defining the preconditions and postconditions, if any, as well as the specific method signature (Douglass, 1999). Third, the purpose of the interface should be defined, as well as when it should and shouldn't be implemented by a class.

Interfaces are cohesive and well defined.

7.2.7 Class Modeling Design Tips

This section summarizes a collection of class modeling design tips and techniques I have found useful over the years, such as:

- Follow the Law of Demeter
- Minimize coupling

DEFINITIONS

Idiom. Describes how to implement a particular part of a pattern, the part's functionality, or the relationship to other parts in the design. Idioms are often specific to a particular programming language.

Interface. The definition of a collection of one or more operation signatures and, optionally, attribute definitions, which comprises a cohesive set of behaviors. Some object languages support the capability for classes and/or components to implement interfaces.

Polymorphism. Different objects can respond to the same message in different ways, enabling objects to interact with one another without knowing their exact type.

Realizes relationship. A type of relationship where an item implements (realizes) a concept or type, such as a standard or an interface.

- Maximize cohesion
- Methods should do something
- Separate commands from queries
- Beware of *connascent* software elements
- Consider adding color to your diagrams

7.2.7.1 Follow the Law of Demeter

Don't talk to strangers.

The Law of Demeter (Lieberherr, Holland, and Riel, 1988; Ambler, 1998a) states that objects should send messages to themselves, a parameter of their methods, their own attributes, an element within a collection that is an attribute, or an object they create. Craig Larman (1998) encapsulates this concept with his "Don't Talk to Strangers" pattern.

7.2.7.2 Minimize Coupling

A class should be dependent on as few other classes as possible.

Coupling is a measure of how much two items, such as classes or methods, are interrelated. When one class depends on another class, we say they are *coupled*. When one class interacts with another class, but doesn't know any of the implementation details of the other class, we say they are *loosely coupled*. When one class relies on the implementation (that is, it directly accesses the data attributes of the other), we say they are *highly coupled*.

A class is coupled to another class when it has knowledge of that other class. Coupling is important because when Class *A* is coupled to Class *B*, a change in *B* could necessitate a change in *A*. As a result, you want to reduce coupling wherever possible. In object-oriented designs, several sources of coupling exist:

1. **Coupling via associations.** Whenever an association exists between two classes, they are coupled. For example, in Figure 7-13, the class "Person" is coupled to "Address" via the "lives at" association: a person object know at what address it lives. Similarly, "Seminar" is coupled to "Course" via the "offering of" association. Furthermore, because this association is bidirectional, "Course" is also coupled to "Seminar." It is important to understand that a class is coupled to another class only when it has knowledge of that other class. Therefore Class *A* can be coupled to Class *B* without *B* being coupled to Class *A*.

2. **Coupling via aggregation and composition.** Aggregation and composition are simply specialized types of association, so they also indicate coupling. In Figure 7-13, the classes "Program" and "Course" are coupled to one another via aggregation.

3. **Coupling via dependency.** Dependencies also indicate coupling between classes in the same manner as association does.

4. **Coupling via collaboration.** In a way, coupling via collaboration is related to coupling via association, aggregation, composition, or dependency (remember, without some sort of relationship you can't have collaboration). The main point here is that collaborations increase coupling—not only does an object know of the existence of other objects, it also collaborates with them. For example, "Program" increases its coupling to "Course" via each collaboration it has with it. Riel (1996) suggests you should minimize the number of collaborations between two classes if possible.

5. **Coupling via realization.** The class "Student" is coupled to the definition of the "Searchable" interface via a realizes relationship. If the definition of the interface changes, the "Student" class needs to be updated to reflect this change.

6. **Direct coupling via inheritance.** Subclasses are highly coupled to the implementations of their superclasses (a subclass knows and does everything its superclass does). For example, in Figure 7-13, the "Student" class is coupled to the "Person" class in this manner. One way to reduce this kind of coupling is not to allow subclasses to modify the values of attributes defined in their superclasses. This implies that you need to invoke accessors instead of directly accessing the values of attributes. While this is a little extra work, it makes your system more maintainable in the long run.

7. **Indirect coupling via inheritance.** Because a class inherits all the relationships and collaborations of its superclass(es), it also inherits any coupling with which the superclasses are involved. In this case, the "Student" class is indirectly coupled to "Address" via inheriting from "Person."

7.2.7.3 Maximize Cohesion

Cohesion is a measure of how much an item, such as a class or method, makes sense. A good measure of the cohesiveness of something is how long describing it takes using only one sentence: the longer it takes, the less cohesive it likely is. You want to design methods and classes that are highly cohesive. In other words, it should be completely clear what a method or class is all about. A good rule of thumb is if you cannot describe a class or method with one sentence in less than 15 seconds, then it probably is not cohesive. Classes should represent only one kind of object, and methods should do one thing and one thing well.

Cohesive items can easily be described in one sentence.

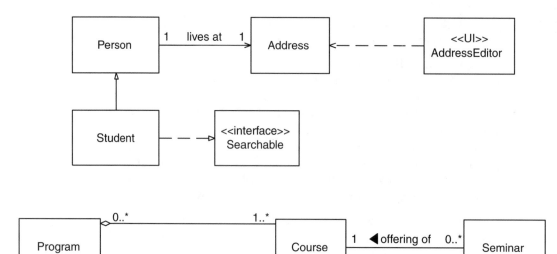

Figure 7-13.
Sources of coupling
in your object-
oriented designs

7.2.7.4 Methods Should Do Something

Although this sounds obvious, in practice this advice is often ignored. Each method of a class should either access or modify the attributes of the class. A method should do something, and not just pass the buck to other methods.

7.2.7.5 Separate Commands from Queries

Asking a question should not change the answer.

This is the Command-Query Separation Principle (Meyer, 1997), a principle stating that functions should not produce abstract side-effects. The basic idea is this: Asking a question (a query), perhaps by invoking a getter or by asking for a calculated value, shouldn't change the state target object. For example, it doesn't make sense that anything should change about a seminar just because you ask how many students are currently enrolled in it. Commands can cause changes in the object. For example, a request to a seminar to enroll a student into itself would obviously change the state of the seminar. The student would be enrolled in it if she is eligible to take the seminar and there is room for her.

7.2.7.6 Beware of Connascent Software Elements

Consistent use of color can improve the understandability of your diagrams.

Connascence (Page-Jones, 2000) is a measure of how well you have applied encapsulation within your system—have you minimized coupling and maximized cohesion. Two software elements are connascent either because of bad design (therefore, fix it) or, by their nature (they

---

DEFINITION

Coupling. The degree of dependence between two items. In general, it is better to reduce coupling wherever possible.

---

fulfill a common goal). For example, mirror hierarchies are connascent because their structures reflect that they fulfill a common goal.

7.2.7.7 Consider Adding Color to Your Diagrams

Coad, Lefebrvre, and DeLuca (1999) provide excellent advice in their book *Java Modeling in Color with UML* for improving the understandability of your diagrams by applying color to them. Your models are part of your communication interface with other developers and, just as user interfaces can be improved by the effective application of color, so can UML diagrams. In addition to applying UML stereotypes to your classes, you can also apply color: Perhaps controller classes are rendered in blue, business entity classes in green, and system classes in yellow. Other uses for color include indicating the implementation language of a class (for example, blue for Java and red for C++), the development priority of a use case (for example red for Phase 1, orange for Phase 2, and yellow for future phases), or the target platform (for example, blue for an application server, green for a client machine, and pink for a database server) for a software element. Deployment modeling is discussed in further detail in Section 7-7.

7.3 Applying Design Patterns Effectively

Design patterns describe a solution to common problems found in the design of systems. I won't discuss every existing design pattern in this section—too many exist to list in one book and people are discovering new patterns every day anyway. However, I will describe two useful design patterns that you should be able to apply immediately to the applications you are developing. These patterns are "Singleton" and "Façade" (Gamma et al., 1995).

DEFINITION

Connascence. Between two software elements, *A* and *B*, the property by which a change in *A* would require a change to *B* to preserve overall correctness within your system.

7.3.1 The Singleton Design Pattern

Discovering classes in your application that should only have one instance is common. Perhaps there should only be one instance of a certain editing screen open at any given time, perhaps you have configuration information you want to store in one place only, or perhaps you have one or more constant values you need to maintain somewhere. In all these examples, you need to have a single instance of the class in question: a single instance of the dialog box, a single instance of the configuration information, and a single instance of the constants.

The Singleton pattern ensures that only one instance of a class exists at any one time.

Singleton (Gamma et al., 1995) is a design pattern that shows how to ensure that only one single instance of a class exists at any one time. In Figure 7-14, you see the definition for an interface describing the Singleton design pattern. Note that a static attribute keeps track of the single instance, and a class method creates the instance if it doesn't already exist. The interface for this pattern is one of the few times I have actually seen a valid use for including an attribute in the definition of an interface. However, this is an invalid use of an attribute within an interface because I have assigned it private visibility instead of public (remember, interfaces define a public interface to be implemented by a class). Although Singleton is a simple pattern, I suspect it is one you will use over and over again when developing object-oriented software.

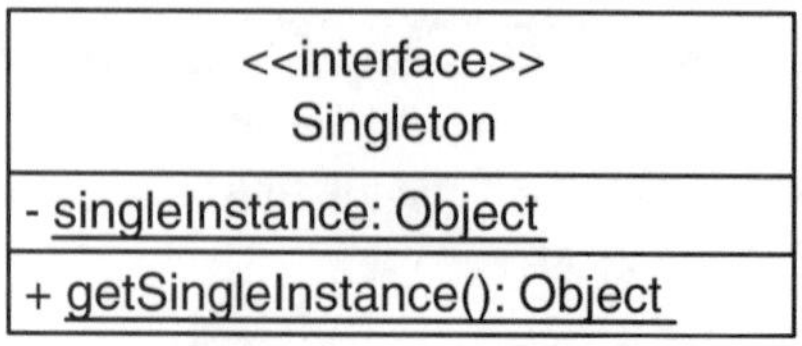

Figure 7-14.
The solution to the Singleton design pattern

<<interface>>
Singleton
- singleInstance: Object
+ getSingleInstance(): Object

7.3.2 The Façade Design Pattern

The purpose of the Façade design pattern (Gamma et al., 1995) is to provide a unified interface to a subsystem or component, making it easier to use. The solution for the Façade pattern is presented in Figure 7-15. The gist of the pattern is that objects external to the subsystem or component send messages to the façade class, which, in turn, routes them to the appropriate "internal" classes and objects.

The Façade pattern has several advantages. First, it provides a simple and standard way to implement components using object technology. The façade class implements the public interface of the component and the "internal classes" implement the behaviors provided by the component. Component modeling is covered in detail in Section 7.6. Second, it provides a mechanism to reduce the coupling within your system because the external classes now interact only with the façade class, not all of the classes internal to your component or subsystem. Third, the external classes are not prevented from collaborating with the internal classes if need be, providing flexibility, albeit at the cost of increased coupling. Finally, because the communication to the internal classes of a component or subsystem are focused through a common point, the façade class, it provides a single point where you can potentially add important system features, such as security access control and load balancing.

7.3.3 Tips for Applying Patterns Effectively

The following tips can help you to apply patterns successfully in your work:

1. **Read widely.** Although patterns became popular in the early-to-mid 1990s within the object community, they have quickly gained prominence and significant work has been accomplished

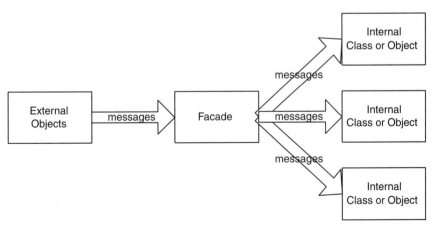

Figure 7-15.
The solution to the Façade design pattern

> **DEFINITIONS**
>
> *Load balancing.* A technique where processing requests are distributed across several nodes, so the overall processing burden is spread as evenly as possible across the nodes.
>
> *Security access control.* The act of ensuring that users of a system may only invoke the behaviors to which they are entitled, including, but not limited to, the manipulation of components, objects, and data.

in a few short years. The end result is that hundreds, if not thousands, of design patterns are published. A good starting point for learning more about all types of patterns, including design patterns, can be found at The Process Patterns Resource Page (*http://www.ambysoft.com/processPatternsPage.html*).

2. **Understand the patterns.** Simply reading about patterns isn't enough; you also need to understand them. Most patterns describe both when and when not to apply them—important information you need to understand to use them successfully.

3. **Patterns are not the solution to everything.** Many patterns are out there at your disposal, but not every design problem can be solved via the application of one or more patterns. The secret is to have a good grasp of what patterns exist and to look them up when you think you have a situation where they can be applied.

4. **Remember that several types of patterns exist.** As you have seen throughout this book, analysis patterns, design patterns, and process patterns are just a few of the types of patterns that exist.

7.4 State Chart Modeling

Develop state chart diagrams for classes that exhibit different behavior depending on their state.

Objects have both behavior and state or, in other words, they do things and they know things. Some objects do and know more things, or at least more complicated things, than other objects. Some objects are incredibly complicated, so complex that developers can have difficulty understanding them. To understand complex classes better, particularly those that act in different manners depending on their state, you should develop one or more UML state chart diagrams (Booch, Jacobson, and Rumbaugh, 1999; Fowler and Scott, 1997; Ambler, 1998a; Douglass, 1999) describing how their instances work.

First, some basic terminology for state modeling. UML state chart diagrams depict the various states that an object may be in and the transitions between those states. In fact, in other modeling languages, it is common for this type of a diagram to be called a state-transition diagram or even simply a state diagram. A state represents a stage in the behavior pattern of an object and, like UML activity diagrams (Chapter 6), it is possible to have initial states and final states. An initial state, also called a creation state, is the one that an object is in when it is first created, whereas a final state is one in which no transitions exit. A transition is a progression from one state to another and will be triggered by an event that is either internal or external to the object.

Figure 7-16 presents an example state chart diagram for the Seminar class during registration. The rounded rectangles represent states; instances of Seminar can be in the "Proposed," "Scheduled," "Open For Enroll-ment," "Full," and "Closed to Enrollment" states. An object starts in an ini-tial state, represented by the closed circle, and can end up in a final state, represented by the bordered circle. This is the exact same notation used by UML activity diagrams, a perfect example of the consistency of the UML.

The arrows in Figure 7-16 represent transitions, progressions from one state to another. For example, when a seminar is in the "Scheduled" state, it can either be opened for enrollment or cancelled. Transitions can also have

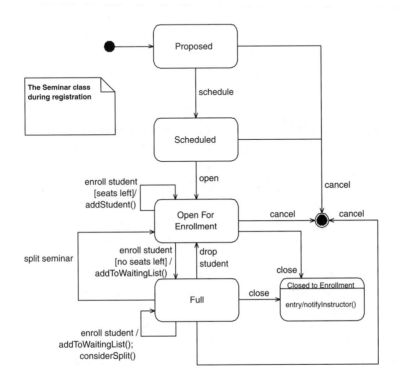

Figure 7-16.
A UML state chart diagram for the Seminar class during registration

guards on them, conditions that must be true for the transition to be triggered. An example of a guard in Figure 7-16 is shown on the transition from the "Open For Enrollment" to the "Closed to Enrollment" state, the UML notation for which is in the format "[guard description]" where the text is free-form. Also possible is to indicate the invocation of methods on your transition, an example of which is shown on the same transition as the guard, the format being "methodName1(), methodName2()," and so forth with the order in the listing implying the order in which they are invoked.

States are represented by attribute values.

States are represented by the values of the attributes of an object. For example, a seminar is in the "Open For Enrollment" state when it has been flagged as open and seats are available to be filled. It is possible to indicate the invocation of methods within a state; for example, upon entry into the "Closed to Enrollment" state the method "notifyInstructor()" is invoked. The general notation for indicating methods within states is shown in Figure 7-17 and is self explanatory: Methods to be invoked when the object enters the state are indicated by the keyword "entry." Methods to be invoked as the object exits from the state are indicated by the keyword "exit." And methods that are invoked while the object is in the state have no keyword. The capability to indicate method invocations when you enter and exit from a state is useful because it enables you to avoid documenting the same method several times on each of the transitions that enter or exit from the state, respectively. I indicate the methods to run during the state when I want to indicate that a method is to be run continously, perhaps a method that polls other objects for information or a method that implements the logic of an important business process.

Transitions are the result of the invocation of a method that causes an important change in state. Understanding that not all method invocations

---

DEFINITIONS

Final state. A state from which no transitions exit. Objects will have zero or more final states.

Guard. A precondition that must be true before a transition may occur.

Initial state. The state an object is in when it is first created. All objects have an initial state. This is often referred to as the *creation state*.

Recursive transition. A transition that leads into the same state from which it originated.

State. Represents a stage in the behavior pattern of an object. A state can also be said to represent a condition of an object to which a defined set of policies, regulations, and physical laws apply.

Transition. A progression from one state to another. A transition will be triggered by an event (either internal or external to the object).

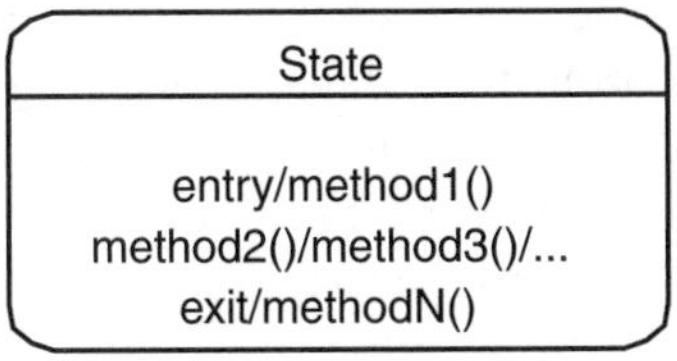

Figure 7-17.
The notation for modeling method invocations within states

will result in transitions is important. For example, the invocation of a getter method likely wouldn't cause a transition because it isn't changing the state of the object (unless lazy initialization is being applied). Furthermore, Figure 7-16 indicates that an attempt to enroll a student in a full seminar may not result in the object changing state, unless it is determined that the seminar should be split, even though the state of the object changes (another student is added to the waiting list). You can see in Figure 7-16 that transitions are a reflection of your business rules. For example, you see that you can attempt to enroll a student in a course only when it is open for enrollment or full, and that a seminar may be split (presumably into two seminars) when the waiting list is long enough to justify the split. You can have recursive transitions, transitions that start and end in the same state, an example of which is the "enroll in seminar" transition when the seminar is full.

Transitions are the result of method invocations and often reflect business rules.

For the sake of convention, we say an object is always in one and only one state, implying that transitions are instantaneous. Although we know this is not completely true (every method is going to take some time to run), it makes life a lot easier for us to assume that transitions take no time to complete.

Objects are always in one and only one state. Transitions are considered instantaneous.

7.4.1 How to Draw a State Diagram

Drawing a state diagram is fairly straightforward and can be described in the following steps:

1. Identify the initial/creation state.
2. Identify the final state(s), if any.
3. Identify as many other applicable, "real-world" states as possible.
4. Identify potential substates.
5. Identify the transitions leaving a state.
6. Identify the target state to which a transition leads.

The first thing you want to do is to identify the creation state and whether any final states exist. In other words, you basically want to identify both the start and the end of an object's life. After you have done

You can find states by looking at the boundary values of your attributes.

this, ask yourself what other states or stages in the life of an object does it pass through? You can often find states by looking at the boundary values of your attributes. For example, when the number of students in a seminar reaches the maximum, it becomes full. "Full" is a valid state because different rules now apply: When a student tries to enroll, he is put on a waiting list and the seminar is a candidate to be split in two.

Complex states often have substates.

Sometimes the behavior of an object is in such a complex state that you need to develop a separate state chart to represent the object. You can easily do this or you may simply decide to model the substates of the state (referred to as the superstate) by drawing a state chart within the state bubble of the superstate. This is an advanced state chart diagramming technique beyond the scope of this book, one that is common for real-time development, but not as common for business application development, a topic covered well by the book *Doing Hard Time* (Douglass, 1999).

Try to identify as many states as possible first, and then look for transitions.

Once you have identified as many states as you can, start looking for transitions. For each state, ask yourself how the object can get out of it, if possible. This will give you a transition. Because all transitions lead from one state to another, ask yourself what new state the transition leads you to (don't forget about recursive transitions that lead to the same state). You should also look at the methods you identified in your class diagram. Some of them will correspond to a transition in your state diagram.

7.4.2 When and Why Should You Draw State Diagrams?

State diagrams are used to document complex classes, often in real-time systems.

State chart modeling is a dynamic modeling technique, one that focuses on identifying the behavior within your system—in this case, behavior specific to the instances of a single class. My style is to draw one or more state chart diagrams when a class exhibits different behavior depending on its state. For example, the "Address" class is fairly simple, representing data you will display and manipulate in your system. Seminar objects, on the other hand, are fairly complex, as you can see in Figure 7-16. This state chart is not complete, however, because seminars have interesting behavior during the school year. Once a seminar becomes closed to enrollment, it is taught by an instructor who will input marks into the university system throughout

---

TIP

State Modeling Often Reveals Potential Error Conditions

Identifying potential error conditions while you are state chart modeling is common because you are constantly asking "should this transition be allowed when the object is in this state?" When the answer is yes, you need to add the transition to your diagram. When the answer is no, you may need to document this potential issue so your programmers develop the proper error-checking code, so the transition is not allowed to occur.

the semester. Eventually, the seminar will finish, the instructor will enter the final marks, and then she will submit the marks so they can be added to each student's official records. This indicates to me that there is still some more modeling to be done. You can take either of two basic approaches: you could expand the existing state chart to include the appropriate new states or you could draw another state chart diagram representing this logic. State diagrams are also useful in real-time environments (which are typically complex).

7.4.3 State Diagrams and Inheritance

Although being able to inherit state diagrams would be nice, it is extremely unlikely this will happen. The definition of inheritance says that although the subclass is similar to the superclass, *it is still different*. The behavior of the subclass is usually different than that of the superclass. This means you need to reconsider the state diagram when you inherit from a class with one. The one good thing is that many of the states and transitions are reusable. You will probably find you either add new states and transitions, or you will redefine some.

The state chart(s) differ between a superclass and its subclasses.

7.5 Collaboration Modeling

A fundamental concept of the Unified Modeling Language is that you use different diagrams for different purposes. Class diagrams model the static nature of your system, sequence diagrams model the logic of usage scenarios, and state chart diagrams model the behavior of complex classes. But what happens when you need to show the behavior of several objects collaborating together to fulfill a common purpose? This is what UML collaboration diagrams (Booch, Jacobson, and Rumbaugh, 1999) can be used for, to provide a birds-eye view of a collection of collaborating objects.

Collaboration diagrams depict a birds-eye view of the interactions between objects.

Collaboration diagrams show the message flow between objects in an OO application and also imply the basic associations (relationships) between classes. Figure 7-18 presents a simplified collaboration diagram for displaying a seminar details screen or page. The rectangles represent the various objects involved that make up the application. The lines between the classes represent the relationships (associations, aggregation, composition, dependencies,

---

DEFINITIONS

Substate. A specific state that is part of a more generalized superstate.

Superstate. A general state that is decomposed into several substates.

or inheritance) between them. The same notation for classes and objects
used on UML sequence diagrams are used on UML collaboration diagrams,
again another example of the consistency of the UML. The details of your
associations, such as their multiplicities, are not modeled because this information is contained on your UML class diagrams; remember, each UML diagram has its own specific purpose and no single diagram is sufficient on its
own. Messages are depicted as a labeled arrow that indicates the direction of
the message, using a notation similar to that used on sequence diagrams. Figure 7-19 summarizes the basic notation for modeling messages on collaboration diagrams. Optionally, you may indicate the sequence number in which
the message is sent, indicate an optional return value, and indicate the
method name and the parameters (if any) passed to it.

*Model return
values only when
it isn't obvious.*

In Figure 7-18, you see that the "Seminar Details" user interface class
collaborates with the seminar object to obtain the information needed to

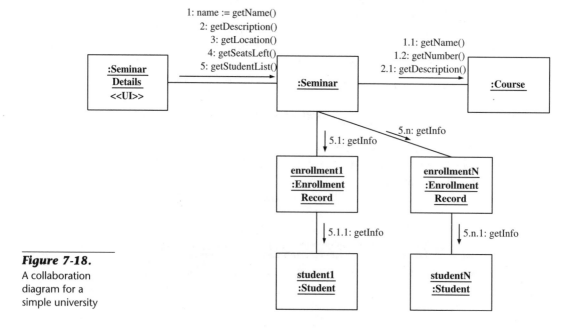

Figure 7-18.
A collaboration
diagram for a
simple university

sequenceNumber: returnValue := methodName(parameters)

Figure 7-19.
The basic notation for invoking a message on a collaboration diagram

display its information. It first invokes the getter method to obtain the name of the seminar. You know this is the first message invoked because its sequence number is one. To fulfill this responsibility, the seminar object then collaborates with the course object that describes it to obtain the name of the course. Notice how I chose to indicate the return value in the description of the first message, but not the second. My rule of thumb is that if the return value is obvious, which is definitely the case with a getter method, then you shouldn't clutter your diagram by indicating the return value. Also notice the numbering scheme I used. The invocation of "getName()" and "getNumber()" on the course object is clearly the result of invoking "getName()" on the seminar object: The name of a seminar is in the format "Course Number: Course Name."

7.5.1 Drawing Collaboration Diagrams

Collaboration diagrams are usually drawn in parallel with class diagrams and sequence diagrams. Class diagrams provide input into the basic relationships between objects, sequence diagrams provide an indication of the message flow between objects, and collaboration diagrams provide a bird's-eye view of the interactions between objects. With collaboration diagramming the basic idea is that you:

1. Identify the scope of the diagram

2. Identify the objects

3. Identify the relationships between the objects

4. Identify the messages passed between the objects

To determine the scope of your diagram, you need to ask yourself what you want to model. I like to use collaboration diagrams to model

In Figure 7-18, instead of modeling each individual invocation of the getter methods to obtain the information, I would need to put together the list of students enrolled in a seminar, I simply modeled a single message "getInfo," which represents all the getter methods. An important modeling philosophy is that adding value is more important than being exact: this technique is a bit of a cheat, but it makes for simpler diagrams.

TIP

Consolidate Getter Invocations on Collaboration Diagrams

the logic of the implementation of a major user interface element, which is what I did in the diagram of Figure 7-18. It is also common to see collaboration diagrams used to model the logic of the implementation of a complex method of a class, particularly one that interacts with a large number of other objects. To determine the objects and the associations needed for your diagram, you merely need to look at your system's design-level class diagram, the topic of Section 7.2, and decide what classes and relationships you need to support the scope of your diagram. To identify the required messages, you work through the logic of what you are modeling in exactly the same manner you did to identify the messages in UML sequence diagrams, as described in Chapter 6.

Although Figure 7-18 applies sequence numbers to the messages, my experience is if you feel the need to use sequence numbers on collaboration diagrams, this is a good indication that you should be using sequence diagrams instead. The main difference between collaboration diagrams and sequence diagrams is that sequence diagrams show the objects and messages involved, as well as the appropriate order for message invocations, for a single use case scenario. Collaboration diagrams, on the other hand, are used to get a big-picture outlook for the system, potentially incorporating the message flow of many use case scenarios.

7.5.2 Collaboration and Inheritance

When it gets right down to it, an object-oriented system is basically a collection of objects working together to get the job done. Therefore, to understand fully how an OO application works, you need to understand how objects collaborate. Figure 7-20 depicts a transcript object requesting the full name of a student object, so it can include the name as part of its output. Because the object is an instance of "Student," your system will first look at the definition of the "Student" class to obtain the definition of the "getFullName()" method. Because this method is not defined in the class, it will traverse up the class hierarchy and look at the definition of the immediate superclass, in this case "UniversityPerson," to discover it is not defined there either. This process continues to the next immediate superclass, "Person," where the definition of the method exists. The method is invoked and the full name of the student is built, being the combination of the person's first name, last name, and middle initials. Important to note is that had the object been an instance of "InternationalStudent," then its overridden version of the "getFullName()" method would have been invoked instead. The general rule is this: When the system is looking for the definition of a method, it starts at the definition of the class of which the object is an instance and works its way up the class hierarchy until it finds the first definition of the method.

DEFINITION

Use case scenario. A single path of logic through one or more use cases. A use case scenario could represent the basic course of action through a single use case, a combination of portions of the basic course replaced by the steps of one or more alternate paths through a single use case, or a logic path spanning several use cases. Use case scenarios are also called usage scenarios.

Meanwhile, Back in Reality

Figure 7-20 depicts an example of what happens conceptually to find the appropriate implementation of a method, but the actual implementation will differ between implementation environments.

7.5.3 When Should You Draw Collaboration Diagrams?

Collaboration diagrams should be drawn whenever you want to fully understand the behavior of an OO application and to show the objects that make up the application and the message flow between them. The reality is that

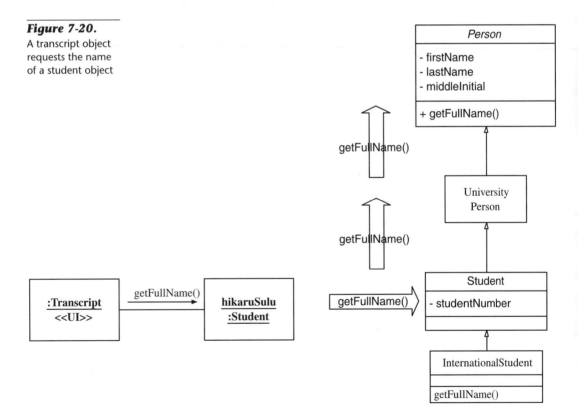

Figure 7-20.
A transcript object requests the name of a student object

*Sequence
diagrams and
collaboration
diagrams are
interchangeable.*

UML sequence diagrams and UML collaboration diagrams are interchangeable, and their usage often boils down to a matter of personal taste.

7.6 Component Modeling

Component-based development (CBD) and object-oriented development go hand-in-hand, and it is generally recognized that object technology is the preferred foundation from which to build components. The Unified Modeling Language includes a component diagram (Booch, Rumbaugh, and Jacobson, 1999; Ambler, 1998a) that can be used both to analyze and design your component-based software. Figure 7-21 presents an example component model for the university system. Components are modeled as rectangles with two smaller rectangles jutting out from the left-hand side. Components implement one or more interfaces, modeled using the same "lollipop" notation that UML class diagrams use. Components have dependencies on the interfaces of other components, modeled using the standard UML dependency notation.

7.6.1 How to Develop a Component Model

The goal of component modeling is to distribute the classes of your system into larger-scale, cohesive components. Identifying components is

Figure 7-21.
An example UML component diagram for the university

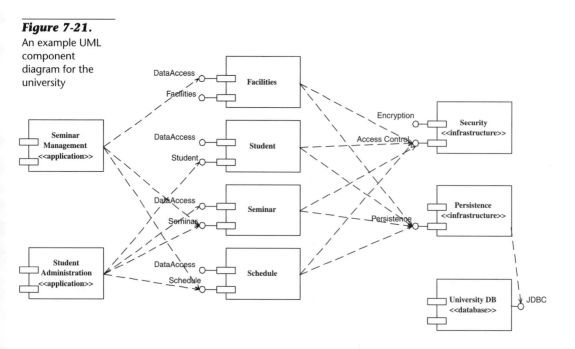

> Collaboration diagrams model interactions between objects, and objects interact with each other by invoking messages on each other. If you want to see the data flow, instead of the message flow, between the portions of a system, then you should consider drawing an activity diagram.
>
> **TIP**
>
> *Collaboration Diagrams Don't Model Data Flow*

the design equivalent of identifying packages (see Chapter 6). This section summarizes a design process, based on the subsystem identification techniques presented in *Designing Object-Oriented Software* (Wirfs-Brock, Wilkerson, and Wiener, 1990) and the distributed object modeling process presented in *Building Object Applications That Work* (Ambler, 1998a), for refactoring a traditional object design for the purposes of deploying it as components. Five steps exist, typically performed in an iterative manner, to componentize your object design:

1. Handle nonbusiness/domain classes
2. Define class contracts
3. Simplify inheritance and aggregation hierarchies
4. Identify domain components
5. Define domain-component contracts

7.6.1.1 Handle Nonbusiness Classes

In Section 7.1, you saw that five types of classes exist from which you will build your applications. User interface classes encapsulate the screens and reports that make up the user interface for your system. Business/domain class implement the fundamental domain types within your application—for example, the "Student" and "Seminar" classes. Controller/process classes, such as "EnrollInSeminar" in Figure 7-3, implement complex business logic that pertains to several classes. Persistence classes encapsulate access to your persistent stores (relational databases, flat files, object bases), and system classes encapsulate operating system features, such as your approach to interprocess communication (IPC). Persistence and system classes are important because they make your system more robust by promoting portability and reusabilty throughout the systems your organization develops.

The easiest part of identifying subsystems is first to deal with user interface classes because they are generally implemented on client machines (such as personal computers, HTML browsers, and Java terminals). I prefer to identify a component for each major portion of the user

Identify components for the user interface classes of your system.

interface for the system, typically one for each type of human actor. I assign these components the stereotype "<<application>>," as you see with the "Seminar Management" and "Student Administration" components of Figure 7-21.

Two basic strategies exist for handing your persistence classes, depending on your general approach to persistence. First, for systems that use "data classes" to encapsulate hard-coded SQL for simple CRUD (create, read, update, delete) behavior, you should deploy their data classes along with their corresponding business classes (more on this later). For example, this persistence strategy would result in a "StudentData" class that corresponds to "Student," a "SeminarData" class that corresponds to "Seminar," and so on. Wherever you choose to deploy "Student," you also automatically deploy the "StudentData" class. Second, for systems that take a more robust approach to persistence, perhaps using a persistence framework or persistence layer, you will typically model a "Peristence" component. This approach was taken by the component model of Figure 7-21: I assigned the stereotype of "<<infrastructure>>" to it to separate it from the business/domain components, which are typically not assigned stereotypes for the same reasons that stereotypes are not assigned to business classes in UML class diagrams.

Assign the <<infrastructure>> stereotype to persistence and system components.

System classes are also assigned to infrastructure components, such as the "Security" component in Figure 7-21, and have the "<<infrastructure>>" stereotype applied to them. Candidate infrastructure components typically include system management facilities that support real-time monitoring and audit logging, a messaging component that wraps middleware services, a printing component, and a file management component.

7.6.1.2 Define Class Contracts

A class contract is any service/behavior of a class that is requested of it. In other words, it is a public method that directly responds to a message from other classes. The best way to think about this is that a collection of class contracts define the external interface, also known as the public interface, of a class. For example, the contracts of the "Seminar" class likely include operations such as "enrollStudent()" and "dropStudent()." For the purpose of identifying components, you can ignore all the operations that aren't class contracts because they don't contribute to communication between objects distributed in different components, simplifying your problem dramatically.

7.6.1.3 Simplify Hierarchies

For the sake of identifying components, your system's inheritance and aggregation hierarchies can often be simplified. For inheritance hierarchies a rule of thumb to follow is that if a subclass doesn't add a new

> **DEFINITION**
>
> **Domain component.** A large-scale component that encapsulates cohesive portions of your business domain.

contract, then it can effectively be ignored and, in general, you can often consider a class hierarchy as a single class. For aggregation and composition hierarchies, you can ignore any "part classes" that aren't associated with other classes outside of the aggregation hieararchy. By collapsing aggregation and inheritance hierarchies, you simplify your model, making it easier to analyze when you define subsystems.

7.6.1.4 Identify Potential Domain Components

A domain component is a set of classes that collaborate among themselves to support a cohesive set of contracts. The basic idea is that classes, and even other domain components, are able to send messages to domain components either to request information or to request that an action be performed. On the outside, domain components appear simple;, actually they appear like any other type of object but, on the inside, they are often quite complex because they encapsulate the behavior of several classes.

A key goal is you want to organize your design into several components in such a way as to reduce the amount of information flowing between them. Any information passed between components, either in the form of messages or the objects that are returned as the result of a message send, represents potential traffic on your network (if the components are deployed to different nodes). Because you want to minimize network traffic to reduce the response time of your application, you want to design your domain components in such a way that most of the information flow occurs within the components and not between them.

Reduce the flow of traffic between components.

To determine whether a class belongs in a domain component, you need to analyze the collaborations it is involved with to determine its distribution type. A *server* class is one that receives messages, but doesn't send them. A *client* class is one that sends messages, but doesn't receive them. A *client/server* class is one that both sends and receives messages. Once you have identified the distribution type of each class, you are in a position to start identifying potential domain components. Heuristics for identifying potential components are as follows:

1. **Server classes belong in a component.** Pure server classes belong in a domain component and often form their own domain components because they are the "last stop" for message flow within an application.

DEFINITION

Contract. Any service/behavior of a class or component that is requested of it.

---

2. **Merge a component into its only client.** If you have a domain component that is a server to only one other domain component, you may decide to combine the two components or, perhaps, the two machines on which the domain components reside can be connected via a high-speed private link, avoiding the need to put the one machine on your regular network.

3. **Client classes don't belong in components.** Client classes don't belong in a domain component because they only generate messages, they don't receive them, whereas the purpose of a domain component is to respond to messages. Therefore, client classes have nothing to add to the functionality offered by a component.

4. **Highly coupled classes belong in the same component.** When two classes collaborate frequently, this is an indication they should be in the same domain component to reduce the network traffic between the two classes. This is especially true when that interaction involves large objects, either passed as parameters or received as return values. By including them in the same domain component, you reduce the potential network traffic between them. The basic idea is that highly coupled classes belong together.

5. **Minimize the size of the message flow between components.** Client/server classes belong in a domain component, but there may be a choice as to which domain component they belong to. This is where you need to consider issues such as the information flow going into and out of the class.

6. **Components should be cohesive.** A fundamental design precept is that a class should be part of a domain component only if it exists to fulfill the goals of that domain component.

7. **Consider potential changes to the components.** Refine your assignment of classes to domain components by considering the impact of potential changes on them. Consider how each change case (change case modeling was discussed in Chapter 3) would affect your design. If you know some classes are likely to change, then you may choose to implement them in one or two components if it makes sense to limit the scope of the changes when they do occur.

> A good rule of thumb is that it should be impossible to reuse the parts of a component on their own, and that you need the entire component for it to be useful. A corollary is if you can reuse a part of a component, this is usually a good indication you have another component.
>
> **TIP**
>
> *Classes Within a Component Should Be Reused Together*

7.6.1.5 Define Domain-Component Contracts

Domain-component contracts are the collection of class contracts accessed by classes outside the domain component (class contracts that are only used by classes within the subsystem are not included). As you would expect, the collection of domain-component contracts form the public interface for a domain component. This step is important because it helps both to simplify your design—users of it only need to understand the public interface of each component to learn how to use it—as well as to decrease the coupling within your design.

Consider several rules of thumb when defining domain-component contracts. When all the contracts of a server class are included in the contracts provided by the domain component of which it is part, consider making the server class its own domain component that is external to the current component. The implication is that when the entire public interface of the server class is needed by the outside world, then encapsulating it within another domain component won't buy you anything. There is a mirror rule of thumb to this one: If none of the contracts of a server class are included in the subsystem contract (that is, these contracts are only accessed by classes internal to the subsystem), then the server class should be defined as a subsystem internal to the present subsystem. The contracts of a subsystem should be cohesive, that is, they should make sense being together. If they don't, then you probably have multiple subsystems.

DEFINITIONS

Client class. A class whose instances send messages to instances of other classes, but don't receive them.

Client/server class. A class whose instances both send messages to instances of other classes as well as receive messages from instances of other classes.

Server class. A class whose instances receive messages, but doesn't send them to instances of other classes.

Booch, Jacobson, and Rumbaugh (1999) suggest you "manage the seams in your system" by defining the major interfaces for your components. What they mean is you want to define the interfaces to components early in design, so you are free to work on the internals of each component without having to worry about how you will affect other components. You have to keep the defined interface stable. They also suggest that components should depend on the interface of other components and not on the component itself. You can see this in Figure 7-21, where dependencies are drawn from components to the interfaces of other components. The advantage of this approach is you can restrict access to a component, potentially making your system more secure and potentially more robust. This decoupling of components enables you to scale each component independently, resulting in greater flexibility and a smoother growth path.

7.6.2 Implementing a Component

Common object-oriented programming languages, such as Java, C++, and Smalltalk, don't natively support components. What this means is, in all three of these languages, it is possible to declare the definition of a class, but not a component. To get around this minor problem, you simply implement façade classes, described in Section 7.3, to implement the interfaces of your components. Façade classes accept messages from objects external to a component and route the message to the appropriate class(es) and object(s) encapsulated within the component. Part of this routing effort may include converting the incoming message into something the internal classes and objects can recognize, as well as converting their response into something the external client objects can understand. In fact, a design pattern called "Adapter" (Gamma et al., 1995) exists for specifically this.

7.7 Deployment Modeling

A UML deployment diagram depicts a static view of the run-time configuration of processing nodes and the components that run on those nodes. In other words, deployment diagrams show the hardware for your system, the software that is installed on that hardware, and the middleware used to connect the disparate machines to one another. You want to create a deployment model for applications that are deployed to several machines. A point-of-sales application running on a thin-client network computer directly accessing a centralized database server would be a good candidate for a deployment model. So would a customer service system deployed using a distributed object architecture such as CORBA

(Common Object Request Broker Architecture). Deployment models are also needed for the design of embedded systems, showing how the hardware and software components work together. In short, all but the most trivial of systems will require a deployment model.

Figure 7-22 presents an example of a UML deployment diagram for the student administration application. The three-dimensional boxes represent nodes, such as computers or switches, and connections between nodes are represented with simple lines. As you would expect, software components, interfaces, and dependencies are indicated using the standard UML notations. In Figure 7-22, stereotypes indicate that the connection between the browser and the application server uses the Internet's standard HTTP protocol, and that Java's Remote Method Invocation (RMI) protocol is used across the connection between the application server and the data server. The components have the same stereotypes as they did on the UML component diagram of Figure 7-21.

7.7.1 How to Develop a Deployment Model

Deployment models are typically developed in parallel with component models. To develop a deployment model, you iterate through the following steps:

1. **Identify the scope of the model.** To develop a deployment model, you should start by identifying the scope of the model, typically a deployment configuration for a single application. My approach is to develop a deployment model for each major configuration of the applications of your overall system. For example,

Figure 7-22.
A deployment diagram for the university information system

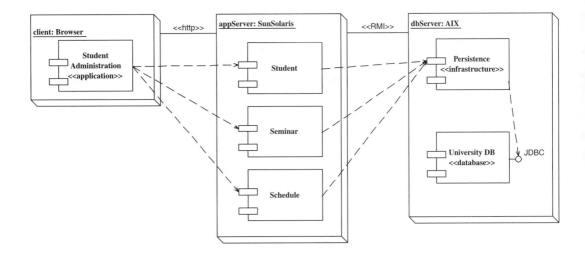

> **TIP**
>
> *Components Should Only Depend on Interfaces*
>
> By making components dependent on the interfaces of other components, instead of on the other components themselves, you enable yourself to replace the component without having to rewrite the components that depend on it. For example, in Figure 7-21, several large-scale domain components depend on the interface to the "Persistence" component to store them in the database. Perhaps the first implementation of this component was developed in-house, but because you quickly found out how complicated persistence can be (see Section 7.8), you instead decided to purchase a persistence framework. To swap this persistence framework into place, you merely need to implement the same interface for it. Had your domain components relied on the actual implementation of your "Persistence" component, instead of its interface, you would have needed to rewrite portions of your domain components to use its new implementation.

Develop a deployment model for each major configuration of your application(s).

if you deploy your "Student Administration" application both as an HTML application that students can use over the Internet and as a stand-alone desktop application deployed on portable computers that will replicate objects to your main application server occasionally, then you likely need a deployment for each of these configurations. I would also be tempted to develop a deployment model for the "Seminar Management" application modeled in Figure 7-21 because it uses different domain components than does the "Student Administration" application and because the university may decide to implement this using different client-side technology (perhaps as a Java application instead of an HTML application).

2. **Identify the distribution architecture.** Do you intend to take a fat-client approach or a thin-client approach? Will your application have two tiers, three tiers, or more? Your distribution architecture strategy will often be predetermined for your application, particularly if you are deploying your system to an existing technical environment. The various distribution architecture strategies are covered in detail in the second book in this series, *Building Object Applications That Work* (Ambler, 1998a).

3. **Identify the nodes and their connections.** Your distribution strategy will define the general type of nodes you will have, but not the exact details. For example, the deployment diagram of Figure 7-22 takes a three-tier client/server approach, telling you that you will have an user interface tier, an application server tier, and a database-server tier. To complete the deployment diagram, you need to decide how each of these tiers will be implemented—

in this case, in a browser, on a Solaris-based server, and on an AIX-based server, respectively—as well as how they will be connected (via HTTP and RMI in this case).

4. **Distribute components to nodes.** The software components, modeled in detail on your UML component diagram, which are applicable to the scope of your deployment model, should then be distributed to each node. This was straightforward using a three-tier approach: Application components are assigned to the client, domain components are assigned to the application server and the "Persistence" component, and the database itself is assigned to the database server. Different distribution architecture strategies naturally have different component distribution heuristics.

5. **Model dependencies between components.** My approach is to combine the dependencies between two components into one. For example, in Figure 7-21, two dependencies exist between the "Student Administration" component and the interfaces of the "Student" component, one to each interface. Yet in Figure 7-22, I show one dependency between the two components (and not to the interfaces of "Student"). This is a matter of personal style: The information is already well documented on the component model, so why repeat it on the deployment model? I could have modeled the dependency to the actual interfaces, as I have shown between the components deployed to the data server in Figure 7-22, but I chose not to do so. Yes, it isn't as accurate, but the diagram is easier to read as a result.

7.7.2 *When Should You Create Deployment Models?*

To determine whether you need to create a deployment model, ask yourself this: If you knew nothing about the system and someone asked you to install it and/or maintain and support it, would you want a description of how the parts of the system fit together? When I ask this question of the project teams I work with, we almost always decide to develop a deployment model. More important, practice has shown that deployment modeling is well worth it. Deployment models force you to think about important deployment issues long before you must deliver the actual system.

Deployment modeling should be performed by both the development/engineering folks responsible for building the system and by operations folks who are responsible for operating and supporting it once in production. The engineers will have a vision as to how to build the system, whereas the operations people will have a better understanding of the current environment in which it will be used.

The development and operations staff should develop deployment models together.

T I P *Consider a Wide Range of Technical Issues*	When you are deployment modeling, you need to consider a bevy of technical issues, such as: What existing systems will yours need to interact/integrate with? How robust does your system need to be (will there be redundant hardware to failover to)? What/who will need to connect to and/or interact with your system and how will they do it (via the Internet, exchanging data files, and so forth)? What middleware, including the operating system and communications approaches/protocols, will your system use? What hardware and/or software will your users directly interact with (PCs, network computers, browsers, and so forth)? How do you intend to monitor the system once it has been deployed? How secure does the system need to be (do you need a firewall, do you need to physically secure hardware, and so forth)?

7.8 Relational Persistence Modeling

If you're one of the lucky few to work in an organization using an object database (ODB), you don't need to read this section. If you are among the majority of developers and are using a relational database (RDB), however, then you need to pay careful attention to this section. Relational databases are often used as the mechanism to make your objects persistent. Because relational databases don't completely support object-oriented concepts, the design of your database is often different than the design of your class diagram. Persistence models—also called *data models* or *entity-relationship (ER) models*—are used to communicate the design of a database, usually a relational database, to both your users and to other developers. At press time, UML doesn't support persistence models.[3]

In Figure 7-23, you see an example of a persistence model for the design of a simple human resources system. In the model are four data entities: "Position," "Employee," "Task," and "Benefit," which, in many ways, are simply classes that have data, but no functionality. The entities are connected by relationships and, although they not shown in Figure 7-23, it is possible to model associations, inheritance, aggregation, and composition on persistence models just as you would in a class model.

7.8.1 Keys and Object Identifiers

A key uniquely identifies a row in a table.

A key uniquely identifies a row of a relational table, a table being the implementation of a data entity in a relational database and a row being

---

[3] I maintain the page *http://www.ambysoft.com/umlPersistence.html* that tracks the progress of these efforts.

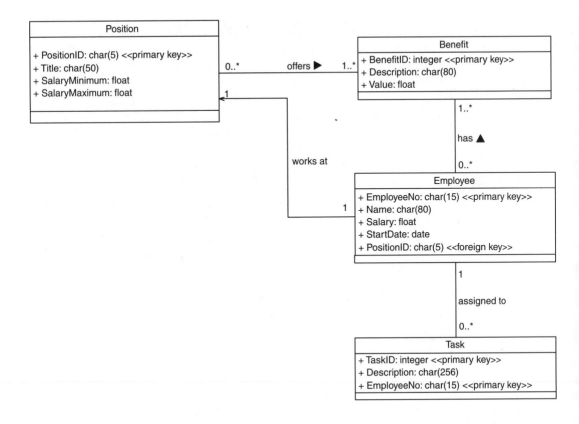

Figure7-23.
A persistence model
for a simple human
resources database

the data equivalent of an instance of a data entity. You have different
ways to use keys. A primary key is the preferred key for a data entity,
whereas a secondary key is an alternative way to access rows within a
table. A foreign key is one or more attributes in a data entity that represent a key, either primary or secondary, in another data entity. Foreign
keys are used to maintain relationships between rows. For example, in
the persistence model in Figure 7-23, you see that the column "Employ-
eeNo" is the primary key of the "Employee" data entity. A column is the
relational equivalent of an attribute of a class. You also see that the "Posi-
tionID" column is the primary key of "Position" and, within the
"Employee" data entity, it is a foreign key to the "Position" data entity
(this is the attribute used to maintain the "works at" association between
the two data entities. Implementing associations using foreign keys is
discussed in detail later in this section. In this book, I indicate keys on
diagrams through the use of stereotypes such as "<<primary key>>,"
"<<secondary key>>," and "<<foreign key>>."

> **DEFINITIONS**
>
> ***Client/server (C/S) architecture.*** A computing environment that satisfies the business need by appropriately allocating the application processing between the client and the server processes.
>
> ***Fat client.*** A two-tiered client/server architecture in which client machines implement both the user interface and the business logic of an application. Servers typically only supply data to client machines with little or no processing done to it.
>
> ***n-tier client/server.*** A client/server architecture separated into *n* layers, where *n* is greater than three.
>
> ***Thin client.*** A client/server architecture in which client machines implement only the user interface of an application.
>
> ***Three-tier client/server.*** A client/server architecture separated into three layers: a client layer that implements the user interface, an application server layer that implements business logic, and a database server layer that implements persistence.
>
> ***Tier*** A layer within a deployment architecture.
>
> ***Two-tier client/server.*** A client/server architecture separated into two layers: an application layer (the client) and a server layer.

7.8.1.1 Persistent Object IDs

Object identifiers (OIDs) are used to identify objects uniquely in a relational database.

You need to assign unique identifiers to your objects so you can identify them. In relational terminology, a unique identifier is called a *key*. In object terminology, a unique identifier is called an *object identifier*[4] (OID). OIDs are typically implemented as full-fledged objects in your OO applications and as large integers or strings in your relational schema.

OIDs enable you to simplify your key strategy within a relational database. Although OIDs don't completely solve the navigation/traversal issue between objects, they do make it easier. You still need to perform table joins, assuming you don't intend to traverse, to read in an aggregate of objects, such as an invoice and all its line items, but at least it is doable. Another advantage is that the use of OIDs enables you to easily automate the maintenance of relationships between objects. When all your tables are keyed on the same type of column(s), in this case OIDs, it becomes straightforward to write generic code to take advantage of this.

---

[4] Throughout this book, I use the term object identifier (OID) to mean the persistent OID that is stored as a key in your relational database. Some object environments have their own internal object identifier scheme in place to identify objects when they are in memory, a scheme to which you likely don't have direct access, but these identifiers are not meant to be persisted. Anyway, when you see the term OID, think "persistent OID."

An OID should be unique within a class hierarchy and, ideally, unique among all objects generated by your organization (something often called *global uniqueness*). For example, will the OID for a customer object be unique only for instances of customer, to people in general, or to all objects? Given the OID value 74656, will it be assigned to a student object, a professor object, and a seminar object? Will it be assigned to a student, but not to a professor (because the "Student" class and the "Professor" class are in the same class hierarchy)? Or, will it only be assigned to a student object and that's it? The real issue is one of polymorphism: It is probable that a student object may one day become a professor object, but likely not a seminar object. To avoid this issue of reassigning OIDs when an object changes type, you at least want uniqueness at the class hierarchy level, although uniqueness across all classes completely avoids this issue.

The level of uniqueness of your OIDs dramatically affects the robustness of your design.

The second issue, that of determining new OIDs, can greatly affect the run-time efficiency of your application. You have several ways (Ambler, 1998a) to generate values for OIDS:

1. **Use the MAX() function (and add 1) on the OID column.** This works when the OID value only needs to be unique within the table, but doesn't scale well because of the extra accesses to your data tables.

2. **Maintain a separate table for storing the next value of a key.** The basic idea is you read the current value, increment it, write it back to the source table, and then use the new value for your key. This is a better strategy, but still does not scale well because of the extra update within your database.

3. **Use Universally Unique Identifiers (UUIDs) from the Open Software Foundation.** UUIDs (Szyperski, 1998) are 128-bit values created from a hash of the ID of your Ethernet card or an equivalent software representation and the current datetime of your computer system. This strategy works well, but it depends on having an Ethernet card (or at least the equivalent of an Ethernet card ID) so, therefore, it is not portable.

4. **Use Globally Unique Identifiers (GUIDs) from Microsoft.** GUIDs follow a similar strategy to UUIDs: they are 128 bits and are a hash of a software ID and the current date/time. The GUID generator will use the Ethernet card ID if it is available and, if so, will be able to generate a globally unique value. Otherwise, it will generate a value that is guaranteed unique only on the machine that generated it. Although GUIDs are interesting, they are not portable and potentially not even unique, depending on your environment.

DEFINITIONS

Column. The relational database equivalent of an attribute of a data entity stored in a relational table.

Data entity. The representation of the data describing a person, place, thing, event, or concept.

Foreign key. One or more attributes within a data entity that represent a primary or secondary key in another table. Foreign keys are used to maintain a relationship to a row in another table.

Key. A data attribute, or collection of data attributes, that uniquely describes a data entity.

Primary key. The preferred key for a data entity.

Relational table. The physical implementation of a data entity within a relational database.

Row. The relational database equivalent of an instance of a data entity stored in a relational table. Also called a *record*.

Secondary key. A key that is an alternative to the primary key for a data entity. Also known as an *alternate key*.

---

5. **Use proprietary database essential generation functions.** Many relational database products include key generation functionality that you can use if needed. These strategies are typically not portable across database vendors and often do not work well in multidatabase environments (the generated values are often unique only within the database they are generated by).

6. **Use the HIGH/LOW approach.** This approach, described in the following Section 7.8.1.2, is a portable, easy-to-develop high-performance technique that results in globally unique values. The only drawback is you need to code and maintain this yourself.

7.8.1.2 The HIGH/LOW Approach to OIDs

HIGH is uniquely assigned from a common source or algorithm. LOW is an incremental value generated at the client.

The basic idea is that a persistent object identifier is in two logical parts: a unique HIGH value you obtain from a defined source and an N-digit LOW value your application assigns itself. Each time a HIGH value is obtained, the LOW value will be set to zero. For example, if the application you are running requests a value for HIGH, it will be assigned the value 1701. Assuming that N (the number of digits for LOW) is also 4, then all persistent object identifiers that the application assigns to objects will be combinations of 17010000, 17010001, 17010002, and so on until 17019999. At

> The object paradigm is based on proven software engineering principles for building applications out of objects that have both data and behavior, whereas the relational paradigm is based on proven mathematical principles for efficiently storing data. The "impedance mismatch" comes into play when you look at the preferred approach to access: With the object paradigm you traverse objects via their relationships, whereas with the relational paradigm, you duplicate data to join the rows in tables. This fundamental difference results in a nonideal combination of the two paradigms, although when have you ever used two different things together without a few hitches? One of the secrets of success for mapping objects to relational databases is to understand both paradigms, and their differences, and then make intelligent trade-offs based on that knowledge.

TIP

Beware the Object-Relational Impedance Mismatch

this point, a new value for HIGH is obtained, LOW is reset to zero, and you continue again. If another application requests a value for HIGH immediately after, it will be given the value of 1702, and the OIDs that will be assigned to objects it creates will be 17020000, 17020001, and so on. As you can see, as long as HIGH is unique, then all values will be unique.

So how do you calculate HIGH? You can do this in several ways. First, you could use one of the incremental key features provided by database vendors. This has the advantage of improved performance—with a four-digit LOW, you have one access on the database to generate 10,000 keys instead of 10,000 accesses. However, this approach is still platform-dependent and might not work for a multidatabase environment. You could also use either GUIDs or UUIDs for the HIGH value, although you still have platform-dependency problems.

A third approach is to implement the HIGH calculation yourself. You could write a portable utility in ANSI-compliant C, PERL, or 100 percent Pure Java that maintains an *M*-digit incremental key. You would either need to have a single source for this key generator within your system or to have multiple sources that, in turn, have an algorithm to generate unique values for HIGH between them. Of course, the easiest way to do so is to apply the HIGH-LOW approach recursively, with a single source that the HIGH-generators collaborate with. In the previous example, perhaps the HIGH server obtained the value of 17 from a centralized source, which it then used to generate values of 1701, 1702, 1703, and so on until 1799, at which point it would then obtain another two-digit value and start over again.

7.8.1.3 Implementing Persistent Object Identifiers
So how do you make this work in the real world? First, you want to implement a factory class (Gamma et al., 1995) that encapsulates your

TIP *OIDs Should Have No Business Meaning*	A critical issue that needs to be pointed out is OIDs should have absolutely no business meaning whatsoever. Nada. Zip. Zilch. Zero. Any column with a business meaning can potentially change, and if there is one thing we have learned as an industry over the years in the relational world it is this: Giving your keys meaning is a fatal mistake. If your users decide to change the business meaning, or if they want to add some digits or make a number alphanumeric, you need to make changes to your database in every single spot where you use that information. Anything used as a primary key in one table is virtually guaranteed to be used in other tables as a foreign key. What should be a simple change, adding a digit to your customer number, can be a huge maintenance nightmare. Yuck. In the relational database, world keys without business meaning are called *surrogate* keys.

algorithm for generating persistent object identifiers. In the case of the HIGH/LOW approach, this class would maintain the LOW value and obtain the HIGH value from the appropriate source.

128 bits is a good size for OIDs.

Second, you need to choose a size for your OID that is big enough to ensure your organization will not run out of OID values. For example, two- and four-digit numbers will not cut it for the HIGH/LOW approach. It is common to see 96-bit or 112-bit values for HIGH, and 16-bit or 32-bit values for LOW. The reason 128-bits is a magic size for many key strategies is because you need that many bits to have enough potential values for persistent object identifiers without having to apply a complex algorithm. The first time a new persistent object identifier is requested the factory will obtain a new HIGH and reset LOW to zero, regardless of the values for HIGH and LOW the last time the factory was instantiated. In the example, if the first application assigned the value of 17010123, and then was shut down; the next time that application runs, it would start with a new value for HIGH, say 1867, and start assigning 18670001, and so on. Yes, this is wasteful, but when you are dealing with 112-bit HIGHs who cares? Increasing the complexity of a simple algorithm to save a couple of bytes of storage is the thought process that gave us the Year 2000 crisis, so let's not make that mistake again.

DEFINITIONS
Object identifier (OID). A unique identifier assigned to objects, typically a large integer number. OIDs are the object-oriented equivalent of keys in the relational world. *Surrogate key.* A key without a business meaning.

A third issue you need to consider is polymorphism, which is a fancy term that means objects can change their type, an issue that becomes important for persistent object identifiers. For example, a chair object may become a firewood object, so if you have a chair object with 12345 as its identifier and an existing firewood object with 12345 as its identifier, then you have a problem when the chair becomes firewood. The problem is you would have to assign the chair a new identifier value, everything that referred to it would need to be updated, and so on. The solution is to make your persistent object identifier values unique across all objects, and not just across types/classes of objects. To achieve this, make the persistent object identifier factory class a Singleton. A Singleton class has only one instance in your memory space, so all objects obtain their identifiers from a central source.

Polymorphism drives the need for using OIDs with a globally unique value.

Fourth, never display the value of the persistent object ID, never allow anyone to edit it, and never allow anyone to use it for anything other than identification. As soon as you display or edit a value, you give it business meaning, which you saw earlier to be a bad idea for keys. Ideally, nobody should even know the persistent object identifier even exists, except perhaps the person(s) debugging your data schema during initial development of your application.

Never use an OID, or keys in general, for anything other than identifying an object.

Fifth, distributed design issues must be considered. You may find you want to buffer several HIGH values to ensure your software can operate in disconnected fashion for quite some time. The good news is that persistent object identifiers are the least of your worries when developing software to support disconnected usage or, perhaps that is the bad news, depending on your point-of-view. You may also decide to store the LOW value locally. After all, when your software shuts down if disconnected, usage is a serious requirement for you.

You can easily make the HIGH/LOW strategy work for disconnected usage.

Finally, because this strategy only works for the objects of a single organization, you may decide to include some sort of unique organization identifier to your keys to guarantee uniqueness of persistent object identifiers between organizations (something often called *galactic uniqueness*). The easiest way to do this is to append your organization's Internet

---

DEFINITIONS

Disconnected usage. The potentially full use of an application when it isn't connected to your organization's network.

Galactically unique OID. A persistent OID with a value that is guaranteed to be unique across all organizations that follow the same value generation strategy.

Globally unique OID. A persistent OID with a value that is guaranteed to be unique within the organization that generated it.

domain name, which is guaranteed to be unique, to your identifiers if you are rolling your own HIGH values or simply to use a UUID/GUID for your HIGH values. You may need to do something like this if your organization shares data with other organizations or if your organization is likely to be involved with a merger or acquisition.

7.8.2 The Basics of Mapping Objects to RDBs

In this section, I describe the fundamental techniques required to map objects successfully into relational databases:

- Mapping attributes to columns
- Mapping classes to tables
- Implementing inheritance in an RDB
- Mapping relationships:
  - one-to-one
  - one-to-many
  - many-to-many
  - association versus aggregation
  - same classes/tables, different relationships

7.8.2.1 Mapping Attributes to Columns

Attributes map to zero or more columns; zero or more attributes map to a single column.

An attribute of a class maps to zero or more columns in a relational database. Remember, not all attributes are persistent. For example, an "Invoice" class may have a "grandTotal" attribute used by its instances for calculation purposes, but not saved to the database. Furthermore, some attributes of an object are objects in their own right; for example, a "Course" object has an instance of "TextBook" as an attribute that maps to several columns in the database (actually, chances are the "TextBook" class will map to one or more tables in its own right). The important thing is this is a recursive definition: At some point, the attribute will be mapped to zero or more columns. Also possible is that several attributes could map to one single column in a table. For example, a class representing an American ZIP code may have three numeric attributes, one representing each of the sections in a full ZIP code, whereas the ZIP code may be stored as a single column in an address table.

7.8.2.2 Mapping Classes to Tables

Classes map to tables, although often not directly. Except for simple databases, you will never have a one-to-one mapping of classes to tables.

In the following sections, I discuss three strategies for implementing inheritance structures to a relational database and an example where dissimilar classes map to one table.

Classes map to one or more tables; one or more classes can map to a single table.

7.8.2.3 Implementing Inheritance in a Relational Database

The concept of inheritance throws in several interesting twists when saving objects into a relational database (Ambler, 1998a). The problem basically boils down to how to organize the inherited attributes within your persistence model. The way in which you answer this question can have a major impact on your system design. There are three fundamental solutions for mapping inheritance into a relational database and, to understand them, I discuss the trade-offs of mapping the class diagram presented in Figure 7-24. To keep the issues simple, I have not modeled all the attributes of the classes. I also haven't modeled their full signatures or any of the methods of the classes. Also, I haven't applied the Business Entity analysis pattern described in Chapter 6 to this hiearchy (I need a simple example, and this one is really straightforward).

You have three basic choices when mapping inheritance hierarchies to a relational database.

7.8.2.3.1 Use One Data Entity for an Entire Class Hierarchy

With this approach, you map an entire class hierarchy into one data entity, where all the attributes of all the classes in the hierarchy are stored in it. Figure 7-25 depicts the persistence model for the class hierarchy of Figure 7-24 when this approach is taken. Notice how a "person-OID" column was introduced for the primary key of the table. I use OIDs in all the solutions to be consistent and to take the best approach I know for assigning keys to data entities.

The advantages of this approach are it is simple, polymorphism is supported when a person changes roles, and ad-hoc reporting is also easy because all the data you need about a person is found in one table. The disadvantages are every time a new attribute is added anywhere in the class hierarchy, a new attribute needs to be added to the table. This

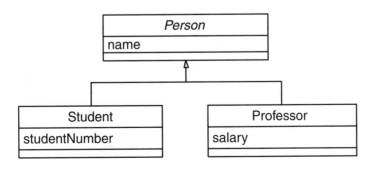

Figure 7-24.
A UML class diagram of a simple class hierarchy

Figure7-25.

Mapping the class
hierarchy to one
single data entity

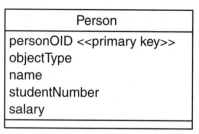

increases the coupling within the class hierarchy. If a mistake is made
when adding a single attribute, it could affect all the classes within the
hierarchy and not just the subclasses of whatever class got the new
attribute. It also potentially wastes a lot of space in the database. I also
needed to add the "objectType" column to indicate if the row represents
a student, a professor, or another type of person. This works well when
someone has a single role, but it quickly breaks down if they have multiple roles (that is, the person is both a student and a professor).

7.8.2.3.2 Use One Data Entity Per Concrete Class
With this approach, each data entity includes both the attributes and the
inherited attributes of the class it represents. Figure 7-26 depicts the persistence model for the class hierarchy of Figure 7-24 when this approach
is taken. Data entities correspond to each of the "Student" and "Professor" classes because they are concrete, but not to "Person" because it is
abstract (indicated by the fact that its name is depicted in italics). Each of
the data entities was assigned its own primary key, "studentOID" and
"professorOID," respectively.

The main advantage of this approach is it is still fairly easy to do ad-hoc
reporting because all the data you need about a single class is stored in only
one table. Several disadvantages exist, however. First, when you modify a
class, you need to modify its table and the table of any of its subclasses. For
example, if you were to add height and weight to the "Person" class, you
would need to add it to both tables, and that's a lot of work. Second, when-

Figure 7-26.

Mapping each
concrete class to a
single data entity

Student	Professor
studentOID <<primary key>> name studentNumber	professorOID <<primary key>> name salary

---

DEFINITION

Ad-hoc reporting. Reporting performed for the specific purposes of a small group of users where it is common for the users to write the report(s) themselves.

---

ever an object changes its role (perhaps you hire one of the graduating students to become a professor) you need to copy the data into the appropriate table and assign it a new OID—once again a lot of work. Third, it is difficult to support multiple roles and still maintain data integrity (it is possible, just harder than it should be). For example, where would you store the name of someone who is both a student and a professor?

7.8.2.3.3 Use One Data Entity Per Class
With this approach, you create one table per class, the attributes of which are the OID and the attributes that are specific to that class. Figure 7-27 depicts the persistence model for the class hierarchy of Figure 7-24 when this approach is taken. Notice how "personOID" is used as the primary key for all three data entities. An interesting feature of Figure 7-27 is that the "person-OID" column in both "Professor" and "Student" is assigned two stereotypes, something not allowed in the UML. My opinion is this is an issue that will need to be addressed by the UML persistence modeling profile and may even necessitate a change in this modeling rule.

The main advantage of this approach is it conforms to object-oriented concepts the best. It supports polymorphism well because you merely have records in the appropriate tables for each role that an object might have. It is also easy to modify superclasses and add new subclasses because you merely need to modify/add one table. This approach has several disadvantages. First, many tables are in the database, one for

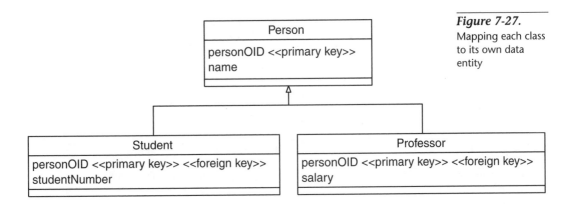

Figure 7-27.
Mapping each class to its own data entity

> **DEFINITIONS**
>
> *Abstract class.* A class that doesn't have objects instantiated from it.
> *Concrete class.* A class that has objects instantiated from it.

every class (plus tables to maintain relationships). Second, it takes longer to read and write data using this technique because you need to access multiple tables. This problem can be alleviated if you organize your database intelligently by putting each table within a class hierarchy on different physical disk-drive platters (this assumes the disk-drive heads all operate independently). Third, ad-hoc reporting on your database is difficult, unless you add views to simulate the desired tables.

7.8.2.3.4 Comparing the Mapping Strategies

Notice how each mapping strategy results in a different model. To understand the design trade-offs among the three strategies, consider the simple change to the class hierarchy presented in Figure 7-28: A "TenuredProfessor" class has been added that inherits from "Professor." Figure 7-29 presents the updated persistence model for mapping the entire class hiearchy into one data entity. Notice how little effort was required to update the model following this strategy, although the obvious problem of wasted space in the database has increased. Figure 7-30 presents the persistence model when each concrete class is mapped to a data entity. With this strategy, I only needed to add a new table, although the issue of how do we handle objects that either

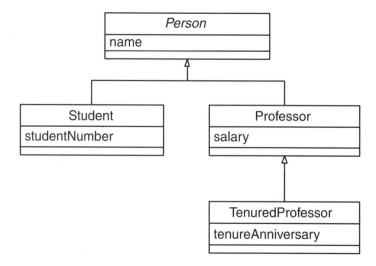

Figure 7-28.
Extending the initial class hierarchy

```
┌─────────────────────────────────────────┐
│                  Person                  │
├─────────────────────────────────────────┤
│  personOID <<primary key>>              │
│  objectType                              │
│  name                                    │
│  studentNumber                           │
│  salary                                  │
│  tenureAnniversary                       │
├─────────────────────────────────────────┤
│                                          │
└─────────────────────────────────────────┘
```

Figure 7-29.
Mapping the extended hierarchy to a single data entity

change their relationship (students become professors) has now become more complex because we have added the issue of promoting professors to become tenured professors. Figure 7-31 presents the solution for the third mapping strategy, mapping a single class to a single data entity. I needed to add a new table, one that included only the new attributes of the "Tenured-Professor" class. The disadvantage of this approach is that it requires several database accesses to work with instances of the new class.

The point to remember is that none of the approaches is perfect. Each has its strengths and weaknesses. The three approaches are compared in Table 7-7.

No mapping strategy is ideal for all situations.

7.8.3 Mapping Associations, Aggregation, and Composition

Not only do you need to map objects into the database, you also need to map the relationships with which the object is involved, so they can be restored at a later date. An object can be involved with four types of relationships: inheritance, association, aggregation, and composition. To

```
┌───────────────────────────────────┐  ┌───────────────────────────────────┐
│              Student              │  │             Professor             │
├───────────────────────────────────┤  ├───────────────────────────────────┤
│  studentOID <<primary key>>      │  │  professorOID <<primary key>>    │
│  name                             │  │  name                             │
│  studentNumber                    │  │  salary                           │
├───────────────────────────────────┤  ├───────────────────────────────────┤
│                                   │  │                                   │
└───────────────────────────────────┘  └───────────────────────────────────┘
```

```
┌───────────────────────────────────────────┐
│               TenuredProfessor             │
├───────────────────────────────────────────┤
│  tenuredProfessorOID <<primary key>>      │
│  name                                      │
│  salary                                    │
│  tenureAnniversary                         │
├───────────────────────────────────────────┤
│                                            │
└───────────────────────────────────────────┘
```

Figure 7-30.
Mapping the concrete classes of the extended hierarchy to data entities

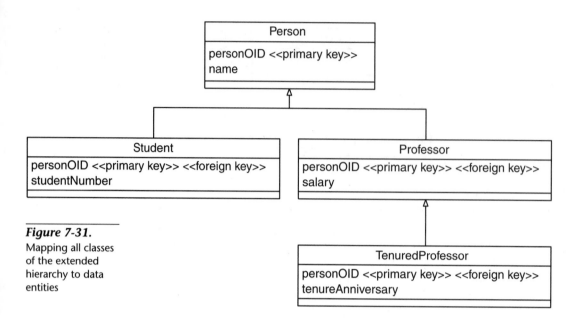

Figure 7-31.
Mapping all classes
of the extended
hierarchy to data
entities

map these relationships effectively, you must understand the difference
between them, how to implement relationships generally, and how to
implement many-to-many relationships specifically.

7.8.3.1 The Difference Between Association and Aggregation/Composition
From a database perspective, the only difference between association and
aggregation/composition relationships is how tightly the objects are
bound to each other. With aggregation and composition, anything you

Table 7-7. Comparing the approaches to mapping inheritance.

Factors to Consider	One table per hierarchy	One table per concrete class	One table per class
Ad-hoc reporting	Simple	Medium	Medium/Difficult
Ease of implementation	Simple	Medium	Difficult
Ease of data access	Simple	Simple	Medium/Simple
Coupling	Very high	High	Low
Speed of data access	Fast	Fast	Medium/Fast
Support for polymorphism	Medium	Low	High

do to the whole in the database, you almost always need to do to the parts. This is not the case with association.

In Figure 7-32 (Ambler, 1998a), you see three classes, two of which have a simple association between them, and two that share an aggregation relationship (actually, composition would likely have been a more accurate way to model this). From a database point-of-view, aggregation/composition and association are different because, with aggregation, you usually want to read in the part when you read in the whole, whereas, with an association, what you need to do isn't always as obvious. The same goes for saving objects to the database and deleting objects from the database. Granted, this is usually specific to the business domain, but this rule of thumb seems to hold up in most circumstances.

7.8.3.2 Implementing Associations in Relational Databases

Relationships in relational databases are maintained through the use of foreign keys. A foreign key is a data attribute that appears in one table that may be part of, or is coincidental with, the key of another table. Foreign keys enable you to relate a row in one table with a row in another. To implement one-to-one and one-to-many relationships, you merely have to include the key of one table in the other table.

In Figure 7-33, you see three tables, their keys (OIDs of course), and the foreign keys used to implement the relationships between them. First, a one-to-one association exists between the "Position" and "Employee" data entities. A one-to-one association is one in which the maximums of each of its multiplicities are one. To implement this relationship, I used the attribute "positionOID," the key of the "Position" data entity. I was forced to do it this way because the association is unidirectional; employee rows know about their position rows, but not the other way around. Had this been a bidirectional association, I would have needed to add a foreign key called "employeeOID" in "Position" as well. Second, I implemented the many-to-one association (also referred to as a one-to-many association) between "Employee" and "Task" using the same sort of approach, the only difference being that I had to put the foreign key in "Task" because it was on the "many" side of the relationship.

Figure 7-32.
The difference between association and aggregation/composition

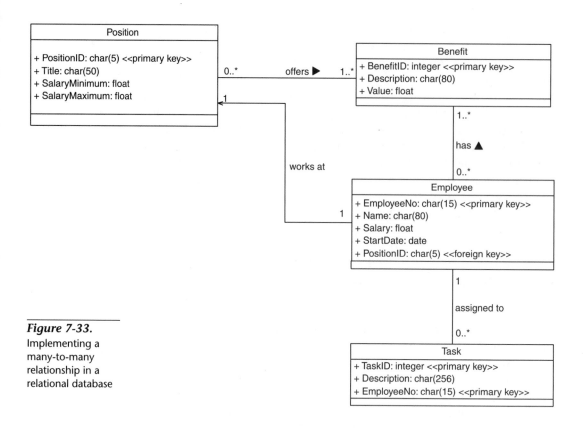

Figure 7-33.
Implementing a
many-to-many
relationship in a
relational database

7.8.3.3 Implementing Many-to-Many Associations

To implement many-to-many relationships, you need the concept of an associative table, a data entity whose sole purpose is to maintain the association between two or more tables in a relational database. Referring to Figure 7-25, you see a many-to-many relationship between "Employee" and "Benefit." In Figure 7-33, you see how to use an associative table to implement a many-to-many relationship. In relational databases, the attributes contained in an associative table are traditionally the combination of the keys in the tables involved in the relationship. The name of an associative table is typically either the combination of the names of the tables that it associates or the name of the association it implements. In this case, I chose ""EmployeeBenefit" over "BenefitEmployee" and "has" because I felt it reflected the nature of the association better.

Notice the application of multiplicities in Figure 7-33. The rule is that the multiplicities "cross over" once the associative table is introduced, as indicated in Figure 7-34. A multiplicity of "1" is always introduced on the

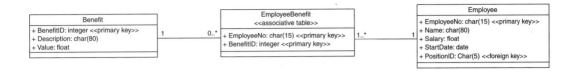

Figure 7-34.
Introducing an
associative table

outside edges, as you can see in Figure 7-34 to preserve the overall multiplicity of the original association. The original association indicated that an employee has one or more benefits and any given benefit is given to zero or more employees. In Figure 7-33, you see this is still true even with the associative table in place to maintain the association.

Important to note is I choose to apply the stereotype "<<associative table>>" rather than the notation for associative classes—a dashed line connecting the associative class to the association that it describes for two reasons. First, the purpose of an associative table is to implement an association, whereas the purpose of an associative class is to describe an association. Second, the approach taken in Figure 7-33 reflects the actual implementation strategy you would need to take using relational technology.

The notation for associative classes is not applicable for associative tables.

7.8.4 Drawing Persistence Models

Drawing persistence models is straightforward and, like class diagramming, is often an iterative process. The five major steps are as follows:

1. **Identify data entities.** Look for any person, place, thing, event, or concept about which you are interested in storing data. If you have a class diagram, it should drive the development of your persistence model using the techniques described previously. If you don't yet have a class diagram, you should.

2. **Identify data attributes.** What information do you want/need to store about each data entity? The easiest way to do this is to map the attributes of your classes to columns in your tables (Section 7.8.2.1).

DEFINITIONS

Many-to-many association. An association where the maximum of both multiplicities is greater than one.

Many-to-one association. An association where the maximum of one multiplicity is one and the other is more than one.

One-to-one association. An association where the maximums of each of its multiplicities is one.

3. **Identify the key attribute(s).** Ask yourself if there are one or more columns that can be used in combination to identify an occurrence (instance) of a data entity. Often, you have several choices for your key, forcing you to choose one and, sometimes, you don't have any columns that can be used for a key, forcing you to introduce new columns to act as the key. As you read in Section 7.8.1, when you are given the choice, you should use OIDs for your keys instead of columns with business meaning.

4. **Identify relationships between data entities.** Identifying relationships between data entities is identical to identifying relationships between classes. The reality is all your important relationships will already be indicated on your class diagrams.

5. **Resolve many-to-many associations.** As described in Section 7.8.3.3, you need to resolve many-to-many associations into two many-to-one associations by introducing an associative table into your persistence model.

7.8.5 When Should You Develop Persistence Models?

Persistence models are used to document the design of a database.

Your class diagram should drive the design of your persistence model, not the other way around.

Persistence models are used to design the schema of your database. You typically need to draw a persistence model whenever you are using a relational database in which to store your objects. The strength of persistence models is data entities are conceptually the same as the tables of a relational database and attributes are the same as table columns.

Although often tempted to use persistence models to drive the development of class diagrams, I tend to shy away from this approach unless I know the persistence model is designed very well, that is, the persistence model is highly normalized. I cover both data and class normalization in detail in *Building Object Applications That Work* (Ambler, 1998a). For now, think of a highly normalized data entity as one that is very cohesive. To use relational technology successfully on object-oriented applications, you should let your class diagram drive the design of your data/persistence model (Ambler, 1998b). In other words, create the class diagram that is right for your application, and then use it to derive the database design for that application.

DEFINITION

Associative table. A table in a relational database used to maintain a relationship between two or more other tables Associative tables are typically used to resolve many-to-many relationships.

7.9 User Interface Design

During design, you continue your user interface prototyping efforts, described in Chapter 6, and, at the same time, "clean up" the overall design of the user interface. This clean-up effort focuses on applying common user interface design principles and techniques, applying your organization's chosen user interface design standards, and evolving your user interface flow diagram. User interface design is a complex task, one that requires a wide range of skills to be successful. Although my advice to most project teams is to hire a user interface design expert onto your team, the reality is few people are available with the appropriate skillset. The reality is most decisions regarding the design of your system's user interface, or affecting its usability, are made by ordinary developers (Constantine and Lockwood, 1999). Therefore, it is important that all developers have an understanding of the basics of user interface design, hence, the need for reading this section.

7.9.1 User-Interface Design Principles

Let's start with the fundamentals of user interface design. Constantine and Lockwood (1999) describe a collection of principles for improving the quality of your user interface design. These principles are as follows:

User interface design is a difficult task requiring a wide range of skills.

1. **The structure principle.** Your design should organize the user interface purposefully, in meaningful and useful ways based on clear, consistent models that are apparent and recognizable to users, putting related things together and separating unrelated things, differentiating dissimilar things, and making similar things resemble one another. The structure principle is concerned with overall user interface architecture.

2. **The simplicity principle.** Your design should make simple, common tasks simple to do, communicating clearly and simply in the user's own language, and providing good shortcuts that are meaningfully related to longer procedures.

3. **The visibility principle.** Your design should keep all needed options and materials for a given task visible without distracting the user with extraneous or redundant information. Good designs don't overwhelm users with too many alternatives or confuse them with unneeded information.

4. **The feedback principle.** Your design should keep users informed of actions or interpretations, changes of state or condition, and errors or exceptions that are relevant and of interest to the user through clear, concise, and unambiguous language familiar to users.

5. **The tolerance principle.** Your design should be flexible and tolerant, reducing the cost of mistakes and misuse by allowing undoing and redoing, while also preventing errors wherever possible by tolerating varied inputs and sequences and by interpreting all reasonable actions.

6. **The reuse principle.** Your design should reuse internal and external components and behaviors, maintaining consistency with purpose rather than merely arbitrary consistency, thus reducing the need for users to rethink and remember.

7.9.2 Techniques for Improving Your User-Interface Design

This section summarizes tips and techniques I have learned over the years that often lead to effective software user interfaces.

1. **Consistency, consistency, consistency.** I believe the most important thing you can possibly do is to ensure that your user interface works consistently. If you can double-click items in one list and have something happen, then you should be able to double-click items in any other list and have the same sort of thing happen. Put your buttons in consistent places on all your windows, use the same wording in labels and messages, and use a consistent color scheme throughout. Consistency in your user interface enables your users to build an accurate mental model of the way it works, and accurate mental models lead to lower training and support costs.

Set organization-wide standards and stick to them.

2. **Set standards and stick to them.** The only way you can ensure consistency within your application is to set user interface design standards, and then stick to them.

3. **Explain the rules.** Your users need to know how to work with the application you built for them. When an application works consistently, it means you only have to explain the rules once. This is a lot easier than explaining in detail exactly how to use each feature in an application step by step.

4. **Support both novices and experts.** Consider the design of a library system within the university. Although a library-catalog metaphor might be appropriate for casual users of the system, students, it probably is not all that effective for expert users, librarians. Librarians are highly trained people who are able to use complex search systems to find information in the library; therefore, you should consider building a set of search screens just for them.

5. **Navigation between major user interface items is important.** If it is difficult to get from one screen to another, then your users will quickly become frustrated and give up. When the flow between screens matches the flow of the work that the user is trying to accomplish, then your application will make sense to your users. Because different users work in different ways, your system needs to be flexible enough to support their various approaches. Interface-flow diagrams, described in Section 7.9.3, should be developed to further your understanding of the flow of your user interface.

6. **Navigation within a screen is important.** In Western societies, people read left to right and top to bottom. Because people are used to this, should you design screens that are also organized left to right and top to bottom when designing a user interface for people from this culture? You want to organize navigation between widgets on your screen in a manner users will find familiar to them.

7. **Word your messages and labels appropriately.** The text you display on your screens is a primary source of information for your users. If your text is worded poorly, then your interface will be perceived poorly by your users. Using full words and sentences, as opposed to abbreviations and codes, makes your text easier to understand. Your messages should be worded positively, imply that the user is in control, and provide insight into how to use the application properly. For example, which message do you find more appealing: "You have input the wrong information" or "An account number should be eight digits in length." Furthermore, your messages should be worded consistently and displayed in a consistent place on the screen. Although the messages "The person's first name must be input" and "An account number should be input" are separately worded well, together they are inconsistent. In light of the first message, a better wording of the second message would be "The account number must be input" to make the two messages consistent.

8. **Understand your widgets.** You should use the right widget for the right task, helping to increase the consistency in your application and probably making it easier to build the application in the first place. The only way you can learn how to use widgets properly is to read and understand the user interface standards and guidelines your organization has adopted.

9. **Look at other applications with a grain of salt.** Unless you know another application has been verified to follow the user

interface standards and guidelines of your organization, don't assume the application is doing things right. Although looking at the work of others to get ideas is always a good idea, until you know how to distinguish between good user interface design and bad user interface design, you must be careful. Too many developers make the mistake of imitating the user interface of poorly designed software.

10. **Use color appropriately.** Color should be used sparingly in your applications and, if you do use it, you must also use a secondary indicator. The problem is that some of your users may be color-blind and if you are using color to highlight something on a screen, then you need to do something else to make it stand out if you want these people to notice it. You also want to use colors in your application consistently, so you have a common look and feel throughout your application.

11. **Follow the contrast rule.** If you are going to use color in your application, you need to ensure that your screens are still readable. The best way to do this is to follow the contrast rule: Use dark text on light backgrounds and light text on dark backgrounds. Reading blue text on a white background is easy, but reading blue text on a red background is difficult. The problem is that not enough contrast exists between blue and red to make it easy to read, whereas blue contrasts well with white.

12. **Align fields effectively.** When a screen has more than one editing field, you want to organize the fields in a way that is both visually appealing and efficient. I have always found the best way to do so is to left-justify edit fields—in other words, make the left-hand side of each edit field line up in a straight line, one over the other. The corresponding labels should be right-justified and placed immediately beside the field. This is a clean and efficient way to organize the fields on a screen.

13. **Expect your users to make mistakes.** How many times have you accidentally deleted some text in one of your files or in the file itself? Were you able to recover from these mistakes or were you forced to redo hours, or even days, of work? The reality is that to err is human, so you should design your user interface to recover from mistakes made by your users.

14. **Justify data appropriately.** For columns of data, common practice is to right-justify integers, decimal align floating-point numbers, and to left-justify strings.

15. **Your design should be intuitable.** In other words, if your users don't know how to use your software, they should be able to determine how to use it by making educated guesses (Raskin, 1994). Even when the guesses are wrong, your system should provide reasonable results from which your users can readily understand and ideally learn.

16. **Don't create busy user interfaces.** Crowded screens are difficult to understand and, hence, are difficult to use. Experimental results (Mayhew, 1992) show that the overall density of the screen should not exceed 40 percent, whereas local density within groupings should not exceed 62 percent.

17. **Group things effectively.** Items that are logically connected should be grouped together on the screen to communicate the fact that they are connected, whereas items that have nothing to do with each other should be separated. You can use whitespace between collections of items to group them and/or you can put boxes around them to accomplish the same thing.

For more information about object-oriented user interface (OOUI) design, I suggest reading Chapter 9 in *Building Object Applications That Work* (Ambler, 1998a), the second book in this series.

7.9.3 User-Interface Flow Diagramming

During design, you will evolve your user interface flow diagram to reflect the design information being captured in your user interface prototype and your sequence diagrams. For example, the initial requirements version of your user interface flow diagram (refer to Figure 3-15) is likely to evolve as the result of your analysis efforts into something resembling the diagram depicted in Figure 7-35.

Notice how the user interface classes of Figure 7-3 are used in Figure 7-35. The classes you discovered during sequencing diagramming were added to this diagram at the time they were identified (that is what iterative development is all about). It is interesting to note the screen flow in Figure 7-35 is different than that of Figure 7-3. The problem is, in the sequence diagram, the fees display screen is opened by the main menu, whereas in the user-

---

DEFINITION

Intuitable. The guesses and presuppositions of users are more likely to be right than wrong and, even when wrong, the results are reasonable responses from the system that are readily understood by the users.

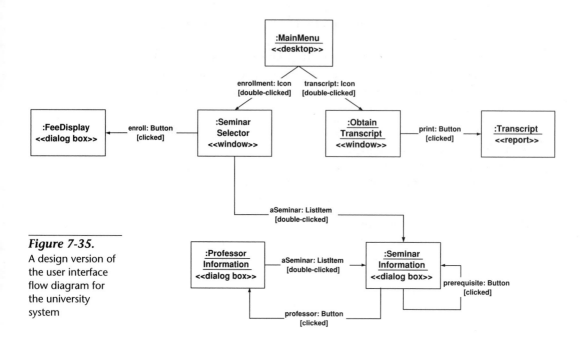

Figure 7-35.
A design version of
the user interface
flow diagram for
the university
system

interface flow diagram, it is opened from the seminar details screen. How
the system should work in this case should be discussed with your subject
matter experts and both diagrams should be updated to reflect their answer.

Also interesting to note is that user interface implementation choices are
now reflected in the UI flow diagram. I have chosen to take a graphical user
interface (GUI) approach to the system's user interface and Figure 7-35
reflects this in several ways. First, the major UI elements are assigned stereotypes, such as "<<window>>" and "<<dialog box>>," concepts that are
applicable to GUIs (as opposed to a stereotype such as "<<HTML page>>").
Second, the types of transitions between the various UI elements are also
GUI-centric: buttons are clicked to get to a new screen or report, icons on the
main menu (the desktop) are double-clicked to get to screens, and so on.

7.9.4 User-Interface Design Standards and Guidelines

Most major platforms have well-defined user interface design guidelines.
Mind you, they are not always followed, but at least they exist, as you see
in Table 7-8. My advice is to:

1. **Adopt an industry standard and modify it as needed.** My
   experience is that the guidelines documents list in Table 7-8 will
   meet from 95 to 99 percent of your UI-design standards needs
   and you simply need to write a several-page addendum to them

Table 7-8. User interface design guidelines for common development platforms

Platform	UI Design Guidelines	Publisher
Apple	*Macintosh Human Interface Guidelines*	Addison-Wesley Publishing Company, Inc., 1993
IBM	*Systems Application Architecture: Common User Access Guide to User Interface Design.*	IBM Corporation, 1993.
Java	*Java Look and Feel Design Guidelines*	Addison-Wesley Publishing Company, Inc., 1999
Microsoft	*The Windows Interface Guidelines for Software Design: An Application Design Guide*	Microsoft Press, 1995

to reflect your specific environment. By adopting industry standards, you not only take advantage of the work of others, you also increase the chance that your application will look and feel like other applications your users purchase or have built.

2. **Follow and enforce the guidelines.** There is no value in "adopting" UI design guidelines if you don't actually follow them. Many developers think they know better, that because they are good programmers, they know everything there is to know about all aspects of development, including user interface design. My experience is that, 99 times out of 100, developers who refuse to conform to industry-recognized user interface standards end up developing horrendous user interfaces. They may think the user interface is fantastic, but their users often find it difficult to learn and to use.

3. **Obtain training in user interface design and in the guidelines.** You and your coworkers need to understand at least the fundamentals of user interface design and the standards your organization has adopted. A two-day user interface design training seminar that includes coverage of your platform's standard design guidelines will be one of the best investments your project team can make.

7.10 Design Tips

This section presents a collection of tips and general words of wisdom for successful object-oriented design.

1. **Focus on the problem, not the techniques.** Your goal is to develop software that supports the efforts of your user community.

Rosenberg and Scott (1999) advise that you should ruthlessly focus on answering the fundamentally important questions about the system you are building and refuse to get caught up in the superfluous modeling issues. I have been on several projects where the most pressing issue to the modelers was the correct usage of extend and include associations on use case diagrams, or which notation to use to develop their persistence models. Interesting issues, but not important ones when your goal is develop a system that works.

2. **Don't forget your technical infrastructure.** During requirements gathering, you will identify nonfunctional requirements, perhaps pertaining to security access control or system performance, technical requirements that must be reflected in your design.

3. **Document your style guidelines.** Throughout this book, I discuss a variety of modeling issues where there are several valid strategies you could take and, for each one, I suggested you choose one strategy and stick with it. For example, do you assume all accessor methods exist or do you show them on your diagrams? Do you assume that the scaffolding code for managing associations exists or do you show it on your diagram? Not only should you choose each strategy, you should also document which strategy you have chosen so everyone on your team and, ideally, within your organization, can follow the same set of modeling practices.

4. **Develop a technical prototype.** Never assume your design works; instead, insist on proving it works by developing a technical "proof-of-concept" prototype (Ambler, 1998b).

5. **Requirements, then analysis, then design, and then code.** Just because you are taking an iterative approach to development doesn't mean you can hack. Fundamentally, you need to determine what is wanted, then determine what you will build, next determine how you will build it, and then finally build it. Think, and then act.

6. **Use Computer Aided System Engineering (CASE) tools effectively.** Many affordable object-oriented CASE tools are on the market and you should consider using one if you are going to be doing a lot of class modeling. CASE tools provide automated support for documenting your class model. Many CASE tools are as easy to use as a paint program: you draw your class model by clicking the appropriate icons and dropping class model symbols onto your diagram. When you double-click a symbol in your

class model, an appropriate editing screen is displayed, which you are expected to fill in. It's that simple. You can either keep your system documentation online in an electronic file or print it to obtain a hard copy

7. **Document complicated things.** If it is complicated, then document it thoroughly (actually, if something is complicated, then spend more time and try to design it so it is simple).

8. **Do not overdocument.** You need to document your design, but you shouldn't overdocument either. Remember, users pay you to build systems, not to document them. There is a fine line between underdocumenting and overdocumenting, and only through experience are you able to find it.

9. **Design for change.** Your users will often request that new features be added to a system. The mark of a good system design is it should be easy to extend and/or modify the functionality of an existing application. To understand the potential changes your system will face, I recommend you develop change cases (Chapter 3) and consider important software engineering principles such as extensibility, maintainability, and portability when you are designing systems.

10. **Design for your implementation environment judiciously.** Take advantage of features of your implementation environment, but don't be stupid about it. Trade-offs are normal, but understand the implications and manage the risks involved. Every time you take advantage of a unique performance enhancement in a product (such as a database, operating system, or middleware tool), you are likely coupling your system to that product and, thus, reducing its portability. To minimize the impact of your implementation environment on your systems, you can layer your software (Section 7.1) and wrap specific features to make them appear general. Wrapping is discussed in detail in *Building Object Applications That Work* (Ambler, 1998a), the second book in this series.

11. **Expect and act on feedback.** Never forget that, as an object designer, you are a mere mortal just like everyone else on your team. Your design will never be perfect, and the people who are "downstream" from you, the programmers and database administrators who will implement your design, will likely challenge portions of your approach. Expect to receive feedback—I suggest you actively seek it—about your work and be prepared to consider it and act accordingly. Not only will your system be the better for it, you will likely learn something in the process.

DEFINITION

Baseline. A tested and certified version of a deliverable representing a conceptual milestone that thereafter serves as the basis for further development and that can be modified only through formal change control procedures. A particular version becomes a baseline when a responsible group decides to designate it as such.

---

12. **Indicate application of patterns.** If you have applied one or more design patterns in your models, and it is likely you always will, then you should document what patterns you have applied and the extent of the change it caused to your model. I often indicate the application of common design patterns, such as "Singleton" and "Façade" presented in Section 7.3, with stereotypes.

7.11 What You Have Learned

This chapter introduced you to the main artifacts of object-oriented design (OOA) and their interrelationships, as depicted in Figure 7-1. You learned that the purpose of design is to define how your system will be built, as opposed to the purpose of analysis (Chapter 6), which is to identify what will be built.

In this chapter, you saw how to apply the key object-oriented design techniques: class modeling, state chart modeling, collaboration modeling, component modeling, deployment modeling, persistence modeling, and user interface prototyping. In Chapter 8, you see how your design efforts bridge the gap between analysis and implementation.

7.12 Review Questions

1. Identify ten common design patterns, taking them from at least three different sources, and summarize each pattern in one or two paragraphs. Describe how each could or could not be applied to your analysis class model for the bank case study (Sections 3.10.1 and 6.10). For the patterns that could not be applied, indicate why you felt they were inappropriate.

2. Modify your analysis class diagram for the bank case study to reflect the application of the design patterns chosen in Question 1.

3. Should the aggregation associations of Figure 7-5 and Figure 7-6 be composition associations instead? Justify why or why not providing references supporting your argument.

4. Section 7.2.4.4 suggests that the precondition(s) of an overriding method must be the same or weaker than those of the method it is replacing and its postcondition(s) must be the same or stronger. Justify why this is true (or why it is not true). Provide at least two examples.

5. Section 7.2.5.4 discusses the use of accessor methods, using a "Date" class as an example. Model a date class, including definitions of the attributes ("year," "month," and "day"), as well as the relevant methods. In addition to being able to represent dates accurately, your model should also be able to calculate the difference in days between two dates and to add or subtract a given number of days from an existing date. Discuss your visibility decisions for each attribute and method in your design.

6. Develop a state chart diagram for a bank account, based on the information in the bank case study in Section 3.10.1.

7. Develop a state chart diagram for the "Seminar" class during a semester, representing the logic described in Section 7.4.2.

8. Develop a UML collaboration diagram to model the act of successfully transferring funds from a checking account to a savings account using an automated teller machine. Remember to include the appropriate controller class(es).

9. Create a component model based on your design class model and other supporting diagrams for your bank case study (Sections 3.10.1 and 6.10). Write a paragraph describing each component and develop an interface(s) for each component.

10. Create a deployment model for the bank case study (Section 3.10.1). Choose a deployment architecture, such as three-tier client/server, as well as appropriate implementation technologies. Write a one-page justification for your choices.

11. Using a development tool of your choice, develop a user interface prototype for the bank case study (Section 3.10.1). Assume you are building the user interface that will be used by human bank tellers (you are not building an automated teller machine). This prototype should reflect your chosen deployment architecture from the previous question (for example, if you chose an architecture that supported only browser-based technology, then your teller application should be browser-based).

12. Create two versions of a persistence diagram to model the fact that a professor may teach many seminars and that a seminar is taught by one or more professors, one using foreign keys in each data entity

and one using an associative table to resolve the association. Compare and contrast the advantages of the two approaches, suggesting when you would want to apply each one.

13. In a persistence diagram, what would be the advantages (if any) and disadvantages (if any) of using an associative table to resolve a many-to-one association?

14. Consider the additional requirements presented in Section 7.11.1. First, update your requirements models to reflect these changes. Then update your analysis models appropriately (hopefully, you baselined your original models), maintaining traceability back to your requirements models. Then update your design models to reflect these changes.

15. When you updated your models to reflect the new requirements presented in Section 7.11.1, what general changes did you need to make? How easy was it to accomplish? What was difficult? Why? What could you have done to ease this change? Present your findings as if it was a report to your organization's senior management.

7.12.1 The Bank Case Study Six Months Later

Your banking system has been in place for six months and it is running fine. During this time, the bank has been preparing to expand into other countries. Not only will the bank do business in the United States, it will also start doing business in Canada, Mexico, Great Britain, and France. The bank wants to be able to do business in each of these countries in their own currencies. For example, Mexican accounts will be handled in pesos, Canadian accounts in Canadian dollars, French accounts in francs, and so on. Because many of their customers do business internationally, it is certain that some customers will have accounts in several countries. ABC's corporate strategy is to be second-to-none in the banking industry. This means it must provide the best service to its customers. As a result, its accounts must be robust. This means if somebody wants to transfer money between an American account and a Mexican account, the bank can do it. If someone wants to deposit $20 in American dollars into a British account, it can do it...and at both a teller and an automated teller machine.

Software is everything that happens outside the code.

Chapter 8

Building Your System: Object-Oriented Programming

What You Will Learn in This Chapter

What is programming?
Why there is more to programming than writing source code
How to implement your object design in Java
How to implement your persistence design in structured query language (SQL)
Programming tips, techniques, and idioms

Why You Need to Read This Chapter

The goal of all your modeling efforts to this point is to ensure that your solution meets the needs of your users in an effective and sufficient manner. To ensure this success, however, programmers must understand how to transition design models into working source code. In this chapter, you learn the basics to develop both object-oriented and persistence code for your system.

The purpose of object-oriented programming is to build your actual system, to develop the code that fulfills your system's design. As you can see in Figure 8-1, your design artifacts, depicted as dashed boxes, drive the development of your source code. As with the previous Figures 3-1, 6-1, and 7-1, the arrows represent "drives" relationships—information in your design model to drive the development of your source code, and vice versa. The most important implication of Figure 8-1 is that design and programming are highly interrelated and iterative. Your programming efforts will quickly reveal weaknesses in your design that need to be addressed. Perhaps the designers were unaware of specific features in the programming environment and, therefore, didn't take advantage of them.

What isn't as obvious in Figure 8-1 is you will focus on two types of source code: object-oriented code, such as Java or C++, and persistence mechanism code, such as data definition language (DDL), data manipulation language (DML), stored procedures, and triggers. Section 8.2 describes how to implement common object-oriented concepts in Java and Section 8.3 describes persistence coding. Your class models, state chart diagrams, user interface prototypes, business rules, and collaboration diagrams drive the development of your object-oriented code, whereas your persistence model drives the development of your persistence code.

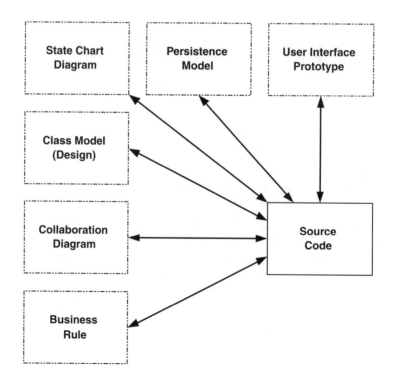

Figure 8-1.
Overview of design artifacts and their relationships

DEFINITIONS

Business rule. A policy your software must satisfy. Business rules are what a functional requirement "knows"—the controls and guidelines fulfilled by the functional requirement. An operating principle or policy of your organization.

Class diagram. Class diagrams show the classes of a system and the associations between them.

Class model. A class diagram and its associated documentation.

Collaboration diagram. A UML diagram that shows instances of classes, their interrelationships, and the message flow between them. Collaboration diagrams typically focus on the structural organization of objects that send and receive messages.

Component diagram. A UML diagram that depicts the software components that comprise an application, system, or enterprise. The components, their interrelationships, interactions, and their public interfaces are depicted.

Data definition language (DDL). Commands supported by a persistence mechanism that enable the creation, removal, or modification of structures (such as relational tables or classes) within it.

Data manipulation language (DML). Commands supported by a persistence mechanism that enables the access of data within it, including the creation, retrieval, update, and deletion of that data.

Deployment diagram. A UML diagram showing the hardware, software, and middleware configuration for a system.

Development/maintenance trade-off. Development techniques that speed the development process often have a negative impact on your maintenance efforts, whereas techniques that lead to greater maintainability negatively impact your development efforts, at least in the short term.

Persistence mechanism. The permanent storage facility used to make objects persistent. Examples include relational databases, object databases, flat files, and object/relational databases.

Persistence model. A model that describes the persistent data aspects of a software system.

Prototype. A simulation of an item, such as a user interface or a system architecture, the purpose of which is to communicate your approach to others before significant resources are invested in the approach.

State chart diagram. A UML diagram that describes the states an object may be in, as well as the transitions between states. Formerly referred to as a *state diagram* or *state-transition diagram*.

Stored procedure. An operation that runs in a persistence mechanism.

Trigger. An operation that is automatically invoked as the result of data manipulation language activity within a persistence mechanism.

User interface (UI). The user interface of software is the portion the user directly interacts with, including the screens, reports, documentation, and software support (via telephone, electronic mail, and so on).

User interface prototype. A prototype of the user interface (UI) of a system. User interface prototypes could be as simple as a hand-drawn picture or as complex as a collection of programmed screens, pages, or reports.

<table>
<tr><td>

TIP

Adopt and Follow Coding Standards and Guidelines.

</td><td>

Your team, and ideally your organization, must come to a consensus as to the standards and guidelines it will follow during development. Programming standards and guidelines are critical to ensuring the work produced by your developers is of the quality your organization requires. Developers should follow the standards and guidelines when working on your application, and reviews should ensure they have done so. These standards and guidelines should be defined/selected by the time programming begins, so your team starts with a solid foundation.

</td></tr>
</table>

8.1 What Is Programming?

There is far more to programming than simply writing code. As you see in the solution to the Program process pattern (Ambler, 1998b) depicted in Figure 8-2, writing source code is just one of many activities. Programming is an iterative activity, one that is driven by your design models and project infrastructure (your chosen development tools, standards, guidelines, and process). The end goal of your programming efforts is to produce a packaged application that can undergo testing in the large (described in Chapter 9).

There is significantly more to programming than writing code.

Figure 8-2 reveals the true complexity of programming. It shows that programmers need to work together with modelers to understand the models and to provide relevant feedback to the modelers. This brings up an important software process issue: If your modelers and programmers are not going to work together effectively, why even bother modeling in the first place? Programmers need to invest the time to prepare their code for inspections, a "testing in the small" activity described in Chapter 9, as well as be actively involved in integration and build efforts. As you would expect, programmers also need to write and document their code and, as I argue later, need to optimize portions of their code only after discovering which code sections need improvement.

Good developers understand the entire development process.

Not only is there more to programming than writing source code, as you have seen in this book, there is more to software development than programming. Until you understand the big picture and how you fit into it, you will never reach your full potential as a developer. I'm not saying you need to be an expert at every part of the development process; however, you do need to understand the fundamentals.

Good developers develop with maintenance in mind, not development.

The second important lesson developers need to learn is there is more to development than just development. You also need to consider production issues, such as maintenance and support. In fact, an application will spend the vast majority of its lifetime in production (postdevelopment). The average computer program spends 80 to 90 percent of its life-

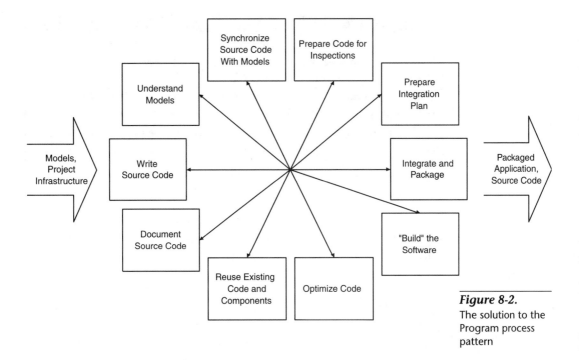

Figure 8-2.
The solution to the
Program process
pattern

time being maintained and supported, and only a small portion being developed. The implication is that you should program with maintenance in mind, fully expecting that one day your source code will need to be updated to reflect new requirements or simply to fix a defect. In Chapter 10, you see that comprehensive software processes such as the Object-Oriented Software Process (Ambler, 1998b; Ambler, 1999) and the enhanced Unified Process (Ambler and Constantine, 2000a–c) include phases for postdevelopment activities.

A related concept is something I call the development/maintenance trade-off—that is, decisions that speed the development process often harm you during maintenance, whereas decisions that improve the maintainability of your system can often increase the time it originally takes you to develop it—at least in the short term. You see, code that is more maintainable is more likely to be reused than code that is not. If the code is hard to maintain, it is also hard to reuse. The factors that make your code maintainable—documentation, paragraphing, intelligent naming strategies, and good design, many of the things we talk about in this chapter—all take time and money during the development process. Although they will pay for themselves many times over during maintenance, the short-term pain is often enough to motivate you to put them off till a later date, a date that more often than not never comes.

The development/ maintenance trade-off boils down to an ounce of prevention being worth a pound of cure.

Your real trade-off is this: Do you invest a little bit of time and effort during development to reduce your future maintenance efforts greatly? I think the answer is yes.

8.2 From Design to Java Code

In this section I show how to translate your object-oriented design into Java source code. The basic concepts are the same for other object-oriented languages, such as C++ and Smalltalk, although the syntax changes. Object-based languages, such as Visual Basic, may not support all the concepts described in this section. In fact, if you are using Visual Basic, I suggest referring to the book *Developing Applications with Visual Basic and UML* (Reed, 1999) as a replacement to this section. It is important to understand that the goal of this section is to introduce you to the fundamental techniques for translating your models into source code. The goal is not to teach you the nuances of the Java programming language.

Figure 8-3 depicts a simple class diagram for the university system, a modified version of several class diagrams presented in Chapter 7. The reason I present a modified version is to keep it simple: The example should depict the major object-oriented concepts you need to understand how to translate into code. It needn't be an accurate reflection of the university system design. As you can see in the diagram, however, I have not strayed far from our initial design; instead, I have simplified it, so I could focus on just what we need and no more.

To translate your object-oriented design into Java, you need to know how to implement:

- Classes
- Instance and static attributes of a class
- Instance and static methods of a class

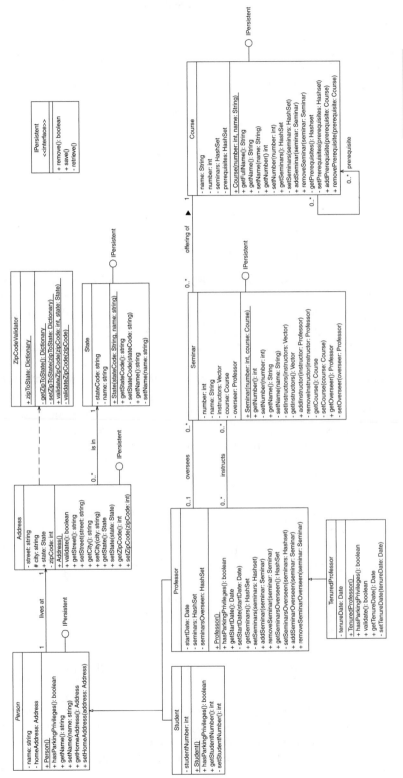

Figure 8-3.
A simple class diagram for the university system

- Constructors

- Accessor methods

- Inheritance

- Interfaces

- Associations, aggregation, and composition

- Dependencies

- Collaboration

- Business rules

8.2.1 Implementing a Class In Java

You should include documentation comments describing a class right above its declaration.

Figure 8-4 presents the beginning of source code to declare of the "Person" class in Java. The class itself is declared on the bottom line of Figure 8-4 and the meaning of each word is described in Table 8-1. At the top is the header documentation for the class, using Java's documentation comment style, describing the class, indicating its author, and version number. "@author" and "@version" are javadoc tags, predefined strings that are parsed by Java's Javadoc utility to generate external documentation for your code (Vermeulen, et al., 2000). The documentation is fairly sparse because there is not much to this class. It is common to document a brief description of the class, any applicable invariants of the class, the author(s) of the class, and its version.

Figure 8-4.
Declaring the "Person" class

```
/**
 * Person encapsulates basic behavior required of
 * employees and students of the University.
 *
 * @author Chris Roffler, Scott Ambler
 * @version 3.0 April 22, 2000  JDK 1.2.2
 **/

abstract public class Person implements IPersistent
```

It is important that your organization set style guidelines for use of comments in Java or in any language. Java has three styles of comments: Documentation comments start with "/**" and end with "*/" characters, C-style comments start with "/*" and end with "*/" characters, and single-line

> In addition to learning the syntax and nuances of the Java language, you also want to learn how to write high-quality code in Java, code that is easy to understand, to maintain, and to enhance. In other words, you want to learn the elements of Java style. To do this, I suggest the following books: *The Elements of Java Style* (Vermeulen, et al., 2000), *Essential Java Style* (Langr, 2000), *Java 2 Performance and Idiom Guide* (Larman and Guthrie, 2000), *Java In Practice* (Warren and Bishop, 1999), and *More Java Gems* (Deugo, 2000).
>
> **TIP**
>
> *Learn the Elements of Java Style*

comments start with "//" and go until the end of the source-code line. I prefer to use documentation comments immediately before declarations of interfaces, classes, methods, and attributes to document them because they are processed by Javadoc to produce external source code documentation. I use C-style comments to document out lines of code that are no longer applicable, but that I want to keep in case my users change their minds or because I want to turn it off temporarily while debugging. Finally, I use single-line comments internally within methods to document business logic, sections of code, and declarations of temporary variables.

Set guidelines for using documentation, C-style, and single-line comments within your organization.

To implement a class in Java, you must first declare it, then declare its attributes, and then define its methods.

Table 8-1. The meaning of each word in the declaration of the "Person" class

Word	Meaning
abstract	Indicates that the class has no instances. If this keyword is not indicated, the class would have been assumed concrete.
public	Indicates that the class is accessible to every other class in your system. If this keyword is not indicated, the class would have assumed to be concrete.
class	Indicates that a class is being declared, the other option being an interface.
Person	The name of the class being declared.
implements	An optional keyword, which indicates a list of interfaces that the class (or, optionally, its subclasses in the case of an abstract) must implement.
IPersistent	An interface that the class implements. Could have been a list of several interface that names separated by commas. Notice how the class diagram in Figure 8-3 indicates that the "Person" class implements the "IPersistent" interface.

DEFINITIONS

Abstract class. A class that does not have objects instantiated from it.

Comment. Documentation in source code.

C-style comment. A style of multiline comment in Java that begins with "/*" characters and ends with "*/" characters.

Documentation comment. A style of multiline comment in Java that begins with "/**" characters and ends with "*/" characters. Also known as a *Javadoc comment.*

Invariant. A set of assertions about an instance or class that must be true at all "stable" times, where a stable time is the period before a method is invoked on the object/class and immediately after a method is invoked.

Javadoc tag. A predefined string of text, beginning with the "@" symbol, which can be embedded in Javadoc comments for formatting purposes. Examples include the "@returns" and "@throws" tags.

Javadoc. A Java utility that parses Java source files for documentation comments to use as a basis from which to generate external code documentation.

Single-line comment. A style of Java comment beginning with the characters "//"—anything following the double-slash to the end of the current line is a comment.

Static attribute. An attribute whose value is all instances of a class. Each instance of a class will share the single value of a static attribute.

Static method. A method that operates at the class level, potentially on all instances of that class.

Visibility. The level of access that external objects have to an item, such as an object's attributes or methods, or even to a class itself.

8.2.2 Declaring Instance Attributes In Java

The declarations for the instance attributes of the "Person" class are depicted in Figure 8-5. The "name" attribute is a simple string, one of Java's primitive types, whereas the "homeAddress" attribute is a full-fledged object, in this case, an instance of the "Address" class depicted in Figure 8-3. Each attribute is assigned private visibility, a design issue I described at length in Chapter 7. The type of an attribute is declared immediately following the visibility, in this case, "string" for the "name" attribute and "Address" for the "homeAddress" attribute. Finally, the name of each attribute is indicated and the statement ends with a semicolon (Java statements end in semicolons).

Figure 8-5.
Declaring the attributes of the "Person" class

```
/**
 * The person's name.
 *
 * @example Troi, Deanna
 */
private string name;

/**
 * The person's home address.
 *
 * @see Address#Address(Person person)
 */
private Address homeAddress;
```

To show you how to implement attributes with different visibilities, I present the declarations for the attributes of the "Address" class in Figure 8-6. You can declare nonprivate attributes, but that is rarely a good idea.

Figure 8-6.
Declaring the attributes of the "Address" class

```
/**
 * The city street of the address
 *
 * @example 1701 Enterprise Way
 */
private   String street;

/**
 * The name of the city
 *
 * @example  Metropolis
 */
protected String city;

/**
 * The state that the address is in
 */
public    State  state;
```

```
/**
 * The zip code that the address is in
 *
 * @example  90210
 */
private    String zipCode;
```

Document your attributes effectively.

In both Figures 8-5 and 8-6, I have used documentation comments to describe each attribute, enabling Javadoc to recognize that I want to include it in my external documentation. I use Javadoc tags in the documentation; "@example"[1] is one of my own devising and "@see" is one of the standard Javadoc tags. As indicated in Chapter 7, I believe in documenting the purpose of an attribute, its invariants (if any), and providing relevant examples that would add value to my source code. The book *The Elements of Java Style* (Vermeulen, et al., 2000), the fifth book in this series, provides an excellent discussion of how to document attributes effectively.

8.2.3 Implementing Instance Methods In Java

Abstract classes may declare abstract methods, methods that must be declared in concrete subclasses.

Instance methods are implemented exactly as you would expect: header documentation should describe the method, the method signature is declared, and the Java statements that implement the code for the method are declared. Figure 8-7 depicts the implementation of the "hasParkingPrivileges()" method of the "Person" class. The declaration of the method signature is similar to the declaration of the class and attributes you saw earlier. First, the visibility of the method is declared; in this case, the method is public (you saw in Chapter 7 that methods can also have protected, private, and default visibility in Java). Next, the optional keyword "abstract" appears, which in Java implies that this class merely defines a method signature that must be implemented by its concrete subclasses. Only abstract classes (you saw in Figure 8-4 that the "Person" class is abstract) may declare abstract methods. The return type of the

---

[1] The term "method" comes from the Smalltalk language. Methods are commonly referred to as member functions in C++ and operations in Java. The Unified Modeling Language takes it one step further to define a method as the logic, the code, of an operation. In the UML, an operation is the combination of its signature (its name, the definition of the parameters passed to it, and what it returns) and its method (the code). This is an interesting distinction to make if you're an academic or CASE-tool builder, but not of much interest if you're an everyday developer. Because I come from a Smalltalk background, throughout this book I use the terms *method, operation,* and *member function* to represent what the UML considers to be an operation.

> ### DEFINITIONS
>
> **Endline comment.** The use of a single-line comment to document a line of source code, where the comment immediately follows the code on the same line as the code. Also known as an *inline comment*.
>
> **Instance attribute.** An attribute that is applicable to a single instance (object) of a class. Each object will have is own value for an instance attribute.
>
> **Invariant.** A set of assertions about an instance or class that must be true at all "stable" times, where a stable time is the period before a method is invoked on the object/class and immediately after a method is invoked.
>
> **Primitive type.** A type of attribute built into a programming language. For example, Java includes primitive types such as int, string, and Boolean.

method then appears, in this case "boolean." Finally, the method name, an open parenthesis, a list of parameter declarations (if any), and a closing parenthesis is indicated. In this case, the name of the method is "hasParkingPrivileges" and there are no parameters.

Figure 8-7.
The "hasParkingPrivileges()" method in the "Person" class

```
/**
 * Indicates whether a person is allowed to park a vehicle
 * at the university.
 *
 * @return true if allowed to park, false otherwise
 */
public abstract boolean hasParkingPrivileges();
```

Figure 8-8 shows the implementation of the "hasParkingPrivileges()" method of the "Professor" class, an example of how a method in a subclass can override (redefine) one in its parent class. Because "Professor" is a concrete class, it must have (or inherit) an implementation of any abstract methods defined in its superclasses. You see in the class diagram of Figure 8-3 that the "Student" class also implements its own version of this method. In this case, it returns false because students aren't allowed to park their cars on university grounds because of a lack of parking spaces. Interesting to note is that the documentation for this method is similar to that of Figure 8-7, the main difference being that the documentation is now more specific.

Subclasses may override some or all of the methods in its superclass(es).

Figure 8-8.
The "hasParkingPrivileges()" method of the "Professor" class

```
/**
    * Indicates that a professor is allowed to park a vehicle
    * at the university.
    *
    * @return true
    */
public boolean hasParkingPrivileges()
{
    return true;
}
```

8.2.4 Implementing Static Methods and Attributes in Java

Static methods potentially operate on all instances of a single class. Similarly, static attributes are applicable to all instances of a single class. In the class diagram of Figure 8-3, static methods and attributes are underlined, the UML standard, whereas instance methods and attributes are not.

In Figure 8-9, you see the implementation of the two validation methods of the "ZipCodeValidator" class, both static methods (note the use of the Java keyword "static" in its declarations). You see that parameters are declared type first, followed by the name, which is opposite of the UML approach to declare the name first, followed by the type. Compare the source code of Figure 8-7 with the class diagram of Figure 8-3 to see what I mean. In fact, the ordering of a method declaration in Java is significantly different than that of UML, something you will easily get used to. As with attributes, the types of parameters may be Java primitive types or full-fledged objects.

Figure 8-9.
Implementing the "validateZipCode()" methods in the "ZipCodeValidator" class

```
/**
    * Verify that the zip code is valid.
    * The zip code should be in a valid format and should be
    * a valid zip code for the given state.
    *
    * @return true if valid, false otherwise
    */
```

```java
static public boolean validateZipCode(String zipCode, State state)
{
  // Check that the zip code only is in the proper format
  if ( ! validateZipCode(zipCode)) {
    return false;
  }
  // Verify that the zip code corresponds to the state
  try {
    String   stateCode = zipCode.substring(0,2);
    int     number = Integer.parseInt(stateCode);
    return isValidState(number, state);
  } catch (Exception e) {
  }
  return false;
}

/**
 *   Validate the format of a zip code
 *
 *   Valid zip codes are in the format NNNNN or NNNNN-NNNN,
 *   for example 90210 and 74656-1701
 *
 *   @return true if the format is valid, false otherwise
 */
static private boolean validateZipCode(String zipCode)
{
  if ( zipCode == null)
    return false;

  // A valid zip code may be in the format NNNNN  (5 digits)
  if ( zipCode.length() == 5) {
    try {
      // Ensure that there is only digits
      Integer.parseInt(zipCode);
      return true;
    } catch (Exception e) {
      return false;
    }
  } else {
    // A valid zip code may be in the format NNNNN-NNNN
    if ( zipCode.length() == 10) {
      // Ensure that a hyphen is in the sixth position
      if ( ! (zipCode.charAt(5) == '-') )
```

```
      return false;

      // Get the first five characters of the zip code
      String str1 = zipCode.substring(0,5);
      // Get the last four characters of the zip code
      String str2 = zipCode.substring(6);

      try {
        // Ensure that the strings only hold digits
        Integer.parseInt(str1);
        Integer.parseInt(str2);
        return true;
      } catch (Exception e) {
        return false;
      }
    }
  }
  return false;
}
```

The source code of Figure 8-9 is interesting for several reasons:

1. **The source code presents an example of overloaded methods**. The methods "validateZipCode(zipCode, State)" and "validateZip-Code(zipCode)" are overloaded. An overloaded method is one where one or more methods exist (within the same class, within its superclasses, or within its subclasses) that have the same name, but different parameters. This is allowed in Java, enabling you to define families of methods similar to each other, but that have different implementations, as you can see in Figure 8-9.

2. **Overloading might not have been appropriate here**. I specifically named the methods in Figure 8-9 the way I did so I could have a simple example of overloading. The reality is that the second method could have been named something like "validateZipCodeFormat(zipCode)" to make its purpose more obvious.

DEFINITION

Override. When you redefine an attribute or method in a subclass we say you override it.

3. **Each method has several return statements**. Note that each of the statements provides an answer of the type defined in the declaration of the methods (in both cases Boolean).

4. **Each method presents an example of Java's exception-handling approach in the form of a "try/catch" structure**. The method invocations and statements within the scope of the try, anything between the opening and closing curly braces, are attempted. If any of them throws an exception, via Java's "throw" statement (see Figure 8-13 for an example of a throw statement), then processing ends at that point and the catch clauses are invoked. In this case, it is possible that the conversion of a string to an integer may fail—the Integer.parseInt() method throws an exception if a string containing nondigit characters is passed to it, something you can look up in the documentation for the Java Development Kit (JDK).

5. **The methods have different visibilities**. In my design, I want the "validateZipCode(zipCode, state)" method to be invoked by other objects, in this case address objects, so they can validate their ZIP codes effectively. Therefore, this method was declared as public. However, the behavior to validate the format of ZIP code, although normalized (Ambler, 1998a) into its own method, does not need to be available to external objects in my design. Therefore, the "validateZipCode(zipCode)" method was declared as private.

6. **The method header documentation is good enough**. As I describe in Chapter 7, in the header documentation for a method, I believe in documenting what a method does and why it does it, any known bugs with the method, any exceptions it throws, any applicable visibility decisions, the return value of the method, how a method changes the object, examples of how to invoke the method, and any applicable preconditions and postconditions.

7. **The internal documentation is good**. I also believe in writing documentation only when it adds value, which is why both methods in Figure 8-9 include just enough internal documentation to make obvious what is happening. Notice how the documentation is written in straightforward business terms such as "Ensure that a hyphen exists in the sixth position" and not "Invoke charAt() with 5 as a parameter and compare it to a hyphen," which is merely an English wording of the statement. Internally within a method you should document any control

structures, what and why the code does something, local variables, difficult or complex code, and the processing order if applicable.

8. **The "validateZipCode(zipCode)" method likely has bugs**. Although I haven't built a test case to validate this, I suspect I can pass the string "-1701," which is an invalid ZIP code, although a valid integer as a string of length five, so it would likely get through my existing code. Object-oriented testing is covered in Chapter 9.

Figure 8-10 depicts the declaration of the static attribute "stateZips" of "ZipCodeValidator." It is declared to be static; therefore, it is accessible by the methods of the class in which it is declared. It is also assigned a value of "null" to initiate its value.

Figure 8-10.
The "zipToState" attribute of the "ZipCodeValidator" class

```
/**
 *  Maps the first two digits of a zip code to the state
 *  that the zip code is in.
 */
static Vector  stateZips = null;
```

8.2.5 Implementing Constructors

Figure 8-11 depicts the constructor for the "Seminar" class, a static method because it applies to the class as a whole, implementing the responsibility to create instances of the class. The Java convention is that the constructor for a class must have the same name as the class itself, including that the first letter of the name is capitalized. This method takes as a parameter the course object of which the object is a seminar and assigns it to the object's "course" attribute. I'm not invoking the getter method for "course" to show you an example of how to do this because invoking getters within a constructor can be dangerous. The problem is, if the getter method checks the value it is passed against that of another attribute of the class, and that attribute is not yet set by the constructor, then an error results. The constructor invokes a method on the course object to maintain the association between the two objects (the implementation of associations is discussed in detail in Section 8.2.9). The "Instructor's" attribute is set to an instance of a new vector that will be used to maintain the association to the "Professor" objects that teach it.

DEFINITIONS

Postcondition. An expression of the properties of the state of an operation or use case after it has been invoked successfully.

Precondition. An expression of the constraints under which an operation or use case will operate properly.

Exception. An indication that an unexpected condition has occurred within some software. In Java, exceptions are "thrown" by methods to indicate potential problems.

Overload. When you define two methods with the same name, but different parameters, we say you *overload* it.

Figure 8-11.
The constructor method of the "Seminar" class

```
/**
 * Public constructor
 *
 * @param The course which describes this seminar
 */
public Seminar(Course course)
{
  this.course = course;
  course.addSeminar(this);

  instructors = new Vector();
}
```

The constructor takes a parameter that is identical in name to one of its instance attributes. Because instance attributes are accessible by the constructor method of a class, a name-hiding problem occurs with this parameter. To resolve it, the method must refer to the attribute using its fully qualified name, in this case, "this.course," to differentiate it from the parameter.

Notice the use of whitespace in Figure 8-11, spaces and blank lines within the source code. Whitespace improves the readability of your code. The spaces around the equal signs make it easier to distinguish where the names of the attributes end on the left and where the new value starts on the right-hand side. More important, the blank line before the statement where the Instructor's attribute is set helps to separate it from the statements that focus on working with the course object.

Whitespace improves the readability of your code.

> ### DEFINITIONS
>
> *Constructor.* A method, typically a static one, whose purpose is to instantiate and, optionally, to initialize an object.
>
> *Name hiding.* This refers to the practice of using the same, or at least a similar, name for an attribute/variable/parameter as for one of higher scope. The most common abuse of name hiding is to name a local variable the same as an instance attribute.
>
> *Whitespace.* Blanks, such as blank lines or spaces.

8.2.6 Encapsulating Attributes with Accessors

Accessors dramatically increase the robustness of your code.

Accessor methods come in two flavors: setters and getters. A setter modifies the value of an attribute, whereas a getter obtains its value. Although accessors add minimal overhead to your code, the reality is that the loss in performance is often trivial compared to other factors (such as questionable database designs). Accessors help to hide the implementation details of your classes and, thus, increase the robustness of your code. By having, at most, two control points from which an attribute is accessed, one setter and one getter, you are able to increase the maintainability of your classes by minimizing the points at which changes need to be made.

Figure 8-12 depicts the implementation of the getter and setter methods for the "homeAddress" attribute of the "Person" class. Both methods do exactly as you would expect. Getters and setters are useful because they enable you to encapsulate important business rules, transformation logic, and/or validation logic that are applicable to your data attributes. For example, Figure 8-13 presents an alternative implementation of the setter method. See how it first verifies the address object that it has been passed is valid by invoking its "validate()" method and, if it is, then it sets the value of the "homeAddress" attribute. If the address is not valid, then it throws an exception (as you saw in Figure 8-9, exceptions are handled by the invoker of a method via Java's try/catch statement).

Figure 8-12.
The getter and setter for the "homeAddress" attribute of the "Person" class

```
/**
 * Gets the person's home address
 *
 * @return homeAddress
 */
```

```
public Address getHomeAddress()
{
    return homeAddress;
}


/**
 * Sets the person's home address
 *
 * @param homeAddress
 */
public void setHomeAddress(Address homeAddress)
{
    this.homeAddress = homeAddress;
}
```

Figure 8-13.
Alternative implementation of the "setHomeAddress()" method

```
/**
 * Sets the person's home address
 *
 * @param homeAddress
 * @return homeAddress
 */
 public Address setHomeAddress(Address homeAddress) throws
InvalidDataException
 {
    // Only set the address if it is valid
    if ( homeAddress.validate() ) {
        this.homeAddress = homeAddress;
    }
    else {
        throw new InvalidDataException();
    }
 }
```

One of the most important standards your organization can enforce is the use of accessors. Some developers don't want to use accessor methods because they don't want to type the few extra keystrokes required (for example, for a getter, you need to type in "get" and "()" above and beyond

> **TIP**
>
> *Accessors Are the Only Place to Access Attributes*
>
> An essential concept with the appropriate use of accessor methods is that the *only* methods allowed to work directly with a attribute are the accessors themselves. Yes, it is possible to directly access a private attribute within the methods of the class in which the attribute is defined, but you don't want to do so because you would increase the coupling within your class.

the name of the attribute). The bottom line is that the increased maintainability and extensibility from using accessors more than justifies their use.

8.2.6.1 Naming Accessors

Getter methods should be given the name "get" + attribute name, unless the attribute represents a Boolean (true or false), and then the getter is given the name "is" + attribute name. Setter methods should be given the name "set" + attribute name, regardless of the attribute type (Gosling, Joy and Steele, 1996). As you see in Table 8-2, the attribute name is always in mixed case with the first letter of all words capitalized. This naming convention is used consistently within the Java Development Kit (JDK) and is what is required for JavaBeans development.

8.2.6.2 Visibility of Accessors

Corresponding getter and setter methods often have different visibilities.

You should always strive to make accessors protected, so only subclasses can access the attributes. You should try to make accessors private if subclasses don't need access to the attribute. Only when an external class or object needs to access an attribute should you make the appropriate getter or setter public. As you see in Figure 8-3, it is quite common for the visibility of corresponding getter and setter methods to be different: in the class "Seminar," you see the "getName()" method has public visibility, yet "setName()" has private visibility. Figure 8-15 reveals the only place the setter method is called is in the getter to formulate the name of the seminar, a combination of the course number, seminar number, and course name.

> **DEFINITIONS**
>
> *Accessor.* An operation used either to modify or retrieve a single attribute. Also known as *getter* and *setter* operations.
>
> *Getter.* A method to obtain the value of a data attribute, or to calculate the value, of an object or class.
>
> *Setter.* A method that sets the value of a data attribute of an object or a class. Also known as a *mutator.*

Figure 8-14.
Invoking accessors within methods.

```
/**
    Increment the counter

    Note: This operation is over documented to explain exactly what
          is happening
*/
public void increment()
{
    int count;  // Used to increment the value of the counter

    count = getCounter();   // Get the current value of the counter
    count = count + 1;
    setCounter( count );    // Sets the incremented value of the
counter
}
```

Figure 8-15.
The getter and setter methods for the "name" attribute of the "Seminar" class

```
/**
 *  Returns the name of the seminar.
 *  The seminar name is the concatenation of the course number
 *  (CCC), the seminar number(SSS), and the name of the
 *  course(NNN) in the format "CCC-SSS NNN"
 *
 *  @return String  Name of the seminar
 *  @example   "CSC 158-2 Introduction to Java Programming"
*/
public String getName()
{
    String newName = new String();

    if ( name == null) {
        // Build the name
        newName += course.getNumber() + " ";
        newName += getNumber();
```

```
        newName += " " + course.getName();

        setName(newName);
    }
    return name;
}
```

*Lazy initialization
adds complexity to
getter methods,
but potentially
increases system
performance.*

The implementation of the "getName()" method in Figure 8-15 is an example of *lazy initialization*, an approach where the value of an attribute is initialized (set) when it is first accessed. The advantage of this approach is that you only incur the expense of obtaining the value when and if you need it. On the surface, this doesn't appear like much of a saving for determining the seminar name, but it could be if the course object resided on another server, needed to be read in from persistent storage, and then needed to have its name transmitted across the network. The main disadvantage of lazy initialization is that your code becomes more complex because you need to check to see if the attribute has been defined yet and, if not, obtain its value. Lazy initialization is typically used when an attribute is expensive to calculate or obtain (perhaps it is very large and would take significant time to transmit across the network) and when it is not always required each time the object is brought into memory.

8.2.6.3 Why Use Accessors?
Accessors improve the maintainability of your classes in the following ways:

1. **Updating attributes**. You have single points of update for each attribute, making it easier to modify and to test. In other words, your attributes are encapsulated.

Table 8-2. Example accessor names

Attribute	Type	Getter name	Setter name
name	string	GetName	setName
homeAddress	Address object	GetHomeAddress	setHomeAddress
persistent	boolean	IsPersistent	setPersistent
zipCode	int	GetZipCode	setZipCode
instructors	Vector of Professor objects	GetInstructors	setInstructors

> **DEFINITION**
>
> *Lazy initialization.* An approach in which the initial value of an attribute is set in its corresponding getter method the first time the getter is invoked.

2. **Obtaining the values of attributes.** You have complete control over how attributes are accessed and by whom.

3. **Obtaining the values of constants**. By encapsulating the value of constants in getters when those values change, you only need to update the value in the getter and not every line of code where the constant is used. Constants are often implemented as static attributes of Java interfaces; therefore, I avoid the inclusion of static attributes in interface definitions in favor of static getter methods.

4. **Initializing attributes**. The use of lazy initialization ensures that attributes are always initialized and are initialized only if they are needed.

5. **Reduction of the coupling between a subclass and its superclass(es).** When subclasses access inherited attributes only through their corresponding accessor methods, this makes it possible to change the implementation of attributes in the superclass without affecting any of its subclasses, effectively reducing coupling between them. Accessors reduce the risk of the "fragile base class problem" where changes in a superclass ripple throughout its subclasses.

6. **Encapsulating changes to attributes.** If the business rules pertaining to one or more attributes change, you can potentially modify your accessors to provide the same capability as before the change, making it easier for you to respond to the new business rules.

7. **Name hiding becomes less of an issue.** Although you should avoid name hiding (giving local variables the same names as attributes), the use of accessors to always access attributes means you can give local variables any name you want. You needn't worry about hiding attribute names because you never access them directly anyway.

> **DEFINITION**
>
> *Name hiding.* This refers to the practice of using the same, or at least similar, name for an attribute/variable/parameter as for one of higher scope. The most common abuse of name hiding is to name a local variable the same as an instance attribute.

You don't have to make all your accessors public.

8.2.6.4 Why Shouldn't You Use Accessors?

The only time you might not want to use accessors is when execution time is of the utmost importance, but it is a rare case, indeed, that the increased coupling within your application justifies this action. Lea (1997) makes a case for minimizing the use of accessors on the grounds that it's often the case that the values of attributes in combination must be consistent and it isn't wise to provide access to attributes singly. He is right, so don't! I think Lea has missed the point that you don't need to make all accessor methods public. When you are in the situation where the values of some attributes depend on one another, then you should introduce methods that do the "right thing" and make the appropriate accessor methods protected or private as needed.

8.2.7 Implementing Inheritance In Java

Figure 8-16 depicts how to have a class inherit from another in Java: with the "extends" keyword when a class is declared. Java only supports single inheritance, the capability of a class to inherit from zero or one classes, as opposed to C++, which supports multiple inheritance, the capability to inherit from zero or more classes. Because "Student" inherits from "Person," we say "Student" is the subclass of "Person" and "Person" is the superclass of the "Student" class.

Figure 8-16.
Indicating that the "Student" class inherits from the "Person" class

public class Student extends Person

8.2.8 Implementing Interfaces In Java

Two aspects of implementing interfaces in Java are the actual definition of the interface itself and the definition of the code for a class to implement that interface.

8.2.8.1 Defining an Interface

In Figure 8-3, you see an interface called "IPersistent." Interface definitions are indicated on UML class diagrams using a class box with the <<interface>> stereotype. In the diagram, I deviated from the common UML notation by indicating the <<interface>> stereotype below the name of the interface, instead of above it. I do this throughout this book because my experience is that the name of the element, be it a class, an interface, or an object, is more important to most developers than its stereotype. Figure 8-17

DEFINITIONS

Inheritance. The representation of an *is a*, *is like*, or *is kind of* relationship between two classes. Inheritance promotes reuse by enabling a subclass to benefit automatically from the entire behavior that it inherits from its superclass(es).

Multiple inheritance. When a class directly inherits from more than one class.

Single inheritance. When a class directly inherits from only one class.

Subclass. If Class *B* inherits from Class *A*, we say *B* is a subclass of *A*.

Superclass. If Class *B* inherits from Class *A*, we say *A* is a superclass of *B*.

depicts the code for the complete definition of the "IPersistent" interface. First, notice how an interface is declared in the same manner as a class, and then the only difference is the use of the "interface" keyword instead of the "class" keyword. Although not indicated here, interfaces can "inherit" from zero or more other interfaces via the "extends" keyword, just like a class. This feature leads many people to claim that Java does, in fact, support multiple inheritance. My opinion is that this is wishful thinking at best. Second, notice how the documentation is similar in style to that of a class: header documentation exists for the interface, as well as for its method definitions. Third, notice how the method definitions don't include a body of source code. The purpose of a Java interface is to define a collection of signatures that a class must implement, not to provide the actual implementation. Fourth, although the methods all return void, accept no parameters, and don't throw any exceptions, it is possible to indicate these just as you would for a method declaration in a class. The reality is these methods should throw exceptions because it is possible for errors to occur within the permanent storage mechanism or anywhere along the communication chain to it. As indicated at the beginning of the chapter, I wanted to keep this as simple as possible.

DEFINITIONS

Interface. The definition of a collection of one or more operation signatures and, optionally, attribute definitions that comprises a cohesive set of behaviors. Some object languages support the capability for classes and/or components to implement interfaces.

Signature. The combination of the name, parameter names (in order), and name of the return value (if any) of a method.

Figure 8-17.
Defining the "IPersistent" interface

```
/**
 * Interface for persistent objects
 *
 * Objects that are persisted must implement this interface
 *
 * @author  Chris Roffler, Scott Ambler
 * @version 4.0 April 28, 2000
 * @since   1.0 January 15, 1999 JDK 1.1.2
 */
public interface IPersistent
{
  /**
   * Remove the object from permanent storage
   *
   * @postcondition  This object will no longer be available to other
   * objects
   *
   * Note: Removal does not necessarily mean deletion, it may simply
   * mean the archival of the object.
   */
  void remove();

  /**
   * Write the object to permanent storage
   *
   * @postcondition  This object is written to permanent storage
   */
  void save();

  /**
   * Retrieve the object from permanent storage
   *
   * @precondition   None. The object does not need to exist in
   * permanent storage.
   * @postcondition  If the object exists in storage it will be brought
   * into memory.
   */
  void retrieve();
}
```

DEFINITIONS

Doclet. A Java API that is an add-on to Javadoc.

Stereotype. Denotes a common use of a modeling element. Stereotypes are used to extend the UML in a consistent manner.

Define a static getter method instead of a static attribute in interfaces.

It is possible to declare static attributes in Java interfaces, although only named constants (you cannot update them). As indicated in my discussion of why you should use accessors in Section 8.2.6, I prefer to use a getter method to return constants (hence, making my code more flexible).

The documentation of the methods in Figure 8-17 is interesting because they use two more of my suggested Javadoc tags: "@precondition" and "@postcondition." These tags are important because they provide a minimal support for design by contract (Meyer, 1997). True support would entail new commands being added to Java, perhaps "precondition" and "postcondition." Because these tags are not yet standard in the Java world, and I don't know when they will be, you need to write a Java doclet to support them if you want to include them in your documentation. I would also use these tags to document the methods implemented in classes.

Interfaces are documented in a similar manner to classes.

8.2.8.2 Implementing an Interface in a Class

It is fairly straightforward to implement an interface in a class. You must declare that the class implements the interface, as you saw in Figure 8-4, and then you must implement methods for the class that conform to the method signature definitions of the interface, as you see in Figure 8-18. Notice the similarity of the method documentation to the original documentation defined within the interface; it is almost identical. Second, notice how the "remove()" method traverses the associations the seminar object has with Instructor objects and the course object it represents. It does this to ensure the referential integrity of your objects (a topic discussed in detail in Section 8.3.1). For the actual code to persist seminar objects, I have merely written comments in their place because persistence coding is covered in detail in Section 8.3.4.

You must declare that the class implements the interface, and then write the methods of the interface for the class.

Figure 8-18.
Implementing the methods of the "IPersistent" interface in the "Student" class

```
/**
 *
 * Remove the seminar from permanent storage
 *
 * @postcondition  This seminar will no longer be available to other
 * objects
```

```
         *
         */
        public void remove()
        {
            if ( instructors != null) {
                // Each instructor of this seminar must have
                // it removed from their list of seminars.
                Enumeration instructorList = instructors.elements();

                while ( instructorList.hasMoreElements()) {
                    Professor professor = (Professor)instructorList.nextElement();
                    professor.removeSeminar(this);
                }
            }
            //
            // Disassociate the Course from this seminar
            //
            if ( getCourse() != null) {
                getCourse.removeSeminar(this);
                setCourse(null);
            }

            // Specific code to remove the seminar from permanent storage
        }


        /**
         * Write the seminar to permanent storage
         *
         * @postcondition  This seminar is written to permanent storage
         */
        public void save()
        {
            // Specific code for to save this seminar
        }

        /**
         * Retrieve the seminar from permanent storage
         *
         * @precondition   None. The seminar does not need to exist in
         * permanent storage.
         * @postcondition  If the seminar exists in storage it will be brought
         * into memory.
```

```
    */
    public void retrieve()
    {
        // Specific code to retrieve this seminar from
        // permanent storage
    }
```

8.2.9 Implementing Associations, Aggregation, and Composition In Java

Relationships—in this section, when I use the term relationship, I mean association, aggregration, and composition—are implemented via the combination of attributes and methods. The attributes describe the relationship, and the methods define and update the relationship. To understand this topic fully, you need to understand how to implement:

- Unidirectional and bidirectional relationships:
  - one-to-one relationships
  - one-to-many relationships
  - many-to-many relationships
- Recursive relationships
- Several relationships between the same classes
- Aggregation and composition

8.2.9.1 Implementing Unidirectional and Bidirectional Relationships

A *unidirectional* association is one that may be traversed in one direction only. For example, in Figure 8-3, you see a unidirectional association from "Person" to "Address." You know it is unidirectional because the association line has an arrowhead pointing from "Person" to "Address." The implication is that person objects know about their address objects, but address objects don't know about the person objects that live there. In the diagram, you see that "Person" has scaffolding code to maintain

Unidirectional associations are straightforward to manage.

DEFINITION

Referential integrity. The assurance that a reference from one entity to another entity is valid. If entity *A* references entity *B*, then entity *B* exists. If entity *B* is removed, then all references to entity *B* must also be removed.

the association, in this case the "homeAddress" attribute and its corresponding getter and setter method (depicted in Figure 8-12). This code is sufficient to manage the association between the two objects, maintaining the fact that a person lives at one and only one address (one-to-many association management is discussed later).

Bidirectional associations are naturally harder to manage than unidirectional associations because they can be traversed in both directions. Here's a little secret: Maintaining a bidirectional association is just like maintaining two unidirectional associations. The only added complication is you need to maintain them both in tandem. In Section 8.2.9.3, I discuss how to implement a bidirectional many-to-one association between "Seminar" and "Course," and I discuss a bidirectional many-to-many association between "Seminar" and "Instructor" in Section 8.2.9.4.

8.2.9.2 Implementing One-to-One Relationships

One-to-one relationships are the easiest to maintain because you only need to have an instance attribute in either one or both classes. For example, in Figure 8-12, you see the code needed to maintain the one-to-one unidirectional association from "Person" to "Address." Had this association been bidirectional code, and an attribute, it would have been needed in the "Address" class as well. One-to-one associations are always implemented as the combination of a simple attribute, such as an instance of "Address" in the case of the "Person" class, and a getter and setter method to manipulate that attribute.

One-to-one associations can also be implemented in a manner similar to how you would do so in a relational database, using a foreign key and methods to manipulate the key. The basic idea is that the unique identifier, the key, for the associated object is known by the other object. This value is then used to retrieve the associated object when it is needed, effectively a use of lazy initialization described in Section 8.2.6.2. Using this approach to maintain the association from "Person" to "Address," you would first need to add an attribute to "Address" to be used to identify it—ideally an object ID (OID), as described in Chapter 7, along with its corresponding getter and setter. This attribute would also be added to "Person," perhaps called "homeAddressOID," along with a getter and setter to manipulate it. The "getHomeAddress()" method of Figure 8-12 must be updated to check if "homeAddress" has been set and, if not, then use the value of "homeAddressOID" to retrieve the appropriate address object.

8.2.9.3 Implementing One-to-Many Relationships

One-to-many relationships, also called *many-to-one* relationships, are a little more difficult to implement. Actually, it is the "many" aspect of the relation-

---

DEFINITIONS

Foreign key. One or more attributes within a data entity that represent a primary or secondary key in another table. Foreign keys are used to maintain a relationship to a row in another table.

Key. One or more columns in a relational data table that, when combined, form a unique identifier for each record in the table.

Object identifier (OID). A unique identifier assigned to objects, typically a large integer number. OIDs are the object-oriented equivalent of keys in the relational world.

---

ship that is the problem, because it cannot be implemented simply as the combination of an attribute, a getter, and a setter. Instead, to manage the "many" part of a relationship, you must use a collection object such as an instance of Java's "Vector" or "Hashset" classes to track the relationship to potentially several other objects. Collection classes enable you to keep track of zero or more items by adding and removing them from the collection as needed. Each type of collection class works differently; for example, an instance of "Hashset" only lets you add one reference to any given object, whereas an instance of "Vector" lets you add as many references as you want to the same object. The "Hashset" class is good to use if you need a unique collection of objects, whereas the "Vector" class is good to use if speed is of the essence. Each collection class has different strengths and weaknesses.

In Figure 8-3, you see a one-to-many bidirectional association between the "Course" and "Seminar" class. The "Seminar" class includes scaffolding to maintain the association to course objects. It has a "course" attribute, a getter and setter for the attribute, and even takes a course object as a parameter to its constructor, the "Seminar(number, course)" method, as you saw in Figure 8-11. To manage the association in the other direction, the "Course" class has an instance attribute "seminars," which is a hashset, and a corresponding getter and setter called "getSeminars()" and "setSeminars()," which work exactly as you would expect. However, because "seminars" is a collection, I also needed to add methods to add and remove objects to and from it, in this case the methods "addSeminar()" and "removeSeminar()," as depicted in Figure 8-19.

The scaffolding to manage the "many" side of an association is slightly more complex than that of a "one" side.

Figure 8-19.
Managing the association from a course to its seminars

```
/**
 * Add a seminar to the course
 */
```

```
public void addSeminar(Seminar seminar)
{
   getSeminars().add(seminar);
}

/**
 * Remove a course from the seminar
 */
public void removeSeminar(Seminar seminar)
{
   getSeminars().remove(seminar);
}
```

*Adopt and then
follow Java
programming
conventions.*

Notice the consistency of the names of the collection attribute, its "add" and "remove" methods, and the role of the objects stored in the collection. As you see in Figure 8-3, I follow this naming convention for all the scaffolding attributes and methods to maintain the "many" portion of an association. The more consistent your code is, the easier it is to understand and to enhance.

Also notice the "addSeminar()" and "removeSeminar()" methods both use the getter method to access the collection and don't directly access the attribute itself. For example, instead of writing "getSeminars().remove(seminar)" I could just as easily have written "seminars.remove(seminar)." Although this code would run slightly faster, it would also lose the information-hiding benefits enabled by accessor methods. This is a trade-off I chose not to make, however. I prefer to optimize code as a last resort, not as a first resort.

8.2.9.4 Implementing Many-to-Many Relationships

Many-to-many relationships require the most amount of work to implement because each object involved in the relationship must maintain a collection of references to the other objects to which it is related. You saw in the previous section how to implement the "many" sides of an association. When using a many-to-many association, you merely need to do this on both sides. Figure 8-20 presents the scaffolding code in the "Professor" class to manage its part of the "instructs" association with instances of "Seminar." Figure 8-21 presents the similar code to manage its part of the association. I didn't include the header documentation or the accessors for the sake of brevity.

DEFINITION

Information hiding. The restriction of external access to attributes.

Figure 8-20.
The scaffolding code in the "Professor" class

```
private HashSet seminars;

public void addSeminar(Seminar seminar)
{
    // If the seminar is not already in the collection add it
    // The if statement avoids an infinite loop managing the association
    if ( ! getSeminars().contains(seminar)) {
        getSeminars().add(seminar);

        // The Seminar should know who instructs it
        seminar.addInstructor(this);
    }
}

public void removeSeminar(Seminar seminar)
{
    // Only perform the removal of the seminar if it is in the collection
    // The if statement avoids an infinite loop managing the association
    if ( getSeminars().contains(seminar)) {
        // Remove the seminar from the collection
        getSeminars().remove(seminar);

        // Update the seminar so that it knows that the professor
        // no longer instructs it
        seminar.removeInstructor(this);
    }
}
```

Figure 8-21.
The scaffolding code in the "Seminar" class

```
private Vector    instructors;

public void addInstructor(Professor professor)
{
    // If the professor does not exist in the collection add it
    // The if statement avoids an infinite loop managing the association
    if ( ! instructors.contains( professor )) {
        getInstructors().add( professor );
```

```
            // Update the other end of the association
            professor.addSeminar( this );
        }
    }

    public void removeInstructor(Professor professor)
    {
        if ( instructors.contains( professor )) {
            getInstructors().remove( professor );

            // Update the other end of the association
            professor.removeSeminar( this );
        }
    }
```

Notice how, in Figure 8-20, the "addSeminar(seminar)" method automatically invokes "addInstructor(professor)" in the "Seminar" class and, in Figure 8-21, that this method does the same thing in the other direction. This code is more robust than that presented in Figure 8-19 because it automates the management of the association in both directions, reducing the chance of introducing a logic error in your code. Also notice the use of whitespace in the parameter list of method invocations in Figure 8-21, as compared to 8-20. Both styles are fine; just pick one and follow it consistently in your code.

8.2.9.5 Recursive Relationships

Recursive relationships are managed using the same techniques as nonrecursive relationships.

Recursive relationships are implemented exactly as nonrecursive associations: that is, with attributes and methods. The only difference is all the scaffolding code is implemented in one class instead of two. In Figure 8-3, you see a course knows its prerequisites, a unidirectional recursive association. Figure 8-22 presents code necessary to maintain this relationship, once again, not including the header documentation or the accessors for the sake of brevity.

Figure 8-22.
The scaffolding code to manage the recursive association of the "Course" class

```
    private HashSet  prerequisites;

    public void addPrerequisite(Course course)
    {
        getPrerequisites().add(course);
    }
```

```
public void removePrerequisite(Course course)
{
    getPrerequisites().remove(course);
}
```

8.2.9.6 Implementing Several Relationships Between the Same Classes

To implement several relationships between the same two classes, you merely implement the appropriate scaffolding code to maintain the relationships. For example, in Figure 8-3, you see that two relationships exist between the "Professor" and the "Seminar" class: "instructs" and "oversees." As you can see in the class diagram, each class has the appropriate scaffolding code to manage both of these associations.

Two classes can have several relationships between them.

8.2.9.7 Implementing Aggregation and Composition

As you might have guessed, aggregation and composition associations are handled exactly the same way as associations. The main difference, from a programming point-of-view, is that aggregation implies a tighter relationship between the two classes than does association, and composition implies an even tighter relationship still. Although Figure 8-3 doesn't include either aggregation or composition associations, the association between "Seminar" and "Course" is tight, in fact, at least as tight as you would see with aggregation (unfortunately the sentence rule doesn't make sense in this case or I would have used aggregation). In Figure 8-23, you see the result of this closeness in the implementation of the "remove()" method in the "Course" class—when a course is removed, its seminars are also removed. This type of lifecycle management code is typical within aggregation and composition hierarchies, as discussed in Chapter 7.

Figure 8-23.
Implementing the "remove()" method in the "Course" class

```
/**
 * Remove a course
 *
 * @postcondition  The course and its seminars will be removed
 */
public void remove()
{
    if ( seminars != null) {
        // Clone the original set because we can't safely remove
        // the items from the set while we iterate over it
```

```
HashSet set  = (HashSet) getSeminars().clone();
Iterator iterator = set.iterator();

// Remove each seminar of this course
while ( iterator.hasNext() ) {
   Seminar seminar = (Seminar) iterator.next();

   // Remove the seminar from the collection
   getSeminars().remove(seminar);
  }
}

// Remove the instance from permanent storage

// Persistence code...
 }
```

Figure 8-23 is interesting because it implements the business rule that, when a course is made unavailable, it is removed from the university catalog, and its seminars must also be made similarly unavailable (remember, removed does not necessarily mean deleted). This is effectively a referential integrity issue. In a relational database, this logic would be implemented as a trigger, discussed in detail in Section 8.3.4. However, my philosophy is that business logic belongs in the business layer, which is implemented using object technology, not in the database. Therefore, I prefer to implement "triggers" in my business code, not in my persistence code.

Meanwhile, Back in Reality
Writing code to enforce referential integrity in your business classes instead of your database only works when all your applications are written this way (and, hopefully, they share a common code base). This situation, however, is rarely the case. Instead, many organizations are in the position that some of their applications, often most, are written assuming that the database(s) will handle referential integrity. In my opinion, this reflects an inappropriate layering of these applications; business logic is then implemented on several disparate architectural tiers, making the applications less robust.

8.2.10 Implementing Dependencies

You don't really implement dependencies in Java; instead, dependencies are simply reflected in the code you write. For example, in Figure 8-3, you see that a dependency exists between the "Address""class and the "ZipCodeValidator" class. This dependency is a reflection of the fact that in the "validate()" method of "Address," it invokes the "validateZipCode(zipCode, state)" method of the "ZipCodeValidator" class, as seen in Figure 8-24. The method is invoked on the class. As you see in the class diagram, it is a static method, so you invoke it on the class and not an instance of the class, returning a Boolean indicating whether the ZIP code is valid.

Dependencies are reflected in method invocations in your code.

Figure 8-24.
Implementing the "validate()" method in the "Address" class

```
/**
 * Validate the address
 *
 * @return true if the address is valid, false otherwise
 */
public boolean validate()
{
    // Code to validate the street, city, and state...

    // Validate the zip code
    return ZipCodeValidator.validateZipCode(zipCode, state);
}
```

8.2.11 Implementing Collaboration in Java

In Chapter 5, you learned that collaboration occurs for one of two reasons: either an object requests information from another object or it requests another object to do something for it. Collaboration is implemented as a method invocation on an object or class. In Figure 8-15, you saw the implementation of the "getName()" method of "Seminar"—to formulate its name, a seminar object must collaborate with its corresponding course to get the base information it needs. Figure 8-24 presents an example of how an address object collaborates with the "ZipCodeValidator" class to determine whether a ZIP code is valid.

Collaboration is a method invocation on an object or class.

8.2.12 Implementing Business Rules

Business rules can be implemented using a variety of methods. For example, the business rules pertaining to the validation of a ZIP code are encapsulated by the "ZipCodeValidator" class. A business rule may also be

Business rules may be implemented as methods, as classes, or using rule engines.

implemented as a method. For example, Figure 8-25 implements the business rule that a tenured professor must receive tenure on or after the day he or she starts with the university. Business rules may also be implemented using business rule engines, software products specifically designed to implement complex rules, a topic that is beyond the scope of this book.

Figure 8-25.
The "validate()" method in the TenuredProfessor class

```
/**
 * A tenured professor must have been given tenure on or after
 * the date that he or she started with the university.
 *
 * @return true if the attribute values are self-consistent, false otherwise
 */
public boolean validate()
{
   if ( this.getStartDate() != null && this.getTenuredAnniversary() != null) {
      long start = this.getStartDate().getTime();
      long tenureDate  = this.getTenuredAnniversary().getTime();

      if ( tenureDate >= start)
         return true;
      else
         return false;
   } else
      return false;
}
```

8.3 From Design to Persistence Code

Relational databases are the most common type of persistence mechanism.

Because the most common type of persistence mechanism is still relational databases, I focus on the basics of how to write code to interact with them. If you aren't using a relational database to store your objects, then you can skip this section if you like. As with Section 8.2, my goal is to introduce the basics of writing persistence code for you, not to present a comprehensive overview of the language.

Figure 8-26 presents a simple persistence model, using the notation described in Chapter 7, for a relational database (RDB) consisting of two tables. The "Seminar" data entity has four columns, one of which is the

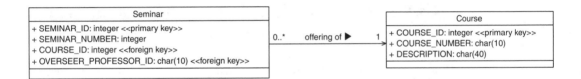

Seminar
+ SEMINAR_ID: integer <<primary key>>
+ SEMINAR_NUMBER: integer
+ COURSE_ID: integer <<foreign key>>
+ OVERSEER_PROFESSOR_ID: char(10) <<foreign key>>

0..*   offering of ▶   1

Course
+ COURSE_ID: integer <<primary key>>
+ COURSE_NUMBER: char(10)
+ DESCRIPTION: char(40)

Figure 8-26.
A simple persistence model

primary key "SEMINAR_ID," the value of which uniquely identifies each row of the table. The column "COURSE_ID" is the primary key of the "Course" table and is a column of "Seminar" used as a foreign key to maintain the association between seminar rows and course rows. This persistence schema is used as the running example for this section.

8.3.1 Strategies for Implementing Persistence Code

You implement the persistence code within your software in several ways. The most common, and least palatable, in my opinion, is to embed Structured Query Language (SQL) statements in your classes. The advantage of this approach is it enables you to write code quickly and it is viable for small applications and/or prototypes; however, two main disadvantages exist. First, it directly couples your business classes with the schema of your relational database, implying that a simple change such as renaming a column or porting to another database results in a rework of your source code. Second, it forces you to write significant amounts of SQL code, at least four statements for simple CRUD (create, retrieve, update, and delete) operations, let alone the additional code required for complex versions of this behavior.

Embedding SQL code in your classes is easy, but a significant development and maintenance burden.

A slightly better approach is one in which the SQL statements for your business classes are encapsulated in one or more "data classes." Once again, this approach is suitable for prototypes and small systems of fewer than 40 to 50 business classes, but it still results in a recompilation (of your data classes) when simple changes to the database are made. Your data "classes" are typically implemented as normal Java classes with embedded SQL, one data class for each business class (for example, "TenuredProfessor" has a corresponding "TenuredProfessorData" class), or as a collection of stored procedures in your database (one or more for

Encapsulating persistence code in data classes is a step in the right direction.

DEFINITION

Rule engine. Software, typically based on artificial intelligence (AI) techniques, used specifically for implementing complex logic in the form of rules.

<table>
<tr><td colspan="1">

DEFINITIONS

Column. The relational database equivalent of an attribute of a data entity stored in a relational table.

Data entity. The representation of the data describing a person, place, thing, event, or concept.

Persistence layer. Software, also known as a *persistence framework*, that encapsulates permanent storage mechanisms, such as relational databases, so application developers don't have knowledge of how or where objects are stored. Persistence layers automate significant portions of the efforts required to persist objects.

Primary key. The preferred key for a data entity.

Relational database (RDB). A permanent storage mechanism in which data is stored as rows in tables. RDBs don't natively support the persistence of objects, requiring the additional work on the part of developers and/or the use of a persistence layer.

Relational table. The physical implementation of a data entity within a relational database.

Row. The relational database equivalent of an instance of a data entity stored in a relational table. Also called a *record* or *tuple*.

</td></tr>
</table>

Persistence layers provide a robust solution that reduces both your development and maintenance burden.

retrieving, one or more for deleting, and so on). The best thing to be said about this approach is you have at least encapsulated the source code that handles the hard-coded interactions in one place, the data classes.

A third approach is to use a persistence layer/framework that maps objects to persistence mechanisms (in this case, relational databases) in such a manner that simple changes to the relational schema don't affect your object-oriented code. The advantage of this approach is that application programmers don't need to know a thing about the schema of the relational database. In fact, they don't even need to know that their objects are being stored in a relational database. Instead of writing code that needs to be tested and maintained over time, someone uses an administration tool to define the mappings between your object schema and your data schema (a topic covered in detail in Chapter 7). The main disadvantage is that there is a performance impact to your applications, a minor one if you buy/build an effective persistence layer, but an impact still happens.

DEFINITIONS

SQL. Structured Query Language.

SQL statement. A piece of SQL code used to retrieve, update, insert, or delete data, or manipulate the schema of a relational database.

8.3.2 Defining and Modifying Your Persistence Schema

To define, update, and remove tables in a relational database, you need to write Data Definition Language (DDL) SQL statements. DDL is straightforward, as you see in Figures 8-27, 8-28, and 8-29. Granted, DDL has a lot more to it than just this. You can use it to define database triggers and stored procedures (discussed in the following section), add indexes on tables to speed data access, and to add views on your database (think of views as virtual tables). Using persistence modeling tools to define your schema is quite common.

Figure 8-27.
SQL statement to create the "Seminar" table

```
CREATE TABLE Seminar (
    SEMINAR_ID              INTEGER NOT NULL,
    COURSE_ID               INTEGER NOT NULL,
    OVERSEER_PROFESSOR_ID   CHAR(10) NULL
);
```

Figure 8-28.
SQL statement to add a column to the "Seminar" table

```
ALTER TABLE Seminar
    ADD SEMINAR_NUMBER INTEGER NULL
```

Figure 8-29.
SQL statement to remove the "Seminar" table

```
DROP TABLE Seminar;
```

8.3.3 Creating, Retrieving, Updating, and Deleting Data

To manipulate the data stored in a relational database, you issue Data Manipulation Language (DML) SQL statements to the database. Figure 8-30 depicts an SQL "INSERT" statement to create a row in a table. You can see that the columns of the table are listed and that the values to insert into those columns are listed—each value maps, in order, to one and only one column in the list. Notice how the "OVERSEER_ID" column has its value

Issue SQL "INSERT" statements to create rows in relational tables.

in quotes. This is because it is a character value, whereas the other columns are numeric, so no quotes are around their values.

Figure 8-30.
SQL statement to insert a row into the "Seminar" table

```
INSERT INTO Seminar
    (SEMINAR_ID, COURSE_ID, OVERSEER_ID, SEMINAR_NUMBER)
VALUES
    (74656, 1234, 'THX0001138', 2)
```

Issue SQL "SELECT" statements to retrieve data from relational tables.

To retrieve data from a database, you can issue an SQL "SELECT" statement. Figure 8-31 presents a straightforward example of retrieving zero or one rows from the database. I know that not more than one row will be returned because the "WHERE" class specifies an exact value for the primary key; in this case, the "SEMINAR_ID" column must have the value 1701. Either a row exists with this key value or it doesn't. There cannot be more than one row with this value by definition (remember, key values must be unique). If a row exists with that value already, and someone tries to insert another row with the same value into the table, the statement will not run and it will result in an error. Figure 8-32 presents a more complex example, one that results in zero or more rows being returned. The "WHERE" clause has two parts: One provides a value for the key (you don't always have to specify values for the key in the "WHERE" clause) and the other provides a wild-card search value for the "OVERSEER_ID" column. The statement also includes an "ORDER BY" clause to specify the sort order of the data rows in the result set.

Figure 8-31.
SQL statement to retrieve a row from the "Seminar" table

```
SELECT * FROM Seminar
WHERE SEMINAR_ID = 1701
```

Figure 8-32.
SQL statement to retrieve several rows from the "Seminar" table

```
SELECT * FROM Seminar
WHERE  SEMINAR_ID > 1701
AND             OVERSEER_ID LIKE 'THX%'
ORDER BY        COURSE_ID, OVERSEER_ID
```

Figure 8-33 presents an example of how to update data in a relational table via an SQL "UPDATE" statement. This is straightforward. You simply specify the values of the columns you want to set, and include an appropriate "WHERE" clause, so the right rows get updated. Updating several rows at once is possible simply by writing a "WHERE" clause that is less specific.

Issue SQL "UPDATE" statements to update data in relational tables.

Figure 8-33.
SQL statement to update a row in a table in the "Seminar" table

```
UPDATE Seminar
   SET   OVERSEER_ID = 'NCC0001701',
SEMINAR_NUMBER = 3
WHERE SEMINAR_ID = 1701
```

To delete data from a relational database, you need to issue an SQL "DELETE" statement, as depicted in Figure 8-34. The syntax of the "DELETE" statement is similar to the syntax of the other types of SQL DML statements, as you can see.

Issue SQL "DELETE" statements to delete data in relational tables.

Figure 8-34.
SQL statement to delete data from the "Seminar" table

```
DELETE FROM Seminar
WHERE  SEMINAR_ID > 1701
   AND              OVERSEER_ID = 'THX0001138'
```

8.3.4 Implementing Behavior in a Relational Database

Behavior is implemented in a relational database using stored procedures and triggers. A *stored procedure* is basically a function/procedure/method that is implemented in a relational database and a *trigger* is a procedure that is automatically invoked as the result of Data Manipulation Language statement invocations. As I discussed in both this and the previous chapter, my philosophy is that business logic should be implemented in your business class, not in your database. However, stored procedures and triggers have their uses.

Several valid uses exist for stored procedures. The first is to encapsulate a legacy data design. Organizations commonly have a significant investment in their existing legacy databases, an investment they are unwilling or unable to do away with. The problem is that the legacy schema is often less than ideal, particularly from an object-oriented

Use stored procedures to wrap legacy schemas and to implement data intensive operations.

point-of-view. One way to deal with this problem is to wrap the legacy schema with stored procedures that present an interface to your database that reflects the design of your object schema. A second use for stored procedures is to implement operations involving significant amounts of data, those that access thousands or millions of data rows, which produce a small result. An example of this would be calculating the average mark received by all students enrolled in either a philosophy or a computer science course. This operation may involve thousands of rows, depending on the number of students enrolled in these types of courses, yet the end result is a single number. It may be more efficient to do the processing in the database instead of transmitting all these rows across the network and calculating the average on another machine.

Triggers should be used to ensure referential integrity when you can't guarantee all applications use the same business classes.

As suggested in Section 8.2.9.7, a valid use for triggers is to use them to ensure referential integrity when your database is accessed by both object-oriented and nonobject-oriented software or, in the case of pure OO organizations, you don't use a common set of business classes. Referential integrity deals with the issue that if object *A* references object *B*, then object *B* must exist. If row *A* references row *B*, then row *B* exists. And when *B* is removed, then all references to *B* must also be removed. Using triggers to implement referential integrity is a lowest-common denominator approach.

Stored procedures and triggers are likely not portable between database vendors, reducing the robustness of your system.

Why don't I like stored procedures and triggers? Because stored procedures and triggers are currently implemented using languages specific to each database vendor, implying that they aren't portable. One of my philosophies is that you should always design your software to be portable because you can count on having to port your software—even something as simple as a "minor" operating system upgrade or database upgrade counts as a port in my books. The good news is that most database vendors are starting to adopt Java as their programming language, indicating to me that stored procedure and trigger code may one day be portable between vendors. At press time, however, this is definitely not the case, so I am leery of any significant use of stored procedures and triggers beyond what I discuss in this section.

DEFINITIONS

Portability. A measure of how easy it is to move an application to another environment (which may vary by the configuration of either their software or hardware). The easier it is to move an application to another environment, the more portable we say that application is.

Wrapper. A collection of one or more classes that encapsulates access to non-OO technology to make it appear as if it is OO.

Wrapping. The act of encapsulating non-OO functionality within a class, making it look and feel like any other object within the system.

8.4 Programming Tips

This section presents a collection of programming tips and techniques, and idioms for improving the quality of your code. Although some Java examples are presented, these tips are, in fact, applicable to a wide range of programming languages.

8.4.1 Techniques for Writing Clean Code

In this section, I cover several techniques that help to separate professional developers from hack coders. These techniques are as follows:

- Document your code
- Paragraph/indent your code
- Paragraph and punctuate multiline statements
- Use whitespace
- Follow the 30-second rule
- Write short, single command lines

8.4.1.1 Document Your Code

If your code is not worth documenting, then it is not worth keeping (Nagler, 1995). Following effective documentation guidelines, described in Chapter 7 and in Section 8.4.2, greatly enhances the quality of your source code.

8.4.1.2 Paragraph/Indent Your Code

One way to improve the readability of a method is to paragraph it; in other words, indent your code within the scope of a code block. Any code within braces, the { and } characters, forms a block. The basic idea is that the code within a block should be uniformly indented one unit (a unit is typically from two to four spaces). Figure 8-35 presents a version of a method that doesn't apply any sort of paragraphing, whereas Figure 8-36 presents a paragraphed version of the same code. Notice how following the flow of logic in the paragraphed version is easier because the indentation visually groups code that is at the same logical scope.

Effective indentation increases the readability of your code.

DEFINITION

Idiom. Describes how to implement a particular part of a pattern, the part's functionality, or the relationship to other parts in the design. Idioms are often specific to a particular programming language.

Figure 8-35.
Unparagraphed source code

```
public boolean validate()
{
if ( this.getStartDate() != null && this.getTenuredAnniversary() !=
null) {
long start = this.getStartDate().getTime();
long tenureDate   = this.getTenuredAnniversary().getTime();

if ( tenureDate >= start)
return true;
else
return false;
} else
return false;
}
```

Figure 8-36.
Paragraphed source code

```
public boolean validate()
{
    if ( this.getStartDate() != null && this.getTenuredAnniversary() !=
null) {
        long start = this.getStartDate().getTime();
        long tenureDate   = this.getTenuredAnniversary().getTime();

        if ( tenureDate >= start)
            return true;
        else
            return false;
    } else
        return false;
}
```

8.4.1.3 Paragraph and Punctuate Multiline Statements

A related issue to paragraphing your code occurs when a single statement requires several lines of code, an example of which appears in Figure 8-37.

DEFINITION

Paragraphing. A technique where you indent the code within the scope of a code block by one unit, usually a horizontal tab, to distinguish it from the code outside the code block. Paragraphing helps to increase the readability of your code.

Notice how I indent the second and third lines one unit, visibly indicating they are still part of the preceding line. Also notice how the final comma in the second line immediately follows the parameter and is not shown on the following line (word processors also work this way).

Figure 8-37.
Paragraphing a multiline statement

```
BankAccount newPersonalAccount = AccountFactory
    createBankAccountFor( currentCustomer, startDate,
    initialDeposit, branch);
```

8.4.1.4 Use Whitespace in Your Code

A few blank lines or spaces, called *whitespace*, added to your Java code can help to make it much more readable by breaking the code up into small, easy-to-digest sections (Ambler, 1998a; Vermeulen, et al., 2000). I like to use a single blank line to separate logical groups of code, such as control structures, and two blank lines to separate method definitions. Without whitespace, the code is difficult to read and to understand. Notice how the readability of the code improves from Figure 8-38 to 8-39, thanks to the simple addition of a blank line between setting the counter and the lines of code to calculate the grand total. Also notice how the addition of spaces around the operators and after the comma also increase the readability of the code. Small things, yes, but they can still make a big difference.

The effective addition of spaces and blank lines in your code increases its readability.

Figure 8-38.
Source code without whitespace

```
counter=1;
grandTotal=invoice.total()+getAmountDue();
grandTotal=Discounter.discount(grandTotal,this);
```

Figure 8-39.
Source code with whitespace

```
counter = 1;

grandTotal = invoice.total() + getAmountDue();
grandTotal = Discounter.discount(grandTotal, this);
```

8.4.1.5 Follow the 30-Second Rule

Well-written code can be understood in fewer than 30 seconds.

I have always believed another programmer should be able to look at a method, a class, or an interface definition and be able to fully understand what it does, why it does it, and how it does it in fewer than 30 seconds (Ambler, 1998a). If he or she cannot, then your code is too difficult to maintain and should be improved. A class is made understandable in fewer than 30 seconds by informative header documentation. A method is made understandable in fewer than 30 seconds by effective heading documentation, adherence to common naming and programming conventions, and effective internal documentation.

8.4.1.6 Write Short, Single Command Lines

Your code should do one thing per line (Ambler, 1998a). Back in the days of punch cards, it made sense to try to get as much functionality as possible on a single line of code because the speed of program execution was partially determined by the number of cards you had. Considering it has been over 20 years since I have even seen a punch card, though, I think we can safely rethink this approach to writing code. Whenever you attempt to do more than one task on a single line of code, you make your code harder to understand. Why do this? You want to make your code easier to understand so it is easier to maintain and enhance. Just as a method should do one thing and one thing only, you should only do one thing on a single line of code. Furthermore, you should write code that remains visible on the screen. My rule of thumb is that you shouldn't have to scroll your editing window to the right to read the entire line of code, including code that uses endline comments.

8.4.2 Techniques for Writing Effective Documentation

Over the years I have found the following philosophies work well:

- Comments should add to the clarity of your code
- Write the documentation before writing the code
- Document why something is done, as well as what is being done

8.4.2.1 Comments Should Add to the Clarity of Your Code

Nagler (1995) points out that the reason you document your code is to make it more understandable to you, your coworkers, and to any other developer who comes after you. The implication is that your documentation should add value. The goal is not to write a lot of documentation, it is to write just enough documentation to explain your work.

Quality, not quantity, is the order of the day.

8.4.2.2 Write the Documentation Before You Write the Code

The best way to document code is to write the comments before you write the code. This gives you an opportunity to think about how the code will work before you write it and ensures the documentation will be written. Alternatively, you should at least document your code as you write it. Because documentation makes your code easier to understand, you are able to take advantage of this fact while you are developing it. The way I look at it, if you are going to invest the time writing documentation, you should at least get something out of it (Ambler, 1998a).

8.4.2.3 Document Why Something Is Being Done, Not Just What

Fundamentally, you can always look at a piece of code and figure out what it does. For example, you can look at the code in Figure 8-40 and determine that a 5 percent discount is being given on orders of $1,000 dollars or more. Why is this being done? Is there a business rule that says large orders get a discount? Is there a limited-time special on large orders or is it a permanent program? Was the original programmer just being generous? I wouldn't know unless it is documented somewhere, either in the source code itself or in an external document (Ambler, 1998a).

Figure 8-40.
Undocumented source code

```
if ( grandTotal >= 1000.00)
{
    grandTotal = grandTotal * 0.95;
}
```

A useful metric for estimating the quality of your code is the number of lines of comment per method (Lorenz and Kidd, 1994; Ambler, 1998a). My experience has been that good methods have more lines of comments than lines of code. Too few comments indicates that other programmers will have a difficult time trying to understand your code and too many comments indicates that you are wasting too much time documenting it.

Related to the number of lines of comment per method is the percentage of methods with comments (Lorenz and Kidd, 1994; Ambler, 1998a).

Good code often has more lines of documentation than lines of "real" code.

T I P

Learn the Elements of C++ Style

To learn how to program effectively in C++, I always suggest reading the books *Advanced C++: Programming Styles and Idioms* (Coplien, 1992), *Effective C++: 50 Specific Ways to Improve Your Programs and Designs* (Meyers, 1992), and *More Effective C++: 35 New Ways to Improve Your Programs and Designs* (Meyers, 1996). Anybody can learn to write C++ code, so you should strive to learn to write excellent C++ code.

Although I instantly want to say this figure should always be 100 percent, the reality is it doesn't have to be. This is because you don't really need to document setters—methods that set the value of attributes.

8.4.3 Miscellaneous

I believe you will find the following observations of value when you attempt to write high-quality source code:

- Get the design right first
- Smaller methods are usually better
- Reduce method response
- Develop in small steps
- Write code that is understandable by everyone

8.4.3.1 Get the Design Right First

Would you feel comfortable walking over a bridge that, instead of being put together with a plan, was put together with only the hard work of a group of construction workers who felt they knew what they were doing? Of course you wouldn't. You would be afraid the bridge could fall down at any minute. Why should your users be comfortable working with software built by a group of programmers who felt they knew what they were doing? How comfortable would you be when you were taking a flight somewhere if you discovered the air-traffic-control system was written without first putting together, and then following, a solid design? Think about it.

The time invested in design pays off during programming.

Have you ever been in a situation where some of the code that your code relies on needs to be changed? Perhaps a new parameter needs to be passed to a method or perhaps a class needs to be broken up into several classes. How much extra work did you have to do to make sure your code works with the reconfigured version of the code that got changed? How happy were you? Did you ask yourself why somebody didn't stop to think about the issues first when the code was originally written, so this didn't happen? That they should have *designed* it first? Of course you did. If you take the time to learn how you are going to write your code before you actually start coding, you will probably spend less time doing it and, potentially, reduce the impact of future changes on your code simply by thinking about the issues first.

Rushing to code results in systems that are fragile, difficult to maintain and extend, and difficult to understand. This can be perilous. The reality is, nevertheless, that the results of design are an incomplete first step and that, during programming and testing, issues will be discovered that require changes to the initial design (Larman, 1998).

8.4.3.2 Smaller Methods Are Usually Better

If you want to write methods that are easy to maintain, then they should be small. One should hope for fewer than 10 statements for Smalltalk code and 30 statements for C++ or Java (Smalltalk is a higher-level language than C++ or Java, resulting in fewer lines of code). Remember, the 30-second rule: somebody should be able to look at any method and completely understand it in under 30 seconds. This implies that methods must be both small and well documented (they should do one thing and one thing only). If methods are difficult to understand, then they are difficult to maintain and enhance, increasing your maintenance costs.

Large methods are difficult to maintain and enhance.

Furthermore, if a method is large, this is a good indication that your code is actually function-oriented, as opposed to object-oriented (Lorenz and Kidd, 1994; Ambler, 1998a). Objects get things done by collaborating with each other and not by doing everything themselves. This results in short methods, not long ones. Although you will occasionally run into long methods, they are few and far between. If your methods are long, this is an indication that a problem exists.

8.4.3.3 Reduce Method Response

Programmers should reduce the method response (Chidamber and Kemerer, 1991; Ambler, 1998a) of a method. *Method response* is a count of the total number of messages sent as a result of a method being invoked. The exact definition of method response is recursive. It is the count of all message sends within a method, plus the method response of each method invoked by those message sends. The reason this is an important metric is that methods with high method-response values indicate that the method is difficult to test, as you have to test all the code that gets invoked. Another potential problem is the potential for high coupling. Remember, the only way an object can send a message to another object is when it knows about that other object, implying that some coupling exists between the two objects. The higher the method response, the greater the chance of coupling.

The more messages that get invoked by a method, the harder it is to test.

There is a problem in that my advice to reduce method response contradicts my advice to write small methods. To get a low method response, you need larger methods. To get smaller methods, you need to increase the method response. This is acceptable because neither measurement is accurate 100 percent of the time. Sometimes methods are large, but nothing is wrong with them. Sometimes they have a high-method response and nothing is wrong with them.

8.4.3.4 Develop in Small Steps

Developing in small incremental steps is significantly faster than developing large portions of code at once.

I have always found that developing in small steps—writing a few methods, testing them, and then writing a few more methods—is often far more effective than writing a whole bunch of code all at once, and then trying to fix it. It is much easier to test and fix 10 lines of code than 100 lines. In fact, I can safely say you could program, test, and fix 100 lines of code in ten 10-line increments in less than half the time than you could write a single 100-line block of code that did the same work. The reason for this is simple. Whenever you are testing your code and you find a bug, you almost always discover that the bug is in the new code you just wrote, assuming the rest of the code was pretty solid to start. You can hunt down a bug faster in a small section of code than in a big one. By developing in small incremental steps, you reduce the average time it takes to find a bug, which, in turn, reduces your overall development time.

I want to point out a small caveat. Developing in small, incremental steps is faster only in interpreted environments such as Smalltalk, which let you see the effects of changes to your code instantly, or on small applications that can be compiled quickly in environments such as C++, which don't support interpreted development. When your application takes several hours to compile, you probably cannot afford to write a few lines, compile it, and then test it.

8.4.3.5 Write Code That Is Understandable by Everyone

Program for people.

Whenever code can only be understood by the original programmer, this is a sign that the person is a bad coder, not the coding genius he likely thinks he is. Most programmers typically work on teams, not alone, and most code is typically maintained by people who weren't its original developer(s). By writing clean, understandable code, you make it easier for others to work with it, increasing the chance they can maintain and enhance the code effectively.

DEFINITION

Method response. A count of the total number of messages sent as a result of a method being invoked.

8.4.3.6 Optimize Your Code Only as a Last Resort

I have left my discussion of Java code optimization for the end of this chapter for a reason: Optimizing your code is one of the last things programmers should be thinking about, not one of the first. My experience is that you should leave optimization to the end because you want to optimize only the code that needs it. Often a small percentage of your code results in the vast majority of the processing time and this is the code you should be optimizing. A classic mistake is to try to optimize all your code, even code that already runs fast enough. Personally, I prefer to optimize the code that needs it, and then move on to more interesting tasks than trying to squeeze out every single CPU cycle.

Optimize last, not first.

8.5 What You Have Learned

In this chapter, you have learned that your design artifacts should drive the development of your source code, as indicated by Figure 8-1. You saw how to implement fundamental object-oriented concepts using the Java programming language, enabling you to transform your models into actual working software. You also learned the fundamentals of writing Structured Query Language (SQL) code to interact with relational database (RDB) technology. Finally, you were introduced to a wealth of programming idioms for writing high-quality source code, regardless of your implementation language.

8.6 Review Questions

1. In addition to the languages mentioned in this chapter—Java, C++, and Smalltalk—name five other object-oriented languages and provide at least two sources (vendors, open-source Web sites, or freeware Web sites) from which you can obtain each language. List three strengths and weaknesses for each language and describe a use for which the language is well suited.

2. What changes would you need to make to the implementation of the "Course" class if its recursive association was bidirectional instead of unidirectional?

3. Develop a "DateRange" class in Java. It should have two attributes: "startDate" and "endDate." Start by modeling this class. What invariants should it exhibit? What methods are needed to ensure these invariants? What visibilities should these methods be assigned? Write the source code for the "DateRange" class based on your model.

4. What did you learn by modeling, and then coding, the "Date Range" class? How far did your source code stray from your initial design? What changes did you need to make to your model? How easy/difficult were the changes to make to your model? In hindsight, what could you have done when you were modeling to minimize the changes you needed to make?

5. Section 8.2.2 discusses the concept of using a combination of foreign keys and lazy initialization to implement relationships between objects. Using this approach, modify the design of Figure 8-3 and write the code to implement the many-to-many association between "Professor" and "Seminar."

6. Compare the strengths and weaknesses of Java's standard collection classes, as well as ObjectSpace's JGL collection classes. Provide an example for when you would use each one.

7. What standard Javadoc tags are available to you? From what you have seen in this chapter and the previous one, what tags do you think are missing? Describe how each tag will be used and provide an example of its use.

Anything worth building is worth testing.

You build a wide variety of artifacts, including models, documents, and source code.

Chapter 9

Object-Oriented Testing

What You Will Learn in This Chapter

How to overcome the misconceptions surrounding object-oriented testing
The Full Lifecycle Object-Oriented Testing (FLOOT) methodology
Techniques for testing your requirements, analysis, and design models
Techniques for testing your code
Techniques for testing your system once it is ready to be deployed
Techniques your users can apply to validate your system
How to write test cases, harnesses, and suites
How to record a defect

Why You Need to Read This Chapter

It isn't enough simply to develop software; you need to develop software that works. As software becomes more complex—you use object technology to deal with this complexity—it becomes harder to test. You can apply a variety of testing techniques throughout the entire software lifecycle, and this chapter describes these techniques.

One of the fundamentals of software engineering is that you should test as early as possible. You want to find and fix defects early in development for two reasons: Most mistakes are made early in the life of a project and the cost of fixing defects increases exponentially the later they are found.

Most defects are introduced into software products early in their lifecycle.

First, technical people are very good at technical tasks such as design and coding—that is why they are technical people. Unfortunately, technical people are often not as good at nontechnical tasks, such as gathering requirements and performing analysis, perhaps another reason why they are technical people. The end result is that developers have a tendency to make more errors during requirements definition and analysis than during design and coding.

The second motivating factor for testing early is that the cost of fixing defects rises the later they are found. This happens because of the nature of software development—work is performed based on work performed previously. For example, modeling is performed based on the information gathered during the definition of requirements. Programming is done based on the models that were developed, and testing is performed on the written source code. If a requirement was misunderstood, all modeling decisions based on that requirement are potentially invalid, all code written based on the models is also in question, and the testing efforts are then verifying the application against the wrong conditions. As a result, errors detected toward the end of the development lifecycle or after the application has been released are likely to be very expensive to fix. On the other hand, errors detected early in the lifecycle, where they are likely to be made, may be much less expensive to fix because you only have to update a few documents.

9.1 Overcoming Misconceptions About Object-Oriented Testing

Developers may have several common misconceptions concerning object-oriented testing. In part, this was due to a scarcity of research in OO testing in the early days of object orientation—people were struggling with concepts, modeling, and programming practices. This was also due in part to the industry's tendency to focus on the front-end of development, on modeling and programming, and not on a less "sexy" subject, such as

---

DEFINITION

Defect. Anything that detracts from your system's capability to meet the needs of your users completely and effectively. Also known as a *bug, fault,* or *feature.*

> **TIP**
>
> *You Can Test More Than Just Code*
>
> As you will see in this chapter, you can test all your deliverables, not just your source code. At a minimum, you can review models and documents, and by doing so, you can find and fix defects long before they get into your code.

testing. I want to address these misconceptions so you have an accurate understanding of object-oriented testing.

9.1.1 Misconception #1: With Objects You Do Less Testing

This is the most dangerous misconception a developer can have, a misconception that is often the result of an incomplete understanding of inheritance. Novice OO developers often assume that because a class has already been tested, they can create subclasses that inherit from it, but they do not have to test the new subclass fully. This assumption is wrong. When a class inherits from another, it is adding new behavior, some of which may be completely new, and some of which may be extensions of existing behavior. A subclass will implement new, and often more complex, business rules than its superclass. These business rules may extend, or conflict with, the rules implemented in the existing classes. The result is that you need to rerun the appropriate test cases originally developed for the superclass on the new subclass to ensure it still works, in addition to test cases associated with the new behaviors. Rerunning tests to ensure existing functionality still works is called *regression testing*, and rerunning the tests of superclasses on subclasses is called *inheritance regression testing*. In other words, you are doing more testing, not less. When you stop to think about it, this makes sense. One of the reasons you adopted OO in the first place is because you want to develop applications that are more complex than those you could have developed following a structured/procedural approach. Therefore, doesn't it make more sense that you would need to do more testing for a more complex application?

The greater the complexity of your software, the more effort you need to invest to test it.

> **DEFINITIONS**
>
> *Regression testing.* The validation that existing software still works after changes have been made.
>
> *Inheritance regression testing.* The act of running the test cases of the super classes, both direct and indirect, on a given subclass.

9.1.2 Misconception #2: Structured Testing Techniques Are Sufficient

Your testing paradigm needs to change to reflect your new development paradigm.

The good news is that this misconception is, in fact, partly correct. The bad news is this misconception is only partly correct. As you see in this chapter, many code-testing techniques, such as boundary-value testing, are still applicable for testing OO code, and many common system and user-testing techniques are applicable for integration testing of your software as a whole. In this chapter, however, you also see that several traditional testing techniques, such as coverage testing, are no longer as important in the OO world. Polymorphism, the capability of objects to change type, negates the value of coverage testing because your code might work today for a given object, but tomorrow might fail after the object changes type. Also, structured testing techniques do not take into consideration the fact that objects encapsulate both data and behavior—the development paradigm has changed. Doesn't it make sense that the testing paradigm should also change?

9.1.3 Misconception #3: Testing the User Interface Is Sufficient

There is far more to your software than its user interface.

Because tool vendors have concentrated on building tools for testing the user interface of an application and they have spent less effort on other aspects of testing, it is easy for developers with little testing experience to assume that testing the user interface is sufficient. Yes, user interface testing is important, but there's more to an application than screens and reports. You have to test all aspects of your application, the ones visible in the user interface and the ones hidden from view.

9.2 Full Lifecycle Object-Oriented Testing (FLOOT)

The *Full Lifecycle Object-Oriented Testing* (*FLOOT*) methodology is a collection of testing techniques to verify and validate object-oriented software. The FLOOT lifecycle is depicted in Figure 9-1, indicating that a variety of techniques are available to you throughout all aspects of software development. Summaries of each FLOOT technique are provided in this section. For further details, refer to Chapter 12 of *Building Object Applications That Work* (Ambler, 1998a).

DEFINITIONS

Coverage testing. The act of ensuring all lines of code are exercised at least once.

Integration testing. The act of ensuring that several portions of software work together.

> **DEFINITION**
>
> *User interface testing.* The testing of the user interface (UI) to ensure it follows accepted UI standards and meets the requirements defined for it. Often referred to as *graphical user interface (GUI)* testing.

9.2.1 Regression Testing

Regression testing is the act of ensuring that changes to an application have not adversely affected existing functionality. Have you ever made a small change to a program, and then put the program into production only to see it fail because the small change affected another part of the program you had completely forgotten about? Regression testing is all about avoiding problems like this. Regression testing is the first thing you should be thinking about when you begin the actual testing in the large of your application. How angry would you get if you took your car into a garage to have a new stereo system installed only to discover afterward that the new stereo works, but the headlights don't? Pretty angry. How angry do you think your users would get when a new release of an application no longer lets them fax information to other people because the new e-mail feature you just added has affected it somehow? Pretty angry.

How do you do regression testing? The quick answer is to run all your previous test cases against the new version of your application. Although

Users expect that all the functionality they had in a previous version of a system will either still exist or will be enhanced by new releases.

Figure 9-1.
The techniques of the Full Lifecycle Object-Oriented Testing (FLOOT) methodology

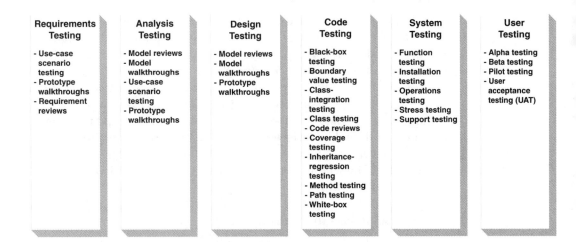

Requirements Testing	Analysis Testing	Design Testing	Code Testing	System Testing	User Testing
- Use-case scenario testing - Prototype walkthroughs - Requirement reviews	- Model reviews - Model walkthroughs - Use-case scenario testing - Prototype walkthroughs	- Model reviews - Model walkthroughs - Prototype walkthroughs	- Black-box testing - Boundary value testing - Class-integration testing - Class testing - Code reviews - Coverage testing - Inheritance-regression testing - Method testing - Path testing - White-box testing	- Function testing - Installation testing - Operations testing - Stress testing - Support testing	- Alpha testing - Beta testing - Pilot testing - User acceptance testing (UAT)

Regression Testing, Quality Assurance

T I P *Take the Time to Test*	Testing is often shortchanged during construction in favor of programming. Many developers apparently feel it is more important to deliver a lot of functionality that may not work properly (they have not tested it) than it is to deliver something small that definitely works. Instead, they should either take the extra time to ensure their application works properly or reduce the functionality of what they are delivering to produce quality work within the same time frame. There is little value in delivering something on time that does not work.

Changes in the design may result in changes to your old testing procedures.

this sounds like a good idea, it often proves not to be realistic. First, you may have changed part of, or even all of, your application's design. This means you need to modify some of the previous test cases. Second, if the changes you have made truly affect only a component of the system, then potentially you only need to run the test cases that affect this single component. Although this approach is a little risky because your changes may have had a greater impact than you suspect, it does help to reduce both the time and cost of regression testing.

Incremental development dramatically increases the importance of regression testing.

It is important to recognize that incremental development makes regression testing critical. (Remember, OO development is incremental in the small.) Whenever you release an application, you have to ensure that its previous functionality still works, and because you release applications more often when taking the incremental approach, this means regression testing becomes that much more important.

9.2.2 Quality Assurance

Quality assurance (QA) is the act of reviewing and auditing the project deliverables and activities to verify that they comply with the applicable standards, guidelines, and processes adopted by your organization. Fundamentally, quality assurance attempts to answer the following questions: "Are you building the right thing?" and "Are you building it the right way?" Quality assurance is critical to the success of a project and should be an integral part of all project stages. At all points during development you should be reviewing your work to ensure its quality.

Quality is in the eye of the beholder.

A key concept in quality assurance is that quality is often in the eye of the beholder, indicating that many aspects exist to software quality, including the following:

- Does it meet the needs of its users?
- Is it on time?
- Is it on budget?

DEFINITION

Quality assurance. The validation that the right thing was built the right way.

- Does it follow standards?
- Is it easy to use?
- Is it reasonably free of defects?
- Is it easy to maintain and to enhance?
- How easy will it integrate into the current technical environment?

9.2.3 Testing Your Requirements, Analysis, and Design Models

You saw earlier that most defects are introduced early in the lifecycle, most often during requirements and analysis activities. You also saw that the earlier you detect an error, the less expensive it is to fix. Therefore, it is imperative for you attempt to test your requirements, analysis, and design artifacts as soon as you can. Luckily, a collection of techniques exists that you can apply to do exactly that. As you see in Figure 9-1, these techniques are use case scenario testing, prototype walkthroughs, requirement reviews, model reviews, model walkthroughs, and user interface testing. These forms of testing are typically performed in parallel with your requirements, analysis, and design efforts to validate this work as early as possible.

9.2.3.1 Use Case Scenario Testing

Use case scenario testing (Ambler, 1998b), covered in detail in Chapter 4, is a testing process in which users are actively involved with ensuring that user requirements are accurate. The basic idea is that a group of subject matter experts (SMEs), with the aid of a facilitator, step through a

Use case scenario testing helps to validate your user requirements.

Looking for quality after the fact in a technical review is only part of the solution, but it is definitely not enough. Quality is a way of life for professional developers who strive to create high-quality deliverables the first time, every time. Developers who do this focus on the customers, the people who will use what they create downstream in the development process. The best developers actively look for new and better ways to do things, constantly trying to improve the quality of their work. Quality is everyone's job, not just that of the quality assurance department.

TIP

Quality Is Everyone's Job

> ### DEFINITIONS
>
> *Model review.* A technical review in which an analysis and/or design model is inspected.
>
> *Model walkthrough.* A less formal version of a model review.
>
> *Peer review.* A style of technical review in which a project deliverable, or portion thereof, is inspected by a small group of people with expertise in the product being reviewed.
>
> *Prototype walkthrough.* A process by which your users work through a collection of use cases using a prototype as if it were the real system. The main goal is to test whether the design of the prototype meets their needs.
>
> *Requirement review.* A technical review in which a requirements model is inspected.
>
> *Technical review.* A testing technique in which one or more development artifacts are examined critically by a group of your peers. A review typically focuses on accuracy, quality, usability, and completeness. Less formal versions of this process are often referred to as walkthroughs or peer reviews.
>
> *Use case scenario testing.* A testing technique in which one or more person(s) validate your domain model (typically a CRC model) by acting through the logic of use case scenarios.

series of defined use cases to verify that your CRC model or analysis-level class model, which they created, accurately reflects the requirements defined by the use cases.

9.2.3.2 Prototype Walkthrough

Prototype walkthroughs quickly verify that your prototype meets the needs of your users.

A prototype walkthrough (Ambler, 1998b), covered in detail in Chapter 4, is a testing process in which your users work through a series of use cases to verify that a user prototype meets their needs. The basic idea is that your users pretend the prototype is the real application and try to use it to solve real business problems described by the scenarios. Granted, they need to use their imaginations to fill in the functionality the application is missing (such as reading and writing objects from/to permanent storage) but, for the most part, this is a fairly straightforward process.

> ### DEFINITION
>
> *Subject matter expert (SME).* A person who is responsible for providing pertinent information about the problem and/or technical domain either from personal knowledge or from research.

DEFINITION

User-acceptance testing (UAT). A testing technique in which users verify that an application meets their needs by working with the software.

Your users sit down at the computer and begin to work through the use cases. Your job is to sit there and observe them, looking for places where the system is difficult to use or is missing features. In many ways, prototype walkthroughs are a lot like user-acceptance tests, described in Section 9.2.6.2. The only difference is that you are working with the prototype instead of the real system.

9.2.3.3 User Requirement Review

A user requirement review is a testing technique in which a group of users and/or recognized experts review your requirements artifacts. Your requirements model—including your use case model, business rule definitions, constraint definitions, and nonfunctional requirements—should be distributed ahead of time to the review participants, so they can work through them in advance. A meeting is often held where everyone gets together to describe the issues and potential defects they found with the requirements model. The purpose of a user requirement review is to ensure that your requirements accurately reflect the needs and priorities of your user community and to ensure your understanding is sufficient from which to develop software.

User requirement reviews ensure that your understanding of the requirements is accurate.

9.2.3.4 Model Reviews and Walkthroughs

A model review, also called a *model walkthrough* or a *model peer review*, is a testing technique in which your modeling efforts are examined critically by a group of your peers. The basic idea is that a group of qualified people, both technical staff and SMEs, get together in a room and evaluate a model that describes all or part of the application you are currently developing. The purpose of this evaluation is to determine if the models not only fulfill the demands of the user community, but also are of sufficient quality to be easy to develop, maintain, and enhance. When model reviews are performed properly, they can have a big payoff because they

Model reviews reveal defects early during development when they are reasonably inexpensive to fix.

The main goal of testing is to find problems in your application so you are able to fix them. If your tests do not find any problems, then it is likely you need to improve your testing efforts.

TIP

Successful Tests Find Errors

often identify defects early in the project, reducing the cost of fixing them. In fact, Grady (1992) reports that 50 to 75 percent of all design errors can be found through technical reviews.

9.2.3.5 User-Interface Testing

The user interface (UI) of an application is the portion the user directly interacts with: screens, reports, documentation, and your software support staff. User interface testing is the verification that the UI follows the accepted standards chosen by your organization and the UI meets the requirements defined for it. User interface testing is often referred to as *graphical user interface (GUI) testing.* User interface testing can be as simple as verifying that your application "does the right thing" when subjected to a defined set of user interface events, such as keyboard input, or something as complex as a usability study where human-factors engineers verify that the software is intuitive and easy to use.

9.2.4 Testing Your Source Code

The language constructs of object-oriented programming languages require new code-testing techniques.

Object-oriented source code is composed of several constructs, including methods (operations), classes, and inheritance relationships. You need test techniques that reflect the fact that you have these new constructs; in other words you need test techniques that reflect the very nature of object orientation. In this section I overview a variety of traditional code testing techniques, such as black-box testing and coverage testing, as well as object-specific testing techniques such as class testing and inheritance-regression testing. Even in the simplest object-oriented programs you will find that you will apply most if not all of these techniques.

Test while you code.

Code-testing techniques are typically applied as you write your source code. One of the driving principles of eXtreme programming, also known as *XP*, is that you should write your testing code first (Beck,

---

DEFINITIONS

Human-factors engineer (HFE). A person who is an expert in the analysis and design of the user interface for an application and/or work environment for your users.

User interface (UI). The portion of software with which the user directly interacts, including the screens, reports, documentation, and software support (via telephone, electronic mail, and so on).

User interface event. An occurrence, often initiated by a user, such as keyboard input, a mouse action, or spoken input captured by a microphone, that causes action within your application.

DEFINITIONS

Black-box testing. The act of ensuring that given input *A* the component/system being tested gives you expected results *B*.

Boundary-value testing. The act of ensuring that unusual or extreme situations are handled appropriately by code.

Class testing. The act of ensuring that a class and its instances (objects) perform as defined.

Class-integration testing. The act of ensuring that the classes, and their instances, that form an application perform as defined.

Code inspection. A form of technical review in which the deliverable being reviewed is source code.

Coverage testing. The act of ensuring that all lines of code are exercised at least once.

Method testing. The act of ensuring that a method (also known as an *operation* or a *member function*) performs as defined.

Path testing. The act of ensuring that all logic paths within your code were exercised at least once. This is a superset of coverage testing.

Unit testing. The act of testing small components of a system to ensure they work.

White-box testing. The act of ensuring that specific lines of code work as defined. This is also referred to as *clear-box testing*.

2000). The idea is, by writing your test code for a given operation before you write the operation itself, it forces you to think about what that operation should do and how it should work, improving the quality of your code. It also ensures that you have testing code available to validate your work, enabling you to run it right away to show that your code works as it should.

9.2.4.1 Black-Box Testing

Black-box testing, also called *interface testing*, is a technique in which you create test cases based only on the expected functionality of a method, class, or application without any knowledge of its internal workings. One way to define black-box testing is that given defined input *A* you should obtain the expected results *B*. The goal of black-box testing is to ensure that the system can do what it should be able to do, but not how it does it. For example, a black-box test for a word processor would be to verify it is able to read a file from disk, and then write it back exactly as it was originally. It is a black-box test because you can run it without having any knowledge of how the word processor reads and writes files.

Black-box testing can be performed without knowledge of how the software was implemented.

Producing the best work possible is everyone's responsibility. At the same time, you need to recognize that because most people are convinced their work is correct, they often miss errors others will find. The best approach is to have developers initially test their own work to get the major defects out of it, and then have a professional test engineer take over the testing of the work to increase the chance of finding all the bugs.

The creation of black-box tests is often driven by the user requirements, typically documented by use cases, for the application. The basic idea is you look at the user requirement and ask yourself what needs to be done to show that the user requirement is met. The advantage of black-box tests is they let you prove that your application fulfills the user requirements defined for it. Unfortunately, black-box testing does not let you show that extra, often technical, features not defined by your users also work. For this, you need to create white/clear-box test cases.

9.2.4.2 Boundary-Value Testing

*Boundary-value
tests validate that
your software
handles unusual
or extreme cases.*

Boundary-value testing is based on the knowledge that you need to test your code to ensure that it can handle unusual and extreme situations. For example, boundary-value test cases for withdrawing funds from a bank account would include test cases such as attempting to withdraw $0.00, $0.01, and –$0.01, a very large amount of money, and perhaps even a large negative amount of money. Furthermore, if a daily limit of $500 exists for withdrawals from automated teller machines, you would want to create tests that verify you could withdraw $500 on a single transaction, but not $500.01, and run the same tests for a collection of transactions that add up to the same amount. The basic idea is you want to look for limits defined either by your business rules or by common sense, and then create test cases to test attribute values in and around those values. The main advantage of boundary-value testing is it enables you to confirm that your program code is able to handle unusual or extreme cases. A serious disadvantage of boundary-value testing is that it is easy for developers to convince themselves they only need to do boundary-value testing. After all, it discovers unusual errors, doesn't it? The reality is you want to find both the usual and unusual errors.

9.2.4.3 Class Testing

*Class testing is
both unit testing
and integration
testing.*

Class testing is both unit testing and traditional integration testing. It is unit testing because you are testing the class and its instances as single units in isolation, but it is also integration testing because you need to verify that the methods and attributes of the class work together. The one assumption you need to make during class testing is that all other classes in the system work. Although this may sound like an unreasonable assumption, it is basically what separates class testing from class-integration testing. The main purpose of class testing is to test classes in isolation, something that is difficult to do if you do not assume everything else works.

9.2.4.4 Class-Integration Testing

Class-integration testing, also known as *component testing*, addresses the issue of whether the classes in your system, or a component of your system, work together properly. The only way classes or, to be more accurate, the instances of classes, can work together is by sending each other messages. Therefore, some sort of relationship must exist between those objects before they can send the message, implying that the relationships between classes can be used to drive the development of integration test cases. In other words, your strategy should be to look at the association, aggregation, and inheritance relationships that appear on your class diagram and in formulating class-integration test cases.

Class-integration testing verifies that your classes work together appropriately.

9.2.4.5 Code Inspections

Code inspections, also known as *code reviews*, often reveal problems that normal testing techniques do not—in particular, poor coding practices that would make your application difficult to extend and maintain. Code inspections verify that you built the code correctly and you built code that will be easy to understand, to maintain, and to enhance. Code inspections can be an effective means for training developers in software engineering skills because reviews reveal areas where they need to improve. Finally, code inspections are a great way to detect and fix problems as early in the coding process as possible. Writing 1,000 lines of code, reviewing it, fixing it, and moving on is better than writing 100,000 lines of code, and then finding out the code is unintelligible to everyone but the people who wrote it.

Code inspections verify that you built the code correctly, aid in the training of developers, and detect potential problems early in the coding process.

Code inspections should concentrate on quality issues, such as:

- Does the code satisfy the design?

- Naming conventions for your classes, methods, and attributes

Object-oriented development is significantly different than structured/procedural development. Many of the techniques you used in the past to test structured applications are either no longer applicable or need to be reworked to meet the new needs of OO development.

TIP

A New Development Paradigm Implies a New Testing Paradigm

- Code documentation standards and conventions

  - Have you documented what a method does?

  - Have you documented what parameters must be passed?

  - Have you documented what values are returned by a method?

  - Have you documented both what and why a piece of code does what it does?

- Writing small methods that do one thing and one thing well

- How to simplify the code

9.2.4.6 Coverage and Path Testing

Coverage testing ensures that all lines of code were tested. Path testing ensures that all logic paths were tested.

Coverage testing is a technique in which you create a series of test cases designed to test all the code paths in your code. In many ways, coverage testing is simply a collection of white-box test cases that together exercise every line of code in your application at least once. Path testing is a superset of coverage testing ensuring not only that all lines of code have been tested, but that all paths of logic have also been tested. The main difference occurs when you have a method with more than one set of case statements or nested IF statements: to determine the number of test cases with coverage testing. You would count the maximum number of paths between the sets of case/nested IF statements and, with path testing, you would multiply the number of logic paths.

The main advantage of coverage testing is it helps to ensure that all lines of code within your application have been tested, although it does not ensure that all combinations of the code have been tested. Path testing, on the other hand, does test all combinations of the code, but it requires significantly more effort to formulate and run the test cases. In most cases, path testing is unrealistic because of the exponential nature of the task.

TIP

Hold Code Inspections Before Significant Testing Occurs

My experience is that code inspections should be performed before testing because, once code has been tested and approved, developers are rarely motivated to have their code inspected. Their attitude is that the code works, so why bother looking at it again? The implication is that you should first inspect your code, act on the recommendations from inspection, and then test it.

> McGregor (1997) points out that the riskier something is, the more it needs to be reviewed and tested. In other words, I would invest significant effort in testing an air traffic control system, but nowhere near as much effort testing a "Hello World" application.
>
> **TIP**
>
> *Test to the Risk of the Artifact*

9.2.4.7 Inheritance-Regression Testing

Without a doubt, the most important part of object-oriented code testing is inheritance-regression testing—the running of the class and method test cases for all the superclasses of the class being tested. The motivation behind inheritance-regression testing is simple: It is incredibly naive to expect that errors have not been introduced by a new subclass. New methods are added and existing methods are often redefined by subclasses, and these methods access and often change the value of the attributes defined in the superclass. It is possible that a subclass may change the value of the attributes in a way that was never intended in the superclass, or at least was never expected. Personally, I want to run the old test cases against my new subclass to verify that everything still works.

9.2.4.8 Method Testing

Method testing is the act of ensuring that your methods, called *operations* or *member functions* in C++ and Java, perform as defined. The closest comparison to method testing in the structured world is the unit testing of functions and procedures. Although some people argue that class testing is really the object-oriented version of unit testing, my experience has been that the creation of test cases for specific methods often proves useful and should not be ignored, hence the need for method testing. Issues to address during method testing include the following:

- Ensuring that your accessor methods work

- Ensuring that each method returns the proper values, including error messages and exceptions

- Basic checking of the parameters being passed to each method

- Ensuring that each method does what the documentation says it does

---

DEFINITION

Accessor. An operation used either to modify or retrieve a single attribute. Also known as *getter* and *setter* operations.

9.2.4.9 White/Clear-Box Testing

White-box tests are formulated based on your knowledge of the code.

White-box testing, also called *clear-box testing* or *detailed-code testing*, is based on the concept that your program code can drive the development of test cases. The basic idea is you look at your code, and then create test cases that exercise it. With white-box testing, you are able to see the internal workings of an application and, with this knowledge, you create test cases that can run specific sections of code.

For example, assume you have access to the source code that reads in files for a word processor. When you look at it, you see that an IF statement determines whether the file being read in is a word-processing file or a simple text file, and then reads it in appropriately. This indicates that you need to run at least three tests on this source code: one to read in a word-processor file, one to read in a text file, and one to read in a file that is neither a word-processor file nor a text file. By looking at the code, you are able to determine new test cases to exercise the different logic paths within it.

The main advantage of white-box testing is it lets you create tests that exercise specific lines of code that may not have been tested by simple black-box test cases. Unfortunately, it does not let you confirm that all the user requirements have been met because it only enables you to test the specific code you have written.

9.2.5 Testing Your System in its Entirety

System testing is performed by developers to verify that your application is ready for user testing.

System testing is a testing process in which you aim to ensure that your overall system works as defined by your requirements. System testing is typically done toward the end of the development lifecycle, enabling you to fix known problems before your application is sent for user testing (Section 9.2.6). System testing is comprised of the following techniques:

- Function testing
- Installation testing
- Operations testing
- Stress testing
- Support testing

9.2.5.1 Function Testing

Function testing is a systems-testing technique in which development staff verifies that their application meets the defined needs of their users. The idea is that developers, typically test engineers, work through the main functionality that the system should exhibit to assure themselves

---

DEFINITIONS

Function testing. A testing technique in which development staff confirm that their application meets the user requirements specified during analysis.

Installation testing. The act of ensuring that your application can be installed successfully.

Operations testing. The act of ensuring that the needs of operations personnel who have to support/operate the application are met.

Stress testing. The act of ensuring that the system performs as expected under high volumes of transactions, high numbers of users, and so on.

Support testing. The act of ensuring that the needs of support personnel who have to support the application are met.

System testing. A testing process in which you find and fix any known problems to prepare your application for user testing.

---

that their application is ready for user-acceptance testing (UAT). During user testing is when users confirm for themselves that the system meets their needs. In many ways, the only difference between function testing and user-acceptance testing is who does it: testers and users, respectively.

Developers perform function testing to validate that their application is ready for user-acceptance testing.

Use cases, covered in detail in Chapter 4, are typically used to develop function test cases because they describe the exact behavior of how your users work with your application. You may find that changes in the design of your application can force you to revisit your use cases to verify that they are still applicable, although these problems should have been identified and fixed during construction.

9.2.5.2 Installation Testing

The installation utility/process for your application is part of your overall application package and, therefore, must be tested. Installation testing is a form of system testing in which the focus is whether your application can be installed successfully. Several important issues should be considered:

- Can you successfully install the application into an environment that it hasn't been installed into before?

- Can you successfully install the application into an environment where it, or a previous version, already exists?

- Is configuration information defined correctly?

- Is previous configuration information taken into account?

- Is online documentation installed correctly?

DEFINITIONS

Test case. A description—including the setup, series of actions, and expected results—of a situation that a software item must support.

Use case. A sequence of actions that provides a measurable value to an actor.

- Are other applications affected by the installation of this one?

- Are there adequate computer resources for the application? Does the installation utility detect this and act appropriately?

9.2.5.3 Operations and Support Testing

Operations and support testing help to ensure that your system can be kept in production once it is deployed.

The goal of operations testing is to verify that the requirements of operations personnel are met, and to ensure that your operations staff will be able to run your application successfully once it is installed. Support testing addresses similar issues except with a support personnel focus. Tourniaire and Farrell (1997) suggest that the needs of your support organization, in addition to those of your operations organization, be tested for before your application is allowed to go into production.

9.2.5.4 Stress Testing

The goal of stress testing is to determine the load/volume levels under which your application no longer works properly.

Stress testing is the process of ensuring that your application works with high numbers of users, high numbers of transactions (testing of high numbers of transactions is also called *volume testing*), high numbers of data transmissions, high numbers of printed reports, and so on. The goal is to find the stress points of your system under which it no longer operates, so you can gain insights into how it will perform in unusual and/or stressful situations.

9.2.6 Testing by Users

User testing, which follows system testing, is composed of testing processes in which members of your user community perform the tests. The goal of user testing is to have the users verify that an application meets their needs. User testing is comprised of the following techniques:

- Alpha testing
- Beta testing
- Pilot testing
- User-acceptance testing (UAT)

> **DEFINITION**
>
> **Volume testing.** A subset of stress testing that deals specifically with determining how many transactions or database accesses an application can handle during a defined period of time.

9.2.6.1 Alpha, Beta, and Pilot Testing

One of the major problems with testing is that you can only test for the problems you know about. Unless you perform the job of your users day-in and day-out, you can never know the needs of the problem domain as well as they do. The implication is that you will never be able to define as many real-life testing scenarios as your users can; therefore, it makes sense to get your users to test for you.

Your users can devise more and better real-life test scenarios than you can.

Two common approaches to this are alpha testing and beta testing (alpha/beta testing is referred to as *pilot testing* for applications being developed for use by internal users). Alpha testing is a process in which you send out software that is not quite ready for prime time to a small group of your users to enable them to work with it and report back to you on the problems they encounter. Although the software is typically buggy and may not meet all their needs, they get a heads-up on what you are doing much earlier than if they waited for you to release the software formally. Beta testing is basically the same process, except the software has many of the bugs fixed that were identified during alpha testing (beta testing follows alpha testing) and the software is distributed to a larger group. The

> **DEFINITIONS**
>
> **Alpha testing.** A testing period in which prerelease versions of software products—products that are often buggy—are released to users who need access to the product before it is to be officially deployed. In return, these users are willing to report back to the software developers any defects they uncover. Alpha testing is typically followed by a period of beta testing.
>
> **Beta testing.** Similar to alpha testing, except the software product should be less buggy. This method is used by software development companies that want to ensure that they meet as many of their clients' needs as possible.
>
> **Pilot testing.** A testing process equivalent to beta testing, which is used by organizations to test applications they have developed for their own internal use.
>
> **User testing.** Testing processes in which the user community, as opposed to developers, performs the tests. User testing techniques include user acceptance testing, alpha testing, beta testing, and pilot testing.

main goal of both alpha and beta testing is to test run the product to identify, and then fix any bugs before you release your application.

9.2.6.2 User-Acceptance Testing (UAT)

Your users are the only ones who can determine if an application truly meets their needs.

After your system testing proves successful, your users must perform user-acceptance testing, a process in which they determine whether your application truly meets their needs. This means you have to let your users work with the software you produced. Because the only person who truly knows your own needs is you, the people involved in the user-acceptance test should be the actual users of the system—not their managers and not the vice presidents of the division they work for, but the people who will work daily with the application. Although you may have to give them some training to gain the testing skills they need, actual *users* are the only people who are qualified to do *user*-acceptance testing. The good news is, if you have function-tested your application thoroughly, then the UAT process will take only a few days to a week at the most.

9.3 From Test Cases to Defects

You define, and then run, a series of tests against testing targets.

The primary purpose of testing is to validate the correctness of the target of your testing efforts. To perform testing, you need to define, and then run, a series of tests against said targets. A test case is the definition of a single test to be performed. To document a test case, you should describe its purpose, the setup work you need to perform before running the test to put the item you are testing into a known state, the steps of the actual test, and the expected results of the test. A test script is the actual steps, sometimes either written procedures to follow or the source code, of a test. You run test scripts against your testing targets. A test suite is a collection of test scripts, and a test harness is the portion of the code of a test suite that aggregates the test scripts. You run your test suite against your test target(s), producing test results that indicate the actual results of your testing efforts. If your actual test results vary from your expected test results, documented as part of each test case, then you have identified a potential defect in your test target(s).

TIP

One Test Is Worth a Thousand Opinions

You can tell me that your application works, but until you show me the test results, I will not believe you.

DEFINITIONS

Defect. Anything that detracts from your application's capability to meet your user's needs completely and effectively. Also known as a *bug*, *fault*, or *feature*.

Test case. The definition of a single test.

Test harness. The portion of the code of a test suite that aggregates the test scripts.

Test script. The steps to be performed to run a test case. Test scripts will be implemented using a variety of techniques, from source code for code tests to written steps for function testing.

Test suite. A collection of test scripts.

Test target. An item, such as a model, document, or portion of software to be tested.

It is not enough for you find a defect; you must also record that you found it. Collecting this information is important for several reasons. First, it provides an accurate description, so the defect may be fixed. Second, it provides the metrics (measurements) you need to analyze and then improve your work practices. This data should be used to avoid defects in the first place, an important key process area, or at least to find defects sooner in the development process to reduce the cost of fixing them. Humphrey (1997) suggests that the following information be recorded about a defect:

Record the detailed information when you discover a defect to aid your repair efforts later.

- Description of the defect
- Date the defect was found
- Name of the person who found it
- Defect type (user interface bug, application crash, and so on)
- Stage in which the defect was found
- Stage in which the defect was introduced
- Stage in which the defect was removed
- Date the work was started
- Date the defect was fixed
- Steps to re-create the defect
- Effort, in work hours or workdays, to fix the defect
- Description of the solution

9.4 What You Have Learned

One of the fundamentals of software engineering is that you should test as early as possible. You want to find and fix defects early in development for two reasons: Most mistakes are made early in the life of a project and the cost of fixing defects increases exponentially the later they are found. Furthermore, you explored and shattered several myths surrounding object-oriented testing, discovering that object-oriented software requires more testing, structured testing techniques are not sufficient for testing object software, and you need to test more than just the user interface of your software. You then discovered that a variety of object-oriented testing techniques are available to you, encapsulated by the Full Lifecycle Object-Oriented Testing (FLOOT) methodology, depicted in Figure 9-1 and summarized in Table 9-1. FLOOT techniques exist to test a range of project artifacts including, but not limited to, models, documentation, and source code.

Table 9-1. The techniques of the FLOOT methodology

FLOOT Technique	Description
Black-box testing	Testing that verifies that an item, when given the appropriate input(s), provides the expected results.
Boundary-value testing	Testing of unusual or extreme situations that an item should be able to handle.
Class testing	The act of ensuring that a class and its instances (objects) perform as defined.
Class-integration testing	The act of ensuring that classes and their instances perform together as expected.
Code review	A form of technical review in which the deliverable being reviewed is source code.
Component testing	The act of validating that a component works as defined.
Coverage testing	The act of ensuring that every line of code is exercised at least once.
Design review	A technical review in which a design model is inspected.
Inheritance-regression testing	The act of running the test cases of the super classes, both direct and indirect, on a given subclass.
Integration testing	Testing to verify that several portions of software work together.
Method testing	Testing to verify that a method (member function) performs as defined.
Model walkthrough	A less formal version of a design review, often held on an impromptu basis.
Path testing	The act of ensuring that all logic paths within your code are exercised at least once.
Prototype review	A process by which your users work through a collection of use cases, using a prototype as if it were the real system. The main goal is to test whether the design of the prototype meets their needs.

Regression testing	The act of ensuring that previously tested behaviors still work as expected after changes have been made to an application.
Requirements review	A technical review in which a requirements model is inspected.
Stress testing	The act of ensuring that the system performs as expected under high volumes of transactions, users, load, and so on.
Technical review	A quality assurance technique in which the design of your application is examined critically by a group of your peers. A review typically focuses on accuracy, quality, usability, and completeness. This process is often referred to as a *walkthrough*, an *inspection*, or a *peer review*.
Use case scenario testing	A testing technique in which one or more person(s) validate your domain model by acting through the logic of use case scenarios.
User interface testing	The testing of the user interface (UI) to ensure that it follows accepted UI standards and meets the requirements defined for it. Often referred to as *graphical user interface (GUI) testing*.
White-box testing	Testing to verify that specific lines of code work as defined. Also referred to as *clear-box testing*.

9.5 Review Questions

1. Compare and contrast "quality assurance" and "testing." What value does each activity add to the development of software? Which is more important? Why?

2. For each of the following collections of artifacts, what type of people would you invite to review them? Justify the presence of each of the reviewers.
   - Use case model and business rules definitions
   - User interface prototype and interface flow diagram
   - Sequence diagrams and analysis-level class model
   - Design-level class model, state charts, collaboration diagrams
   - Design-level class model, persistence model

3. When you are inspecting source code, what other artifacts would potentially prove useful as reference material in the review? Explain how each item would be useful.

4. Compare and contrast black-box testing and white-box testing. Provide examples for how you would use these two techniques in combination with method testing, class testing, and class-integration testing.

5. Define a collection of test cases for one of your business classes (pick an interesting one). For each test case, indicate the type(s) of test it is (class test, white-box test, and so on).

6. Compare and contrast coverage testing and path testing. Discuss the feasibility of each approach.

7. Develop a Java class that would run tests against the "validateZipCode (zipCode)" method of the "ZipCodeValidator" class described in Chapter 8. Start by defining and documenting test cases for the method, test cases that your class must then implement.

8. Develop a set of test cases for your DateRange class of Chapter 8 and a test suite of one or more classes to run those tests.

A software process enables you to navigate the complexity
of software development, operations, and support successfully.

Chapter 10

Putting It All Together: Software Process

Why You Need to Read This Chapter

Developing software is difficult and developing large-scale, mission-critical
software is very difficult. Experience shows that software professionals who follow
an appropriate, proven software process have greater chances of succeeding.
To be successful at applying object technology, you must understand the
object-oriented software process.

Object technology is appropriate for many, but not all, environments.

As you have seen in this book, and as you have likely experienced yourself, software development is a complex endeavor. You could choose to ignore this inherent complexity, as many developers do to their misfortune, or you could seek to understand how to manage the complexity of software development. A software process defines activities and roles; interrelationships develop, operate, and support software. This includes the topics covered in this book—requirements, analysis, design, programming, and testing—and supporting activities such as project management, quality assurance, enterprise management, operations, and support. Furthermore, to be successful, you need to understand that object-oriented development techniques are ideal for several types of systems; yet are not so ideal for others. Just as you don't want to try to fit a square peg into a round hole, you don't want to use object-orientation (OO) for projects where it doesn't make sense.

The software process for object technology is similar, yet still different from that of structured technology.

How do you develop applications using object-oriented technology? If you have read any articles or books about OO, one of the first things you read was that the OO paradigm is different than the procedural paradigm. This is true. On the one hand, the OO paradigm is based on the concept that applications should be built from interacting objects that have both data and functionality. The procedural paradigm, on the other hand, is based on the concept that applications should be built from collections of functions and procedures, perhaps organized into modules that read and write external data. The difference appears subtle; however, practice shows that it is, in fact, vast.

The "fact" that OO development is iterative is a myth. OO development is really serial in the large and iterative in the small.

Another thing you may have read is that OO development is iterative. This statement is only partly true. The main components of OO development—modeling, programming, and testing in the small (formerly known as unit testing)—are, in fact, performed iteratively. Professional software development is comprised of far more than just these three things. You have several aspects of project initiation to contend with, all of which should be done long before development begins. You eventually have a code freeze, perhaps several over time, after which you perform testing in the large (see Chapter 9) and, hopefully, deliver the application. After delivery and the application is up and running in production, you need to track change requests, including both enhancements and problem reports; therefore, the application may be updated in the future. In short, OO development is iterative in the small, but serial in the large.

OO development is typically incremental, but not always.

You may have also heard that OO development is incremental; in other words, applications are built and released a portion at a time. This can also be true, but doesn't necessarily have to be this way. I have been involved in many OO projects over the years, many that took an incremental approach, and some did not.

An important point to be made is that there's a lot more to OO development than writing code. There is also a lot more to it than creating use cases, user interface prototypes, and class models. OO development is about creating applications that solve the needs of your users. It is about doing this in such a way that the applications you build are timely, accurate, and of high quality. You need a range of skills or, at least, your project team together needs a range of skills, to be successful.

Successful OO development is hard.

10.1 What Is So Different About Object-Oriented Development?

I want to start this chapter with a discussion of why object orientation is different from the structured/procedural paradigm. My experience is that OO development:

1. **Requires you work more with your users.** Users can and should perform the majority of the requirements and analysis efforts on a project. This is radically different when compared to structured development, where developers interview users, perhaps do some prototyping, and then produce some sort of analysis document (sometimes). With a little bit of guidance, many of the requirements and analysis techniques presented in this book, such as use cases and Class Responsibility Collaborator (CRC) models, can easily be performed by your users.

2. **Puts a greater emphasis on analysis and design.** As you saw in this book, you do CRC modeling, prototyping, use case modeling, sequence diagramming, class modeling, and a variety of other types of modeling when taking an OO approach. These are all analysis and design tasks. If you don't get the analysis and design right, it doesn't matter how good of a programmer you are.

3. **Offers benefits that are achieved throughout the entire development lifecycle.** This means you need to understand how OO changes requirements, analysis, design, and testing, in addition to OO programming. That's why this book describes the entire development lifecycle, and not just analysis and design.

4. **Requires a new mindset on the part of developers.** You have to work more with your users. You have to concentrate more on analysis and design. Communication and modeling skills become imperative. This won't be an easy transition, but it is a one you *must* make to be successful in you career.

5. **Requires a culture change within IS departments.** Individual developers must look at their job from a new perspective. As a group, they must change the way in which they work together to

The OO paradigm changes the way you interact with your users and fellow developers.

serve the needs of their clients to be successful. Namely, the OO software process requires a change in your development culture.

10.2 What Is a Software Process?

What is a software process? A software process is a set of project phases, stages, methods, techniques, and practices that people employ to develop and maintain software and its associated artifacts (plans, documents, models, code, test cases, manuals, and so forth). Furthermore, not only do you need a software process, you need one that is proven to work in practice, a software process tailored to meet your exact needs. In this chapter, I present several leading processes: the Object-Oriented Software Process (OOSP), the Unified Process, the Microsoft Solutions Framework (MSF), the OPEN Process, Xtreme Programming (XP), and Catalysis. I present these processes so you can be aware of them, their strengths and weaknesses, and adopt and combine them as is appropriate for your efforts.

To put the software process into better perspective, Figure 10-1 depicts the scope of the various approaches to process, showing that the development process is a subset of the software process that, in turn, is a subset of the enterprise processes of your organization. The figure also indicates the key factors that influence your process, including your organization's culture, your architecture, the tools you use, the standards you follow, the legislation that is appropriate to your firm, and the external processes of the organizations with which yours interacts (such as your customers). While your organization's software process is an important and complex thing, it is only part of the overall picture and it can be influenced by factors that aren't under your complete control.

Figure 10-1.
The scope of processes

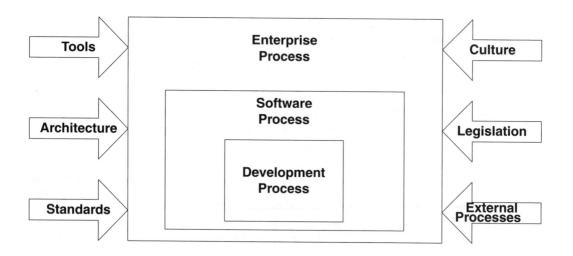

10.3 Why Do You Need a Software Process?

An effective software process enables your organization to increase its productivity for several reasons. First, by understanding the fundamentals of how software is developed, you can make intelligent decisions, such as knowing to stay away from SnakeOil v2.0, the wonder tool that claims it automates fundamental portions of the software process. Second, it enables you to standardize your efforts, promoting reuse and consistency between project teams. Third, it provides an opportunity for you to increase quality through industry best practices, such as code inspections, configuration management, change control, and architectural modeling.

An effective software process enables you to increase productivity, reuse, consistency, and quality on your projects.

An effective software process also improves your organization's operations and support efforts in several ways. First, it should define how to manage change and to allocate maintenance changes appropriately to future releases of your software, streamlining your change process. Second, it should define first how to transition software smoothly into operations and support, and then how your operations and support efforts are actually performed. Without effective operations and support processes, your software will quickly become shelfware.

Why adopt an existing software process or improve your existing process using new techniques? The reality is that software is growing more complex and, without an effective way to develop and maintain that software, the chances of succeeding will only be reduced. Not only is software getting more complex, we're also being asked to create more software simultaneously. Most organizations have several software projects currently in development and have many times that in production, projects that need to be managed effectively. The nature of the software we're building is also changing, from the simple batch systems of the 1970s that structured techniques are geared toward, to the interactive, international,

---

DEFINITIONS

Development process. A process that focuses on the development aspects of a system, including requirements definition, modeling, programming, testing, and delivery of the system.

Enterprise process. The overall process of a single organization, encompassing the processes of all aspects of the organization.

Process. The definition of the steps to be taken, the roles of the people performing those steps, the artifacts being created, and the artifacts being used to fulfill a purpose that provides value to someone or some organization.

Software process. A process that describes how to develop, operate, and support one or more systems.

user-friendly, 7/24, high-transaction, high-availability online systems at which object-oriented and component-based techniques are aimed. And while you're doing that, you're asked to increase the quality of the systems you're delivering and to reuse as much as possible, so you can work more quickly and more cheaply. This is a tall order, one that is nearly impossible to fill if you can't organize and manage your staff effectively, and a software process provides the basis to do just that.

10.4 From Waterfall/Serial Development...

Let's consider the history of the concept of software process. The waterfall approach, popularized in the 1970s, was the first generally accepted software process, a process based on a serial approach to system development. The basic idea is that development proceeds serially throughout the life of the project, with the efforts of the development team proceeding from one project phase to another, as depicted in Figure 10-2. This is called the *waterfall* approach because development flows from one phase to another, just as water flows from one level to the next one below it.

The waterfall approach does not truly reflect how software is developed.

The main disadvantage of the waterfall approach is that it doesn't completely reflect the way systems are developed. Nobody really does all the analysis first, and then all the design, and so on. What typically happens is, during design and programming, developers often find they don't have all the information they need to do their work, so they need to go back and do some more analysis. During testing, problems are found and often

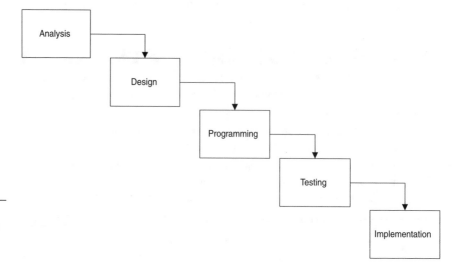

Figure 10-2.
The serial waterfall approach to development

> **DEFINITION**
>
> *Waterfall approach.* An approach to building applications where development efforts proceed in a serial manner from one project stage to another.

are fixed by going back to previous stages and redoing some of the work. The point is that the waterfall approach needs to include backward arrows so developers can rework some of their previous efforts.

A second disadvantage is that the serial nature of the waterfall approach makes it difficult to update and/or improve on the analysis performed earlier in the project. Today, most organizations face an operating environment in which the rules change quickly: Competitors introduce competing products, regulations change, and new technologies provide alternative ways for delivering functionality. The end result is that you need to update your analysis/design regularly to react to these changes. If you don't, you run the risk of implementing an application that no longer meets the needs of your users. Unfortunately, the waterfall approach does not support a changing environment very well.

The waterfall approach does not easily support dynamic environments.

The third disadvantage, at least a perceived disadvantage, is the waterfall approach often leads to large, documentation-heavy, monolithic systems. I write "perceived" because monolithic systems are in no way the direct result of the waterfall approach. Instead, they are the result of the teams that chose to build them that way. I have seen small systems successfully developed using the waterfall approach. The waterfall approach is one of many techniques/processes you use to build systems. If you misuse a process, then who is to blame: you or the process?

People claim that using the Waterfall SDLC always leads to monolithic systems. This is a myth.

When should you use a waterfall approach? A serial approach to application development has proven quite effective for building large, mission-critical applications, especially those projects whose requirements are well known or that at least can be well defined.

10.5 ...to Iterative Development...

In the 1980s, personal computers had a dramatic impact on the way information system (IS) professionals looked at software development. Systems no longer had to work on multimillion-dollar machinery, they no longer had to take years to develop, and they no longer had to remain in the domain of the data-processing department. Almost overnight, organizations were deploying software on computing equipment that cost only several thousand dollars. Software for personal computers was often written in several weeks, often written with either the direct involvement of users and, sometimes, even by users themselves. New

The serial approach began giving way to the iterative approach in the mid-1980s.

technology brought with it new demands that, in turn, forced developers to reconsider the way software was developed. As a result, many developers began to take an iterative approach to software development, instead of the traditional serial approach.

The best known iterative approach to development is the spiral approach (Boehm, 1988), in which developers build systems by first doing a little bit of analysis, then some prototyping, then some design, then some coding, and so on until the application is complete. Notice how the Spiral approach is depicted in Figure 10-3. It shows development being comprised of several project phases; each one is performed several times throughout the development of an application.

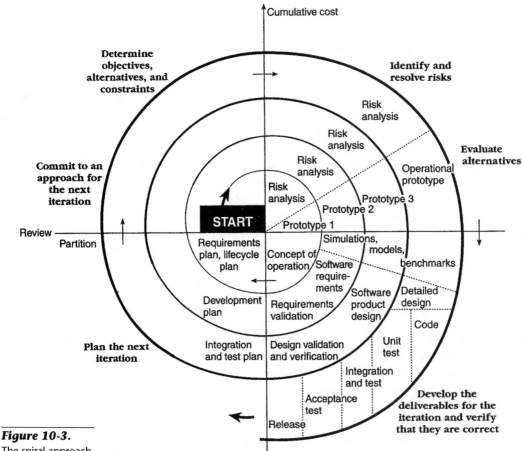

Figure 10-3.

The spiral approach to software development

Source: Adapted from "A Spiral Model of Software Development and Enhancement" (Boehm 1988).

The main advantage of the spiral approach is it is a more realistic look at software development because it recognizes that you often must revisit each project phase throughout the development process. It also directly includes prototyping as a project phase, providing the opportunity to include users to a greater extent. The disadvantages of the spiral approach are that it is complex and it still is not completely accurate. Consequently, you sometimes realize during one phase that you need to go back immediately and redo a previous one, perhaps going from prototyping directly back to analysis, without continuing to the next phase.

Iterative development has proven an effective approach to developing applications whose requirements are not well known at the beginning of the project. Iterative development supports the exploration and definition of "fuzzy" requirements by enabling developers and users to work closely together to define them, to build a potential solution, and then to evaluate the solution, repeating this process where necessary to flesh out the application. Iterative development is well suited for rapidly changing environments because it enables you to discover and react to those changes in a timely and efficient manner.

Iterative development is suitable for rapidly changing business environments.

A significant disadvantage of iterative development is that it is often difficult to define deliverables for the project—you often never finish any given stage until the application is complete; therefore, it is difficult to deliver anything. I personally don't agree with this argument because, at any given time during the project, you always have an example of work to show for your efforts. You have the requirements you have already identified, you have a (partial) design based on those requirements, you have code written that supports the design, and, hopefully, you have test results verifying your work to date. Yes, it might not be pretty and it might not be complete, but you should always be in a position where, if asked, you could clean up your work and produce an "official" set of deliverables representing what you have done.

It can be difficult, but not impossible, to define deliverables when taking the iterative approach.

10.6 ...and Incremental Development

One valid way to develop applications is to take an incremental approach. The basic idea is, instead of building an application all at once, producing a single "big-bang" release, you deliver the application in smaller releases, delivering portions of the required functionality in each release (releases are also referred to as *product baselines*). Each release is effectively a miniproject, which incorporates all the development components that a large project has; the only difference is the scope is smaller. The required functionality is delivered to the user community, the difference being that it is done in portions, instead of all at once.

With an incremental approach, you deliver software in several smaller releases.

Incremental development results in getting portions of an application out sooner, and often getting out the entire application sooner.

Figure 10-4 depicts the difference between releasing your software as a large, single "big-bang" release or in a series of smaller, incremental releases. Notice how, by taking an incremental release strategy, the first incremental release is typically the largest one. This is because you have to get a lot of basic infrastructure work done to support the application, such as development of the basic business classes needed by the application and the installation of any hardware, software, or middleware to support it. Second, the overall effort needed to release the application is less than that for a single, big-bang release. Just as it is easier to eat your dinner by taking several smaller bites than it is to try to consume it all in a single bite, it is often easier to develop an application in several releases than it is to try to do it all at once.

A small minority of projects can only be delivered in one, single release.

Several advantages exist to incremental development. First, an incremental approach enables you to get functionality into the hands of your users quicker, an important feature in today's hypercompetitive business environment. Second, because your application is being used sooner, you increase the opportunity to find and fix any mistakes you have made during development, enabling you to make tactical changes sooner. Third, the incremental approach to application development is generally less expensive and less risky than the big-bang approach over the long run because it is easier and less expensive to develop several small releases than one large one.

The main disadvantage of incremental development is that it does not apply to all system projects. Would you be willing to fly out of an airport whose air-traffic control system is only 60-percent complete? Probably not, although most application projects can be organized so the application is delivered in several incremental releases; only a small minority cannot be.

Figure 10-4.
Incremental releases
"one big bang"

10.7 The Development Process Presented in This Book

Throughout this book, I present a minimal software process for developing software using object-oriented techniques. I say it is minimal because I have focused on the core activities of software development: requirements, analysis, design, programming, and testing. I have not covered other important topics such as project management, metrics, architecture, and system deployment. Nor have I covered topics that would make it a true software process, such as the operation and support of your system once it is put into production. I took this approach because I wanted to present the fundamental techniques you are likely to require on your first object technology project.

This book presents the core development techniques required for your first object-oriented project.

What is the process you have seen so far? From a serial-in-the-large point-of-view, depicted in Figure 10-5, you saw that requirements (Chapter 3) drives your analysis efforts (Chapter 6), which, in turn, drives your design efforts (Chapter 7), which then drives your programming efforts (Chapter 8). All these activities are then verified and validated by the Full Lifecycle Object-Oriented Testing (FLOOT) techniques described in Chapters 4 and 9. As you would expect, Figure 10-5 is straightforward and not much different from the serial approach presented in Figure 10-2. A more interesting viewpoint, I believe, is to consider the software process from the point-of-view of the artifacts of OO development described in this book. Figure 0-6 is an amalgam of the chapter overview figures—Figures 3-1, 6-1, 7-1, and 8-1—presented for the artifacts of OO requirements, analysis, design, and programming, respectively. The diagram's boxes, such as Collaboration Diagram and Essential Use Case Model, represent artifacts and the arrows represent "drives" relationships. For example, you see that information in your design class model drives the development of your source code. Although your requirements-oriented artifacts drive

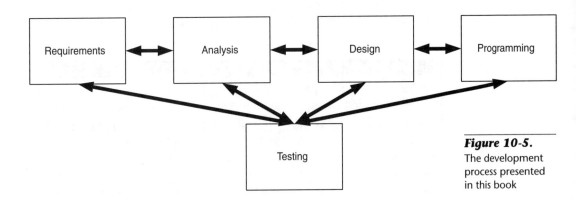

Figure 10-5.
The development process presented in this book

your analysis-oriented artifacts, and so on, the arrows are double-headed because the process is actually iterative in the small: artifact *A* drives changes to artifact *B*, which may provide feedback that motivates changes to artifact *A*. In *Process Patterns* (Ambler, 1998b), I describe the Detailed Modeling process pattern, the solution for which is similar to Figure 10-6. In many ways, Figure 10-6 is the evolution of that pattern solution.

10.8 Process Patterns of the Object-Oriented Software Process (OOSP)

Process patterns are the reusable building blocks from which you may tailor a software process.

Let's expand the scope of our discussion from the development process presented in this book to a full-fledged software process. Figure 10-7 depicts the lifecycle of the Object-Oriented Software Process (OOSP), comprised of a collection of process patterns. A process pattern is a collection of techniques, actions, and/or tasks (activities) that solve a specific software process problem taking the relevant forces/factors into account. Just as design patterns describe proven solutions to common software design problems, process patterns present proven solutions to common software process problems. Process patterns were originally proposed by James Coplien in his paper "A Generative Development-Process Pattern Language" in the first *Pattern Languages of Program Design* book (Addison-Wesley, 1995). I believe three scales of process patterns exist: phase process patterns, stage process patterns, and task process patterns. A phase process pattern depicts the interactions between the stage process patterns for a single project phase, such as the Initiate and Deliver phases of the OOSP (Ambler, 1998b). A stage process pattern depicts the tasks, which are often performed iteratively, of a single project stage such as the Program and Model stages (Ambler, 1998b). Finally, task process patterns address lower-level process issues, such as the Reuse First process pattern (Ambler, 1999), which describes how to achieve significant levels of reuse within your organization and the Technical Review process pattern, which describes how to organize reviews and inspections. The three scales of process patterns are conceptually similar

---

DEFINITIONS

Artifact. A document, model, file, diagram, or other item that is produced, modified, or used during the development, operation, or support of a system.

Full lifecycle object-oriented testing (FLOOT). A testing methodology for object-oriented development that comprises testing techniques, which, taken together, provide methods to verify that your application works correctly at each stage of development.

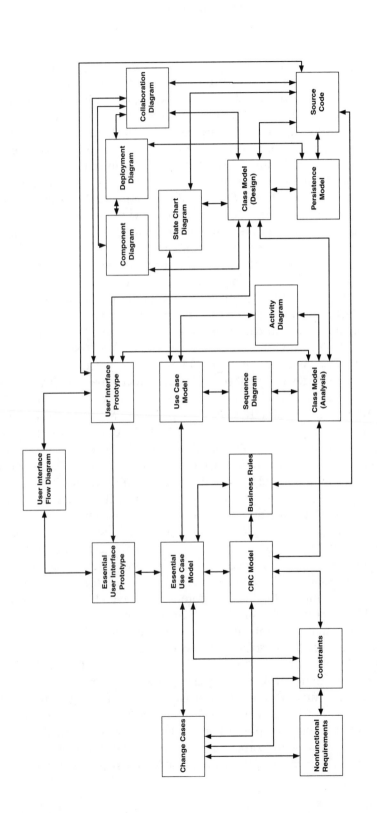

Figure 10-6.
The iterative techniques described in this book

to the scale of other types of patterns. In the modeling world, you have architectural patterns, design patterns, and programming idioms.

I believe an important feature of a process pattern is that it describes what you should do, but not the exact details of how you should do something. Process patterns are an excellent mechanism for communicating approaches to software development that have proven to be effective in practice. When applied together in an organized manner, process patterns can be used to construct a software process for your organization, as you see with the OOSP lifecycle of Figure 10-7. Because process patterns do not specify the exact details of how to perform a given task, you can use them as reusable building blocks from which you may tailor a software process that meets the specific needs of your organization.

In Figure 10-7, you see that four project phases exist within the OOSP: Initiate, Construct, Deliver, and Maintain and Support, each of which is described by a corresponding phase-process pattern. Also notice the fourteen project stages in the OOSP: Justify, Define and Validate Initial Requirements, Define Initial Management Documents, Define Infrastructure, Model, Program, Test in the Small, Generalize, Test in the Large, Rework, Release, Assess, Support, and Identify Defects and Enhancements. Each of these stages is described by a stage process pattern. The process patterns of the Initiate and Construct phases are described in *Process Patterns* (Ambler, 1998b) and those of the Deliver and Maintain, and Support phases in *More Process Patterns* (Ambler, 1999), the third and fourth books, respectively, in this series. Project stages are performed in an iterative manner within the scope of a single project phase. Project phases, on the other hand, are performed in a serial manner within the OOSP.

The OOSP defines both project and cross-project tasks.

As you can see, OOSP has more to it than just its phases and stages. The "big arrow" at the bottom of the diagram indicates important tasks critical to the success of a project that apply to all stages of development. These tasks include quality assurance, project management, training and education, people management, risk management, reuse management, metrics management, deliverables management, and infrastructure management. The important thing to note is that several of these tasks are applicable at both the project and cross-project (program) levels. For example, risk management should be performed for both a single project and for your portfolio of software projects. It is no good if each project is relatively risk-free, but as a collection they become quite risky. Deliverables management, which includes configuration management and change control functions, is also applicable for both a single project and for a collection of projects because the collection of projects may share a single artifact, such as common source code. Infrastructure management, where you evolve your corporate processes, standards, guidelines, and architectures, is a concept that is applicable across several projects, but

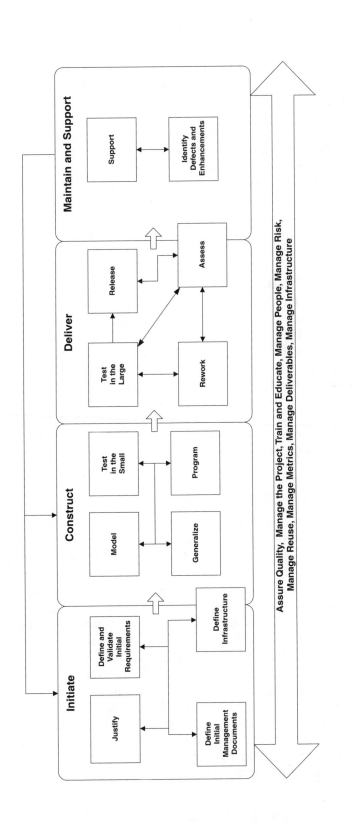

Figure 10-7.
The Object-Oriented Software Process (OOSP) lifecycle

also applies to a single project because that project team needs guidance and support to use your organization's software infrastructure.

OOSP has several strengths. First, it is a comprehensive approach to the software process, taking the entire lifecycle into account. Second, it honestly portrays the fact that large-scale, mission-critical software is serial in the large and iterative in the small. Contrary to popular belief, real-world development isn't purely iterative. Third, it explicitly supports program/infrastructure processes, enabling large-scale reuse and effective management of your portfolio of software projects. Fourth, significant work is being done in process patterns and organizational patterns, with a large body of knowledge being posted online almost daily (see *http://www.ambysoft.com/processPatternsPage.html* for links). Fifth, the OOSP lifecycle explicitly includes the Maintain and Support phase (which, in hindsight, should have been more aptly named the Production phase, but nobody's perfect) to remind developers constantly that they need to take maintenance and support considerations into account as they create software. Finally, OOSP explicitly includes items that have a tendency to fall through the cracks. This is why there is a need to generalize your work if you intend to make it reusable: the need to perform risk management, to perform quality assurance, and to assess your project and project team once your software has been delivered.

The main disadvantage of OOSP is it explicitly indicates the inherent complexity of developing, operating, and supporting software. This can be quite daunting for some people.

10.9 The Unified Process

The enhanced lifecycle is the evolution of the Unified Process into a full-fledged software process.

The Unified Process (Kruchten, 1999) is the latest endeavor of Rational Corporation, the same people who introduced what has become the industry-standard modeling notation, the Unified Modeling Language (UML). Figure 10-8 depicts the enhanced lifecycle for the Unified Process (Ambler 2000a; Ambler 2000b; Ambler 2000c). Along the bottom of the diagram, you see that any given development cycle through the Unified Process should be organized into what Rational calls *iterations*. Although I would argue that the term *increments* is likely a better term than *iterations*, the basic concept is, at the end of each iteration, you produce an internal executable that can be worked with by your user community. This reduces the risk of your project by improving communication between you and your customers. Another risk-reduction technique built into the Unified Process is the concept that you should make a go/no-go decision at the end of each phase. If a project is going to fail, then you want to stop it as early as possible in its lifecycle. This is an important concept in an industry with upward to an 85 percent failure rate (Jones, 1996).

The Inception phase is where you define the project scope and define the business case for the system. The initial requirements for your software are identified. Basic project management documents are started during the Inception phase, including the initial risk assessment, the estimate, and the project schedule. The Elaboration phase focuses on detailed analysis of the problem domain and the definition of an architectural foundation for your project. The Construction phase, often the heart of software projects, is where the detailed design for your application is developed, as well as the corresponding source code. The purpose of the Transition phase is to deliver the system to your user community. There is often a beta release of the software to your users, typically called a *pilot release* within most businesses, in which a small group of users work with the system before it is released to the general community. The Production phase, one of my enhancements over the original version of the Unified Process (Kruchten, 1999), represents the portion of the software lifecycle after a system has been deployed. As the name of the phase implies, its purpose is to keep your software in production until it is either replaced with a new version—from a minor release such as a bug fix to a major new release—or it is retired and removed from production.

Figure 10-8.
The enhanced lifecycle for the Unified Process

The Unified Process has several strengths. First, it is based on sound software engineering principles such as taking an iterative, requirements-driven, and architecture-based approach to development. Second, it provides several

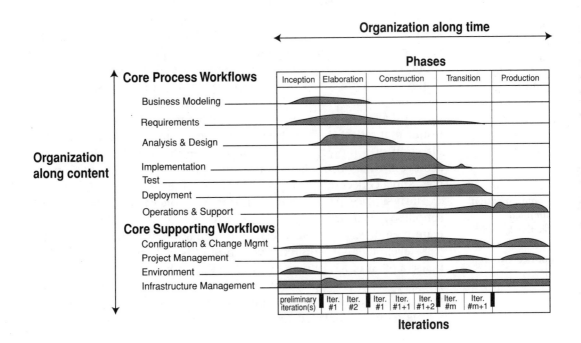

mechanisms, such as a working prototype at the end of each iteration and the go/no-go decision point at the end of each phase, which adds management visibility into the development process. Third, Rational Corporation has made, and continues to do so, a significant investment in its Rational Unified Process product, an HTML-based description of the Unified Process that your organization can tailor to meet its exact needs.

10.10 Other Processes

In addition to the process patterns of the Object-Oriented Software Process and the Unified Process, you may want to consider several other leading software processes. These processes are as follows:

- eXtreme Programming (XP)
- Microsoft Solutions Framework (MSF)
- The OPEN Process
- Catalysis

10.10.1 eXtreme Programming (XP)

eXtreme Programming (XP) focuses on the things that lead to the successful development of software.

Better known as XP, eXtreme programming is a lightweight software process that is aimed at small-sized teams operating in an environment of ill-understood and/or rapidly changing requirements. XP, described in Kent Beck's *eXtreme Programming Explained: Embrace Change* (Beck, 2000) and online at *www.extremeprogramming.com*, makes two fundamental promises. For programmers, XP promises to focus every day on the things that matter most, the things that lead to the successful development of software. For users and managers, XP promises they will get the most value from their software development investment, see concrete results that reflect their goals every few weeks, and be able to change the direction of a project as needed without undue penalty. How does XP achieve this? By being based on a core set of values, some basic principles, and a collection of proven software-engineering practices.

Communication, simplicity, feedback, and courage are the four core values of XP.

The best place to begin with XP is at its four core values: communication, simplicity, feedback, and courage. Effective communication—between team members, with your users, with management, with any other project stakeholder—is required if your project is to be successful. Simplicity is also a pillar of XP. In many ways an XP team bets it can do the simplest job today to solve a problem, and then pay a little more tomorrow if needed to fulfill new requirements. The alternative is to make something a little more complicated today and bet you actually need it tomorrow.

By obtaining feedback as early as possible, regarding whether a portion of your code works or whether your entire system meets the needs of its users, you know that what you are doing is the right thing. Finally, your team needs the courage to refactor/rework its code (Fowler, 1999) when it discovers it doesn't meet new requirements very well, to stick to its chosen approach when the going gets tough, and to make the hard decisions required to deliver their software.

The four core values of XP lead to its simple, but effective, primary principles. The first one, rapid feedback, is achieved by XP's practices of continuous testing and integration, as well as its inclusion of user experts on the development team. XP believes project teams should assume simplicity, they should treat every problem as if it can be solved with the simplest of approaches, and the team should trust in its ability to add complexity later only when it is needed. The principle of incremental change states that any problem should be solved with the smallest series of changes that makes sense, similar to my own advice to develop in small steps. The principle of embracing change recognizes that requirements do change, technologies change, strategies change, techniques change, and people change—you may as well accept this and revel in it. Performing quality work is also a fundamental XP principle because not only does nobody like doing a careless job, they also don't like being on the receiving end of careless work. In addition, XP promotes many supporting principles, such as supporting personal growth by teaching learning, making a small initial investment to motivate paring of requirements and approaches to those that are the most simple, playing to win instead of playing not to lose, concrete experiments to prove an approach, open and honest communication, working with people's instincts and not against them, everyone accepts responsibility, you should travel light and only develop and maintain critical artifacts, and you should aim for honest measurements to facilitate true understanding of how well your project is progressing.

XP promotes a collection of key principles, such as embracing change, quality work, rapid feedback, and assuming simplicity.

The XP software process is comprised of several practices. And the interesting thing is that XP itself reflects the principles it preaches: XP is simple and it travels light in that it has no more processes than it absolutely needs and no fewer than what is required to be successful. The primary goal of the planning game practice is to define the scope of the project through the development and prioritization of stories, effectively lightweight use cases used to describe your business requirements. Part of the planning game is to allocate decision-making authority appropriately: Technical people make technical decisions and business people make business decisions. Although this sounds simple in theory, in practice many projects run into difficulties when people make decisions outside the scope of their expertise. One goal of the planning game is to organize your project into

You organize your project into small releases via the planning game.

small releases, another key practice of XP. A common best practice of software development is to organize large development efforts into several smaller incremental releases, to reduce the risk on your project and to help you get functionality into the hands of your users sooner.

Your project's metaphor drives your simple design that you may need to refactor as your project evolves.

At the beginning of an XP project, you define the metaphor your team will follow, XP's equivalent of your project architecture. An example of a metaphor is that your software will work just like a collection of storage bins on a conveyor belt. Your project metaphor provides a common focus for your team that drives its design and development efforts. XP also supports the concept of simple design, often driven by Beck's Class Responsibility Collaborator (CRC) modeling technique described in Chapter 3. The XP principles of traveling light and simplicity suggest you invest just enough effort in your models to facilitate your development effort and no more; thus, if a whiteboard drawing is good enough to get the job done, then that's all you should do. Although this may appear alarming to developers who prefer a more formalized approach to modeling, the XP practice of refactoring (Fowler, 1999) your work when needed enables you to model only to the level you need to. When an XP team realizes its current approach is not working, which happens, it must slowly refactor/rework its code to meet the new requirements it must fulfill.

Two heads are better than one.

Often one of the most difficult XP practices for people to adopt is pair programming, the concept that developers should work together in teams of two, a practice that reflects the fact that developers are more productive working together than separately (two heads are better than one). One developer works at the keyboard, while the other sits over his shoulder providing advice and insight, and pops in and takes over development when his partner runs into problems. Part of the planning game is the acceptance of work assignments, based on stories, by developers. One of the rules of XP is that everyone works in pairs; therefore, whenever one person accepts some work, someone must also jump in and work with her, resulting in continually changing work-pair combinations during your projects. Pair programming supports teamwork and communication within your team.

Collective ownership and coding standards promote teamwork among developers.

A related practice is that of collective ownership, the idea being that any team member can work on any of your team's development artifacts, including the source code. Collective ownership requires everyone on the project to trust each other and to have the courage to share their work with others. Both pair programming and collective ownership are supported by the XP practice of coding standards, of all project team members following a common set of development guidelines. Java programming teams may find the coding standards described in *The Elements of Java Style* (Vermeulen, et al., 2000), the fifth book in this series, to be a good source of Java coding standards.

Testing is also a key practice of XP and, in many ways, XP takes testing to the extreme by suggesting you write your testing code before you write your "real" code. This is complimentary to the advice presented in Chapter 9 that you should test early and test often. By continuously testing your code, it gives you the confidence that your code actually works, as well as resulting in cleaner code of higher quality. XP project teams also follow the practice of continuous integration, of building your system regularly (daily, if not several times a day) enabling you to test your software to ensure that it actually works.

Testing and continuous integration are key practices of XP.

The last two key practices of XP are that you work a 40-hour week and you have an onsite customer. Developers can't work effectively if they're tired or burned out, so a fundamental rule of XP is you can't work overtime for more than two weeks in a row. The onsite customer enables an XP team to explore business requirements as it needs to and gives it direct access to someone who can make key business decisions, including project scope definition, quickly.

To adopt XP successfully, you need to recognize it is an all-or-nothing software process. If you are doing everything but pair programming, then you are not doing XP. If you are developing a massive requirements document and design model first, before you start coding, then you are not doing XP. If you are not testing and integrating your code continuously, then you are not doing XP. If you don't have access to knowledgeable users who have the ability to make key requirements and scoping decisions about your system, then you are not doing XP.

XP is an all-or-nothing process.

XP, when followed properly, brings several strengths to the table. Its customer focus increases the chance that the software you write will actually meet the needs of your users, which, in turn, increases the chances of success for your project. Its focus on small, incremental releases decreases the risk on your project, both by showing that your approach works and by putting functionality in the hands of your users, enabling them to provide timely feedback regarding your work. Continuous testing and integration helps to increase the quality of your work, once again increasing your project's chances for success. Finally, the buzzword value of XP makes it attractive to programmers who normally would be unwilling to adopt a software process, enabling your organization to manage its software efforts better.

Several potential problems occur with XP. XP is geared toward a single project, developed and maintained by a single team, but the reality in many organizations is that some aspects of software development (such as data management and release management issues) are outside the scope of control of a project manager. XP is particularly vulnerable to "bad apple" developers who don't work well with others, who think they know it all, and/or who are not willing to share their "superior" code with others. Although these developers are a hindrance to any project and often prove extremely harmful to your organization in the long run, XP's reliance on communication and teamwork implies that these types of developers simply cannot be tolerated on your team. My advice is to try to help them see the error of their ways and, if it appears they are unable to work together effectively on your XP team, to make them aware of other opportunities elsewhere that desperately need their "phenomenal" skills and expertise.

10.10.2 The Microsoft Solutions Framework (MSF)

The Microsoft Solutions Framework (MSF) is a collection of processes, principles, and practices that helps organizations be more effective in their creation and use of technology to solve their business problems. MSF does this by providing rigorous guidance that is flexible enough to be adapted to meet the needs of the project and the organization. Originally based on best practices within Microsoft product development and IT organizations, MSF was created in 1994 and developed into standardized training courses to promote consistency and effectiveness within the Microsoft Consulting Services (MCS) organization and now within Microsoft customers.

MSF is composed of six core workflows, which Microsoft chooses to call models, which are as follows:

1. **The Enterprise Architecture Model.** This workflow provides a consistent set of guidelines for rapidly building enterprise architecture through versioned releases. This process aligns information technology with business requirements through four perspectives: business, application, information, and technology.

2. **The Team Model.** This workflow provides a flexible structure for organizing teams on projects, emphasizing clear roles and responsibilities, as well as clear goals for team success, and increasing team-member accountability through its structure as a team of peers.

3. **The Process Model.** This workflow provides project structure and guidance through a project lifecycle that is milestone-based, iterative, and flexible. It describes the phases, milestones, activities, and deliverables of a project and its relationship to the Team Model. Using this model helps you improve project control, minimize risk, improve quality, and shorten delivery time.

4. **The Risk Management Model.** This workflow provides a structured and proactive way for managing risk on projects. It sets forth a discipline and environment of proactive decisions and actions to assess continuously what can go wrong, determine what risks are important to deal with, and implement strategies to deal with those risks.

5. **The Design Process Model.** This workflow provides a three-phase, user-centric approach that enables a parallel and iterative design, including conceptual, logical, and physical design phases. This is similar conceptually to the requirements, analysis, and design phases presented in this book.

6. **The Application Model.** This workflow provides a logical three-tier (user interface, business/domain, data/system) services-based approach to designing and developing software applications.

Although the MSF is a step in the right direction, at press time, my opinion is that it isn't yet ready for prime time. However, considering the source, my advice is to keep an eye on this process for two reasons: First, Microsoft has a large user base, many of whom may consider adopting all or portions of MSF. Second, I fully expect people to enhance and extend MSF with proven techniques from other leading processes. Time will tell.

The Microsoft Solutions Framework (MSF) still needs work, but likely has a bright future.

10.10.3 *The OPEN Process*

The OPEN consortium, a group of individuals and organizations promoting and enhancing the use of object-oriented technology, has developed the OPEN Process, a comprehensive software process. The OPEN Process is aimed at organizations using object and component technology, although it can easily be applied to other software development technologies. Also similar to the Unified Process, OPEN was initially created by the merger of earlier methods: MOSES, SOMA, Firesmith, Synthesis, BON, and OOram. The OPEN Process supports the UML notation, the Object Modeling Language (OML) notation, and any other OO notation to document the work products the OPEN process produces. The shape of the lines and bubbles may change, but the fundamentals of the software process remain the same. You can find more information about the OPEN process at *www.open.org.au*.

The OPEN Process is a mature software process for the development of object-oriented software.

10.10.4 *Catalysis*

Catalysis (D'Souza and Wills, 1999) is a next-generation approach for the systematic business-driven development of component-based systems. Catalysis defines a systematic and flexible process to help users and developers share a clear and precise vocabulary. It combines different

Catalysis is a software process for component-based development using UML.

DEFINITION

Object Modeling Language (OML). An alternative to the Unified Modeling Language (UML), promoted by the OPEN Consortium (*www.open.org.au*).

views into an integrated whole; specifies and designs component interfaces so they work together readily; implements components; develops new software using object and component technologies; integrates heterogeneous and legacy components or systems into new development; builds robust models and designs of business and technical components; and reuses domain models, architectures, interfaces, code, and process based on patterns. Catalysis got its start in 1992 and has been used in a variety of organizations and problem domains. You can find more information about the Catalysis process at *www.catalysis.org*.

10.11 When to Use Objects

When should you consider using object technology and object-oriented (OO) techniques? A range of situations exist when OO is appropriate to develop the following:

1. **Complex systems.** The easiest way to deal with complexity is to break it down into smaller components, and then deal with each component in turn. The OO paradigm is based on the concept of defining systems based on a collection of interacting objects. This strategy enables you to break down a complex system into smaller components—in this case, collections of similar objects called *classes*. It is easier to deal with one class at a time than it is to deal with the entire system as a whole.

2. **Systems that are prone to change.** When the system you are developing is prone to change, you should consider taking an OO approach to developing it. Remember, OO leads to systems that are extensible (easy to change). With the ever-increasing pace of change in the business world that our systems are designed to support, extensibility becomes more and more important as time goes on. If your business rules change, your systems must also change.

3. **Systems with graphical user interfaces (GUIs).** GUIs are complicated. Consider how much programming must go into something as simple as a window. A window can be moved, resized, opened, closed, minimized, maximized, and so forth. Would you want to have to program that yourself? I sure wouldn't. Call me lazy, but I would rather let somebody else write it, and then reuse his work (most likely through the use of inheritance).

4. **Systems that are based on the client/server model.** In the client/server (C/S) model, a client machine (usually a PC or workstation) is connected to one or more servers (usually a high-powered PC, mini, or mainframe) via a network. Client machines

provide the front-end (the interface), while the server(s) provide access to data and functionality. In a way, doesn't a server sound a lot like a class? While there is a little more to it than that, in the second volume in this series, you see the only way to design client/server systems effectively is to take an OO approach.

5. **Electronic commerce (e-commerce) applications.** Object- and component-based technologies are the norm for the development of e-commerce applications for doing business over the Internet.

6. **Integrated systems.** Object technologies are well suited for enterprise application integration (EAI) efforts. This is because they can be used to develop wrappers around nonobject technology, so they may be integrated into your organization's overall systems.

7. **Systems where structured techniques don't seem to work.** Many organizations are turning to OO techniques because the use of structured techniques failed for a new application. We need to remember that structured techniques were created in the mid-1970s, when we were developing large, mainframe-based, batch-transaction processing systems. Now, in the 2000s, we are developing PC-based online systems with GUI front-ends and Internet-based e-commerce systems. It should come as no surprise that structured techniques are not sufficient for today's needs.

8. **Systems within an organization that is willing to try new approaches.** For OO to be successful, your organization must be willing to try a new approach to development. Virtually all organizations want to develop complex, GUI, and/or Internet-based applications, yet few are willing to modify the way they approach systems development. The systems we are creating today are completely different than those of only five or ten years ago. The systems have changed and so must your approach. Managers and developers alike must be willing to cast aside their preconceived notions and embrace the OO mindset. Only then will your project succeed.

10.12 When Not to Use Objects

Although object technology and object-oriented techniques are versatile, they are not necessarily ideal for all situations. You may not want to use OO to develop the following:

1. **Systems for which structured techniques are ideal.** Structured techniques were specifically created for a certain style of system. As discussed earlier, these systems are typically large, mainframe-based,

> ### DEFINITIONS
>
> **E-commerce.** E-commerce, also known as *electronic commerce* or *Internet-based commerce*, focuses on the use of technology to support the selling of products and services electronically.
>
> **Enterprise application integration (EAI).** The integration of disparate software applications into a cohesive whole to support new and complex business processes.
>
> **Wrapper.** A collection of one or more classes that encapsulates access to non-OO technology to make it appear as if it is OO.

batch-transaction applications. If this is what you are developing, then structured techniques are likely your best choice.

Object-oriented techniques and technologies are not appropriate for every situation, but they are appropriate for most.

2. **Systems when you cannot use OO throughout the entire development lifecycle.** Because the benefits of OO are achieved throughout the entire development lifecycle, it is not advisable to use OO if you cannot do OO programming. Similarly, you should not try to use an OO language if you only have a structured design from which to base it. The paradigms are fundamentally different and trying to combine them can be difficult.

10.13 What You Have Learned

A software process is a set of project phases, stages, methods, techniques, and practices that people employ to develop and maintain software and its associated artifacts (plans, documents, models, code, test cases, manuals, and so on). In this chapter, I presented the leading processes—the Object-Oriented Software Process (OOSP), the Unified Process, the Microsoft Solutions Framework (MSF), the OPEN Process, eXtreme Programming (XP), and Catalysis—so you may understand the options you have open to you. Finally, I discussed when to use OO and when not to use it. The situations for this are summarized in Table 1-1.

Software development, maintenance, and support are complex endeavors, ones that require good people, good tools, good architectures, and good processes to be successful. The software process is a significant part of the solution to the software crisis, something your organization has likely ignored to its peril. We are at the cusp of a new millennium. Now is the time to learn from our past mistakes—the time to choose to succeed.

Table 10-1. When and when not to use OO

When to use OO	When not to use OO
To develop complex systems	To develop large, mainframe-based, batch-transaction systems
To develop systems that are prone to change	To develop systems when you cannot use OO for the entire development process
To develop systems with graphical user interfaces	
To develop client/server systems	
To develop e-commerce systems	
To support enterprise application integration	
To develop systems where structured techniques do not seem to work	
To develop systems in an organization that is willing to try new approaches	

10.14 Review Questions

1. Compare and contrast iterative development, serial development, and incremental development. In what combinations can you combine these three approaches effectively? For each combination suggest a type of system that it would work well for and justify why it would.

2. What workflow(s) can be removed safely from the enhanced lifecycle for the Unified Process? Justify your answer. If no workflows can be removed justify why.

3. Are XP and the Unified Process compatible? If so, how could the techniques of eXtreme Programming (XP) be used to enhance the Unified Process (or vice versa)? If not, why not? Justify your answer.

4. Discuss the statement: "There are two ways for a software project to fail. First, to fail to follow a software process. Second, to follow a software process."

The software is everything outside of the code.

Chapter 11
Where to Go From Here

What You Will Learn in This Chapter

What is the post-2000 (P2K) software environment?
What are the techniques and technologies of the P2K software environment?
What introductory resources exist for P2K techniques and technologies?
What roles/positions do software professionals hold on object-oriented projects?
How can you continue your object-oriented learning process?

Why You Need to Read This Chapter

Your skills, and how you apply them, are significant determinants of your success as a software professional. By reading this book, you have gained the fundamental knowledge required to begin learning object technology and techniques, and this chapter provides insight into the next steps that further your learning process.

You have made it to the end of the book. You know all about object orientation and now you are an object expert who is ready to develop large-scale, mission-critical software. Well, not quite. Realistically, you have learned some useful concepts and techniques, you have seen how they all fit together, and you have applied them by working through the review questions and case studies. You are now in a good position to continue your learning process, a process that is likely to last throughout your entire career. This chapter provides insight into where the software profession currently is, where it is going, what skills will be needed over the next few years, and how you can obtain those skills.

11.1 The Post-2000 (P2K) Environment

You will spend the rest of your career learning new skills.

The software profession was significantly influenced by the Y2K crisis during the last part of the 1990s—new development was postponed or even cancelled in favor of diverting resources to resolving the Y2K crisis and, as a result, many organizations put off investment in adopting new technologies and techniques. Now that the Y2K crisis has passed, we are faced with the realities of the post-2000 (P2K) software environment, an environment dominated by the techniques described in this book.

In the P2K environment, you will apply new paradigms, such as the object-oriented and component-based paradigms, new development processes that are iterative and incremental, new technologies such as Java and CORBA, and new techniques such as use case modeling. Object-development techniques were overviewed in this book, and the key technologies and techniques applicable to the P2K environment are summarized in this section. To understand the P2K environment, you must consider the following:

- New software strategies
- Enabling technologies
- Leading-edge development techniques
- Modern software processes
- Object programming languages
- How to gain P2K skills

11.1.1 New Software Strategies

The 2000s will be dominated by two key software strategies: enterprise application integration (EAI) and electronic commerce (e-commerce). EAI is the integration of disparate software applications into a cohesive whole to support new and complex business processes. Middleware and

> **DEFINITIONS**
>
> *Post-2000 (P2K) environment.* The collection of technologies and techniques—for the most part object-oriented and component-based—that organizations are deploying within their information technology (IT) departments.
>
> *Year 2000 (Y2K) crisis.* The need for organizations in the late 1990s to update and/or replace software that was written to store the year as two digits instead of four.

component technologies, such as CORBA and COM+-compliant tools that are described in the following sections are often used to support EAI. A good place to start is *www.eaiforum.com*, as is the book *Enterprise Application Integration* (Linthicum, 2000). Also, wrapping, a topic covered in detail in *Building Object Applications That Work* (Ambler, 1998a), is an important skill for EAI developers.

E-commerce, also known as *electronic commerce* or *Internet-based commerce*, focuses on the use of technology to support the selling of products and services electronically. Organizations that have been successful at e-commerce include Dell Computer (*www.dell.com*), a retailer of computer hardware and software; Amazon.com (*www.amazon.com*), a retailer of products including books, videos, and music CDs; and Ebay (*www.ebay.com*), an online auction site. The best resource for e-commerce is the magazine *The Industry Standard* (*www.thestandard.com*), which is published in both paper and electronic formats.

11.1.2 Enabling Technologies

Several enabling technologies, in addition to the object programming languages described in Section 11.1.5, are predominant in the P2K environment. These technologies are as follows:

- CORBA
- COM+
- Enterprise JavaBeans (EJB)
- XML
- Persistence layers/frameworks

1. **Common Object Request Broker Architecture (CORBA).** CORBA is an industry-standard approach to distributed object computing, first introduced in the late 1980s, that is defined and maintain by the Object Management Group (OMG). In the early 1990s, CORBA

promised to be the standard environment for object-oriented development but, in practice, CORBA has proven to be a significant force in the middleware arena in the 2000s. A great place to start learning about CORBA is at *www.omg.org/corba/beginners.html*.

2. **COM+.** This is the latest incarnation of Microsoft's Component Object Model (COM). COM was the evolution of Microsoft's Object Linking and Embedding (OLE) and ActiveX technologies, which then evolved into the Distributed Component Object Model (DCOM) and now into COM+. COM+ is a proprietary approach to distributed component development for the Microsoft platform. Visit *www.microsoft.com/com* for a collection of links to white papers, presentations, and case studies about COM-based technologies.

3. **Enterprise JavaBeans (EJB).** EJB is a component architecture for the development and deployment of component-based distributed business applications. Applications written following the EJB architecture are scalable, transactional, and multiuser secure. These applications may be written once, and then deployed on any server platform that supports the EJB specification. EJB lets developers obtain and use enterprise-class services to create mission-critical applications. The best place to start with EJB is *java.sun.com/products/ejb* online and with the book *Mastering Enterprise JavaBeans* (Roman, 1999).

4. **Extensible Markup Language (XML).** An industry-standard approach to data sharing, an important enabling technology for EAI and e-commerce. The Web site *www.xml.org* is the best place to start when learning XML.

5. **Persistence layers.** A persistence layer (also known as a *persistence framework*) automates the storage, retrieval, and deletion of objects from persistent storage, such as a relational database, via the use of mapping metadata. If a relational database is used to store objects, then the mapping metadata relates an attribute of an object to the column of a database table where it is stored. Persistence layers hide the data schema from your objects, increasing the robustness of your software and increasing your development productivity by dramatically reducing the amount of code you need to write (if any) to persist your objects. I cover persistence layers in detail in *Building Object Applications That Work* (Ambler, 1998a), the second volume in this series. You may also want to download the white paper I have posted at *www.ambysoft.com/persistenceLayer.html*, which describes the design of a persistence layer.

DEFINITIONS

Middleware. Technology that enables software deployed on disparate computer hardware systems to communicate with one another.

Object Management Group (OMG). An industry-recognized standards body responsible for standards such as the Unified Modeling Language (UML) and the Common Object Request Broker Architecture (CORBA).

11.1.3 Leading-Edge Development Techniques

As a developer working in the P2K environment, you are likely to use most or all of the following development techniques:

- Component-based development (CBD)
- Incremental development
- Iterative development
- Object orientation
- Patterns
- Unified Modeling Language (UML)
- Usage-centered design
- Use case modeling

1. **Component-based development (CBD).** An approach to development in which software is deployed as collections of interacting components, each of which encapsulate a defined set of behaviors. Any type of technology can be used to implement components, including both object-oriented and structured languages. Common approaches to components include the CORBA Component Model (CCM) from the Object Management Group, Enterprise JavaBeans (EJB) from Sun Microsystems, and COM+ from Microsoft. The best place to start learning about CBD is the book *Component Software: Beyond Object-Oriented Programming* (Szyperski, 1998) and the Web site *www.componentsoftware.org*.

2. **Incremental development.** An approach to software development that organizes a project into several releases instead of one "big-bang" release. This enables you to deploy software earlier to your users and reduces risk to your project by supporting feedback from your users regarding initial releases. Incremental development was discussed in detail in Chapter 10.

3. **Iterative development.** A nonserial approach to software development. In other words, you may do a little bit of requirements engineering, some modeling, some implementation, some testing, some more modeling, some more implementation, some more requirements engineering, and so on. With an iterative approach, the order in which you perform activities is not set in stone. Iterative development reduces the risk to your project and development time by enabling you to apply techniques at the point where they are most effective for your project. Iterative development was discussed in detail in Chapter 10.

4. **Object orientation.** A software paradigm based on the concept that software should be built from objects that exhibit both state (data) and behavior (process). Based on ideas first introduced in the late 1960s, object orientation became popular in the 1980s with languages such as Smalltalk and C++, and became the de facto approach to new development in the 1990s with C++ and Java. The most valuable resource on the Web for object developers is the Cetus Links on Objects and Components, *www.cetus-links.org*. As a next step, I recommend reading *Applying UML and Patterns* (Larman, 1998), which examines object-oriented analysis and design, and the topics of Chapters 6 and 7, respectively, in greater detail, and my own book *Building Object Applications That Work* (Ambler, 1998a), which covers a range of object-oriented topics from the point-of-view of an object developer.

5. **Patterns.** A pattern is a solution to a common problem taking relevant forces into account, supporting the reuse of proven techniques and approaches of other developers. Patterns come in many different varieties, including design patterns, analysis patterns, process patterns, architectural patterns, organizational patterns, programming idioms, and even antipatterns (approaches proven not to work in practice). Analysis patterns were discussed in Chapter 6, design and architectural patterns in Chapter 7, programming idioms in Chapter 8, and process patterns in Chapter 10. Within the object modeling world patterns have formed the basis for a common language between modelers. For example, hearing statements such as "that's a singleton" or "this is an implementation of strategy" referring to the Singleton and Strategy design patterns is common. A useful range of pattern resources is referenced at *www.cetus-links.org/oo_patterns.html*, including both introductory and advanced materials.

6. **Unified Modeling Language (UML).** The UML is an industry-standard modeling language that defines the notation and seman-

tics for object-oriented modeling. The book *UML Distilled* (Fowler and Scott, 1997) is an excellent introduction to the techniques of the UML and is a great book to read after this one if you are interested in learning more about the UML. In *Building Object Applications That Work* (Ambler, 1998a) and *Process Patterns* (Ambler, 1998b) I present an overview of the techniques and how they all work together, similar in concept to the overviews I presented in each of the modeling chapters in this book (3, 6, and 7). Visit *www.omg.org* for more details. I also maintain a Web page at *www.ambysoft.com/ umlAndBeyond.html* of links to key resources on the Web.

7. **Usage-centered design.** A streamlined and systematic approach for devising software closely fitted to the genuine needs of users, software that is not only more useful and easier to use, but also simpler and easier to construct. Essential use cases and essential user interface prototypes (mock-ups), described in Chapter 3, are examples of usage-centered design techniques. To learn more about usage-centered design, the best place to start is the book *Software for Use* (Constantine and Lockwood, 1999).

8. **Use case modeling.** Use case modeling is a requirements engineering technique that was popularized in the early 1990s within the object-oriented development community. As you saw in Chapter 3, use case models, comprised of a use case diagram and a collection of use cases, are used to document the behavioral requirements for a system. The best book I have ever read about use cases is *Applying Use Cases* (Schneider and Winters, 1998); I highly recommend it.

11.1.4 Modern Software Processes

The technologies and techniques of the P2K environment are complex and, as you saw in Chapter 10, developers who want to apply them effectively need modern software processes that reflect this complexity. These processes include the following:

- eXtreme Programming (XP)
- Object-Oriented Software Process (OOSP)
- OPEN Process
- Unified Process

1. **eXtreme Programming (XP).** A deliberate and disciplined approach to software development that stresses communication, simplicity, feedback, and confidence. XP focuses on working

with users, on simple and elegant development, and on testing. To learn XP, start with the book *Extreme Programming Explained* (Beck, 2000) and the Web site *www.extremeprogramming.com*.

2. **Object-Oriented Software Process (OOSP).** OOSP, covered in detail in Chapter 10, is a collection of process patterns that together describe a complete process for developing, maintaining, and supporting software. OOSP is based on the concept that large-scale, mission-critical software development is serial in the large and iterative in the small, delivering incremental releases of software in Internet time. The OOSP is the topic of my books *Process Patterns* (Ambler, 1998b) and *More Process Patterns* (Ambler, 1999). I maintain "The Process Patterns Resource Page" (*www.ambysoft.com/processPatternsPage.html*) of references to process patterns and related resources.

3. **OPEN Process.** A sophisticated and comprehensive software process promoted by the OPEN Consortium (*www.open.org.au*) for the efficient development of software. To learn the OPEN process, I suggest starting with the book *The OPEN Process Specification* (Graham, Henderson-Sellers, and Younessi, 1997).

4. **Unified Process.** The Unified Process is a process based on iterative and incremental approaches for software development. The enhanced lifecycle of the Unified Process, described in detail in Chapter 10, extends the techniques of the Unified Process to be a complete software process that is applicable to large-scale, mission-critical software. To learn more about the Unified Process, start with the book *The Rational Unified Process* (Kruchten, 1999), and then follow with *The Unified Software Development Process* (Jacobson, Booch, and Rumbaugh, 1999), as well as my series regarding the enhanced lifecycle (Ambler 2000a; Ambler 2000b; Ambler 2000c).

11.1.5 Object Programming Languages

Object programming languages, including both object-oriented and object-based languages, are by far the preferred languages for P2K development. These languages include the following:

- C++
- Eiffel
- Java
- Object COBOL

- Object Pascal
- Smalltalk
- Visual Basic

1. **C++.** A hybrid object-oriented programming language that adds object-oriented features to the C programming language. C++ is used for processing intensive software applications, particularly systems programming and e-commerce development. C++ is a primary language for P2K development. A range of introductory C++ books are available to you, most of which are listed online at *www.cetus-links.org/oo_c_plus_plus.html*. For advanced C++, I always suggest the books *Advanced C++* (Coplien, 1992), *Effective C++* (Meyers, 1992), and *More Effective C++* (Meyers, 1996) because they teach you the techniques to program in C++ .

2. **Eiffel.** A "pure" object-oriented programming language. Eiffel is a niche language, one with a small market share, that is used by organizations that are serious about software engineering. A variety of Eiffel resources are referenced at *www.cetus-links.org/oo_eiffel.html*. The book *Eiffel: The Language* (Meyer, 1992) is the definitive book about the language.

3. **Java.** An object-oriented programming language based on the concept of "write once, run anywhere" (WORA). Java software runs on standard Java Virtual Machines (JVMs), enabling reasonable portability between platforms. Java is likely to become the primary language for P2K development because of its portability and versatility (Java code can be deployed to browsers, on application servers, and even with databases). A range of Java resources is referenced at *www.cetus-links.org/oo_java.html*, including both introductory and advanced materials. A good online tutorial is posted at *java.sun.com/docs/books/tutorial/index.html* and I highly suggest the book *The Elements of Java Style* (Vermeulen, et. al., 2000), the fifth book in this series.

4. **Object COBOL.** A hybrid object-oriented programming language that extends COBOL with object-oriented concepts. Object COBOL floundered throughout the 1990s because of the inordinate focus within the COBOL community on the Y2K crisis, instead of on advancing the state of the art. Object COBOL may enjoy a resurgence in popularity as vendors introduce new P2K development tools. Time will tell. An assortment of Object COBOL resources is referenced at *www.cetus-links.org/oo_cobol.html*. I have found the books *Object-Oriented COBOL* (Arranga and Coyle, 1996)

and *Standard Object-Oriented COBOL* (Chapin, 1997) to be good places to start, particularly if you are already an experienced COBOL developer. (I programmed in COBOL in the late 1980s. Shhhh...don't tell anyone.)

5. **Object Pascal.** A hybrid object-oriented programming language that extends Pascal with object-oriented concepts. Object Pascal is a niche language, albeit one with a reasonably large niche, that is likely to continue well into the 2000s, but is unlikely to become a major player in the P2K languages market. A range of Object Pascal resources is referenced at *www.cetus-links.org/ oo_delphi.html*.

6. **Smalltalk.** A pure object-oriented programming language. Smalltalk was first developed in the 1970s by Xerox Parc, a research and development division of Xerox corporation that was popularized in the late 1980s and early 1990s for business application development. Smalltalk is now a niche language that was eclipsed by C++ and Java, more for marketing concerns than technical ones, in the late 1990s. It is doubtful that Smalltalk will enjoy a resurgence in popularity. A variety of Smalltalk resources is referenced at *www.cetus-links.org/oo_smalltalk.html*. I was a Smalltalk developer during the early-to-mid-1990s, and I have found the books *Discovering Smalltalk* (Lalonde, 1994) and *Smalltalk Best Practice Patterns* (Beck, 1997) to be fantastic resources.

DEFINITIONS

Java virtual machine (JVM). An abstract computing machine that supports a defined set of instructions. JVMs are what make Java portable; Java code is compiled into standard byte-code that can be run on any platform with a JVM.

Object programming language. Any programming language that is either object-oriented or object-based.

Object-based programming language. Any programming language that natively supports some, but not all, of the properties of an object-oriented language. Example: Visual Basic.

Object-oriented programming language. Any programming language that natively supports the object-oriented concepts of inheritance, classes, objects, polymorphism, and message passing. Examples: Java and C++.

Write once, run anywhere (WORA). A marketing pitch for the Java language, which points out Java's cross-platform nature.

7. **Visual Basic.** An object-based programming language developed by Microsoft Corporation that extends Basic with several object-oriented concepts. Visual Basic is effectively the workhorse of the Microsoft application-development environment, versions of which are used as macro languages within a range of Microsoft products. Visual Basic is a significant language within the P2K environment, at least for applications written for Microsoft platforms. The best place to start learning Visual Basic is at Microsoft's "Visual Basic Start Page," *msdn.microsoft.com/vbasic*. You are also likely to find *Developing Applications with Visual Basic and UML* (Reed, 1999) to be a good book to read after this one if you are a VB developer.

11.1.6 Internet Development Languages

To support Web-based and e-commerce development, you are likely to work with languages such as:

- HTML
- Perl
- CGI scripts

1. **Hypertext Markup Language (HTML).** HTML is an industry-standard definition of a platform-independent file format for sharing information. HTML pages are the de facto standard approach for user interfaces on the World Wide Web (WWW). The NCSA has an excellent guide to HTML for beginners posted at *www.nsca.uiuc.edu/General/Internet/HTMLPrimer.html*.

2. **Perl (practical extraction and report language).** Perl is a scripting language originally developed for the automation of UNIX system administration tasks that are now commonly used for Web-based software development. Perl includes report creation facilities, editing and data manipulation features, graphical user interface (GUI) features, programming features, and the capability to invoke other programs. The Web page *www.ebb.org/PickingUp-Perl/* is an online tutorial about the Perl programming language that is an excellent place to start learning Perl.

3. **Common gateway interface (CGI).** CGI is a simple protocol used to communicate between Web forms and your program. The page *www.jmarshall.com/easy/cgi* provides an excellent overview of CGI and how to work with it.

> ## DEFINITION
>
> ***Graphical user interface (GUI).*** A style of user interface composed of graphical components, such as windows and buttons.

11.2 Skills for Specific Positions

You saw in Chapter 10 that the complexity of the software process provides a range of opportunities for developers. In this section, I discuss the common roles you may one day possess and the skills you will need in order to be successful. These roles are as follows:

- Business analyst
- IT senior manager
- Object modeler
- Persistence administrator
- Persistence modeler
- Programmer
- Project manager
- Quality assurance engineer
- Software architect
- Test engineer

11.2.1 Business Analyst

Business analysts need requirements gathering and validation skills, as well as object-oriented analysis skills.

A business analyst works with the future users of a system to identify the fundamentals of their business problem, their requirements for the system, how they will likely work with the system, and how they will likely need the system to evolve over time. Chapters 3, 4, and 6 (which covered requirements gathering, requirements validation, and object-oriented analysis, respectively), described the techniques that business analysts use on a daily basis.

11.2.2 IT Senior Manager

Information technology (IT) senior managers oversee the software efforts of an organization. IT senior managers need a basic understanding of the technology being used within the organization, particularly the business implications of that technology, and they must have a solid grasp of the organization's chosen software process. IT senior managers must be trained in the deliverables, the processes, the resources needed, the differences as compared to the old way of doing things, and the risks associated with transitioning to the P2K software environment. At first, many IT senior managers have difficulties with the concept of iterative development because most of the development artifacts, such as the requirements model and the software design, are evolved throughout the project and are not delivered in a serial fashion at defined milestones. IT senior managers need training in the fundamentals of the technology and techniques of the P2K software environment previously described in Section 11.1. An understanding of e-commerce is also critical for IT senior management, as it is likely the key business driver within your organization.

11.2.3 Object Modeler

Object modelers are responsible for the analysis and design of object-oriented software; therefore, they must be skilled in a range of modeling techniques that you have seen in this book. In the past, it was common to see software professionals specialize in one type of modeling, such as data modeling or process modeling, but experience has shown this strategy to be ineffective and even dysfunctional. The Unified Modeling Language defines many types of models because no single model is sufficient to meet all of your needs. By focusing on one type of model to the detriment of others, you ignore many critical modeling issues, producing software that performs poorly or is difficult to maintain. Object modelers must understand a range of modeling techniques and how they all fit together. Furthermore, they need training and education in design patterns, analysis patterns, and architectural patterns to be effective. Modelers that focus on design issues, particularly distributed design, will likely need training in distributed development technologies such as CORBA, Enterprise JavaBeans (EJB), and/or Microsoft's COM+. Modelers will need to learn usage-centered design skills or at least introductory-level user-interface design skills.

Object modelers need a range of modeling skills, including UML and usage-centered design techniques, as well as a knowledge of the underlying implementation technologies.

11.2.4 Persistence Modeler

A persistence modeler, more commonly called a *data modeler* in the structured world, is responsible for the development and maintenance of physical persistence models. For new applications, as you saw in Chapter 7, persistence modelers are needed to develop the physical persistence model based on the object-oriented models for your software. For development involving an existing legacy data schema, the norm for most software projects, persistence modelers may be needed to develop models of the data schema, if they don't already exist, and to aid in the object to data storage mapping efforts as needed. Persistence modelers need to understand the object-oriented models of the UML, how to develop persistence models based on the object-oriented model, how to map objects to relational databases, and the nuances of the permanent storage mechanism(s) used to persist your objects. How to map objects to relational databases is covered in the second volume in this series, *Building Object Applications That Work* (Ambler, 1998a).

11.2.5 Persistence Administrator

A persistence administrator, called a *database administrator* (DBA) in the structured world, is responsible for the care and support of your permanent storage mechanisms and, thus, needs expertise in these products. Persistence administrator roles are often expanded to include the administration of the object-to-relational mappings used by your persistence layer. The roles of persistence administrator and persistence modeler often blur because of the reduced responsibilities for persistence modelers within the object world.

11.2.6 Programmer

The job of a software programmer is to implement and initially test source code based on the models for your system. No more and no less. Programmers need to work closely with both modelers and test engineers, implying that they need to understand at least the basics of object-oriented and component-based modeling and testing. Furthermore, programmers need training and education in design patterns, programming idioms, the programming language with which they are working, and the fundamentals of software engineering, such as the implications of concepts such as coupling and cohesion.

11.2.7 Project Manager

Project managers need broad knowledge of a range of skills.

Project managers are responsible for the organization and management of a software project. They face a complex environment in which to work: Many of the complexities arise from the application of iterative and incremental development techniques. Furthermore, with the worsening shortage of skilled software professionals, project managers are finding that team building and people management skills are becoming even more critical to their success, not just the scheduling and estimating skills that the majority of software project management books focus on. Project managers need broad knowledge of a range of skills, particularly in the software process, but also in people-management skills. A good book to read to learn more about project management is *Software Project Management* (Royce, 1998).

> **DEFINITIONS**
>
> **Permanent storage.** Any physical medium to which data can be saved, retrieved, and deleted. Potential permanent storage mechanisms for objects include relational databases, files, and object databases.
>
> **Physical persistence model.** A model, often called a *physical data model*, that depicts the physical data schema to be implemented in your permanent storage mechanism.

11.2.8 Quality Assurance Engineer

A quality assurance engineer is responsible for ensuring that developers build software according to the accepted standards and processes within the organization. Quality assurance engineers need to be trained in the techniques of the deliverables they are involved with reviewing, as well as in the software process in general. Training in common patterns is also important so quality assurance engineers can detect when a model or document has, or has not, followed accepted approaches to development. My experience is that a few quality assurance engineers have difficulty with the concept of software artifacts that evolve over time, particularly those experienced with structured technologies, and they struggle with issues such as how to review an artifact that is partially complete. Quality assurance engineers need to have an open mind and to focus initially on whether an artifact is "moving in the right direction" rather than whether it is complete.

Quality assurance engineers need an open mind to be effective in following iterative and incremental development practices.

11.2.9 Software Architect

Two types of software architects exist: a project software architect and an enterprise software architect. A project software architect focuses on the identification and proving of a software architecture for a system based on its initial requirements and the existing enterprise architecture of your organization. An enterprise software architect focuses on the software architecture for your organization, considering such issues as enterprise application integration (EAI), reusable frameworks, and a common software infrastructure. Software architects need training and education in the technologies and techniques of the P2K environment, people skills (they'll be supporting project teams and interacting with senior business management), and the fundamentals of your organization's business. Training in patterns, obviously architectural patterns, but also design, analysis, and process patterns is also important. A great book to read is *Software Architecture in Practice* (Bass, Clements, and Kazman, 1998).

> ### DEFINITIONS
>
> **Design pattern.** A pattern that describes a solution to a design problem.
>
> **Idiom.** An idiom describes how to implement a particular part of a pattern, the part's functionality, or the relationship to other parts in the design. Idioms are often specific to a particular programming language.
>
> **Pattern.** A pattern is a solution to a common problem taking relevant forces into account, effectively supporting the reuse of proven techniques and approaches of other developers.

11.2.10 Test Engineer

Test engineers need skills in traditional and object-oriented testing techniques, as well as the development languages in which the code is written.

Test engineers are responsible for the verification that software fulfills the requirements from which it was built. Test engineers need to learn a large repertoire of testing techniques, such as those of the Full Lifecycle Object-Oriented Testing (FLOOT) methodology presented in Chapter 9. As software becomes more complex, the testing tools and techniques an organization uses to validate software also become more complex. Test engineers need training in object-oriented and traditional testing techniques. They also need training in the relevant programming languages to enable them to develop test harnesses (and to see through the false claims of developers who tell them they can do less testing with objects and components, not more). A good book to read is *Testing Object-Oriented Systems* (Binder, 1999) to receive a thorough grounding in object-testing techniques.

11.3 Continuing Your Learning Process

In the software industry, the norm is for software professionals to learn on the job, which has significant implications for you. Although some software professionals are fortunate enough to work for organizations that are willing to invest in the training and education of their staff,

> ### DEFINITION
>
> **Software architecture.** The set of significant decisions about the organization of a software system, the selection of the system's structural elements and their interfaces; the definition of the behavior and structure of those elements, and the definition of the associations and interactions between those elements; the composition of the elements into progressively larger subsystems; and the definition of the architectural style that guides the efforts of software architects.

many are not. In this section, I discuss a collection of techniques you can use to continue your learning process:

- Take general introductory training
- Gain hands-on experience
- Obtain mentoring
- Work in a learning team
- Read, read, read
- Take advanced training

11.3.1 Take General Introductory Training

If possible, you should take several introductory training courses in object-oriented technologies. Table 11-1 indicates several courses, their descriptions, and typical lengths of time (assuming an eight-hour day) in the order in which you should consider taking them. Depending on your role within your organization, you may choose not to take all the courses (for example, business analysts may choose not to take a programming course).

11.3.2 Gain Hands-on Experience

You can read all you want, and you should, and take dozens of training courses, but you don't really learn something until you try it. If you currently aren't on a software project that is using the object-oriented techniques in which you want to gain experience, then you need either to transfer to another project within your organization, find employment at another firm, or work at home with object technology.

Apply the skills you learn in class and in books.

11.3.3 Obtain Mentoring

An object mentor is someone experienced with object orientation who guides novices through the learning process, showing them how to use

---

DEFINITIONS

Education. The teaching skills and knowledge that are typically applicable over the student's entire career.

Mentoring. The process of having an experienced professional impart his or her expertise to novices following a hands-on basis.

Training. The teaching of specific, narrowly focused skills to people who are often immediately applicable to the current position of the student.

TIP *Understand What Your Suppliers and Customers Do*	A rule of thumb I follow is that you should have a basic understanding of the jobs of the people who provide you with input and of those to whom you provide input. Therefore, an object-oriented designer should understand the basics of object-oriented analysis and of object-oriented programming.

object technologies and techniques. The best mentors have several years of experience in object technologies and techniques, mentoring experience, and good communication skills. If your organization doesn't have a formal mentoring process, and few do, then consider identifying potential experts yourself, and either work closely with them or ask them for help learning the new skills you need. Most people will be flattered that you asked and more than happy to help you.

Table 11-1. Suggested introductory training courses in object orientation

Course	Description	Length
Introduction to Object-Oriented Concepts	Overview of the concepts discussed in Chapter 5, as well as the techniques presented throughout this book.	One to two days
Introduction to the ABC Process	Overview of the fundamentals of a leading software process (that is, the OOSP, Unified Process, or XP).	One day
Introduction to Object-Oriented Requirements and Analysis	Hands-on course applying techniques, such as use case modeling, user interface prototyping, sequencing diagramming, and class modeling presented in Chapters 3, 4, and, 6.	Three to five days
Introduction to Object-Oriented Design	Hands-on course applying techniques such as class modeling, state chart modeling, collaboration modeling, and persistence modeling presented in Chapter 7.	Three to five days
Introduction to the XYZ Language	Hands-on course covering the fundamentals of programming in the appropriate programming language (that is, Java or C++) for your environment.	Five to ten days
Introduction to Object-Oriented Testing	Hands-on course describing the fundamentals of object-oriented testing.	Two to five days

Have you ever noticed that the people who come prepared to a course, who know something about the material before attending the class, tend to get a lot more out of it than people who go into it cold? My advice is to take advantage of this observation and prepare before taking any course. Because the training and education process is iterative, the implication is that you will quickly get into a cycle of "read some books," "take some training," "do some reading," and so on. I maintain a suggested reading list at *www.ambysoft.com/books.html,* which includes books that are appropriate for supporting introductory, intermediate, and advanced courses in object orientation. Before you begin your training efforts, you should also ask the training instructors what books they recommend.

11.3.4 Work in a Learning Team

An effective way to learn new skills is to work in a learning team, a small group of people given the task of working together to learn a particular subject. Learning teams are often asked to produce a small application for the company, perhaps something for the human resources or marketing departments. They are usually asked to spend from 20 to 50 percent of their working hours on the miniproject, devoting the rest of their time to current responsibilities. The best learning teams are made up of people who have different skills and who are from separate areas in a systems department. Perhaps one is a manager, another a systems programmer, another an analyst, and so on. This range of skills and backgrounds enables the team to approach the learning process from several directions, increasing its learning opportunities.

A learning team is a small group of people assigned to learn a particular subject.

11.3.5 Read, Read, Read

I cannot stress enough that for your learning efforts to be successful you must read, read, read. You should read a wide range of books. I suggest reading one book a month just to keep up with changes in the industry. I also suggest reading magazines, such as *Software Development* (I write the object column for *SD*), the *Journal of Object-Oriented Programming,* and *Java Developer's Journal.* Finally, Web sites such as the "Cetus Object and

Read at least one book and several magazines each month.

It is common for experienced developers, especially the really good ones, to convince themselves initially that they have been doing this new stuff all along. This is because object-oriented software techniques include many important structured software-engineering principles that you likely already use. Familiarity with some of the underlying principles, the ones usually taught in the introductory classes and introductory books such as this one, make it easy to convince yourself that you've been doing this stuff all along, although the reality is that you haven't.

Components Links" (*www.cetus-links.org*) provide current links to a range of information regarding object orientation.

11.3.6 Take Advanced Training

After several months of hands-on experience under the tutelage of an experienced mentor, the next step is to return to the classroom for advanced training in specific skills. These courses will either be advanced versions of the ones listed in Table 11-1 or courses in specialized skills or technologies. For example, an advanced modeling course is likely to concentrate on analysis and design patterns, and an advanced programming course will convey a series of programming tips and tricks. The experience you have gained gives you the knowledge that you need to understand and absorb the material presented in the advanced courses.

11.4 What You Have Learned

The P2K software environment is complex, an environment in which you will work with a range of technologies and techniques. This chapter introduced you to the primary P2K technologies and techniques, and provided references to good sources of information to learn more about them. You were also introduced to the common roles that software professionals fulfill in today's organizations to provide insight as to where you might like to take your career. Finally, several strategies for continuing your learning process were presented, providing you with avenues to increase your knowledge of object-orientation and of the P2K technologies and techniques.

11.5 Parting Words

Object technology and object-oriented development techniques are the norm, not the exception, for software development today. Object orientation is complex, as you have seen from the range of techniques presented in this book, although it is a paradigm you can easily adopt if you like. One of my fundamental beliefs is that choosing to succeed is one of the most difficult decisions you can make. For software professionals, you choose to succeed when you choose to adopt the object-oriented paradigm. May you live long and prosper.

Glossary

Abstract class. A class that does not have objects instantiated from it.

Abstraction. The essential characteristics of an item, such as a class or operation.

Accessor. An operation used either to modify or retrieve a single attribute. Also known as *getter* and *setter* operations.

Activity diagram. A UML diagram used to model high-level business processes or the transitions between states of a class (in this respect , activity diagrams are effectively specializations of state chart diagrams).

Actor. A person, organization, or system that is external to the system you are developing.

Actor class. A representation of an actor that appears in your use case model.

Ad-hoc reporting. Reporting performed for the specific purposes of a small group of users where it is common for the users to write the report(s) themselves.

Aggregation. The representation of "is part of" associations.

Alpha testing. A testing period in which prerelease versions of software products (that are often buggy) are released to users who need access to the product before it is officially deployed. In return, these users are willing to report any defects they uncover back to the software developers. Alpha testing is typically followed by a period of *beta testing* (see also).

Alternate course of action. An infrequently used path of logic in a use case that is the result of an alternate way to work, an exception, or an error condition.

Alternate key. See *Secondary key*.

Analysis error. An analysis error occurs when a requirement is missing, when a requirement is misunderstood, or when an unnecessary requirement is included.

Analysis pattern. A pattern that describes a solution to a common business/analysis issue.

Anonymous object. An object appearing on a UML Sequence or Collaboration diagram that has not been given a name; instead, the label is simply an indication of the class, such as ": Invoice."

Antipattern. The description of a common approach to solving a common problem, an approach that in time proves to be wrong or highly ineffective.

Application backlog. The average amount of time it takes for the systems department to start the development of a system as measured from the time that the idea for the project was first conceived.

Application server. A server on which business logic is deployed. Application servers are key to an *n*-tier client/server architecture.

Artifact. A document, model, file, diagram, or other item that is produced, modified, or used during the development, operation, or support of a system.

Associative table. A table in a relational database that is used to maintain a relationship between two or more other tables. Associative tables are typically used to resolve many-to-many relationships.

Attribute. Something that a class or object knows. An attribute is basically a single piece of data or information.

Audit logging. The recording of information to identify an action that is of interest to the system, when the action took place and whom/what took the action.

Base use case. A use case that is extended by another via an extend association.

Baseline. A tested and certified version of a deliverable representing a conceptual milestone, which thereafter serves as the basis for further development, and that can be modified only through formal change control procedures. A particular version becomes a baseline when a responsible group decides to designate it as such.

Basic course of action. The main path of logic that an actor follows through a use case. Often referred to as the *happy path* because it describes how the use case works when everything works as it normally should.

Behavioral requirement. The functional tasks your system must support.

Beta testing. Similar to alpha testing except the software product should be less buggy. This method is used by software development companies who want to ensure they meet as many of their clients' needs as possible.

BFC. Better, faster, cheaper.

Bidirectional association. An association that may be traversed in both directions.

Bug. See *Defect*.

Building. The process by which a software product is created from its base source code. This is the act of compiling and linking source code in compiled languages such as Java and C++, or packaging code in languages such as Smalltalk.

Bulk setter. A setter method that updates several interdependent attributes as one transaction. Bulk setter methods invoke the individual setter methods for each attribute as needed. See also *setter.*

Business analyst. Someone who works with the future users of a system to identify the fundamentals of their business problem, their requirements for the system, how they will likely work with the system, and how they will likely need the system to evolve over time.

Business class. Business classes are places, things, concepts, and events that are pertinent to your problem domain. Often referred to as *domain classes* or *analysis classes.*

Business rule. A policy that your software must satisfy. Business rules are what a functional requirement "knows"—the controls and guidelines that are fulfilled by the functional requirement. A business rule is an operating principle or policy of your organization.

Business/domain class. Business/domain classes implement the concepts pertinent to your business domain such as "customer" or "account." Business/domain classes are usually found during the analysis process. Although business/domain classes often focus on the data aspects of your business objects, they will also implement methods specific to the individual business concept.

C++. A hybrid object-oriented programming language that adds object-oriented features to the C programming language.

Callback. An approach where one object indicates that it wants to be sent a message once its request has finished processing; in effect it wants to be "called back."

Cardinality. Represents the concept of "how many?" in associations.

Catalysis. A next-generation software process for the systematic business-driven development of component-based systems.

CCM. CORBA Component Model.

Change case. A change case describes a potential requirement that your system may need to support in the future.

Change-case model. The collection of change cases applicable to your system.

Class. A template from which objects are created (instantiated). Although in the real world, Doug, Wayne, John, and Bill are all "student objects," we would model the class "Student" instead.

Class diagram. Class diagrams show the classes of a system and the associations between them.

Class hierarchy. See *Inheritance hierarchy.*

Class model. A class diagram and its associated documentation.

Class normalization. The process by which you refactor the behavior within a class diagram in such a way as to increase the cohesion of classes while minimizing the coupling between them.

Class Responsibility Collaborator (CRC) card. A standard index card that has been divided into three sections, one indicating the name of the class that the card represents, one listing the responsibilities of the class, and the third listing the names of the other classes that this one collaborates with to fulfill its responsibilities.

Class Responsibility Collaborator (CRC) model. A collection of CRC cards that model all or part of a system.

Classifier. A mechanism that describes behavioral or structural features. Classifiers include use cases, classes, interfaces, and components.

Class-type architecture. A defined approach to layering the classes that comprise the software of a system. The interaction between classes is often restricted based on the layer to which they belong.

Clear-box testing. See *White-box testing.*

Client. A single-user PC or workstation that provides presentation services and appropriate computing, connectivity, and interfaces relevant to the business need. A client is also commonly referred to as a *front end.*

Client class. A class whose instances send messages to instances of other classes, but do not receive them.

Client/server (C/S) architecture. A computing environment that satisfies a business need by appropriately allocating the application processing between the client and the server processes.

Client/server class. A class whose instances both send messages to instances of other classes, as well as receive messages from instances of other classes.

Cohesion. The degree of relatedness within an encapsulated unit (such as a component or a class).

Collaboration diagram. A UML diagram that shows instances of classes, their interrelationships, and the message flow between them. Collaboration diagrams typically focus on the structural organization of objects that send and receive messages.

Column. The relational database equivalent of an attribute of a data entity stored in a relational table.

COM+. The latest incarnation of Microsoft's Component Object Model (COM). COM was the evolution of Microsoft's Object Linking and Embedding (OLE) and ActiveX technologies, which then evolved into the Distributed Component Object Model (DCOM) and now into COM+.

Comment. Documentation in source code.

Commercial package. Software that is developed for sale.

Common gateway interface (CGI). A simple protocol used to communicate between Web forms and your program.

Common Object Request Broker Architecture (CORBA). CORBA is an industry-standard, proven approach to distributed object computing, although in practice CORBA has also proven to be a significant force in the middleware arena. CORBA is defined and maintained by the Object Management Group (OMG).

Component. A cohesive unit of functionality that can be independently developed, delivered, and composed with other components to build a larger unit.

Component diagram. A UML diagram that depicts the software components that comprise an application, system, or enterprise. The components, their interrelationships, interactions, and their public interfaces are depicted.

Component testing. See *Class-integration testing.*

Component-based development. An approach to development in which software is deployed as collections of interacting components, each of which encapsulate a defined set of behaviors.

Composition. A strong form of aggregation in which the "whole" is completely responsible for its parts and each "part" object is only associated with the one "whole" object.

Computer-aided system engineering (CASE) tool. Software that supports the creation of models of software-oriented systems.

Concrete class. A class that has objects instantiated from it.

Concurrency. The issues involved with allowing multiple people simultaneous access to a shared resource, such as an object or persistent storage.

Connascence. Between two software elements, A and B, the property by which a change in A would require a change to B to preserve overall correctness within your system.

Constraint. A global requirement, such as limited development resources or a decision by senior management, that restricts the way you develop a system.

Constructor. A method, typically a static one, whose purpose is to instantiate and optionally initialize an object.

Contract. Any service/behavior of a class or component that is requested of it.

Controller. A class that implements business/domain logic, coordinating several objects to perform a task.

Controller/process class. Controller/process classes implement business logic that involves collaborating with several business/domain classes or even other controller/process classes.

Convenience inheritance. See *Implementation inheritance.*

Coupling. The degree of dependence between two items. In general, it is better to reduce coupling wherever possible.

Coverage testing. The act of ensuring that each line of code is exercised at least once.

Creation state. See *Initial state.*

CRUD. Create, retrieve, update, delete. The basic functionality of a persistence mechanism.

C-style comment. A style of multiline comment in Java that begins with "/*" characters and ends with "*/" characters.

Data definition language (DDL). Commands supported by a persistence mechanism that enable the creation, removal, or modification of structures (such as relational tables or classes) within it.

Data dictionary. A repository of information about the layout of a database, the layout of a flat file, the layout of a class, and any mappings among the three.

Data entity. The representation of the data describing a person, place, thing, event, or concept.

Data manipulation language (DML). Commands supported by a persistence mechanism that enables the access of data within it, including the creation, retrieval, update, and deletion of that data.

Data model. See *Persistence model.*

Data modeler. See *Persistence modeler.*

Database administrator (DBA). See *Persistence administrator.*

Database proxy. An object that represents a business object stored in a database. To every other object in the system, the database proxy appears to be the object it represents. When other objects send the proxy a message, it immediately fetches the object from the database and replaces itself with the fetched object, passing the message on to it.

Database server. A server that has a database installed on it.

Data-flow diagram (DFD). A diagram that shows the movement of data within a system between processes, entities, and data stores. Data-flow diagrams, also called process diagrams, are primary artifacts of structured/procedural modeling.

Defect. Anything that detracts from your application's capability to completely and effectively meet your user's needs. Also known as a *bug, fault,* or *feature.*

Dependency relationship. A dependency relationship exists between class *A* and *B* when instances of class *A* interact with instances of class *B*. Dependency relationships are used when there is no direct relationship (inheritance, aggregation, or association) between the two classes.

Dependent class. A fine-grained class typically identified through the normalization of an attribute into a full-fledged class.

Deployment diagram. A UML diagram showing the hardware, software, and middleware configuration for a system.

Design pattern. A pattern that describes a solution to a common design issue.

Destructor. A method whose purpose is to remove an object completely from memory.

Development process. A process that focuses on the development aspects of a system, including requirements definition, modeling, programming, testing, and delivery of the system.

Development/maintenance trade-off. Development techniques that speed the development process often have a negative impact on your maintenance efforts, whereas techniques that lead to greater maintainability negatively impact your development efforts, at least in the short term.

Diagram. A visual representation of a problem or solution to a problem.

Disconnected usage. The potentially full use of an application when it is not connected to your organization's network.

Distributed objects. An object-oriented architecture in which objects running in separate memory spaces (that is, different computers) interact with one another transparently.

Doclet. A Java API that is an add-on to Javadoc.

Documentation comment. A style of multiline comment in Java that begins with "/**" characters and ends with "*/" characters. Also known as a *Javadoc comment.*

Domain component. A large-scale component that encapsulates cohesive portions of your business domain.

Domain model. A representation of the business/domain concepts, and their interrelationships, applicable to your system. A domain model helps to establish the vocabulary for your project.

EAI. See *Enterprise application integration.*

E-commerce. E-commerce, also known as *electronic commerce* or *Internet-based commerce*, focuses on the use of technology to support the selling of products and services electronically.

Education. The teaching skills and knowledge that are typically applicable over the student's entire career.

Eiffel. A "pure" object-oriented programming language.

Electronic Data Interchange (EDI). An industry-standard approach to sharing data between two or more systems.

Encapsulation. The grouping of related concepts into one item, such as a class or component.

Endline comment. The use of a single-line comment to document a line of source code where the comment immediately follows the code on the same line as the code. Also known as an *inline comment.*

End-to-end prototyping. See *Technical prototyping.*

Enterprise application integration (EAI). The integration of disparate software applications into a cohesive whole to support new and complex business processes.

Enterprise JavaBeans (EJB). EJB is a component architecture, defined by Sun Microsystems, for the development and deployment of component-based distributed business applications.

Enterprise process. The overall process of a single organization, encompassing the processes of all aspects of the organization.

Enterprise software architect. Someone responsible for the software architecture of your organization.

Essential model. A model intended to capture the essence of a problem through technology-free, idealized, and abstract descriptions.

Essential use case. A simplified, abstract, generalized use case that captures the intentions of a user in a technology and implementation- independent manner.

Essential use case model. A use case model comprised of essential use cases.

Essential user interface prototype. A low-fidelity prototype of a system's user interface that models the fundamental, abstract characteristics of a user interface.

Exception. An indication that an unexpected condition has occurred within some software. In Java, exceptions are "thrown" by methods to indicate potential problems.

Extend association. A generalization relationship where an extending use case continues the behavior of a base use case. The extending use case accomplishes this by inserting additional action sequences into the base use case sequence. This is modeled using a use case association with the <<extend>> stereotype.

Extending use case. A use case that extends another use case via an extend association.

Extensibility. A measure of how easy it is to add new features to, to extend, existing software. If item *A* is easier to change than item *B*, then we say that item *A* is more extensible than item *B*.

Extensible Markup Language (XML). An industry-standard approach to data-sharing, an important enabling technology for EAI and e-commerce.

Extension point. A marker in a use case where extension is allowed.

Extreme programming (XP). A deliberate and disciplined approach to software development that stresses communication, simplicity, feedback, and confidence. XP focuses on working with users, on development that is simple and elegant, and on testing.

Facilitator. Someone responsible for planning, running, and managing modeling sessions.

Fat-client. A two-tiered client/server architecture in which client machines implement both the user interface and the business logic of an application. Servers typically only supply data to client machines with little or no processing done to it.

Fault. See *Defect*.

Feature creep. The addition, as development proceeds, of new features to a system that are beyond what the original specification called for. This is also called *scope creep*.

Final state. A state from which no transitions lead out. Objects have zero or more final states.

Flow chart. A diagram depicting the logic flow of a single process or method. Flow charts were a primary artifact of structured/procedural modeling.

Foreign key. One or more attributes within a data entity that represent a primary or secondary key in another table. Foreign keys are used to maintain a relationship to a row in another table.

Framework. A reusable set of prefabricated software building blocks that programmers can use, extend, or customize for specific computing solutions.

Full lifecycle object-oriented testing (FLOOT). A testing methodology for object-oriented development that comprises testing techniques that, taken together, provide methods to verify that your application works correctly at each stage of development.

Function testing. A testing technique in which development staff confirms that their application meets the user requirements specified during analysis.

Functional cohesion. A measure of how well the behaviors of an item make sense when considered as a whole.

Galactically unique OID. A persistent OID with a value that is guaranteed to be unique across all organizations that follow the same value-generation strategy.

Getter. A method to obtain the value of a data attribute, or to calculate the value, of an object or a class.

Globally unique OID. A persistent OID with a value that is guaranteed to be unique within the organization that generated it.

Goldplating. The addition of extraneous features to a system.

Graphical user interface (GUI). A style of user interface composed of graphical components such as windows and buttons.

GUI testing. See *Uuser interface testing*.

Has-a relationship. See *Include association*.

Human-factors engineer (HFE). A person who is an expert in the analysis and design of the user interface for an application and/or work environment for your users.

Hypertext markup language (HTML). Industry-standard definition of a platform-independent file format for sharing information. HTML pages are the de facto standard approach for user interfaces on the World Wide Web (WWW).

Idiom. An idiom describes how to implement a particular part of a pattern, the part's functionality, or the relationship to other parts in the design. Idioms are often specific to a particular programming language.

Implementation inheritance. When inheritance is applied simply for convenience, even though it doesn't make sense to say that the subclass "is a" superclass.

Include association. A generalization relationship denoting the inclusion of the behavior described by a use case within another use case. This is modeled using a use case association with the <<include>> stereotype. Also known as a "uses" or a "has a" relationship.

Incremental development. An approach to software development that organizes a project into several releases instead of one "big-bang" release.

Information hiding. The restriction of external access to attributes.

Inheritance. The representation of an "is a," "is like," or "is kind of" relationship between two classes. Inheritance promotes reuse by enabling a subclass to benefit automatically from the entire behavior that it inherits from its superclass(es).

Inheritance hierarchy. A set of classes that are related through inheritance. Also referred to as a *class hierarchy*.

Inheritance regression testing. The act of running the test cases of the super classes, both direct and indirect, on a given subclass.

Initial state. The state an object is in when it is first created. All objects have an initial state. This is often referred to as the *creation state*.

Inline comment. See *Endline comment*.

Installation testing. The act of ensuring that your application can be installed successfully.

Instance. Just as we say that a data record is an occurrence of a data entity, we say that an object is an instance of a class.

Instance attribute. An attribute that is applicable to a single instance (object) of a class. Each object has its own value for an instance attribute.

Instance method. A method that operates on a single instance (object) of a class.

Instantiate. When we create a student object, we say that we instantiate it from the class "Student."

Integration plan. A plan that describes the schedule, resources, and approach to integrating the elements of a system.

Integration testing. The act of ensuring that several portions of software work together.

Interface. The definition of a collection of one or more operation signatures, and optionally attribute definitions, that comprises a cohesive set of behaviors. Some object languages support the capability for classes and/or components to implement interfaces.

Interface navigation diagram. See *User interface-flow diagram*.

Interface testing. See *Black-box testing*.

Interface-flow diagram. See *User interface-flow diagram*.

Internet-based commerce. See *E-commerce*.

Inter-process communication (IPC). The act of having software interact with one another even though running on two separate pieces of hardware .

Intuitable. The guesses and presuppositions of users are more likely to be right than wrong and, even when wrong, the results are reasonable responses from the system that are readily understood by the users.

Invariant. A set of assertions about an instance or class that must be true at all "stable" times, where a stable time is the period before a method is invoked on the object/class and immediately after a method is invoked.

Invoke. Object *A* sends message *X* to object *B* by invoking (calling) the *X* method implemented by object *B*.

Iterative development. A nonserial approach to software development where you are likely to do some requirements definition, some modeling, some programming, or some testing on any given day.

Java. An object-oriented programming language based on the concept of "write once, run anywhere."

Java virtual machine (JVM). An abstract computing machine that supports a defined instruction set. JVMs are what makes Java portable: Java code is compiled into standard byte-code that can be run on any platform with a JVM.

Javadoc. A Java utility that parses Java source files for Javadoc comments to use as a basis from which to generate external code documentation.

Javadoc comment. See *Documentation comment.*

Javadoc tag. A predefined string of text, beginning with the "@" symbol, that can be embedded in documentation comments for formatting purposes. Examples include the "@returns" and "@throws" tags.

Joint application development (JAD). A structured, facilitated meeting in which modeling is performed by a group of people. JADs are often held for gathering user requirements or for developing system designs.

JVM. See *Java Virtual Machine.*

Key. A data attribute, or collection of data attributes, that uniquely describes a data entity; in a relational database a key is one or more columns in a table that, when combined, form a unique identifier for each record in the table.

Layering. The organization of software collections (layers) of classes or components that fulfill a common purpose.

Lazy initialization. An approach in which the initial value of an attribute is set in its corresponding getter method the first time the getter is invoked.

Learning team. A small group of people given the task of working together to learn a particular subject.

Lifeline. Represents, in a sequence diagram, the life span of an object during an interaction.

Load balancing. A technique where processing requests are distributed across several nodes so the overall processing burden is spread as evenly as possible across the nodes.

Lock. An indication that a table, record, class, or object is reserved so work can be performed on the item. Typically, a lock is established, the work is performed, and the lock is removed.

Maintainability. A measure of how easy it is to add, remove, or modify existing features of a system. The easier a system is to change, the more maintainable we say that system is.

Maintenance burden. The need for software organizations to invest money in the support, operation, and enhancement of existing hardware.

Major user interface element. A large-grained item such as a screen, HTML page, or report.

Many-to-many association. An association where the maximum of both multiplicities is greater than one.

Many-to-one association. An association where the maximum of one multiplicity is one and the other is more than one.

Mentoring. The processes of having an experienced professional impart his or her expertise to novices following a hands-on basis.

Message. A request from one object, the sender, to another, the target. Messages are implemented as a method invocation on the target object.

Message-invocation box. The long, thin, vertical boxes that appear on sequence diagrams, which represent invocation of an operation on an object or class.

Method. Something that a class or object does. A method is similar to a function or procedure in structured programming and is often referred to as an *operation* or *member function* in object development.

Method response. A count of the total number of messages sent as a result of a method being invoked.

Microsoft Solutions Framework (MSF). A software process defined and promoted by Microsoft.

Middleware. Technology that enables software deployed on disparate computer hardware systems to communicate with one another.

Minor user interface element. A small-grained item such as a user input field, menu item, list, or static text field.

Mirror hierarchies. Two or more class hierarchies that because they are each model concepts that are highly related, take on similar structures to one another.

Model. An abstraction describing a problem domain and/or a solution to a problem domain. Traditionally, models are thought of as diagrams plus their corresponding documentation although nondiagrams, such as interview results and collections of CRC cards, are also considered to be models.

Model review. A technical review in which an analysis and/or design model is inspected.

Model walkthrough. A less formal version of a model review.

MSF. See *Microsoft Solutions Framework*.

Multiple inheritance. When a class directly inherits from more than one class.

Multiplicity. UML combines the concepts of cardinality and optionality into the single concept of multiplicity.

Mutator. See *setter*.

Name hiding. This refers to the practice of using the same, or at least a similar, name for an attribute/variable/parameter as for one of higher scope. The most common abuse of name hiding is to name a local variable the same as an instance attribute.

Node. A computer, switch, printer, or other hardware device.

Nonfunctional requirement. The standards, regulations, and contracts to which your system must conform; descriptions of interfaces to external systems that your system must interact with; performance requirements; design and implementation constraints; and the quality characteristics to which your system must conform.

Note. A modeling construct for adding free-form text to UML diagrams.

n-Tier client/server. A client/server architecture in which client machines interact with application servers, which in turn interact with other application servers and/or database servers.

Object. A person, place, thing, concept, event, screen, or report. Objects both know things (that is, they have data) and they do things (that is, they have functionality).

Object COBOL. A hybrid object-oriented programming language that extends COBOL with object-oriented concepts.

Object Constraint Language (OCL). A formal language, similar to structured English, to express side-effect-free constraints within UML models.

Object database (ODB). A permanent storage mechanism, also known as an *objectbase* or an *object-oriented database management system (OODBMS)*, that natively supports the persistence of objects.

Object Database Management Group (ODMG). A standards body responsible for the standard definition for object-oriented databases and the Object Query Language (OQL).

Object identifier (OID). A unique identifier assigned to objects, typically a large integer number. OIDs are the object-oriented equivalent of keys in the relational world.

Object Management Group (OMG). An industry-recognized standards body that is responsible for standards such as the Unified Modeling Language (UML) and the Common Object Request Broker Architecture (CORBA).

Object modeler. Someone who is responsible for the analysis and design of object-oriented software.

Object Modeling Language (OML). An alternative to the Unified Modeling Language (UML), promoted by the OPEN Consortium (*www.open.org.au*).

Object Pascal. A hybrid object-oriented programming language that extends Pascal with object-oriented concepts.

Object programming language. Any programming language that is either object-oriented or object-based.

Object space. The memory space, including all accessible permanent storage, in which objects exist and interact with one another.

Objectbase. See *Object database.*

Object-based programming language. Any programming language that natively supports some, but not all, of the properties of an object-oriented language. Example: Visual Basic.

Object-oriented database management system (OODBMS). See *Object database.*

Object-oriented paradigm. A development strategy based on the concept of building systems from reusable components called objects.

Object-oriented programming language. Any programming language that natively supports the object-oriented concepts of inheritance, classes, objects, polymorphism, and message passing. Examples: Java and C++.

Object-Oriented Software Process (OOSP). A collection of process patterns that together describe a complete process for developing, maintaining, and supporting software. OOSP is based on the concept that large-scale, mission-critical software development is serial in the large, iterative in the small, delivering incremental releases of software in Internet time.

ODMG. Object Database Management Group, a consortium of most of the ODBMS vendors who together set standards for object databases.

OML. See *Object Modeling Language.*

One-to-many association. See *Many-to-one association.*

One-to-one association. An association where the maximums of each of its multiplicities is one.

OO. This is an acronym that is used interchangeably for two terms: Object-oriented and object orientation. For example, when we say OO programming, we really mean object-oriented programming. When we say this is a book that describes OO, we really mean it is a book that describes object orientation.

OOCRUD. Object-oriented create, retrieve, update, and delete.

OPEN Process. A sophisticated and comprehensive software process defined and promoted by the OPEN Consortium (*www.open.org.au*) for the efficient development of software.

Open-source software (OSS). Fully functioning software whose source code is available free of charge. Changes, either new features or bug fixes, are often made to open-source software by its users, changes that are then made available (usually) free of charge to the entire user community.

Operations testing. The act of ensuring that the needs of operations personnel who have to support/operate the application are met.

Optimistic locking. An approach where an item is locked only for the time that it is accessed. For example, if a customer object is edited, a lock is placed on it in the persistence mechanism for the time that it takes to read it in memory, and then it is immediately removed. The object is edited, and then when it needs to be saved, it is locked again, written out, and then unlocked.

Optionality. Represents the concept "do you need to have it?" in associations.

OQL. Object Query Language, a standard proposed by the ODMG for the selection of objects. This is basically SQL with object-oriented extensions that provide the capability to work with classes and objects, instead of tables and records.

Overload. When you define two methods with the same name, but with different parameters, we say you overload it.

Override. When you redefine an attribute or method in a subclass, we say you override it.

Package. A UML construct that enables you to organize model elements into groups.

Paradigm. An overall strategy or viewpoint for doing things. A paradigm is a specific mindset.

Paragraphing. A technique where you indent the code within the scope of a code block by one unit, usually a horizontal tab, to distinguish it from the code outside the code block. Paragraphing helps to increase the readability of your code.

Pattern. A pattern is a solution to a common problem taking relevant forces into account, effectively supporting the reuse of proven techniques and approaches of other developers.

Peer review. A style of technical review in which a project deliverable, or portion thereof, is inspected by a small group of people with expertise in the product being reviewed.

Perl (practical extraction and report language). A scripting language originally developed for the automation of UNIX system administration tasks, which are now commonly used for Web-based software development.

Permanent storage. Any physical medium to which data may be saved, retrieved, and deleted. Potential permanent storage mechanisms for objects include relational databases, files, and object databases.

Persistence. The issue of how objects are permanently stored.

Persistence administrator. Someone who is responsible for the care and support of your permanent storage mechanisms. Commonly called database administrators (DBAs) in the structured world.

Persistence class. Persistence classes provide the capability to store objects permanently. By encapsulating the storage and retrieval of objects via persistence classes, you are able to use various storage technologies interchangeably without affecting your applications.

Persistence framework. See *Persistence layer.*

Persistence layer. Software, also known as a *persistence framework*, that encapsulates permanent storage mechanisms, such as relational databases, so application developers do not have knowledge of how or where objects are stored. Persistence layers automate significant portions of the efforts required to persist objects.

Persistence mechanism. The permanent storage facility used to make objects persistent. Examples include relational databases, object databases, flat files, and object/relational databases.

Persistence model. A model that describes the persistent data aspects of a software system.

Persistence modeler. Someone who is responsible for the development and maintenance of physical persistence models. Commonly called a *data modeler* in the structured world.

Persistent association. An association that is permanent or at least semipermanent in nature, which must be saved as permanent storage (that is, it must be persisted).

Persistent object. An object that is saved to permanent storage.

Pessimistic locking. An approach where an item is locked for the entire time it is in memory. For example, when a customer object is edited, a lock is placed on the object in the persistence mechanism, the object is brought into memory and edited, and then eventually the object is written back to the persistence mechanism and the object is unlocked.

Physical persistence model. A model, often called a *physical data model*, that depicts the physical data schema to be implemented in your permanent storage mechanism.

Pilot testing. A testing process equivalent to beta testing that is used by organizations to test applications they have developed for their own internal use.

Polymorphism. Different objects can respond to the same message in different ways, enabling objects to interact with one another without knowing their exact type.

Portability. A measure of how easy it is to move an application to another environment (which may vary by the configuration of either software or hardware). The easier it is to move an application to another environment, the more portable we say that application is.

Post-2000 (P2K) environment. The collection of technologies and techniques, for the most part object-oriented and component-based, that organizations are deploying within their information technology (IT) departments.

Postcondition. An expression of the properties of the state of an operation or use case after it has been invoked successfully.

Precondition. An expression of the constraints under which an operation or use case will operate properly.

Primary key. The preferred key for a data entity.

Primitive type. A type of attribute built into a programming language. For example, Java includes primitive types such as int, string, and boolean.

Problem space. The scope of your business domain being addressed by your system.

Process. The definition of the steps to be taken, the roles of the people performing those steps, the artifacts being created, and the artifacts being used to fulfill a purpose that provides value to someone or some organization.

Process antipattern. An antipattern that describes an approach and/or series of actions for developing software that is proven ineffective and often detrimental to your organization.

Process diagram. See *Data-flow diagram.*

Process pattern. A collection of general techniques, actions, and/or tasks (activities) that address specific software process problems considering the relevant forces/factors.

Programmer. Someone who implements and initially tests source code based on the models for your system.

Project infrastructure. The tools, standards, guidelines, processes, and other supporting artifacts used by your project team.

Project manager. Someone who is responsible for the organization and management of a software project.

Project scope. The definition of the functionality that will, and will not, be implemented by a project.

Project software architect. Someone who is responsible for the identification and proving of a software architecture for a system based on its initial requirements and the existing enterprise architecture of your organization.

Project stakeholder. Anyone who could be materially affected by the implementation of a new system or application.

Project success. A project is considered a success when it is on time, on budget, and meets the needs of its users.

Proof-of-concept prototyping. See *Technical prototyping.*

Prototype. A simulation of an item, such as a user interface or a system architecture, the purpose of which is to communicate your approach to others before significant resources are invested in the approach.

Prototype walkthrough. A process by which your users work through a collection of use cases using a prototype as if it were the real system. The main goal is to test whether the design of the prototype meets their needs.

Pure inheritance. Inheritance in which the subclass does not override any behavior implemented by its superclass(es). The subclass is free to add new behavior.

Quality assurance. The validation that something was built the right way.

Quality assurance engineer. Someone who is responsible for ensuring that developers build software according to the accepted standards and processes within your organization.

Read into memory. When you obtain the data for an object from persistent storage, but do not intend to update it.

Read lock. A type of lock indicating that a table, record, class, or object is currently being read by someone else. Other people may also obtain read locks on the item, but no one may obtain a write lock until all read locks are cleared.

Realizes relationship. A type of relationship where an item implements (realizes) a concept or type, such as a standard or an interface.

Record. See *Row.*

Recursive association. An association in which the objects involved in it are instances of the same class. For example, people marry people.

Reference manual. A document, either paper or electronic, aimed at experts who need quick access to information.

Referential integrity. The assurance that a reference from one entity to another entity is valid. If entity *A* references entity *B*, then entity *B* exists. If entity *B* is removed, then all references to entity *B* must also be removed.

Regression testing. The validation that existing software still works after changes have been made.

Relational database (RDB). A permanent storage mechanism in which data is stored as rows in tables. RDBs do not natively support the persistence of objects, requiring additional work on the part of developers and/or the use of a persistence layer.

Relational table. The physical implementation of a data entity within a relational database.

Requirement review. A technical review in which a requirements model is inspected.

Requirements analyst. A person responsible for the gathering/elicitation, documentation, and validation of requirements.

Requirements model. The collection of artifacts, including your use case model, user interface model, domain model, change-case model, and supplementary specification that describes the requirements for your system.

Responsibility. An obligation that a class must fulfill, such as knowing something or doing something.

Retrieve into memory. When you obtain the data for an object from persistent storage and intend to update it.

Role. The context that an object takes within an association. For example, a person can have the role of "husband" within a family.

Root class. The topmost class in an inheritance hierarchy.

Row. The relational database equivalent of an instance of a data entity stored in a relational table. Also called a *record* or *tuple*.

Rule engine. Software, typically based on artificial intelligence (AI) techniques, used specifically for the purpose of implementing complex logic in the form of rules.

Scaffolding. Additional code, often complete methods and attributes, required to make your design work. Programmers often introduce scaffolding; it is not modeled as part of analysis and often not even as part of design.

Scope creep. See *Feature creep*.

Scribe. A person responsible for recording information as it is identified.

Secondary key. A key that is an alternative to the primary key for a data entity. Also known as an *alternate key*.

Security access control. The act of ensuring that users of a system may only invoke the behaviors they are entitled to, including, but not limited to, the manipulation of components, objects, and data.

Sequence diagram. A UML diagram that models the sequential logic; in effect, the time ordering of messages between objects.

Server. One or more multiuser processors with shared memory that provides computing connectivity, database services, and interfaces relevant to the business need. A server is also commonly referred to as a *back end*.

Server class. A class whose instances receive messages, but do not send them to instances of other classes.

Setter. A method that sets the value of a data attribute of an object or class. Also known as a *mutator*.

Signature. The combination of the name, parameter names (in order), and name of the return value (if any) of a method.

Simple Network Management Protocol (SNMP). A standard protocol that specifies how to simply communicate status, often in near real-time, of system services. SNMP is used to monitor the status of the various software and hardware components of a system.

Single inheritance. When a class directly inherits from only one class.

Single-line comment. A style of Java comment beginning with the characters "//"—anything following the double-slash to the end of the current line is a comment.

Smalltalk. A pure object-oriented programming language.

Software architect. See *Enterprise software architect* and *Project software architect.*

Software architecture. The set of significant decisions about the organization of a software system, the selection of the system's structural elements, and their interfaces; the definition of the behavior, structure of those elements, the definition of the associations, and interactions between those elements; the composition of the elements into progressively larger subsystems; and the definition of the architectural style that guides the efforts of software architects.

Software configuration management (SCM). A collection of engineering procedures for tracking and documenting software and its related artifacts throughout their lifecycles to ensure that all changes are recorded and the current state of the software is known and reproducible.

Software port. The migration of software from one platform to another. You will often need to port software to other operating systems, other database systems, and even other hardware platforms.

Software process. A process that describes how to develop, operate, and support one or more systems.

Solution space. The problem space being addressed by your system plus the non-domain functionality required to implement your system.

SQL. Structured Query Language.

SQL statement. A piece of SQL code used to retrieve, update, insert, or delete data, or to manipulate the schema of a relational database.

State. Represents a stage in the behaviour pattern of an object. A state can also be said to represent a condition of an object to which a defined set of policies, regulations, and physical laws apply.

State chart diagram. A UML diagram that describes the states an object may be in, as well as the transitions between states. Formerly referred to as a *state diagram* or a *state-transition diagram.*

Static attribute. An attribute whose value is applicable to all instances of a class. Each instance of a class shares the single value of a static attribute.

Static method. A method that operates at the class level, potentially on all instances of that class.

Stereotype. A stereotype denotes a common use of a modeling element. Stereotypes are used to extend UML in a consistent manner.

Stored procedure. An operation that runs in a persistence mechanism.

Stress testing. The act of ensuring that the system performs as expected under high volumes of transactions, high numbers of users, and so on.

Subclass. If class *B* inherits from class *A*, we say that *B* is a subclass of *A*.

Subject matter expert (SME). A person who is responsible for providing pertinent information about the problem and/or technical domain either from personal knowledge or from research.

Substate. A specific state that is part of a more generalized superstate.

Superclass. If class *B* inherits from class *A*, we say that *A* is a superclass of *B*.

Superstate. A general state that is decomposed into several substates.

Supplementary Specification. An artifact where all requirements not contained in your use case model, user interface model, or domain model are documented.

Support testing. The act of ensuring that the needs of support personnel who have to support the application are met.

Support user's guide. A brief document, usually a single page, that describes the support services for your application that are available to your user community. This guide includes support phone numbers, fax numbers, and Web site locations, as well as hours of operation and tips for obtaining the best services.

Surrogate key. A key without a business meaning.

System boundary box. A rectangle optionally included on a use case diagram that depicts the scope of your system.

System class. System classes provide operating-system-specific functionality for your applications or they wrap functionality provided by other tool/application vendors. System classes isolate your software from the operating system (OS), making your application portable between environments, by wrapping OS-specific features.

System layer. The collection of classes that provide operating-system-specific functionality for your applications or that wrap functionality provided by non-OO applications, hardware devices, and/or non-OO code libraries.

System testing. A testing process in which you find and fix any known problems to prepare your application for user testing.

System use case. A detailed use case that describes how your system will fulfill the requirements of a corresponding essential use case, often referring to implementation-specific features, such as aspects of your user interface design.

System use case model. A use case model comprised of system use cases.

Technical prototyping. The act of creating a prototype to validate that your proposed solution works. Often called *proof-of-concept* prototyping or *end-to-end* prototyping.

Technical review. A testing technique in which one or more development artifacts are examined critically by a group of your peers. A review typically focuses on accuracy, quality, usability, and completeness. Less formal versions of this process are often referred to as *walkthroughs* or *peer reviews*.

Temporal cohesion. A measure of whether the behaviors of an item occur during the relatively same time period.

Test case. The definition of a single test; a description—including the setup, series of actions, and expected results—of a situation that a software item must support.

Test engineer. Someone who is responsible for verifying that software fulfills the requirements for which it was built.

Test harness. The portion of the code of a test suite that aggregates the test scripts.

Test script. The steps to be performed to run a test case. Test scripts are implemented using a variety of techniques, from source code for code tests to written steps for function testing.

Test suite. A collection of test scripts.

Test target. An item, such as a model, document, or portion of software, to be tested.

Testing. The validation that the right thing was built.

Thin client. A two-tiered client/server architecture in which client machines implement only the user interface of an application.

Three-tier client/server. A client/server architecture that is separated into three layers: a client layer that implements the user interface, an application server layer that implements business logic, and a database server layer that implements persistence.

Tier. A layer within a deployment architecture.

Top-down design. When you have a problem that you cannot easily deal with, break it down into small problems. Break those problems down, until you are finally left with a collection of small problems that you can deal with one at a time.

Traceability. The ease of which the features of one artifact—perhaps a document, model, or source code—may be related/traced to the features of another.

Training. The teaching of specific, narrowly focused skills that are often immediately applicable to the current position of the student.

Transaction. A single unit of work that either completely succeeds or completely fails. A transaction may be one or more updates to an object, one or more reads, one or more deletes, or any combination thereof.

Transition. A progression from one state to another. A transition is triggered by an event (either internal or external to the object).

Transitory association. An association that is not permanent and not saved to permanent storage. Transitory associations are modeled in UML as dependency relationships.

Transitory object. An object that is not saved to permanent storage.

Trigger. An operation that is automatically invoked as the result of data manipulation language activity within a persistence mechanism.

Tuple. See *Row*.

Tutorial. A document, either paper or electronic, aimed at novice users who need to learn the fundamentals of an application.

Two-tier client/server. A client/server architecture that is separated into two layers, an application layer (the client) and a server layer.

Unidirectional association. An association that may be traversed in only one direction.

Unified Modeling Language (UML). The definition of a standard modeling language for object-oriented software, including the definition of a modeling notation and the semantics for applying it, as defined by the Object Management Group (OMG).

Unified Process. A development process for object-oriented and component-based software.

Usability. Highly usable systems are easy for people to learn how to use and easy for people to use productively, they make it easy to remember from one use to another how to use them, and they help people to make fewer mistakes.

Usage-centered design. A modeling methodology that focuses on the work that users are trying to accomplish and on what the software needs to supply via the user interface to help users accomplish their goals.

Usage scenario. See *Use case scenario.*

Usage-centered design. A streamlined and systematic approach for devising software closely fitted to the genuine needs of users, software that is not only more useful and easier to use, but also simpler and easier to construct.

Use case. A sequence of actions that provide a measurable value to an actor.

Use case diagram. A diagram that shows use cases, actors, and their interrelationships.

Use case model. A model comprised of a use case diagram, use case definitions, and actor definitions. Use case models are used to document the behavioral requirements of a system.

Use case scenario. A single path of logic through one or more use cases. A use case scenario could represent the basic course of action through a single use case, a combination of portions of the basic course replaced by the steps of one or more alternate paths through a single use case, or a logic path spanning several use cases. Use case scenarios are also called *usage scenarios.*

Use case scenario testing. A testing technique in which one or more person(s) validate your domain model (typically a CRC model) by acting through the logic of use case scenarios.

User acceptance testing (UAT). A testing technique in which users verify that an application meets their needs by working with the software.

User interface (UI). The user interface of software is the portion the user directly interacts with, including the screens, reports, documentation, and software support (via telephone, electronic mail, and so on).

User interface class. A screen, menu, or report that is part of the user interface for your system. A class that provides the means for users to interact with the system. User interface classes typically define a graphical user interface for an application, although other interface styles, such as voice command, handwritten input, or HTML, are also implemented via user interface classes.

User interface testing. The testing of the user interface (UI) to ensure that it follows accepted UI standards and meets the requirements defined for it. Often referred to as *graphical user interface (GUI) testing.*

User interface-flow diagram. A diagram that models the interface objects of your system and the relationships between them; also known as an *interface-flow diagram*, a *windows navigation diagram*, or an *interface navigation diagram.*

User manual. A document, either paper or electronic, aimed at intermediate users who understand the basics of an application, but who may not know how to perform all applicable work tasks with the application.

User testing. Testing processes in which the user community, as opposed to developers, performs the tests. User testing techniques include user acceptance testing, alpha testing, beta testing, and pilot testing.

User interface event. An occurrence, often initiated by a user, such as keyboard input, a mouse action, or spoken input captured by a microphone, that causes action within your application.

User interface model. A model comprised of your user interface prototype, user interface-flow diagram, and any corresponding documentation regarding your user interface.

User interface prototype. A prototype of the user interface (UI) of a system. User interface prototypes could be as simple as a hand-drawn picture or a collection of programmed screens, pages, or reports.

Uses relationship. See *Include association.*

Utility. If a system does something worthwhile, something of sufficient value to justify the investment in it, it has utility.

Version control tool. A software tool used to check in/out, define, and manage versions of project artifacts.

Visibility. The level of access that external objects have to an item, such as an object's attributes or methods, or even to a class itself.

Visual Basic. An object-based programming language developed by Microsoft that extends Basic with several object-oriented concepts.

Volume testing. A subset of stress testing that deals specifically with determining how many transactions or database accesses an application can handle during a defined period of time.

Waterfall approach. An approach to building applications where development efforts proceed in a serial manner from one project stage to another.

Whitespace. Blank lines or spaces in source code.

Windows navigation diagram. See *User interface-flow diagram.*

Wrapper. A collection of one or more classes that encapsulates access to non-OO technology to make it appear as if it is OO.

Wrapping. The act of encapsulating non-OO functionality within a class, making it look and feel like any other object within the system.

Write lock. A type of lock indicating that a table, record, class, or object is currently being written to by another source. No one may obtain either a read or a write lock until this lock is cleared.

Write once, run anywhere (WORA). A marketing pitch for the Java language that points out Java's cross-platform nature.

WYSIWYG. What You See Is What You Get.

WYSIWYN. What You See Is What You Need.

XML. See *Extensible markup language.*

XP. See *Extreme programming.*

Year 2000 (Y2K) crisis. The need for organizations in the late 1990s to update and/or replace software that was written to store the year as two digits instead of four.

References and Recommended Reading

Consider reading at least several of the object-oriented development books in the following list. Object orientation is a young field and you'll find a lot of value in learning several related, yet different, techniques. Reading other, non-object books would also be wise.

Ambler, S. W. (1998a). *Building Object Applications That Work: Your Step-By-Step Handbook for Developing Robust Systems with Object Technology*. New York: Cambridge University Press.

Ambler, S. W. (1998b). *Process Patterns—Building Large-Scale Systems Using Object Technology*. New York: Cambridge University Press.

Ambler, S. W. (1999). *More Process Patterns—Delivering Large-Scale Systems Using Object Technology*. New York: Cambridge University Press.

Ambler, S. W. and Constantine, L. L. (2000a). *The Unified Process Inception Phase*. Gilroy, CA: CMP Books.

Ambler, S. W. and Constantine, L. L. (2000b). *The Unified Process Elaboration Phase*. Gilroy, CA: CMP Books.

Ambler, S. W. and Constantine, L. L. (2000c). *The Unified Process Construction Phase*. Gilroy, CA: CMP Books.

Apple (1993). *Macintosh Human Interface Guidelines*. Reading, MA: Addison Wesley Publishing Co.

Arranga, E. C., and Coyle, P. C. (1996). *Object-Oriented COBOL*. New York: Cambridge University Press.

Bass, L., Clements, P., and Kazman, R. (1998). *Software Architecture in Practice*. Reading, MA: Addison Wesley Longman, Inc.

Beck, K., and Cunningham, W. (1989). *A Laboratory for Teaching Object-Oriented Thinking*. Proceedings of OOPSLA '89, pp. 1–6.

Beck, K. (1997). *Smalltalk Best Practice Patterns*. Upper Saddle River, NJ: Prentice Hall PTR.

Beck, K. (2000). *Extreme Programming Explained—Embrace Change*. Reading, MA: Addison Wesley Longman, Inc.

Bennett, D. (1997). *Designing Hard Software: The Essential Tasks*. Greenwich, CT: Manning Publications Co.

Binder, R. (1999). *Testing Object-Oriented Systems: Models, Patterns, and Tools*. Reading, MA: Addison Wesley Longman, Inc.

Boehm, B. W. (1988). *A Spiral Model of Software Development and Enhancement*. IEEE Computer, pp. 61–72, 21(5).

Booch, G., Rumbaugh, J., and Jacobson, I. (1999). *The Unified Modeling Language User Guide*. Reading, MA: Addison Wesley Longman, Inc.

Buschmann, F., Meunier, R., Rohnert, H., Sommerlad, P., and Stal, M. (1996). *A Systems of Patterns: Pattern-Oriented Software Architecture*. New York: John Wiley & Sons.

Chapin, N. (1997). *Standard Object-Oriented COBOL*. New York: John Wiley & Sons.

Chidamber S. R., and Kemerer, C. F. (1991). *Towards a Suite of Metrics for Object-Oriented Design*. OOPSLA '91 Conference Proceedings, Reading, MA: Addison-Wesley Publishing Company, pp. 197–211.

Coad, P. (1992). *Object-Oriented Patterns*. Communications of the ACM, 35(9), pp. 152–159.

Coad, P., and Mayfield, M. (1997). *Java Design: Building Better Apps and Applets*. Englewood Cliff, NJ: Prentice Hall.

Constantine, L. L. (1995). *Constantine on Peopleware*. Englewood Cliffs, NJ: Yourdon Press.

Constantine, L. L., and Lockwood, L. A. D. (1999). *Software for Use: A Practical Guide to the Models and Methods of Usage-Centered Design*. New York: ACM Press.

Coplien, J. O. (1992). *Advanced C++: Programming Styles and Idioms*. Reading, MA: Addison-Wesley Publishing Company.

Coplien, J. O. et al. (1995). *Pattern Languages of Program Design*. Reading, MA: Addison Wesley Longman, Inc., pp. 183–237.

DeMarco, T. (1997). *The Deadline: A Novel About Project Management*. New York: Dorset House Publishing.

Deugo, D. (2000). *More Java Gems*. New York: Cambridge University Press.

Douglass, B. P. (1999). *Doing Hard Time: Developing Real-Time Systems with UML, Objects, Frameworks, and Patterns*. Reading, MA: Addison Wesley Longman, Inc.

D'Souza, D. F., and Wills, A. C. (1999). *Objects, Components, and Frameworks with UML: The Catalysis Approach.* Reading, MA: Addison Wesley Longman, Inc.

Fowler, M. (1997). *Analysis Patterns: Reusable Object Models.* Menlo Park, CA: Addison Wesley Longman, Inc.

Fowler, M., and Scott, K. (1997). *UML Distilled: Applying the Standard Object Modeling Language.* Reading, MA: Addison Wesley Longman, Inc.

Fowler, M. (1999). *Refactoring: Improving the Design of Existing Code.* Menlo Park, CA: Addison Wesley Longman, Inc.

Gamma, E., Helm, R., Johnson, R., and Vlissides, J. (1995). *Design Patterns: Elements of Reusable Object-Oriented Software.* Reading, MA: Addison-Wesley Publishing Company.

Gosling, J., Joy, B., and Steele, G. (1996). *The Java Language Specification.* Reading, MA: Addison Wesley Longman Inc.

Graham, I., Henderson-Sellers, B., and Younessi, H. (1997). *The OPEN Process Specification.* New York: ACM Press Books.

Graham, I., Henderson-Sellers, B., Simons, A., and Younessi, H. (1997). *The OPEN Toolbox of Techniques.* New York: ACM Press Books.

Grady, R. B. (1992). *Practical Software Metrics for Project Management and Process Improvement.* Englewood Cliffs, NJ: Prentice-Hall, Inc.

Hunt, N. (1996). "Testing Object-Oriented Code: Unit Testing." New York: SIGS Publications, *Journal of Object-Oriented Programming,* February, 1996, 8(9), pp. 18–23.

Humphrey, W. S. (1997). *Managing Technical People: Innovation, Teamwork, and the Software Process.* Reading, MA: Addison-Wesley Longman, Inc.

IBM (1993). *Systems Application Architecture: Common User Access Guide to User Interface Design.* IBM Corporation.

Jacobson, I., Booch, G., and Rumbaugh, J. (1999). *The Unified Software Development Process.* Reading, MA: Addison Wesley Longman, Inc.

Jacobson, I., Christerson, M., Jonsson, P., and Overgaard, G. (1992). *Object-Oriented Software Engineering—A Use Case Driven Approach.* Wokingham, England: ACM Press.

Jones, C. (1996). *Patterns of Software Systems Failure and Success.* Boston, MA: International Thomson Computer Press.

Kanerva, J. (1997). *The Java FAQ.* Reading, MA: Addison Wesley Longman Inc.

Kruchten, P. (1999). *The Rational Unified Process: An Introduction.* Reading, MA: Addison Wesley Longman, Inc.

Lalonde, W. (1994) *Discovering Smalltalk.* Redwood City, CA: The Benjamin/Cummings Publishing Company, Inc.

Langr, J. (2000). *Essential Java Style: Patterns for Implementation.* Upper Saddle River, NJ: Prentice Hall PTR.

Larman, C. (1998). *Applying UML and Patterns: An Introduction to Object-Oriented Analysis and Design.* Upper Saddle River, NJ: Prentice Hall PTR.

Larman, C., and Guthrie, R. (2000). *Java 2 Performance and Idiom Guide: Guidelines for Java 2 Performance, Coding, and Testing.* Upper Saddle River, NJ: Prentice Hall PTR.

Lea, D. (1997). *Concurrent Programming in Java: Design Principles and Patterns.* Reading, MA: Addison Wesley Longman Inc.

Leffingwell, D., and Widrig, D. (2000). *Managing Software Requirements: A Unified Approach.* Reading, MA: Addison Wesley Longman, Inc.

Lieberherr, K., Holland, I., and Riel, A. (1988). *Object-Oriented Programming: An Objective Sense of Style.* OOPSLA '88 Conference Proceedings. New York: ACM Press.

Linthicum, D. S. (2000). *Enterprise Application Integration.* Reading, MA: Addison Wesley Longman, Inc.

Lorenz, M., and Kidd, J. (1994). *Object-Oriented Software Metrics.* Englewood Cliffs, NJ: Prentice-Hall.

Maguire, S. (1994). *Debugging the Development Process.* Redmond, WA: Microsoft Press.

Mayhew, D. J. (1992). *Principles and Guidelines in Software User Interface Design.* Englewood Cliffs, NJ: Prentice Hall.

McConnell, S. (1996). *Rapid Development: Taming Wild Software Schedules.* Redmond, WA: Microsoft Press.

McGregor, J. D. (1997). *Quality Assurance: Planning for Testing.* New York: SIGS Publications, *Journal of Object-Oriented Programming,* February, 1997, 9(9), pp. 8–12.

Meyer, B. (1992). *Eiffel: The Language.* Upper Saddle River, NJ: Prentice-Hall PTR.

Meyer, B. (1997). *Object-Oriented Software Construction, Second Edition.* Upper Saddle River, NJ: Prentice-Hall PTR.

Meyers, S. (1992). *Effective C++: 50 Specific Ways to Improve Your Programs and Designs.* Reading, MA: Addison-Wesley Publishing Company.

Meyers, S. (1996). *More Effective C++: 35 New Ways to Improve Your Programs and Designs.* Reading, MA: Addison-Wesley Publishing Company.

Microsoft (1995). *The Windows Interface Guidelines for Software Design: An Application Design Guide.* Redmond, WA: Microsoft Press.

Nagler, J. (1995). *Coding Style and Good Computing Practices.* *http://wizard.ucr.edu/ ~nagler/coding_style.html*

Page-Jones, M. (1995). *What Every Programmer Should Know About Object-Oriented Design.* New York: Dorset House Publishing.

Page-Jones, M. (2000). *Fundamentals of Object-Oriented Design in UML.* New York: Dorset-House Publishing.

Raskin, J. (1994). *Intuitive Equals Familiar.* Communications of the ACM, 37 (9), pp. 17–18.

Reed, Jr., P. R. (1999). *Developing Applications with Visual Basic and UML.* Reading, MA: Addison Wesley Longman, Inc.

Robertson, S., and Robertson, J. (1999). *Mastering the Requirements Process.* Harlow, England: ACM Press.

Roman, E. (1999). *Mastering Enterprise JavaBeans and the Java 2 Platform, Enterprise Edition*. New York: John Wiley & Sons.

Rosenberg, D., and Scott, K. (1999). *Use Case Drive Object Modeling with UML: A Practical Approach*. Reading, MA: Addison Wesley Longman, Inc.

Ross, R. G. (1997). *The Business Rule Book, 2nd Ed*. Houston, TX: Business Rules Solutions, Inc.

Royce, W. (1998). *Software Project Management: A Unified Framework*. Reading, MA: Addison Wesley Longman, Inc.

Rumbaugh, J., Jacobson, I., and Booch, G., (1999). *The Unified Modeling Language Reference Manual*. Reading, MA: Addison Wesley Longman, Inc.

Schneider, G., and Winters, J. P. (1998). *Applying Use Cases: A Practical Guide*. Reading, MA: Addison Wesley Longman, Inc.

Software Engineering Institute (1995). *The Capability Maturity Model: Guidelines for Improving the Software Process*. Reading, MA: Addison-Wesley Publishing Company, Inc.

Sun Microsystems (1999). *Java Look and Feel Design Guidelines*. Reading, MA: Addison-Wesley Publishing Company, Inc.

Szyperski, C. (1998). *Component Software: Beyond Object-Oriented Programming*. New York: ACM Press.

Tourniaire, F., and Farrell, R. (1997). *The Art of Software Support: Design and Operation of Support Centers and Help Desks*. Upper Saddle River, NJ: Prentice Hall PTR.

Vermeulen, A., Ambler, S. W., Bumgardner, G., Metz, E., Misfeldt, T., Shur, J., and Thompson, P. (2000). *The Elements of Java Style*. New York: Cambridge University Press.

Warner, J., and Kleppe, A. (1999). *The Object Constraint Language: Precise Modeling With UML*. Reading, MA: Addison Wesley Longman, Inc.

Warren, N., and Bishop, P. (1999). *Java in Practice: Design Styles and Idioms for Effective Java*. Harlow, England: Addison Wesley Longman Limited.

Weiss, E. H. (1991). *How to Write Usable User Documentation*. Phoenix, AZ: The Oryx Press.

Wiegers, K. (1996). *Creating a Software Engineering Culture*. New York: Dorset House Publishing.

Wiegers, K. (1999). *Software Requirements*. Redmond, WA: Microsoft Press.

Wilkinson, N. M. (1995). *Using CRC Cards: An Informal Approach to Object-Oriented Development*. New York: Cambridge University Press.

Wirfs-Brock, R., Wilkerson, B., and Wiener, L. (1990). *Designing Object-Oriented Software*. Englewood Cliffs, NJ: Prentice-Hall.

Yourdon, E. (1997). *Death March: The Complete Software Developer's Guide to Surviving "Mission Impossible" Projects*. Upper Saddle River, NJ: Prentice-Hall, Inc.

Web-Based Resources

CETUS Links: *http://www.cetus-links.org*

The OPEN Web site: *http://www.open.org.au*

The Process Patterns Resource Page: *http://www.ambysoft.com/processPatternsPage.html*

Rational Unified Process: *http://www.rational.com/products/rup*

Scott Ambler's Online Writings: *http://www.ambysoft.com/onlineWritings.html*

Index